This history text is an authentic contemporary record of early STAR TREK, written with the cooperation of its original producer, with reproductions of much of the actual material used—memos, letters, etc. Is is not available on audio or videotape, although students making field trips to Earth may wish to visit the Smithsonian Institute where one of STAR TREK's visualizations (flatscreen) may be viewed.

Because the material is authentic mid-20th-century *writing*, it has more to offer than simple informational history: cultural sociologists, for instance, can learn much of the amusing sexual taboos of the time, the laughable prejudice against alien life forms, ritual suicide as practiced in big business; economists can study annual fluctuations and trends of the era; for language students this record, written at the very time that the show was being produced, is of course a gold mine.

But our main subject is predictive history—or science fiction as it was then known. Science fiction in written form has a very long history, going back at least to Lucian of Samosata. It first became "popular" in the 19th century, when virtually every leading writer of the day, including Mark Twain, James Fenimore Cooper, Herman Melville, and Henry James, contributed notable works to the genre.

But it was in the first half of the 20th century that science fiction really came into its own in the written form. The visual mass media, however, lagged behind the new ideas and sophisticated concepts then familiar to s.-f. aficionados for a full fifty years—until the advent of STAR TREK in the 1960's.

For the first time a major television network was persuaded to try something more than standard horror scripts with bug-eyed monsters. Months of planning and design went into the attempt to create, to realize in practical, working form, a visual reality of the future. The overall design of the ship itself—

the U.S.S. *Enterprise*—went through at least ten major variations and several hundred drawings (with assists from the Rand Corporation and NASA); the Navy inspected the bridge as a model for a possible communications center; hospitals requested information about the ship's sick bay with its revolutionary diagnostical beds; the beep system was adopted by various official agencies. In short, STAR TREK rapidly developed a devoted fan-following of topflight scientists, engineers, and educators who recognized the ingenuity and foresight behind the fictional façade; science-fiction buffs who for the first time could see in concrete form much that they had been reading about for years; and of course a whole new generation of young people to whom possible futures were a reality rather than a dream.

Nevertheless, having to tread the TV tightrope of combining mass appeal while retaining some cerebral content, STAR TREK maintained only a precarious position on the national network grid. It is significant that it managed to do this despite mediocre Nielsens (an inaccurate "ratings" system of the mid-20th century) and the worst possible "time slot" (on the twenty-four-hour cycle in use at the time).

Today, as with so many of the predictive extrapolations of science fiction, much of STAR TREK's imaginative thinking has become fact. With perspective it is possible now to look back and study this remarkable prototype of so much that was to follow—the first mass-media visualization of the future—and to nod across the centuries to the brilliant minds that forecast a good part of our own present.

As historians and students of predictive history, we need make no guesses. This is how it really happened. . . .

# THE MAKING OF STAR TREK

Stephen E. Whitfield

•

Gene Roddenberry

Written
By
**Stephen E. Whitfield**

BALLANTINE BOOKS • NEW YORK

SBN 345-01705-095

FIRST PRINTING: September, 1968
SECOND PRINTING: December, 1968
THIRD PRINTING: January, 1969
FOURTH PRINTING: April, 1969
FIFTH PRINTING: July, 1970
SIXTH PRINTING: October, 1970

Printed in the United States of America

BALLANTINE BOOKS, INC.
101 Fifth Avenue, New York, N.Y. 10003
An Intext Publisher

To

Orval and LaVila Pierce

who gave me a warm, friendly shelter
and escape from a stormy sea

Beyond

The rim of the star-light

My love

Is wand'ring in star-flight

I know

He'll find in star-clustered reaches

Love,

Strange love a star woman teaches.

I know

His journey ends never

His star trek

Will go on forever.

But tell him

While he wanders his starry sea

Remember, remember me.

"Theme from STAR TREK"
Lyrics by Gene Roddenberry

# CONTENTS

# Introduction

My first personal contact with STAR TREK was in August, 1966. At the time I was employed by an advertising agency in Phoenix, Arizona. One of the agency's accounts was AMT Corporation, a manufacturer of scale model plastic hobby kits. AMT had acquired the merchandising rights on the U. S. S. *Enterprise* and intended to market a scale model plastic kit of the STAR TREK spaceship. Part of my job became one of working closely with Desilu Studios and NBC-TV in order to generate publicity that would reflect favorably on AMT and, hopefully, future sales of the *Enterprise* model kit.

Let me say at the outset that I have always been a strong science fiction buff. For years I have devoured the writings of Heinlein, Bradbury, Sturgeon, Asimov, and a host of others. With the STAR TREK assignment, I knew immediately what Br'er Rabbit meant when he said, "Please don't throw me in the brier patch."

During the months that followed, I made frequent visits to the studio and got to know some of the staff members fairly well. One in particular was Matt Jefferies, STAR TREK's highly imaginative art director. We quickly discovered a mutual interest in flying, and a strong friendship developed.

In May, 1967, Matt sent me a copy of The STAR TREK Guide, a set of guidelines laid out by series creator Gene Roddenberry for use by the show's many writers and directors. At that point I considered myself quite familiar with the show, partly because of the work I had been doing for AMT and partly because I had seen virtually every episode that had been on the air.

My first reading of The STAR TREK Guide opened up a whole new world to me. Here was an immense wealth of background data totally new to me and equally fascinating.

My immediate reaction to that first reading was, "What a nifty basis for a STAR TREK book!"

Several days later I was in Gene Roddenberry's office, explaining the book idea to him. Gene was immediately excited by the project. He not only gave it his blessing, but gave me carte blanche access to the studio in order to assist my research for the book.

In retrospect, I am surprised that Gene agreed to the project at all. I was an unpublished author in the book market, did not even live in the area, and was so totally unfamiliar with television production that I didn't even know enough about it to know what questions to ask. Perhaps it was simply that no one else had suggested the idea to him before.

The book began as a rather simple, uncomplicated idea. It did not stay that way very long.

Initially, the concept was simply one of explaining the various elements that went into the making of the show. In the year of research that followed, this concept underwent many changes. In the television production area, I was a babe in the woods. The more deeply I became involved in research, the more I came to know the principals involved, and the more I learned about the "realities of life," the more convinced I became that the book must encompass more than elements of production. People were and are what makes the thing go. While the book would cover the nuts and bolts of production, it must also cover the people who are, in fact, STAR TREK.

A tape recorder became my constant companion. I interviewed everyone from the Vice President of Television Production all the way down to the man who sweeps the floor on the set. As I did so, one of my earliest observations was underscored again and again by all with whom I spoke.

I was immediately impressed by the uniqueness of the STAR TREK production crew. From the executive producer on down, there seems to be a tremendous esprit de corps. Everyone seems to feel an intense loyalty to STAR TREK, an overriding desire to make this production excellent in quality and one that reflects their own best efforts.

This early impression was so strong that I concluded that someone, probably Gene Roddenberry, had deliberately gone out and hand-picked the key people involved. I have since learned that this is, in essence, exactly what happened.

Having at last finished the writing of this book, I am still convinced the STAR TREK group is indeed a truly unique group of people, perhaps like no other group in the world. This is as it should be. STAR TREK is a unique show, like no other in the world.

The book that follows attempts to tell the story, from an "outsider's" point of view, of the making of an hour-long weekly television series, the history of how it began and what makes it go. To my knowledge it is the first such attempt to tell the history of a telelvision series—the most difficult and ambitious telelvision series ever produced.

The book is therefore an inside look at television as well. It is often funny, sometimes ridiculous, perhaps even (to those in the TV industry) a trifle naïve, and occasionally tragic. But it is also true. In telling the story, I have tried to give the reader a behind-the-scenes glimpse into all areas of television activity—from scriptwriting to casting problems, from stardom to Hollywood parties, from selling a television series to fighting to keep it on the air.

While Gene Roddenberry collaborated with me on this project, I would like to make it clear that the words and points of observation expressed in this book are mine. In many cases I have used quotes from individuals and excerpts from printed material in order to underscore a particular point or activity. In such cases, I have acknowledged the source. In all other respects, however, the observations and the words expressing them are mine.

Many people have assisted me throughout the course of writing this book. In this regard, I owe Gene Roddenberry more than words can say. He is a pretty fantastic guy and often made the difference between disaster and success as this book began to take shape.

At 6′3″, Gene is a tall man, an impressively commanding figure. He is one of that rare breed of men who consider themselves the mildest and gentlest of people but somehow always dominate their surroundings. His hair is slightly grey at the temples, full, thick, and perpetually touseled. Even under the best of conditions, Gene's clothes take on the comfortably worn appearance usually associated with absent-minded professors.

In contrast to his imposing stature, Gene's hands are of medium size, with long, slender, almost delicate fingers. And yet they are capable of bone-crushing handshakes. I mention the hands because I have observed this same characteristic in other highly creative men. It seems to be one of nature's trademarks.

Roddenberry is very much concerned *for* mankind. I have found him to be warm-hearted (almost to a fault), compassionate, and deeply sensitive. On the lighter side, he has a delightful sense of humor, and possesses that enviable ability to "play it straight" while completely and thoroughly putting a person on.

I am personally convinced Roddenberry's creative abilities and interests border on the genius. He has a brilliant, inquisitive mind, a fact attested to by the wide range of activities to which he is drawn. He is an excellent goldsmith and lapidarist, an avid motorcyclist, shoots a pretty fair game of pool, and is equally "at home" in the cockpit of a sailboat or an airplane. More than once Gene's sense of design and intuitive feeling for the harmonious blending of colors have been employed in maintaining the excellence for which STAR TREK has been noted.

His interest in the future of man is obvious in the STAR TREK series. He is intrigued by the idea of what *is* possible through man's advancing technology, and is concerned that he learn to improve himself before his technology destroys humanity.

Because Gene is modest and shows acute embarrassment at personal accolades, it was necessary for me to withhold this statement about him from the manuscript, which I had agreed to let him read and approve. Otherwise, he would have insisted on deleting my remarks. To that extent, I broke my agreement with him. . . . so sue me, Gene!

In the area of editorial assistance, Dorothy Fontana deserves a special word of appreciation. She came to my rescue on more than one occasion, and was of enormous help in keeping this book on the right track.

I would also like to acknowledge the assistance of several

other people, without whose help this book would not have been possible: Bob Justman, Eddie Milkis, Matt Jefferies, Gregg Peters, Bill Theiss, Penny Unger, Rick Carter, Sylvia Smith, Kellam De Forest, and the entire production crew of STAR TREK. I am also most grateful to: Howard McClay and Frank Wright of Paramount's Publicity Department for providing most of the photographs that appear in this book; and Joseph Westheimer Co. for providing the photographs used to illustrate optical processes. I would like to personally thank Miss Bonnie Trost for the herculean task of typing this manuscript. Her long evening and weekend hours devoted to this effort could undoubtedly have been more enjoyably spent elsewhere.

In retrospect, I am amazed the series ever got on the air in the first place. I am also convinced that anyone who wants to produce a television series (particularly one as complex as STAR TREK) has to be (1) an absolute genius and (2) completely out of his mind.

STEPHEN E. WHITFIELD

The technical achievement some eight years ago of the ability to detect reasonable manifestations of intelligent life over interstellar distances has stimulated far-reaching theoretical studies of these matters. Some minor attempts at the detection of possible extraterrestrial radio signals have been carried out in the United States and the Soviet Union. Although the conclusions to be drawn from the theoretical studies are still controversial, the most widely accepted key points to emerge are as follows:

(1) There has probably been and is at present in the universe an enormous number of life-bearing planets, most of which have evolved an intelligent, technical species. . . .

Excerpt from *Prospects in the Search for Extraterrestrial Civilizations,* by F. D. Drake, Center for Radiophysics and Space Research, Cornell University, Ithaca, New York

Part I

BIRTH PANGS

Chapter 1

## As It Was in the Beginning

THE TELEVISION WRITER-PRODUCER FACES AN ALMOST IMPOSSIBLE TASK WHEN HE ATTEMPTS TO CREATE AND PRODUCE A QUALITY TV SERIES. ASSUMING HE CONCEIVED A PROGRAM OF SUCH MEANING AND IMPORTANCE THAT IT COULD ULTIMATELY CHANGE THE FACE OF AMERICA, HE PROBABLY COULD NOT GET IT ON THE AIR OR KEEP IT THERE!*

> Gene Roddenberry
> Creator and Executive
> Producer, STAR TREK

Although Roddenberry was certain the above statement was true, he still dreamed of finding a television series idea that might be the exception to the rule. In 1960 he began to put together a science-fiction idea that seemed promising. He called it STAR TREK. He knew it would at first be considered "too risky," "too different," "impossible to produce." But if he could get it past those hurdles, get it on the air, he might have every writer-producer's dream package.

He decided he had to make it appear on the outside to be nothing more than safe, acceptable adventure stuff. But like a Trojan horse, the series idea would conceal a few surprises. Roddenberry was determined to break through television's censorship barrier and do tales about important and meaningful things. He was certain television's audience was not the collection of nitwits that networks believed it to be. By using

---

* Quotes from Gene Roddenberry throughout the book are printed in this distinctive type face, for easy identification. All *other* statements, opinions, or recountings of events are the words of S.E.W., unless otherwise identified.

science fiction yarns on far-off planets, he was certain he could disguise the fact that he was actually talking about politics, sex, economics, the stupidity of war, and half a hundred other vital subjects usually prohibited on television.

"What d'you mean it's too complicated, Sam? Hell, it's just another horse opera except that they ride a spaceship instead of a nag."

"Sure it uses some complicated words. Throw-away stuff! Flavor! The same way 'Dragnet' used police jargon."

"What's it like? 'Wagon Train'! 'Wagon Train' to the stars, get it?"

Roddenberry developed his ideas into something called a "Series Format" . . . an outline, a framework . . . the skeleton on which a new concept in television science fiction was to be built.

This outline has been reprinted on the pages that follow—in its *original* form. Although certain changes were made later, what follows is the *same* outline that sold STAR TREK as a new series.

Read the outline carefully. It is valuable information for any aspiring writer. It is a good example of how to outline a series idea—the approach used by the pros. It is also an interesting comparison between STAR TREK in the beginning and STAR TREK today.

## STAR TREK
### Created by
### Gene Roddenberry

STAR TREK will be a television "first" . . .
A one-hour science-fiction series *with continuing characters.*
Combining the most varied in drama-action-adventure with complete production practicality.
And with almost limitless story potential.

• • • •

STAR TREK is a new kind of television science fiction *with all the advantages of an anthology, but none of the limitations.* How? Astronomers express it this way:

$$Ff^2 (MgE) - C^1Ri^1 \times M = L/So*$$

Or to put it in simpler terms:

. . . The number of stars in the Universe is so infinite that if only *one in a billion* is a sun with planets . . .

. . . and if only *one in a billion* of all these planets is of Earth size and composition . . .

. . . the Universe would still contain approximately 2,800,000,000,000,000,000,000,000,000,000 planets capable of supporting oxygen-carbon life . . .

. . . or (by the most conservative estimates of chemical or organic probability) something like three million worlds with a good possibility of intelligent life and social evolution similar to our own.

. . . .

Or to put STAR TREK into the language of television . . .

THE FORMAT is "Wagon Train to the Stars"—built around characters who travel to other worlds and meet the jeopardy and adventure which become our stories.

THE TIME could be 1995 or even 2995—close enough to our times for our continuing cast to be people like us, but far enough into the future for galaxy travel to be fully established.

THE FAMILIAR LOCALE is their vessel—the U.S.S. *Enterprise,* a naval cruiser-size spaceship. (In the initial draft of the format, the ship was the U.S.S. *Yorktown.*) The vessel (a permanent set) includes bridge, control rooms, crew quarters and facilities, science labs and technical departments, plus passen-

---

* There is an interesting story about this formula later in the book.

ger and cargo accommodations. These compartments contain the wide range of personalities, some becoming Guest Star roles for stories aboard ship or on the worlds we visit.

THE LEAD ROLE is *Captain Robert T. April,* mid-thirties, an unusually strong and colorful personality, the commander of the cruiser.

OTHER CAST REGULARS are a variety of excitingly different types: *"Number One,"* a glacierlike, efficient female who serves as ship's Executive Officer; *José "Joe" Tyler,* the brilliant but sometimes immature Navigator; *Mr. Spock,* with a red-hued satanic look and surprisingly gentle manners; *Philip "Bones" Boyce,* M. D., ship's doctor and worldly cynic; and uncomfortably lovely *J. M. Colt,* the Captain's Yeoman.

· · · ·

The STAR TREK springboard to 3,000,000 worlds . . .

(Excerpted from orders to Captain Robert T. April)

III. You are therefore posted, effective immediately, to command the following: The U. S. S. *Enterprise.*
   Cruiser Class—Gross 190,000 tons
   Crew Complement—203 persons
   Drive—space-warp
   Range—18 years at light-year velocity
   Registry—Earth, United Spaceship
IV. Nature and duration of mission:
   Galaxy exploration and investigation;
   5 years
V. You will patrol the Ninth Quadrant, beginning with Alpha Centauri and extending to the outer Pinial Galaxy limit.
VI. Consistent with the limitations of your vessel and equipment, you will confine your landings and contacts to Class "M" planets approximating Earth-Mars conditions.

VII. You will conduct this patrol to accomplish primarily:

    (a)  Earth security, via exploration of intelli-
gence and social systems capable of a
galaxial threat, and

    (b)  Scientific investigation to add to the
Earth's body of knowledge of alien life
forms and social systems, and

    (c)  Any required assistance to the several
Earth colonies in this quadrant, and the
enforcement of appropriate statutes af-
fecting such Federated commerce vessels and traders as you may contact in the
course of your mission.

• • • •

The STAR TREK key is the bold establishing of . . .

GALAXY TRAVEL FULLY PERFECTED. April and his
crew, unlike our limited astronauts of today, *are in
charge of their own destiny, must find their own
answers to the jeopardies they meet on far-off
worlds*. The perfected spaceship concept allows us
to move efficiently from story to story, freeing the
audience from tiresome details of technology and
hardware. Our aim is drama and adventure.

THE U.S.S. ENTERPRISE. A permanent set, also provides us with a familiar week-to-week locale. There
is even a suggestion of current naval terminology
and custom which helps link our own "today" with
STAR TREK's "tomorrow."

As with "Gunsmoke" 's Dodge City, "Kildare" 's
Blair General Hospital, our Cruiser is a complete
and highly varied community; we can, at any time,
take our camera down a passageway and find a
guest star (scientist, specialist, ordinary airman, passenger or stowaway) who can propel us into a new
story.

THE SIMILAR WORLDS CONCEPT. Just as the laws of

matter and energy makes probable the other planets of Earth composition and atmosphere, certain chemical and organic laws make equally probable wide evolution into humanlike creatures and civilizations with points of similarity to our own.

All of which gives extraordinary story latitude— ranging from worlds which parallel our own yesterday, our present, to our breathtaking distant future.

. . . .

STAR TREK *keeps all of Science Fiction's variety and excitement, but still stays within a mass audience frame of reference . . .*

By avoiding "way-out" fantasy and cerebral science theorem and instead concentrating on problem and peril met by our very human and very identifiable continuing characters.

Fully one-third of the most successful of all Science Fiction is in this "practical" category. Tales of exotic "methane atmosphere worlds with six-headed monsters" are rare among the Science Fiction classics. The best and most popular *feature highly dramatic variations on recognizable things and themes.* But even within these limits, there are myriad stories, both bizarre and shocking, plus a few monsters legitimus. Space is a place of infinite variety and danger.

. . . .

Some other STAR TREK keys . . .

PLANET LANDINGS. The cruiser itself stays in space orbit, rarely lands upon a planet. Recon parties (small groups, featuring continuing characters) are set down via an energy-matter scrambler which can "materialize" them onto the planet's surface. This requires maximum beam power and is a tremendous drain on the cruiser's power supply. It can be done only across relatively short line-of-sight distances. Materials and supplies can also be moved in this same manner, but require a less critical power expenditure.

Landings are made for a wide variety of reasons —scheduled ports of call, resupplying the cruiser, aid to Earth colonies, scrutiny of an Earth commercial activity, collection of rare animal or plant specimens, a courtesy call on alien life contacted by earlier exploration, a survey of mineral deposits, or any combination of scientific, political, security, or supply needs.

Recon party landings always include dangerous unknowns—no amount of monitoring and observation from cruiser orbit can guarantee complete knowledge of all conditions down there. They can be attacked by alien life, totally ignored, and sometimes even find themselves forced to pose as members of a strange planet's society.

ALIEN LIFE. Normal production casting of much of this alien life is made practical by the SIMILAR WORLDS CONCEPT. To give continual variety, use will, of course, be made of wigs, skin coloration, changes in noses, hands, ears, and even the occasional addition of tails and such.

As exciting as physical differences, and often even more so, will be the universe's incredible differences in social organizations, customs, habit, nourishment, religion, sex, politics, morals, intellect, locomotion, family life, emotions, etc.

LANGUAGE. Simplified by the establishment of a "telecommunicator" device early in the series. Carried in a pocket, little more complicated than a small transistor radio, it is a "two-way scrambler" that appears to be converting all alien language into English and vice versa.

WEAPONRY. Equally basic and simplified. The cruiser is armed with Lasser (sic.) Beams for self-protection. Crew side arms are rifles and pistols which can be adjusted to fire either simple bullets, explosive projectiles, or hypodermic pellets which stun or tranquilize.

* * * *

And finally, the STAR TREK format allows production-budget practicality . . .

. . . by extensive use of a basic and amortized standing set (U.S.S. *Enterprise*) . . .

. . . plus amortization also of miniaturization (i.e., the cruiser in space or orbit) . . .

. . . permits through its "similar world concept" a wide use of existing studio sets, backlots, and local locations, plus unusually good use of in-stock costume, contemporary and historical . . .

. . . minimizes special effects and process by establishing simplified equipment and methods (stet weapons, no space suits, etc.).

* * * *

PRINCIPAL CHARACTER: *Robert T. April*. The "Skipper," about thirty-four, Academy graduate, rank of Captain. Clearly the leading man and central character. This role, built about an unusual combination of colorful strengths and flaws, is designated for an actor of top repute and ability. A shorthand sketch of Robert April might be: "A space-age Captain Horatio Hornblower," constantly on trial with himself, lean and capable both mentally and physically.

Captain April will be the focus of many stories—in still others he may lead us into the introduction of a guest star around whom that episode centers.

A strong, complex personality, he is capable of action and decision which can verge on the heroic—and at the same time lives a continual battle with the self-doubt and the loneliness of command.

As with such men in the past (Drake, Cook, Bougainville, and Scott), April's primary weakness is a predilection to action over administration, a temptation to take the greatest risks onto himself. But, unlike most early explorers, he has an almost compulsive compassion for the rights and plights of others, alien as well as human.

OTHER CONTINUING CHARACTERS: *The Executive Officer.* Never referred to as anything but "Number One," this officer is female. Almost mysteriously female, in fact—slim and dark in a Nile Valley way, age uncertain, one of those women who will always look the same between years twenty and fifty. An extraordinarily efficient space officer, "Number One" enjoys playing it expressionless, cool—is probably Robert April's superior in detailed knowledge of the equipment, departments, and personnel aboard the vessel. When Captain April leaves the craft, "Number One" moves up to Acting Commander.

*The Navigator.* José (Joe) Tyler, Boston astronomer father and Brazilian mother, is boyishly handsome, still very much in the process of maturing. An unusual combination, he has inherited his father's mathematical ability. José Tyler, in fact, is a phenomenally brilliant mathematician and space theorist. But he has also inherited his mother's Latin temperament, fights a perpetual and highly personalized battle with his instruments and calculators, suspecting that space—and probably God, too—are engaged in a giant conspiracy to make his professional and personal life as difficult and uncomfortable as possible. Joe (or José, depending on the other party) is young enough to be painfully aware of the historical repute of Latins as lovers—and is in danger of failing this challenge on a cosmic scale.

*Ship's Doctor.* Philip Boyce, M.D., is a highly unlikely space traveler. Well into his fifties, he's worldly, humorously cynical, makes it a point to thoroughly enjoy his own weaknesses. He's also engaged in a perpetual battle of ideas and ideals with José. Captain April's only real confidant, "Bones" Boyce considers himself the only realist aboard, measures each new landing in terms of the annoyances it will personally create for him.

*The First Lieutenant.* The Captain's right-hand man, the

working-level commander of all the ship's functions—ranging from manning the bridge to supervising the lowliest scrub detail. His name is Mr. Spock. And the first view of him can be almost frightening—a face so heavy-lidded and satanic you might almost expect him to have a forked tail. Probably half Martian, he has a slightly reddish complexion and semi-pointed ears. But strangely—Mr. Spock's quiet temperament is in dramatic contrast to his satanic look. Of all the crew aboard, he is the nearest to Captain April's equal, physically, emotionally, and as a commander of men. His primary weakness is an almost catlike curiosity over anything the slightest "alien."

*The Captain's Yeoman.* Except for problems in naval parlance, J. M. Colt would be called a yeo-woman. With a strip-queen figure even a uniform cannot hide, Colt serves as Captain's secretary, reporter, bookkeeper—and with surprising efficiency. She undoubtedly dreams of serving Robert April with equal efficiency in more personal departments.

Chapter 2

## Creation

I STARTED OFF WRITING SHOWS FOR ZIV.
THEY WERE VERY BAD SHOWS, "MR. DISTRICT
ATTORNEY," "HIGHWAY PATROL," AND SO
FORTH. WHICH WAS FINE, BECAUSE THEY
DIDN'T REQUIRE MUCH KNOWLEDGE OR ABIL-
ITY IN ORDER TO SELL A SCRIPT, AND IN THE
MEANTIME YOU LEARNED ABOUT WRITING.
WHAT "DISSOLVE INTO" MEANS, AND THAT
SORT OF THING.

Gene Roddenberry

Roddenberry's interest in science fiction dated back to his
junior high school days when a classmate lent him a battered
copy of *Astounding Stories*. He never seriously considered
becoming a writer of science fiction or anything else until the
late 1940's, when he found himself a pilot for Pan American
Airways' New York–Calcutta run with a lot of time on his
hands.

His first sales were to flying magazines. In 1949 he left the
airways to move to Los Angeles and investigate the possibilities in the new medium called television. He discovered to his
chagrin that there was precious little television going on in
Los Angeles at that time.

Having a family to support, he looked for a job and
found it with the Los Angeles Police Department. He wrote
his first script for television in 1951, under an assumed
name, since moonlighting was frowned upon.

The following year he wrote a science-fiction script called

31

"The Secret Defense of 117," which was later aired on Chevron Theater.*

During the years that followed, Gene's interest in science fiction continued. From time to time he would jot down ideas and file them away. In the back of his mind, he began to toy around with the idea of doing a science fiction series someday.

In 1954 Gene suddenly discovered that his TV-writing hobby was earning him four times the amount he was then receiving as a police sergeant. He promptly quit the department and turned to writing full time. A writing stint on "West Point" was followed by an assignment to "Have Gun, Will Travel."† He eventually became head writer on that show. In the years that followed, he wrote scripts for such shows as "Kaiser Aluminum Hour," "Four Star Theater," "Naked City," "Dr. Kildare," and just about every other show that was going on, at one time or another.

By 1963 he had created and was producing (at MGM) his first television series, "The Lieutenant."

WHEN A WRITER BEGINS TO HIT WELL AS A FREE-LANCE WRITER, HE RAPIDLY DEVELOPS NEW STRENGTHS AND ABILITIES. IF LUCKY, HE BECOMES VERY MUCH IN DEMAND. HE CAN PICK UP A PHONE AND HAVE AN ASSIGNMENT AT ANY TIME HE WISHES.

EVENTUALLY THE REALIZATION BEGINS TO SET IN THAT, ALTHOUGH HE KNOWS THE BUSINESS AND IS DOING WELL AT IT, HE IS STILL DOING PIECEWORK. IF HE STOPS WRITING, THE MONEY STOPS COMING IN. THE MONEY MAY BE GREAT, BUT THERE IS DAMNED LITTLE SECURITY IN IT FOR HIS FAMILY.

IN TELEVISION THE ONLY WAY TO GET

---

* Ricardo Montalban starred in this show and many years later was a guest star in a STAR TREK episode.

† His episode titled "Helen of Abajinian" won him a Writer's Guild Award for Best Western. By then he was beginning to be regarded as one of the outstanding writers in television.

THAT SECURITY IS TO OWN A PIECE OF THE ACTION. TO OWN A SERIES SO THAT WHEN THERE ARE ROYALTIES AND PROFITS SOMEDAY, YOU WILL HAVE THEM. BUT SECURITY WAS ONLY PART OF THE REASON WHY I MADE THE JUMP FROM WRITER TO WRITER-PRODUCER.

PRIOR TO "THE LIEUTENANT" I HAD WRITTEN SOME OTHER PILOTS. THEY WERE PRODUCED BY OTHER PEOPLE, AND NONE OF THEM SOLD. I BEGAN TO SEE THAT TO CREATE A PROGRAM IDEA AND WRITE A SCRIPT SIMPLY WASN'T ENOUGH.

THE STORY IS NOT "TOLD" UNTIL IT'S ON CELLULOID. TELLING THAT FINAL STORY INVOLVES SOUND, MUSIC, CASTING, COSTUMES, SETS, AND ALL THE THINGS THAT A PRODUCER IS RESPONSIBLE FOR. THEREFORE IT BECAME APPARENT TO ME THAT IF YOU WANT THE FILM TO REFLECT ACCURATELY WHAT YOU FELT WHEN YOU WROTE THE SCRIPT, THEN YOU HAVE TO PRODUCE IT, TOO.

THIS IS WHY TELEVISION WRITERS TEND TO BECOME PRODUCERS.

PRODUCING IN TELEVISION IS LIKE STORYTELLING. THE CHOICE OF THE ACTOR, PICKING THE RIGHT COSTUMES, GETTING THE RIGHT FLAVOR, THE RIGHT PACE—THESE ARE AS MUCH A PART OF STORYTELLING AS WRITING OUT THAT SAME DESCRIPTION OF A CHARACTER IN A NOVEL.

ALTHOUGH THE DIRECTOR PLAYS AN IMPORTANT ROLE IN THIS, THE DIRECTOR IN TELEVISION COMES ON A SHOW TO PREPARE FOR A WEEK, SHOOTS FOR A WEEK, AND THEN GOES ON TO ANOTHER SHOW. UNLIKE THE PRODUCER, HE IS NEITHER THERE AT THE BEGINNING OF THE SCRIPT NOR RARELY THERE FOR LONG AFTER YOU END UP WITH SOME 25,000 FEET OF FILM WHICH NOW HAS

TO BE CUT AND PASTED TOGETHER INTO
SOMETHING UNIFIED.

THERE IS IMMENSE CREATIVE CHALLENGE
AND PLEASURE IN TAKING ALL OF THESE
THINGS AND PUTTING THEM TOGETHER INTO
SOMETHING THAT WORKS  IN A SHOW SUCH
AS STAR TREK, ALMOST EVERYTHING YOU DO
. . . FROM THE FASHIONING OF GARMENTS,
TO FIGURING OUT WHAT A BED LOOKS LIKE
CENTURIES FROM NOW, AND SO ON . . . IS
EVEN MORE CHALLENGING AND EXCITING
TO DO.

During 1963 MGM asked Gene to come up with an idea
for a new series. They were afraid (a fear later justified) that
"The Lieutenant" would not be picked up for another season.

For some reason television seems to run in cycles. At that
time, programming was nearing the end of the "true-to-life-
Defenders" type of cycle. All trends indicated a cycle back to
action-adventure. This cycle later spawned such shows as "I
Spy" and "The Man From U.N.C.L.E." When Gene suggested he'd been playing with a science-fiction adventure
script idea, MGM expressed a willingness to look at it.

As production on "The Lieutenant" neared its end, Gene
began to finalize the series format he had been developing.

In creating STAR TREK, Gene was, in fact, attempting to
destroy three widely accepted Hollywood myths.

First that "science fiction" and "fantasy" were the same.
He insisted that the television audience was ready to accept
the first, but that the difference between the two was important.

Science fiction is based either on fact or well-thought-out
speculation. It is an extension of current knowledge or of a
theory worked out in enough detail to seem at least "possible." Once having established known or theoretical scientific
ground rules, the true science fiction story adheres to them all
the way. With fantasy, on the other hand, you can say, "This
man has the power to blink his left eye and he will disappear," and never explain how or why he can do that. For that
reason the audience finds it difficult to identify with charac-

ters and situations in a fantasy. Roddenberry was convinced
that they would identify with science-fiction characters if he
set believable ground rules and stuck to them.

The second myth (one of the things that has made science
fiction shows so bad in the past) is that most writers and producers viewed science fiction as an entirely separate branch
of literature in which the basic rules of drama do not
apply. In doing a police show or a hospital show or a Western, they followed the essentials of drama and worked to create belief in the character, build ascending climaxes in the
story, orchestrate the characters around a basic theme, and so
on. Yet when those same people approached science fiction,
they ignored all those dramatic principles. Thus, most science
fiction shows were littered with gadgets and bug-eyed monsters and mad scientists, but rarely included realistic characters, believable story situations, or any real drama.

Roddenberry insisted that literature is literature, be it
called science fiction, Shakespeare, or Cowboys and Indians.
You must work to make your characters come to life
whether riding a horse in Dodge City or sitting in a captain's
chair far out in space. The audience must think, "I am
there." They must believe they are sitting in that saddle or
in that chair and it's all happening to *them*.


WHAT'S BEEN WRONG WITH SCIENCE FIC-
TION IN TELEVISION AND IN MOTION PIC-
TURES FOR YEARS IS THAT WHENEVER A
MONSTER WAS USED, THE TENDENCY WAS TO
SAY, "AH, HA! LET'S HAVE A BIG ONE THAT
COMES OUT, ATTACKS, AND KILLS EVERY-
ONE." NOBODY EVER ASKED "WHY?" IN ANY
OTHER STORY, IF SOMETHING ATTACKS (A
BEAR, A MAN, OR WHATEVER), THE AUTHOR
IS EXPECTED TO EXPLAIN, "HERE IS WHY IT IS
THE WAY IT IS, HERE ARE THE THINGS THAT
LED IT TO DO THIS, HERE IS WHAT IT WANTS."

A CLASSIC EXAMPLE OF DOING THIS RIGHT
WAS ONE OF OUR MOST POPULAR EPISODES,

WRITTEN BY GENE COON,* ENTITLED "THE DEVIL IN THE DARK." THE "HORTA" WAS AN UNDERGROUND CREATURE WHICH ATTACKED A GROUP OF MINERS. IN THE END THEY FIND OUT THAT IT ATTACKED BECAUSE—SURPRISE —IT WAS A MOTHER! IT WAS PROTECTING ITS EGGS BECAUSE THE MINERS WERE DESTROYING THEM IN THE BELIEF THAT THEY WERE JUST STRANGE-LOOKING MINERAL FORMATIONS.

WITH THIS UNDERSTOOD, THE HORTA SUDDENLY BECAME UNDERSTANDABLE, TOO. IT WASN'T JUST A MONSTER—IT WAS SOMEONE. AND THE AUDIENCE COULD PUT THEMSELVES IN THE PLACE OF THE HORTA . . . IDENTIFY . . . FEEL! THAT'S WHAT DRAMA IS ALL ABOUT. AND THAT'S ITS IMPORTANCE, TOO . . . IF YOU CAN LEARN TO FEEL FOR A HORTA, YOU MAY ALSO BE LEARNING TO UNDERSTAND AND FEEL FOR OTHER HUMANS OF DIFFERENT COLORS, WAYS, AND BELIEFS.

The third myth involved the belief that it was impossible to weave continuing characters into television science fiction. Until STAR TREK, all television's science fiction had been anthologies.

Yet, Roddenberry noted, virtually every other television series on the air, with mass audience appeal, had a cast of familiar, continuing characters. "Bonanza" is a classic example. A family group. You get to know them, feel comfortable with them. One of the earliest examples was "Gunsmoke." Chester, Doc, Kitty, and Matt. Chester became a familiar figure to people everywhere. Many sent him worried advice about his bad leg. Others wondered if Matt and Kitty had an "understanding." Some argued whether Doc was drinking too much, considering his responsibilities.

In addition to the familiar faces, television found familiar

---

* Coon took over STAR TREK producer chores after Roddenberry moved to executive producer.

surroundings important, too. In the case of "Have Gun, Will Travel," Paladin's home base was the Carlton Hotel, San Francisco, 1872. Whatever his incredible adventures, he ended up back there. And it was somehow comfortable to know that he (and the audience who lived the adventures with him) had a home.

These were the elements that Gene set about weaving into the STAR TREK format: science fiction which adhered to the proven rules of drama, a cast of continuing characters, and a familiar home base from which to operate.

As the last days of "The Lieutenant" drew to a close, Gene submitted the completed STAR TREK series format to MGM. Their reaction was not enthusiastic. They did say they liked the idea enough to consider it and perhaps do something about it . . . sometime.

Gene waited for a decision. And waited. And waited.

After three or four months it became obvious that nothing would happen with MGM. The format was submitted to several other studios. The wording may have varied slightly, but the answers always boiled down to: "It's an interesting idea, but it's not only too different, it's physically and financially impossible to do as a weekly television series."

Then Gene's agent called with the rumor that Desilu Studios was desperate for television properties. He suggested that Gene submit the STAR TREK format to them. In April, 1964, on the basis of the STAR TREK format, plus several other series ideas Gene outlined verbally, Desilu signed Gene to a three-year contract to make television pilots * for them.

Almost immediately STAR TREK was to be dealt a setback.

The ink had hardly dried on the contract before Oscar Katz (at the time, Executive Vice President in Charge of Television Production at Desilu) announced a meeting had been arranged with CBS. Format in hand, Gene prepared to sell his idea.

Present at the meeting were James Aubrey (then President

---

* A "pilot" is like a sample episode from the proposed series and contains all of the normal elements of that series—setting, main characters, type of story, etc. Until recently when sky-rocketing production costs made it impractical, a pilot film was usually required in order to sell a series to one of the networks.

of CBS) and a dozen other CBS vice presidents and executives. The meeting was by no means a "special audience." There were at least fifteen other people waiting outside to explain their proposed series ideas to the CBS officials.

Gene talked for almost two hours, outlining his ideas for the series, explaining ways in which a science-fiction series could be made on budget, and ways it could be made to appeal to a mass audience. He discussed the problems with science fiction in the past, outlined his suggestions for solving them. Aubrey and the others expressed a great deal of interest in what he said. They were particularly interested in his ideas on spaceship design, the types of stories to do, how to cut costs, and other technical aspects that Gene had developed. At the end of the two hours, and after having been questioned closely by most of those present, he thought he had sold them. Then they said, "Thank you very much. We have one of our own that we like better.* But we do appreciate your coming in."

MY ATTITUDE WAS, "YOU S.O.B.'S, WHY DIDN'T YOU TELL ME THAT AFTER THE FIRST TEN MINUTES? IF YOU WANT TECHNICAL ADVICE AND HELP, HIRE ME AND PAY ME FOR IT!" IT'S LIKE CALLING A DOCTOR AND HAVING HIM ANALYZE YOU FOR TWO HOURS AND THEN TELLING HIM, "THANK YOU VERY MUCH FOR PINPOINTING WHAT'S WRONG, AND I'VE DECIDED TO GO TO ANOTHER DOCTOR FOR THE TREATMENT."

Although Gene was understandably angry, CBS may have simply felt that his idea of an adult science fiction series would not reach a mass audience (it almost didn't) and therefore was not commercial enough. Television is in the business of advertising products to a mass audience. Since advertising rates depend on the size of the audience, there is a tendency to "play it safe."

Television has become "big business," with tens of millions

---

* "Lost in Space."

at stake on each program. It takes an extraordinary network executive to gamble on a "special" kind of show that might have only a limited audience.*

As one highly placed network executive said, "Roddenberry, I like you, I like the kind of ideas you talk. I'm a rebel myself. But I'm responsible to stockholders who expect to see a profit every year. If we try to make a television series out of this idea of yours and the series bombs out, we stand to lose a lot of money and I'll be blamed for trying something too different. If the stockholders get upset, I might find myself out of a job."

There are only three major networks, three markets. And one had already turned STAR TREK down. The proposed series had not gotten off to a very encouraging start.

---

* If one has to choose, the college-level audience must be ignored, since they are a minority.

Chapter 3

## A Spark of Life

INTOLERANCE IN THE 23RD CENTURY? IM-
PROBABLE! IF MAN SURVIVES THAT LONG, HE
WILL HAVE LEARNED TO TAKE A DELIGHT IN
THE ESSENTIAL DIFFERENCES BETWEEN MEN
AND BETWEEN CULTURES. HE WILL LEARN
THAT DIFFERENCES IN IDEAS AND ATTITUDES
ARE A DELIGHT, PART OF LIFE'S EXCITING
VARIETY, NOT SOMETHING TO FEAR. IT'S A
MANIFESTATION OF THE GREATNESS THAT
GOD, OR WHATEVER IT IS, GAVE US. THIS IN-
FINITE VARIATION AND DELIGHT, THIS IS
PART OF THE OPTIMISM WE BUILT INTO STAR
TREK.

Gene Roddenberry

The situation in April, 1964, must have been pretty bad.
Both for Gene Roddenberry and for Desilu Studios.

STAR TREK, frankly, was a giant risk. The series format indicated an extremely expensive series and represented a completely new and untried concept. Any studio deciding to un-
derwrite the cost of a pilot would have to do so with the full
knowledge that it might take a half-million-dollar bath in the
process.

Most of the studios around town were doing fairly well at
that time. Television had not yet begun to lose its audience,
and few television executives felt they needed to take giant
risks on new ideas.

By comparison, the situation at Desilu was grim. If a studio like MGM could be termed a major-leaguer, Desilu was

little more than a farm club. In the previous eight years they had made a dozen different pilots, spent millions of dollars in the process, and had produced only losers. Except for the durable "I Love Lucy," Desilu had become largely a rental operation, leasing space and facilities to other production companies. (In fact, "Lucy" was the *only* TV series Desilu had at the time.)

Desilu needed to sell a series to a network—a quality series if possible. By proving the studio's limited facilities were capable of first-class production departments, new talent might be attracted. Also, in case of studio sale, the value would be increased. Roddenberry's needs were simpler: he wanted STAR TREK on the air.

His decision to sign with Desilu was undoubtedly a compromise on his part. STAR TREK would be difficult enough to make under the best of conditions. At a small, ill-equipped studio the task would be doubly difficult.

Gene returned from the disappointing CBS meeting and continued to develop other studio properties, while awaiting a chance with another network. Until that happened, he was completely stymied.

Primarily because of money.

Best estimates for the STAR TREK pilot placed production cost in excess of a half-million dollars. Although more has ben spent on some pilots, it was still high and a considerable gamble for a small studio.

If pilot costs are high, the odds against success are astronomical. One network official recently stated that of the twenty-eight to thirty new shows (pilots) considered by his network every season, only four or five would actually go on the air. The whole process is a celluloid crap game, and the house has all the odds against the players.

The first major break came in early May, 1964. Desilu's Oscar Katz had kept busy, and the format was submitted to Mort Werner, NBC-TV Vice President in Charge of Programming. Werner's courage makes him a rarity in the television game. He liked the idea of doing a show like STAR TREK, but wanted to see it more fully developed. Primarily with Werner's backing, NBC committed about $20,000 in "story money." Under the agreement, Gene would write three stories based on his series concept, NBC would choose one of them, from which Gene would then write the pilot script.

With story money in hand, Gene could now afford to concentrate on developing the idea into a script.

About this time he brought in a talented young woman named Dorothy (D. C.) Fontana to double as both assistant and secretary. Dorothy had worked with Gene on "The Lieutenant," had eight television scripts (mostly Westerns) to her credit, and was later to play an important part in the series.*

STAR TREK's space ship was bound to be a major undertaking and Gene requested Desilu's art department to begin submitting sketches immediately. The exact appearance and shape of the U.S.S. *Enterprise* was anyone's guess at this point, but the decision was made that the ship must be large enough to carry a crew of several hundred people. There were many arguments on this point. Everyone seemed to feel that by the time we reach STAR TREK's future, automation will have developed to such a highly perfected degree that six or eight people would be capable of running virtually any size spaceship. And, indeed, they probably could.

Two things affected the decision in favor of a large ship crew.

The first was the fact that a group of several hundred people aboard a multilevel ship would provide a greater variety of characters to use in the series. Secondly, the larger the vessel, the greater the variety of control rooms, labs, recreation facilities, and other locations aboard.

WE CAN WALK DOWN THE CORRIDOR ANY DAY AND FIND A GUEST STAR WORKING IN THE BIOLABORATORY, OR SOMEWHERE. AFTER WE DECIDED ON THIS MANY PEOPLE, WE DISCOVERED THAT IT DID MAKE SENSE. IF THIS STARSHIP IS DOING ALL THE THINGS WE

---

* Within about two years D. C. Fontana, an exceptionally fine writer, was promoted to script consultant. She has written a number of STAR TREK scripts, and many of them have proved to be among the series' most popular episodes.

SAY IT DOES, WE ARE GOING TO HAVE TO
HAVE SPECIALIZED PEOPLE AND EQUIPMENT
TO COVER EVERY POSSIBLE SCIENCE.

WE BELIEVED THAT EVEN IN OUR ERA OF
STAR TREK, MACHINES WILL NOT BE ABLE TO
REASON AS MAN CAN REASON.

MOREOVER, MEN (AND WOMEN) ON LONG
SPACE VOYAGES WILL BE MENTALLY AND
PHYSICALLY HEALTHIER IF THEY ARE PART
OF A COMMUNITY—THE LARGER AND MORE
VARIED THE COMMUNITY, THE BETTER.

In order to create a believable character for a story, you
must give him a background, a personality, interests, mannerisms, and all the other things you notice in a real flesh-and-
blood person. The more believable and multidimensional, the
better. The same thing is true of the setting, or environment, in
which the characters live and operate.

Gene's insistence upon the Believability Factor, as it has
come to be known, imposed tremendous problems from the
very beginning. It continues to do so even today.

The series format hinted that the *Enterprise* "rarely lands
upon a planet." This was quickly changed to "never."

LAND A SHIP FOURTEEN STORIES TALL ON A
PLANET SURFACE EVERY WEEK? NOT ONLY
WOULD IT HAVE BLOWN OUR ENTIRE WEEKLY
BUDGET BUT JUST SUGGESTING IT PROBABLY
WOULD HAVE RUINED MY REPUTATION IN
THE INDUSTRY FOREVER.

There was also a dramatic reason involved in the decision.
Any type of spaceship landing must necessarily be a time-
consuming operation.

THIS IS ONE OF MANY INSTANCES WHERE A
COMPROMISE FORCED US INTO CREATIVE
THOUGHT AND ACTUALLY IMPROVED WHAT
WE PLANNED TO DO.

IF SOMEONE HAD SAID, "WE WILL GIVE YOU

THE BUDGET TO LAND THE SHIP," OUR STO-
RIES WOULD HAVE STARTED SLOW, MUCH TOO
SLOW. THE FACT THAT WE DIDN'T HAVE THE
BUDGET FORCED US INTO CONCEIVING THE
TRANSPORTER DEVICE—"BEAM" THEM DOWN
TO THE PLANET—WHICH ALLOWED US TO BE
WELL INTO THE STORY BY SCRIPT PAGE TWO.

The concept of "Class M" planets (those approximating
Earth conditions) was a compromise with production costs.
While the billions and billions of planets scattered throughout
this galaxy undoubtedly contain many weird life forms, the
cost, in makeup and special costumes, makes their frequent
appearance on a weekly television show prohibitive. Class M
planets, on the other hand, will contain aliens, but generally
of a humanoid type, bringing makeup and costuming costs
within the realm of reason.

If estimates in the series format were anywhere near
accurate (a couple of million Class M planets), the *Enterprise* had plenty of places to cruise to.

It was decided to emphasize in stories that the ship operated
in a far-flung corner of the galaxy, creating more exciting
story possibilities. The Captain would have to make decisions
entirely on his own. He would carry responsibilities in a way
few men have ever experienced before.

It was also decided the *Enterprise* should not return to the
Earth of STAR TREK's period. To do so would mean highly
complex sets. More important, not having the *Enterprise* return to Earth would avoid complex arguments (and possibly
fatal disagreements with network and sponsors) on how our
present social and economic system finally evolved.

But it was believed reasonable to assume that a "Federation" will exist—a "United Federation of Planets." Some of
the member planets would be Earth Colonies, and others
would be friendly aliens.

There is nothing strange or new in the concept of a galac-
tic-wide federation. It is a normal, logical progression from
what we know today. The history of this Earth is replete with
examples of small city-states, countries, and even religious
groups joining together in a "union," "congress," or "federation." As man reaches out into the stars and makes contact

with other intelligent life forms, it is entirely probable that some sort of cooperative union will result—if not from a need for mutual self-defense, then certainly to enjoy the benefits of interplanetary trade and commerce.

> THESE THINGS AREN'T SO DIFFERENT, AND THEY CERTAINLY DON'T MAKE US GENIUSES. ANY PERSON OF AVERAGE IQ CAN MAKE AN ANALYSIS OF WHERE WE WERE TWENTY YEARS AGO, WHERE WE ARE TODAY, AND WITH THAT CAN MAKE A PRETTY SHREWD GUESS AS TO WHERE WE WILL BE TOMORROW.

By the end of June the three story outlines had been completed and forwarded to NBC.

Although the network was interested in the proposed series, they nevertheless had many reservations about the feasibility of the project. NBC wanted a quality television series. They still considered Gene a novice at the game of producing and they were not at all sure that a small studio like Desilu could produce what was, in effect, a small science-fiction movie every week. Science-fiction movies are often complex, time-consuming projects and usually require a maximum of ten to twelve weeks just to photograph. Assuming the series went on the air, with television's limited budgets, each segment would have to be filmed in five or six days! STAR TREK's story outlines indicated a highly complex show. Could each segment actually be filmed in the time required and maintain the high production standards proposed?

The network also seriously questioned the proposed use of opticals (visual illusions). Heretofore, optical trick photography was considered feasible only for fairly high-budget motion pictures and often took months to complete. If STAR TREK were to use the opticals indicated in Roddenberry's format, new optical methods had to be invented!

Of the three stories submitted, and despite their reservations, NBC chose one entitled "The Cage." * The script based

---

* At this point Mr. Spock was only a hazy outline and bore little resemblance to the present character. Also at this point NBC knew very little of Gene's plans for a character with pointed ears.

on that story eventually became known as "The Menagerie" and as a two-part episode won the International Hugo Award for filmed science fiction.

This was the beginning of STAR TREK, a show that has not only affected television but has played a significant role in readying the audience for the recent interest in major motion picture science fiction. That original story has never before been printed. And, in fact, rarely will a professional writer make a pre-script story outline available to the general public. By special permission of its creator, the original story, "The Cage," as it was first written and in its entirety, is here presented as Chapter 4 of Part I.

Chapter 4

## Star Trek

## "THE CAGE"
Pilot Story Outline *

By:

Gene Roddenberry
First Draft
6-29-64

I. ACT ONE

1. The U.S.S. *Enterprise,* cruising toward its next port of call, intercepts an emergency astro-wave signal sent out fourteen years previously from survivors of a spaceship which had disappeared years ago. The message states that the ship had run into difficulty, attempted to set down on planet Sirius IV, crashed. The survivors have since been using fading power, hoping their radio appeals would be intercepted by some passing ship. We get a good look at the operation of the U.S.S. *Enterprise* as Captain Robert April diverts it toward Sirius IV.

2. The *Enterprise* orbits the planet, the ship's electroscopes locating the wrecked spaceship and focusing a picture of it onto the giant picture screen at the bridge. Radio contact is established, and they hear a strange, atonal recitation voice of one of the survivors. Navigator José Tyler is a bit suspicious of some

---

* A "story outline," of which this is an excellent example, is used by all professional TV and film writers as the "blueprint" for the script. STAR TREK fans will see here that Roddenberry made a number of significant changes between finishing this outline and writing the actual script which followed.

of this message, plus the fact the fading ship's power has lasted this long. But everything else seems to make sense. Robert April selects a recon party of himself, Mr. Spock, José, and ship's doctor Philip Boyce, and they step into the transporter chamber. We get our first look at this procedure, too, as it beams them to materialize on the planet surface far below.

3. The landing party is beamed to materialize on arid, rocky Sirius IV a quarter mile from the wrecked ship. They move in carefully, maintaining defense security, come upon a small encampment containing the few half-starved survivors who are almost unable to believe that rescue is finally here. One of these is a young woman, Vina, provocatively lovely, showing so few effects of the ordeal that Dr. Boyce becomes suspicious, and he finds other things that somehow do not seem to make sense to his medical mind.

At an appropriate moment we pull back and realize all this is also being watched on a strange-shaped televisor screen by crablike creatures. Although in no way human, they are obviously intelligent and have digital capabilities via six multiclawed arms and legs. The screen goes into a close-up on several of the *Enterprise* recon party members, finally centers and stays on Captain April. The crab-creature at the televisor controls turns from the screen, using claw-snap and clatter for speech, and two other of the creatures respond to the message and depart.

4. At the survivor encampment, routine recon party security has been abandoned in the excitement of finding survivors. Dr. Boyce reaches April with his warning, April is diverted by the girl Vina who seems to understand those doubts and wants to tell him something important. She moves with him to an odd-shaped geological formation and, standing directly in front of him, she suddenly disappears! The entire survivor group and encampment have disappeared in the same moment, and the recon party

from the *Enterprise* stands totally alone, stunned, separated from each other, and momentarily defenseless. And in the same instant the two crab-creatures silently emerge from a trapdoor in the rock formation immediately behind April, expertly enmeshing him in a plastic bag of extraordinary strength, drag the struggling *Enterprise* captain back into a metal-lined underground passage as his struggles grow feebler and he falls unconscious. Mr. Spock and navigator Tyler race there, Laser guns out blasting away at the rock, earth, and strange vegetation which camouflage the entry, succeeding only in exposing a gray metal cap which their Laser beams will not penetrate or even mark.

5. Captain Robert April awakes, rolls to his feet, checking to find his weapons have been taken. He still has his small telecommunicator which has slipped down inside his shirt during the struggle. He starts to pull it out, freezes as he becomes aware his "cell" is enclosed on the fourth side by a fully transparent panel and crab-creatures stand outside watching him. He palms the telecommunicator, moves to the transparent wall. Outside, his captivity is creating considerable interest among the creatures; we can hear the snapping and clattering of their claws and external armor-skeleton. April stealthily tunes his telecommunicator until the clattering noises blend into an atonal translation.

6. The reciting voice makes it plain April is in a "zoo," his cage only one of many that line the corridor outside. The "Keeper" is lecturing the others on his estimation of this sample of protein-life they have captured. The others out on the planet surface cannot interfere, since their power and weaponry is of a rather primitive Laser-beam type. This particular one in the enclosure seemed the healthiest and most alert of the lot, the best choice for the "experiment."

FADE OUT

II.   ACT TWO

1. We are outside April's enclosure, the crab-creatures continuing to discuss their specimen. As with
   the similar creatures who died in the spaceship crash
   years ago on their planet, the intellectual processes
   seem as primitive as the weaponry. It was quite simple to bait them in with messages and images of an
   encampment of surviving fellow creatures. Apparently they have little ability to distinguish imagery
   from reality. And if the observers will tune in on this
   biped protein-creature's mind, the Keeper will dem-
   onstrate.

2. Inside the enclosure, April has begun to attempt
   communication with the crab-creatures. Absolutely
   ignored, he tries to rap on the transparent wall. Still
   failing to get their attention, he finds a water container on the floor, moves to strike it against the
   transparent wall. In mid-motion the water container
   suddenly becomes an odd-shaped short sword; he is
   wearing beryllium armor, using a shield to protect
   himself from similarly armed hairy manlike creatures who are attacking him, trying to get at the
   woman he protects. Exotically dressed, this is the il-
   lusion-woman Vina whom we previously met at the
   "survivors' encampment." April is stunned to find
   himself in this position but cannot shake off the reality of it when a sword cut draws blood on his left
   upper arm and he is forced to fight back in defense.
   A blow from one of the hairy bipeds sends him spinning, and his telecommunicator falls out of his shirt
   to the ground. Protecting himself with his shield, he
   scrambles to regain it.

3. We are back with the crab-creatures, watching April
   inside the enclosure, in the same position scrambling
   on the floor for the telecommunicator he has
   dropped. The water container is still in his hand, his
   other arm raised as if holding a shield, protecting
   himself from the enemies he is fighting in the illu-

sion. Scrambling back to his feet, he continues the
sword play, shouting back to the also nonexistent girl
to get away while she can.

The Keeper, via the atonal voice, is explaining
that this is the planet Endrex II on which the subject
once landed and was involved in a similar incident.
A female has been inserted into this illusion to dem-
onstrate how deeply these bipeds are moved by danger to their females.

One of the crab-creatures inquires about the small
telecommunicator in April's hand, and the Keeper
correctly identifies it as a simple language translator
device. They're letting the subject retain it in the
event they wish to communicate with him.

4. Inside the enclosure, the illusion is suddenly over
and Bob April finds himself back in his cage, wield-
ing the water container like a sword, disheveled and
perspiring. All the crab-creatures are departing except for the Keeper, who moves to a sort of desk at
the end of the corridor of enclosures containing various life specimens from other parts of the universe.
(These enclosures are staggered so that we can see
little of the others from April's location.)

In addition to the water container, April's cage
contains a spongelike epiloid that can serve as a bed,
covered with a filmy metallic blanket; a decorative
pool of surging water that has something of a splash-
ing fountain in the center—the enclosure spotlessly
clean and bare, utilitarian but not unattractive. There
are no visible exits or ingresses, no crannies, no holes
—April is hopelessly trapped.

A voice—April whirling to find the girl Vina, now
in a metallic dress approximating the filmy blanket,
in the cage with him, watching him. An unusual conversation—April, defiant and angry, is not interested
in wasting time on illusions which come and go like
snapping a light switch off and on. Vina laughingly
agrees she has no real substance, that she is a product of his mind, and as such she is naturally at-

tracted to him. Isn't that the male dream image of a
woman, one who cannot resist? And Vina does seem
almost compulsively attracted to April, strangely
playing the seductress. He tries to ignore her, works
with his telecommunicator to produce a maximum
radio signal. Vina tells him they are far underground
with a half-mile of solid balsite rock insulating them
from the planet's surface. There is no way for a
radio system to penetrate this and give the spaceship
a bearing on him. Vina also seems to be fully aware
of all of the spaceship's capabilities and systems, the
limitations of its power, the use of the matter-energy
scrambler by which men and material can be transported from the ship to the planet's surface, April's
status as commander, and so on. Being made up as
she is of April's thoughts and memories, she knows
this and much more. Even secrets about himself he
has never admitted to a human being, terrestrial or
otherwise. Then, seeming annoyed by the fact that
he won't answer, she disappears as abruptly as she
arrived.

5. On the U.S.S. *Enterprise* the recon party has returned and reported April's capture to "Number
One." The resources of the *Enterprise* are being organized for location and rescue. In this, utilizing
conflicts of viewpoint and attitude, we continue to
explore the series' regular characters. Philip Boyce,
M.D., has made the most accurate analysis of the life
below. Mr. Spock has fairly close estimations on the
science of this civilization, plus observations of the
planet composition and structure. Youthful navigator
Joe (José) Tyler is irritated at the caution of the
others, insists upon an attack in force, is already utilizing his brilliance in determining how some combination of ship's power might penetrate the planet's
surface to locate underground passages, even permit
radio waves to operate through what appears to be
solid rock so that some communication can be established. Lovely J. M. Colt, the Captain's yeoman,
is enough concerned for April's safety that she slips

in her duties and draws a rebuke from a seemingly emotionless "Number One."

6. The commander of the U.S.S. *Enterprise* is asleep on the odd-shaped bed in his cage. Outside, the Keeper has been joined by another crab-creature, and they hover over a screen watching the sleeping man. Back to Robert April, then the surface of the bed shimmers and begins to change, the covering over his body going from metallic cloth to brocade satin. Then a slim hand reaches in and shakes him. April awakes, finds the lovely illusion Vina with him again. He is lying in a richly appointed bed in a luxurious room. She wears a robe that can only be from the Renaissance period, addressing him as "M'Lord" as she tells him she has arrived in answer to his request. Despite what April says, she continues as if some romantic tryst had been arranged between them. April tries reason, finally becomes so annoyed that he raises his voice, and a pike-bearing man-at-arms enters from the double doors, thinking his "master" has called out in alarm, apologizes quickly upon seeing Vina, exits again. April angrily goes to the window, looks out, and finds the scene that of Renaissance Venice, his building a palace at the edge of the old city's central piazza.

The lovely Vina persists in playing it as a lovers' rendezvous until it becomes obvious April has no intention of succumbing. Then, amused, she drops her role as Renaissance seductress and tries to accomplish the same through a logical analysis of his position. Why not relax and go along with the illusion? It's pleasant, isn't it? Everything looks real, feels real; the pleasure can be equally real. And he can't deny that this is out of his own daydreams. And it's a fine one. The more intelligent the man, the more colorful and more pleasant the variety of his dreams. Imagination is superior to real life; there is no flesh and blood to be hurt; he can even relax and delight in those secret evil things that lurk in the back of every man's mind. All he has to do is think about it and he'll live it.

7. April, on the other hand, can guess all of this is being watched by the alien life which imprisons him, and he damned well will not perform for their amusement and edification. And he is beginning to have some doubts about Vina. Is she completely a figment of his imagination? April baits her into talking about the crab-creatures, their civilization and their planet. Seeming willing to please him in all ways, she explains that the intelligent crablike race had once lived on the planet's surface but that recurring wars, overpopulation, and exhaustion of the planet's mineral and vegetable resources had eons ago forced the planet's scientists to band together and begin burrowing into deep underground communities to protect themselves from the certain destruction of civilization above. The creatures who have captured April are the descendants of this scientific society. The surface civilization died long ago, leaving the surface of Sirius IV the arid waste found by the *Enterprise* recon party. The crab-creatures are advanced far beyond man's capabilities, gave up space travel long ago as vastly less efficient and pleasant than utilizing the power of pure thought.

April questions this sharply, and Vina admits this has been discovered a mistake that has seen the crab-creatures lose their old vigor and disciplines; they are incapable now of creating and building or even repairing their marvelous underground cities and machines. They sit at their televisors, living and reliving experiences and emotions in the thought-records left behind by their forebears. Even the "zoo" is part of this—the cages holding descendants of creatures brought back hundreds of centuries ago from other planets, living exotic experiences and emotions from specimens, too. Thought-imagery has, in fact, become a vicious drug by which the crab-creatures have become incapable of experience and

emotion of their own. They have become so totally
dependent on the minds of others that it will ultimately destroy the surviving crab-creatures as effectively as war and pestilence destroyed their ancestors
on the surface.

8. Captain Robert April finds himself sitting in the
   exact same position as an instant ago but now on the
   bed in his cell; Vina also sitting beside him in the
   same position but now back in the metallic cloth
   dress. She is in mid-sentence, adding, "Unless the ac-
   quisition of an animal like you allows them to. . . ."
   She trails her words as she, too, realizes the Renaissance illusion is over, stops frightened. April is not
   willing to let it stop there. For one thing, she can't
   be totally a creature of his mind. He has never seen
   her before, never even imagined her. Why does she
   keep reappearing? And how can a figment of his
   mind tell him things he does not know? His mind
   contains no information on the inhabitants of this
   planet. Is she one of the crab-creatures in the
   thought-guise of an Earth woman? Her expression
   changes, as if by a sudden decision, and she quickly
   says, "I am real, as real as you are. We're . . . well,
   like Adam and Eve. If they can. . . ." Vina van-
   ishes in mid-sentence as if she had suddenly been
   taken away before she could complete the statement.

                                             FADE OUT

III.  ACT THREE

1. On the surface of planet Sirius IV, a recon party
   under the direction of "Number One" has brought
   one of the vessel's huge matter-converters to the planet's surface, is focusing it on the sealed tunnel entrance at the outcropping of rock where April was
   captured. Using enormous force, risking dangerous
   depletion of the *Enterprise*'s energy, they attempt to
   cut through the stubborn metal. It glows red, then
   white-hot, but stubbornly resists even the maximum
   force of the converter. "Number One" calls the ship

where navigator José is deep in computation on ways to look into the planet's rock crust. He has gone down one blind alley after another without result. He now wants to orbit and probe with electromagnetic waves. If the intelligence beneath is using any form of radio, this would distort their magnetic field, give them some estimation of the location and extent of the civilization below.

2. April is being fed. The Keeper is able to pass material objects through the transparent wall which April himself cannot penetrate. It is a small vial of heavy dark liquid. To encourage April to eat, the Keeper finally communicates—the atonal voice explaining that April's chemical processes have been analyzed as completely as his thought processes and that the vial contains a protein-carbohydrate mixture more than adequate for nourishment and health. If April wishes, it will be quite simple to create for him the illusion that the vial is a banquet table spread with whatever food April cares to draw from his memory. April rejects this and challenges the Keeper. Why should he not let himself die of starvation rather than continue as a captive? The Keeper unemotionally recites that this is impossible since they are perfectly capable of creating for him illusions of hunger so continuing and powerful that he would be unable to resist. Or there is the unpleasant alternative of punishing him. . . .

April is instantly writhing in brimstone, a sulfurous, smoky hellfire place where flame licks at him from all sides and screams of pain are wrenched from him. It lasts only a few seconds and he is back facing the Keeper through the transparent wall. This is a sample from a childhood tale April once read and remembers. There are even more unpleasant things in April's mind. Does he care for another sample of punishment?

April bargains with his Keeper. What is the identity of the image Vina? He'll take his food if the

Keeper will answer that question. The Keeper hesitates, then, as unemotionally as always, recites that April has already guessed the truth. There was a single survivor from the Earth ship crash on the planet surface, a female. They found this specimen interesting, particularly the fact that it responded well to this planet's conditions. They repaired her injuries and have kept her, waiting until another Earth ship passed through the galaxy. The U.S.S. *Enterprise* was baited here by the false radio message so that they could secure a male specimen of the same species. Life for April and Vina will be made extremely pleasant, indeed much more pleasant than could ever be possible for him or the woman in any other galaxy or on any other planet in the Universe. April starts to set the vial down, the Keeper continuing "For example. . . ."

3. April, in precisely the same posture and motion, setting down a china coffee cup into a saucer. He and Vina are in a penthouse overlooking an Earth city, circa 2049 A.D. The young woman, acting as his wife, is moving to refill his cup and is stating that their friend Varjos Miller has four tickets on the Tahiti jet. It might be fun for the weekend. It's less than thirty minutes away, and the Federated Park Commission is doing a festival of the old island outrigger races, fishing, village ceremonies, and so on. During this, Vina's voice fades under and the Keeper's unemotional recitation voice is heard explaining that April can live on Earth in his own time, enjoying all of its pleasures. Or. . . .

April finds himself in an almost fairybook vine-covered cottage on one of the rural can-farms of Mars, still with Vina, in different garb and background. She is continuing her sentence, saying that the Colonists Grange Society is also planning Barth races and that there will be a fifty-mile sled ride down the Great Slopes the next evening. Does he remember how they first met on one of these Martian

"hay rides"? During which Vina's voice has again
faded under, and the Keeper's voice recites that
April can also live in simpler ways . . . or he can
live in wild excitement . . . in any one and every
one of ten thousand places he has visited or even
imagined. . . .

April finds himself on Protos VI, cushioned in
barbaric splendor in one of that planet's eerie rain-
bow gardens, facing a magnificent feast across which
Vina and sinuous green dancing girls of that world
perform for him, the long-eared courtiers subser-
viently bowing and scraping. Vina, whirling in the
barefoot dance, makes a misstep, falls, and a giant
Protos slave is on her with a whip, viciously lashing,
and a courtier is in quickly, bowing and humbly
apologizing, promising the girl will be destroyed
immediately. April, despite his knowledge that this is
only imagery, is forced to his feet, appalled, shouting
for the slave to stop beating the girl.

And in the same instant he finds himself on his
feet back in the cage, biting off his words. The crab-
creature Keeper is watching him through the transparent wall. A voice at his elbow says she is pleased
that he does seem to care for her, and April whirls
to find Vina standing next to him. The Keeper scut-
tles off back to his "desk."

Vina waits only long enough for the Keeper to
leave, and she reveals she is holding a space-boat ax
out of sight behind her body. She took it from the
wreckage, has been hiding it since. The corridor outside is empty, and if he can use the ax to break
through the transparent wall, they can escape. The
crab-creatures are relatively slow and weak, and they
long since stopped carrying weapons. April swings
hard at the transparent wall. It gives slightly, he
swings again harder, the Keeper outside scuttling toward an alarm signal as April finally crashes through
with the girl behind him. She screams for him to
stop the creature before it can reach the mechanism.
April leaps across the corridor, swinging the ax, and

destroys the machine. The crab-creature attacks him, and April defends himself, dispatching the Keeper. He and Vina turn to flee down the corridor.

4. No alarm has been sounded, the "zoo" corridor is empty, and despite Vina's frantic urging to leave immediately, April cannot resist looking into the glass front enclosures that line the corridor. The first is a shocker—a huge six-legged spider-anthropoid with saber tooth fangs throws itself directly at him, stopped only by the transparent wall. Snarling and screaming in fury, the creature flings itself again and again at April, trying to get to him through the barrier. Vina identifies this as the spider-ape of a Rigel planet group.

At the next, a writhing mass of intertwined, hissing, snakelike bodies with vague humanoid faces and atrophied arms. Another enclosure contains incredibly delicate and elongated (special camera lens) winged "angel" creatures, perched on ledges of what appears to be a "zoo" mock-up of a wispy sky-spire city. And another, mongoose-like rodents, but clothed and weaponed like a feudal civilization, complete with a tiny castle, moat, ramparts, etc. It's night; oil lamps can be seen burning through the tiny toy-sized windows. This last civilization April himself has seen —the intelligent Lemur-life of a Class M planet in the Arcturus system.

At the end of the corridor is a low hatchway door shaped to fit the crab-creature shape. April forces it open, and the two flee down a long tubelike metallic corridor—directly into a group of angry crab-creatures blocking their way.

5. Back on the U.S.S. *Enterprise*, navigator José has continued probing the planet electromagnetically, finally picks up interference at one point. Probing more deeply, he finds his instruments are able to analyze it as a feeble signal up through the rock from April's telecommunicator. Computing rapidly, José gets a fix on depth and angle. Sending a recon party

down will be highly risky—if the vector is a fraction of a degree off, the rescue party could find themselves materialized inside solid rock instead of a cavern or passageway. "Number One" insists on leading the rescue party; José demands that he be a member and take the risk of his own computations. Yeoman Colt also volunteers, and Mr. Spock is selected as the fourth member. They arm themselves and prepare to be transported down. One of the spaceship technicians is frowning over his instruments, whirls and tries to warn them he is getting some sort of "feed back." But it's too late. The transporter has been energized, and "Number One" and Colt are dematerializing already. But José and Mr. Spock remain as they are—*for some reason only the women are being transported!*

6. "Number One" and Yeoman Colt arrive inside April's "zoo cage" *sans* weapons. And find themselves watching the strange spectacle of Captain April holding the hand of the young woman Vina, both their eyes glazed like sleepwalkers, legs moving in a slow motion as if trying to escape from something in a dream. Then April and Vina stop, come back to reality, realizing where they are. The Keeper, alive and unharmed, stands outside the glass wall watching them. The escape has been merely another illusion.

The Keeper is amused. There is no need for additional male specimens so their transportation was blocked off. But the arrival of two additional females is quite welcome. Obviously the specimen named April does not care for the first female, and so he now has two alternate choices.

                                                        FADE OUT

IV. ACT FOUR

1. Aboard the *Enterprise*, all controls on the transporter have gone dead. Their scanners, communicators, all contact with the planet has been lost. José can

hardly believe the only answer his computations offer —that the civilization below has devices capable of using pure thought to warp time and dimension to their needs. The *Enterprise* has no way to counter this. Attack on the planet would be as foolhardy as an ant attacking an elephant.

2. In April's cage Vina fills April, "Number One," and Colt in on why they are there. At first, during her five years of captivity, she believed the crab-creatures' desperate attempts to attract a male Earth man to the planet were merely so the Earth specimens could have offspring and not die out, adding some new and different Earth illusions to the menagerie. But she had grown to realize there is a deeper need behind all this. The crab-creatures are dying out. Their ability to live other lives, painlessly and effortlessly, completely without danger to themselves, has drained their vitality and courage. Even their creativity. The great science civilization has stagnated; the machinery left by their ancestors is falling into disrepair; none of them care to repair it or even know how it works. Their once proud capacity for adventure, risk, travel, all the things that make growth and life possible, has atrophied away.

The Keeper, watching them through the transparent wall, now interrupts, pleased with their capacity for logic. This, with their high degree of adaptability, makes them ideally suited to the formation of communities on the surface of the planet, a parasite civilization which will exist to serve as farmers, technicians, and even scientists. The crab-creatures who control their minds will mete out illusions of pleasure and pain as it becomes necessary to evolve them and their descendants into a life of unselfish service. Robert April interrupts, pointing out a flaw in all this. The human creature is incapable of surviving in imprisonment. The Keeper disagrees, points out that the first and most powerful impulse of life is for survival. Although they will have no freedom of choice, those who adapt will have wish-fulfillment reward more pleasant than possibly anywhere else in the Universe. Meanwhile the male specimen April can have any one of the females, or all of them. The choice is his . . . now.

3. At that moment, again in mid-word and mid-motion, April and the three women find themselves upon the planet's surface. The Keeper's voice can be heard continuing. They will immediately begin guided lives of labor, pleasure, and punishment. Wrong-thinking is prohibited, and the training of their children will be strictly controlled. The crab-creatures will patiently wait the generations necessary for them to build their parasite civilization of trained, right-thinking servants. For the use of themselves and their descendants, the zoological gardens will furnish a variety of plant life and certain animals which can be domesticated. If they will look at their belts, they will find their Laser weapons have been returned so that shelter and tools can be fashioned. Plus their telecommunicator instruments which will provide translation until the science language of the planet is learned by them. They are completely controlled; there is no possible escape. Any thought of contact with their space vessel . . . interrupted by "Number One" who has taken out her telecommunicator, but falls to the ground writhing and crying out in pain. The Keeper continues that, as they can see, wrong-thinking is not only useless but will also be severely punished. Yeoman Colt, showing an unsuspected streak of determined courage, starts to say, "I will not . . .", also begins suffering an illusion of intense pain.

It is later, a violet-sky evening, April and the women sitting waiting, wondering. Suddenly "Number One" realizes she has been thinking of the ship and rescue and has not been punished. April nods, has realized the same. For a moment at least they're free to do and think as they wish. He slowly draws his Laser gun, adjusts the setting on it. Vina looks at him, frightened, begins to plead. She has been here so many years; the Keeper was right when he promised there could be pleasure that exceeds imagination. She has cooperated with them and discovered this. April has seen only the smallest sample of possibility. "Number One" interrupts, insisting to April, "Now! Before they stop us!" Yeoman Colt, although frightened, also nods at April. Vina throws herself at him, trying to stop him, frantically screaming the crab-creatures are actually kind and gentle; they can give unimaginable pleasure if you cooperate with them. . . . April interrupts, saying he has no right to force their decision on her. For them, they prefer death. He has set the gun for a hypo-pellet; death is instant, painless. . . .

April raises the gun, aims carefully at "Number One," then finds himself unable to move. A clatter of external skeleton is heard, then April is finally released to turn and find the Keeper and a group of other crab-creatures there, facing him. Strangely, there is something of sadness in the Keeper's atonal reciting voice. They have been probing deep in his and the other women's memories, tracing the violent history of their race. April was right; although Man's history is savage in the extreme, it has been almost always a fight against some form of captivity, even if death was the price of escape. Intelligent life here on Sirius IV has the same history, but it was assumed to be unique to this planet.

There is another parallel between them and Earth life. To kill is considered wrong. Their laws do not permit them to be responsible for death to another creature . . . even if it means the death of their own civilization. They will seek other solutions. If it is the will of the Creator of the Universe that they live, a solution will be found in time. They're now all free for transport to the space vehicle. An angle on Vina . . . as she protests. April can't possibly understand, but she has been here too long, enjoyed the dreams too long. She does not want to go back. And as she talks, we see the slow aging from a lovely youthful woman to an almost grotesque middle-aged woman, bearing the scars and burn marks of a spaceship crash. Trying to hide her face from April, she frantically pleads for the crab-creatures to keep her here. She is not like the others—she *wants* captivity. She doesn't want reality, she wants dreams . . . please!

The Keeper asks April his wish. Do they desire to take the survivor specimen with them? Then, before April can answer, the crab-creature Keeper intones that he reads April's answer and understands.

4. Aboard the U.S.S. *Enterprise,* Mr. Spock is working at the transporter's dead controls, then reacts as the machine hums back into life. Images begin to form in the materialization chamber, and April, "Number One," and J. M. Colt appear, step out into the room, alive and unharmed. What they say to each other about hoping this escape is not another illusion doesn't make much sense to the rest of the crew.

Yeoman Colt, always very much the female, wonders which of them April would ultimately have picked. April, half-amused at Colt, admits the dream-Vina was much more eager and cooperative than either the Yeoman or "Number One." This gets him a sharp look from the usually imperturbable Ex-executive Officer, who excuses herself, moving off to take up her station on the bridge. J. M. Colt would probably exhibit more jealousy, too, except for the rank between herself and her captain. Navigator José Tyler, always the Latin, is instantly interested, wondering whether or not this "illusion" was beautiful? April nods, adds that there is nothing lovelier than an illusion. Or more dangerous. As the civilization on Sirius IV has discovered. When they're under way, he'll work with Dr. Boyce and the science lab technicians on a report for Earth on the narcotic danger of illusion. By the time Man develops the full power of his mind, he'd better be well aware of that fact.

"Number One" and the crew on the bridge are standing by for orders. Captain Robert April gives the command that will head the *Enterprise* back on its former course, leaving Sirius IV behind in the distance. A shot of a space vessel picking up speed into hyperdrive and . . .

FADE OUT

Chapter 5

## Inside a Television Studio

We can send a missile to the moon and send back pictures, but we can't produce a television series without sixty-five people running around using antiquated lamps and everything else. It's true. You've been on the stages and seen the junk we're using. If you want to move a lamp, you've got to get four guys to move the damn thing. It's very strange. We've got a camera that weighs hundreds of pounds!

> A studio executive, discussing
> production problems

A great many changes have taken place at Desilu Studios since the day in 1964 when Gene Roddenberry first brought STAR TREK to the studio. For one thing, Desilu no longer exists. In the summer of 1967, both Desilu Studio and Paramount Studio were sold to Gulf and Western Corporation. Since the two studios were located side-by-side on adjoining pieces of property, Gulf and Western merged the two into one large production facility, under the name of Paramount Studios.

The merger was greeted with mixed reactions among many people, but it has nevertheless resulted in the creation of a major studio with full-fledged production facilities.

A studio is like a small city . . . a city behind high walls, protected by armed guards at the gates. It is a vast complex of buildings and open spaces of land, containing discarded bits and pieces of old sets, broken-down wagons, dusty automobiles, fake river boats, and numerous other items guaranteed to delight the heart of a discerning junk man. The materials may be old, but they are also eternal. From time to time an item will be resurrected, given a new coat of paint, made to look presentable, and used once more in yet another motion picture or television series episode. I am continually amazed at the results that can be achieved from what appears to be, on the surface, a vast array of debris.

Towering over the studio and dominating all are the huge sound stages. These are monolithic structures containing thousands of square feet of empty space (like the interior of some giant-sized gymnasium) into which are crammed hundreds of pieces of equipment, a collection of structures known as "sets" (which simulate reality), a complex array of catwalks and scaffolding overhead, and far too many people.

Although the setting is not at all glamorous, the studio visitor is almost always impressed with "the glamour of it all." Why this is so remains a mystery to me. I only know that I have felt the same way myself.

A major studio usually produces both motion pictures and television. The studio generally functions in two distinct ways. First, there are shows that rent facilities from the studio and in which the studio has no ownership. Second, there are shows that the studio produces on its own or in cooperation with the independent production companies, such as in the case of Roddenberry's Norway Productions which is the studio's partner in making STAR TREK.

Supporting an entire studio operation requires the services of several thousand employees and a wide variety of facilities. These include departments and services such as legal, research, electrical, publicity, transportation, sound recording, music scoring, casting, property shop, construction, special effects, commissary (restaurant), art department, security, first aid, fire, film editing, sound stages, office for production company staffs and stars, barbershop, etc.

These facilities cost a great deal of money to maintain. In order to cover their cost, the studio charges the independent production company a fee for their use. An hour-long television series may be charged as much as $35,000 per episode for these facilities. Other productions may add another $150,000 to that episode budget. Costs are recouped from the sale of the show to the network and profits, if any (and they are rare in television today), are then shared with the independent producer and other partners.

To the home viewing audience, the most glamorous aspect of a television series is its star. He is their idol, he can do no wrong—at least as long as the Nielsen ratings say he's popular. The star, however, is much like the analogy of the iceberg. What you see on the surface is only one tenth of what is hidden below the surface.

The cast of a show (the only people connected with the show who are seen on camera) represent only a fraction of the total number of people required to prepare the show for its eventual viewing on the Big Eye. The remaining members of the production crew are the unsung heroes of television. They take no bows before the lights, they are rarely interviewed by *TV Guide*. They seldom see their names in bright lights. Without them, there would be no stars and no show.

Producing a television series is a complex operation. The process is broken down into three primary phases: pre-production or planning; production or filming; and post-production or final assembly. Each phase involves a group of people who are specialists in that phase.

In overall command is the executive producer, in this case, Gene Roddenberry, a man who, more than anyone else, *is* STAR TREK. He created the series and supervises all who are involved in breathing life into the creation. During the critical first two seasons, he was the final arbiter, the ultimate authority in all basic decisions. He is actively involved in all phases of the production process, including casting, scripts, makeup, set design, sound, and editing. During the third year, having built a trained production unit, he has now begun to turn the daily production reins over to his producers, while he operates in the more traditional Executive Producer role of administrative and policy decisions.

Second-in-command is the producer. As the chief executive officer of the production, the producer is involved with daily problems arising in all departments. In television today, the producer is usually a writer, and much of his time and effort is devoted to story and script. He often rewrites the scripts ("properties") submitted by writers on assignment. The producer is responsible for the successful completion of the entire production process from first vague story idea to final completed film.

The producer's right-hand man is the associate producer. On STAR TREK, because of its production complexities, this post has always been filled by a man selected for his knowledge of the intricate facets of all the phases of production. Hs is concerned with the "how-to" of every phase of film-making—can the desired effect be achieved, and if not, what can be substituted that will be as good or better? He frequently points out details in a proposed script that will pose problems somewhere along the line, and will then suggest solutions to them. After filming has been completed, and the post-production phase begins, the associate producer rides herd on the editing, special optical effects, sound effects, and music score.

Since there are usually four or five shows in various stages of preparation simultaneously, no one person could possibly keep up with all of them at the same time. This is where the assistant to the producer comes in. Although involved to some degree in all phases of production on STAR TREK, the assistant to the producer usually finds himself concentrating on the complex opticals proposed during the planning phase of each show and the follow-up so vital in the third phase. He works closely with the optical houses in the preparation of these special film effects and supervises their addition to the actual piece of film involved, in the final phase. He is therefore strongly involved in the third phase of production and frequently assists the associate producer in editing, dubbing (preparing the sound track), and scoring (preparing the music track).

The inherently expensive nature of a television series production, coupled with the numerous unexpected expenses that may arise every day, makes it vitally important to have someone in a position to keep track of the day-to-day costs. On STAR TREK this person has the title of unit production manager.

The unit production manager wears two hats. First of all, it is his responsibility to try to keep the show within budget, both for the individual episode as well as for the entire series. To do this, he must constantly be aware of how many people are needed during the course of each day's shooting, and whether or not the show can get by with one person less here or there. He must also keep track of the proposed and the actual expenses incurred by all departments and be ready to recommend cuts (or alternate methods) should one of them appear to be in danger of going over budget. Secondly, the unit production manager acts as a liaison between the various department heads and the people who are actually involved in the filming on the set. He becomes involved in such details as hiring the crew members (excluding the actors and extras) who may be needed on the set, making sure the sets are ready to shoot on time, seeing that the stars' dressing rooms are maintained in a clean, neat condition, and a host of other matters surrounding the daily filming activities.

Very often the activities the foregoing gentlemen find themselves involved in are the direct result of ideas generated by the script consultant (or story editor). The script consultant's job is primarily one of rewriting scripts, as well as writing a certain number of original scripts for the series. It is not at all unusual for the script consultant to rewrite completely a script that has been purchased from a free-lance writer. Sometimes this is necessary in order to bring a script more into line with STAR TREK format. At other times it is necessary simply to make the script more feasible to shoot, from a cost standpoint.

Together with the executive producer's assistant and three secretaries, these men and women comprise what is generally referred to by the crew as the front office. They maintain the heading that keeps the starship on its course.

Also involved during the planning stage are several other persons whose collective talents strongly affect the visual impression made by the show. One of these is the art director. He is responsible for the design and construction of all the sets used on each show, including those aboard the *Enterprise,* as well as those depicting the many and varied alien cultures visited from time to time.

When the art director has finished building his set, the set decorator moves in and "dresses" the set. This could mean adding chairs, candlesticks, paintings, an antique bellows forge, or anything else that might be needed by the local natives on Polaris IX.

Since guest stars and extras appear on each show, the casting director for the studio becomes involved. He makes recommendations on who he thinks should play the particular roles, based on who is available around town at that particular time and on his knowledge of actor ability and experience. He sets interviews, recommends contract terms, and works closely with the producer who must make the ultimate casting decisions.

Another person vitally important to the planning phase is the costume designer. During this preproduction stage, the costume designer creates the necessary costumes that will be used during the filming phase of the show. It is safe to say that costume designs have gone a long way toward making STAR TREK a visually interesting and stimulating show.

The remaining members of a production crew are divided almost totally between the second and third phases of the production.

During the filming phase the director reigns supreme. Through the course of the six or seven days it takes to film one episode, all personnel on the set are tuned in (or should be) to the desires of the director. Each director spends about one week in the planning stage before he must step onto the set and "get the show on the road." On the set the director is very much like the conductor of a symphony orchestra. He must coordinate a variety of elements into a creative, artistic expression of the whole. This generally includes the supervision of thirty or forty crewmen on the set, besides the actors and actresses involved.

All of these people have very specific duties assigned to them. When filming time may cost as much as $200 per minute, there can be no mistake about whose responsibility it is to do what. For this reason, the visitor to the shooting set will find a tremendous number of people hurrying about, in what appears to be organized chaos. A partial listing of these people and their duties would include:

1. First Assistant Director: second-in-command to the director, who prepares shooting schedules for each

day's activities, reports on progress of filming, etc. He also controls all physical facets of filming on the stage. All crew members report to him.

2. Second Assistant Director: a "leg man" for the first assistant director, and one who is, in effect, training for an eventual position as first assistant director.

3. Script Supervisor: keeps a record of the content of each individual camera shot ("take"). He cues actors' dialogue and makes certain the action "matches" from shot to shot.

4. Cinematographer or Director of Photography: is responsible for the composition of each individual type of shot and its "movement," or lack of same. He is responsible for the lighting of each scene and its artistic effect.

5. Special Effects: creates specialized, exotic equipment, such as control panels with blinking lights, voice-actuated circuits, lamps that spout "blue flame." Also creates explosions, smoke effects, fog, etc.

6. Sound Mixer: controls the quality and nature of the "live" sound and music on the shooting set.

7. Property Master: is responsible for the maintenance and availability of all hand props used in the show.

8. Gaffer: is responsible for handling of the lighting equipment, and the men involved in that activity.

9. Makeup Artist: is responsible for both routine and specialized (alien) makeup of all actors and actresses.

These are only a few of the many people actively involved in the second phase of the production, although many more are required in the course of the "on set" activities.

In the third phase of production, the primary people involved are the film editors (the ones who actually cut the pieces of film shot every day into one long coherent piece of film), the sound effects man (responsible for the creation of the special sound effects that will be added to the sound track), and the music editor (supervises the addition of the music to the sound track) and the dubbing team who combine dialogue, music, and sound effects into a single balanced, dramatic sound track.

Each and every one of the people is vitally necessary to the production of every episode. The entire operation is a highly complex, well-oiled machine. Everyone must know his job and perform it to almost split-second timing. At stake are five million dollars spent to produce one year's required number of episodes of STAR TREK plus the career reputations of dozens of professionals in the most highly competitive industry of all.

Chapter 6

## A Blueprint for Starflight

Gene created a totally new universe. He invented a starship, which works, by the way, and is a logical progression from what we know today. He created customs, morals, modes of speaking, a complete technology. We have a very rigid technology on the show. We know how fast we can go. We know what we use for fuel. We know what our weapons will do. And Gene invented all these things. He did a monumental job of creation. He created an entire galaxy, and an entire rule book for operating within that galaxy, with very specific laws governing behavior, manners, customs, as well as science and technology. Now that's a hell of a job. He didn't create a show. He created a universe, and it works, and it works well. This was a massive, titanic job of creation. One of the most impressive feats of its kind that I've ever seen. You can submit our ship or our technology or anything you want to NASA and they will say, "Well, it's pretty far out, but I don't see why it shouldn't work." Nobody can tell us that it's scientifically impossible or that it won't work.

> Gene Coon, former
> producer on STAR TREK

NBC's selection of "The Cage" (June, 1964) meant that Roddenberry could start writing the pilot script. He immediately began a period of intensive research to develop a more detailed background for the series.

To look back over those early days is to realize that the enormity of the task was staggering. Simply to create a new television series about everyday life is a big enough job in itself. But Roddenberry was attempting to create an entirely new environment . . . a new way of life . . . a whole new universe. With STAR TREK, *everything* used on the show had to be designed from scratch. Equipment, tools, clothing, weapons, furniture, even knives and forks—almost everything will be different two or three centuries from now.

Do the children of STAR TREK's time ride tricycles? Is the telephone a thing of the past? Do they use flush toilets? Will people write letters the way we do now, on paper and mailed in an envelope? Surely they will have evolved a more efficient method of communicating with each other!

At every turn he was faced with such questions and needed answers—sound, logical, believable answers that would be accepted by the viewers. Gene plunged into the monumental task of creating the detailed framework within which STAR TREK would operate.

Even before NBC had given the green light for a script, Gene had begun contacting technical experts for advice and information. One of the earliest replies to his inquiries was from a World War II Air Force pilot comrade:

WEAPONS EFFECTS AND TEST GROUP
HEADQUARTERS, FIELD COMMAND
DEFENSE ATOMIC SUPPORT AGENCY
SANDIA BASE, ALBUQUERQUE, NEW MEXICO

25 May 1964

Mr. Gene Roddenberry
Desilu Studios
780 N. Gower Street
Hollywood 38, California

Dear Rod:

I have studied your letter and STAR TREK with a great deal of interest. I think you have a great idea, and it should go good if you can keep technical details from detracting from your drama. I see you already recognize this in your approach.

I think the big problem in science fiction is to maintain plausibility without having to explain in detail. You know when Dick Tracy's two-way radio wristwatch came out years ago—it seemed plausible, although only a few advanced scientists knew that solid-state physics and miniature circuitry would make it possible. On the other hand, the plausibility of the space ship in that comic strip is not established. I think the problem is that today's TV public know a few basic facts about space travel problems that must be accounted for before establishing plausibility. This does not require detailed technical justification but an accounting for in a routine manner.

To answer your query instead of trying to be an expert in your business, let me assure you I will be only too happy to put you in touch with personnel from Rand and/or the Space Technology Labs or the AF Space System Division. I am planning a trip to L.A. within four to five weeks—I would attempt to make it sooner if you have an urgent deadline to meet. I could give you a letter of contact, but I would like to kick the idea around with you a bit so I know the kind of contacts which could give you the best help. If, however, the time is pressing, let me know at once and I'll arrange something from here.

I am going to forward a copy of STAR TREK to a physicist at Rand—he is a retired AF type and I can count on him to keep it to himself—he is a creative scientific thinker and will appreciate your concepts.

> Sincerely,
> Donald I. Prickett
> Colonel, USAF

The "physicist at Rand" referred to in the letter above turned out to be a Mr. Harvey P. Lynn. A man of exceptional intelligence and broad scientific knowledge, Mr. Lynn later served as a consultant to STAR TREK, on his own time, for almost a year and a half. A great deal of the technical accuracy built into STAR TREK in the beginning is directly attributed to the guidance and counseling of Mr. Lynn.

Gathering information was one thing. Getting studio people to *use* that information in futuristic terms was something else again. Roddenberry found that most of the people who were supposed to be helping him were not oriented to science fiction at all. As a result, he had difficulty, as time went on, in getting them to look at things from a "different" point of view.

A typical example of this problem occurred during a heated exchange with a greensman. A greensman is a person responsible for providing shrubbery, greenery, and that sort of thing for use on the sets. Gene had been after this fellow to bring him some alien-looking plants. No matter how many times Gene carefully explained what he had in mind, this fellow would always come back with an ordinary-looking potted plant. Finally, in desperation, Gene grabbed the plant, pulled it out of the pot, and stuck it back in, upside down. The bare roots of the plant sort of dangled there in the sunlight, looking nakedly grotesque. "There!" shouted Gene. "Now we've got an alien-looking plant!" The astonished greensman looked at Gene, looked back at the plant, then walked away, shaking his head.

For the first six months Roddenberry was called "Crazy Gene."

People used to call each other on the phone and say, "Have you heard what Crazy Gene wants to do now?"

WELL, IT WAS ALL SO NEW AND STRANGE TO THEM. LIKE YOU CALL SOME UNSUSPECTING PRODUCTION MAN ON THE PHONE, AND HE SAYS, "HELLO," AND YOU SAY, "WHAT DOES IT COST TO PAINT A GIRL GREEN?" YOU GET A LONG SILENCE!

The "green woman" (a character Gene wanted to use in the pilot) alone created a number of recurring problems.

Knowing that the green-skinned alien woman was coming up in the pilot, he decided to shoot some test footage to get the right shade of green on film. He brought in an actress, had

Fred Philips, the newly hired makeup artist, apply green makeup to her face, and then shot some test footage. Now, Fred Philips is an exceptionally fine makeup artist, and recognized as a top pro in the business. He did a thorough job with the makeup and was quite satisfied with the results.

Imagine everyone's surprise, upon viewing the developed film the next day, to find the actress's face just as normally pink-skinned as ever! There was no trace of green.

Gene's orders to Fred Philips: "Paint her greener!" The following day the test film again showed her as pink-skinned as ever. Even Fred was dumbfounded. Recalling the incident, he says, "We did this three days in a row. We had her so green you couldn't believe it, and she still kept coming back pink! Finally we figured out what was happening. The technician over at the film lab would receive the film every day and run it through the development solution. As the image formed on the film, he kept saying to himself, 'My God, this woman is green!' And so he kept correcting the film developing process in order to turn her back to normal skin color again!"

The accomplished actress Susan Oliver later played the part of the alien woman in the pilot and was almost totally covered with green body makeup. During filming she became very tired, and a doctor was called in to give her a vitamin B shot. The doctor arrived, but no one bothered to tell him what his patient looked like. He went over to Susan's dressing room, knocked, the door swung wide, and suddenly he was confronted with an all-green woman! He was so flustered that it took him almost five minutes just to find a spot to administer the shot.

During the rest of the summer and into the early fall of 1964, major effort was devoted to the following principal areas: development of the shooting script that would be submitted to NBC for approval; research aimed at developing and verifying the scientific validity of the technology that STAR TREK would express; finalizing the design of the U.S.S. *Enterprise;* and designing, on paper, the sets that would be required for the pilot.

Among those who were first to join the growing nucleus of STAR TREK staff members and crew were Pato Guzman and

Matt Jefferies. Pato is a volatile Chilean and a man of exceptional creative ability as an art director. Matt Jefferies, assigned to the show as the assistant art director, is an equally creative designer, with a background that suited him well to the series. He is an experienced pilot, a member of the Aviation Writers Society, a nationally acknowledged aviation historian, and has an educational background in areas of aeronautical engineering.

Matt Jefferies' first meeting with Roddenberry came on the same day he returned from a thirty-day vacation. He had been working on the "Ben Casey" series and expected to pick up where he had left off prior to his vacation. To his surprise, he was told that he would not go back to the "Casey" series. A man named Roddenberry would be in his office about ten that morning and would explain the new show that Matt would be working on.

About 10:00 A.M. Gene came in, accompanied by Herb Solow.* After introductions, Gene quickly outlined what the series would be all about, saying, "We're a hundred and fifty or maybe two hundred years from now. Out in deep space, on the equivalent of a cruiser-size spaceship. We don't know what the motive power is, but I don't want to see any trails of fire. No streaks of smoke, no jet intakes, rocket exhaust, or anything like that. We're not going to Mars, or any of that sort of limited thing. It will be like a deep-space exploration vessel, operating throughout our galaxy. We'll be going to stars and planets that nobody has named yet." He then got up and, as he started for the door, turned and said, "I don't care how you do it, but make it look like it's got power."

Matt Jefferies couldn't believe he'd heard it right. Someone had just walked in and casually, matter-of-factly, asked for the almost impossible. Even our own scientists hadn't been able to come up with a design such as he'd just heard described.

According to Matt, the *Enterprise* design was arrived at by

---

* At the time, Herb Solow was assistant to Oscar Katz at Desilu. Later, when Katz left Desilu, Solow was promoted to Vice President in Charge of Television Production. Even in STAR TREK's darkest moments Solow was a staunch ally.

a process of elimination. "For years I had been collecting material on space exploration and activities from friends of mine in companies like North American, Douglas, NASA, and TRW. After Roddenberry's visit I brought all that stuff to the studio, along with everything else we could get our hands on. We pinned the stuff up on the wall and said, 'This we will *not* do.' We wanted to establish a basis of design to work from, but we didn't want the *Enterprise* to look like something currently planned for our space program. We knew that by the time the show got on the air, this type of thing would be old hat. We had to go further than even the most advanced space scientists were thinking.

"We also drew on a lot of research material on Flash Gordon and Buck Rogers. Again we said, 'This we will not do.' There have been a lot of things that took place in those comic strips that have proven out today, but pictorially we felt they were hokey. They used a lot of air-foil fins and rocket tube-like shapes that had no feeling of practicality or necessity. Roddenberry insisted everything be believable. We had to base it all on fairly solid scientific concepts, project it into the future, and try to visualize what the fourth, fifth, or tenth generation of present-day equipment would be like. So, working within those limits, Pato and I sat down and began to sketch out ideas. When we had about two walls covered with these sketches, we called Roddenberry in and he looked them over. Damn it but he can be irritating. He liked only a piece of this one or a small part of that one, but none of our ideas had what he really was looking for. So we did twenty-some more designs, using the few elements he had said he liked.

"Again we called him in. This time people from the sales department came with him, as well as people from the production office, and Harvey Lynn from the Rand Corporation. Again the designs were narrowed down to four or five things he liked. We started the process all over again.

"By the third time around he had two sheets of eight or ten drawings, plus a half dozen good-sized renderings. One of them was the beginning of the design finally chosen and one that I liked very much . . . an upper, saucer-shaped hull, a cigar-shaped lower hull, and two engine pods. Before calling

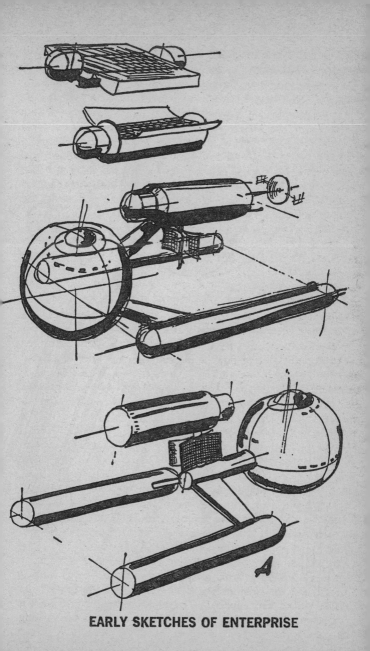

**EARLY SKETCHES OF ENTERPRISE**

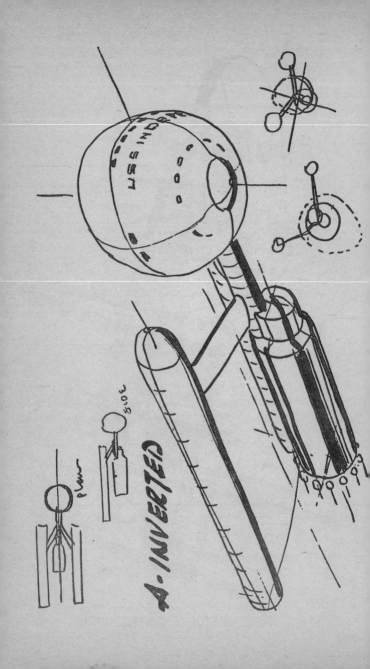

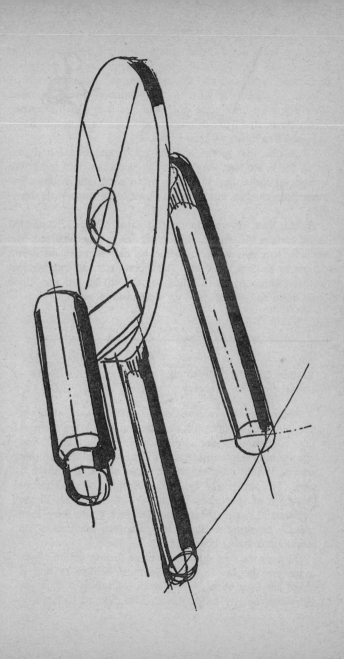

everyone in again, I did a little fast model building. I went
down to the mill [woodworking shop], grabbed a couple of
chunks of wood, and had the men turn out a saucer shape on
a lathe. In about thirty-five or forty minutes I had a model.
We hung it up on a piece of thread and then called everyone
in. Oddly enough, the original model was hung upside down
as opposed to the way we use it now.

"Based on that model and the color rendering I had prepared for it, Roddenberry felt we were on the right track. We
wound up shortening the main pylon strut and made a few
other little changes and then sat down to do some scale drawings."

By this time, several months had gone by and Gene wanted
to be certain this was it before the design was finalized. His
concern was evident in a memo he had sent several weeks
earlier to Kellam De Forest. De Forest runs an independent
research company, with offices on the studio lot, and Gene
had contracted with him to provide basic research services.

TO:                         DATE:    August 25, 1964
Kellam De Forest-Research   SUBJECT:  RESEARCH—
FROM: Gene Roddenberry      STAR TREK PILOT

Reference our science-fiction series STAR TREK, we
are dangerously near the time we must settle on a shape
and configuration for our spaceship of the future, but
are running into considerable difficulty in settling on that
design. Would much appreciate your checking if there is
any "far out," very futuristic selection of sketches or
drawings of spaceships which we could examine. Please
understand, we're talking more *science fiction* here than
we are anything available in space tech manuals or on
scientific drawing boards today.

Perhaps the best direction will be science fiction magazines and books. It would be most helpful to find if
there has ever been any collection of such sketches and
drawings, or any surveys or articles devoted to the subject.

Please do not hesitate to call me directly here at Extensions 298 or 495 if you have any questions.

Gene Roddenberry

While the hassle with the *Enterprise* was going on, attention also had to be devoted to the interior design of the set, notably the bridge. One of the early concepts established was expressed in the following memo:

TO: Pato Guzman      DATE: July 24, 1964
FROM: Gene Roddenberry      SUBJECT: STAR TREK

More and more I see the need for some sort of interesting electronic computing machine designed into the U.S.S. *Enterprise,* perhaps on the bridge itself. It will be an information device out of which April and the crew can quickly and interestingly extract information on the registry of other space vessels, space flight plans for other ships, information on individuals and planets and civilizations, etc.* This should not only speed up our storytelling but could be visually interesting.

Gene Roddenberry

As Gene continued to collect information, he would, in turn, disseminate this information to those concerned, in an effort to stimulate thinking and thereby finalize some of the details under discussion. The following is typical of the information he passed around during that time:

### RODDENBERRY NOTES—STAR TREK

Discussion with various scientists on the STAR TREK series resulted in the following comments:

---

* The beginning thoughts on what was to evolve into Mr. Spock's library–computer station.

The spaceship probably would have some "day and night" schedule, a period of subdued lighting simulating night. The Homo sapien is so adjusted to alternating work and rest that it would become essential.

There is no doubt that information will be fed into future computers via voice—i.e., simply talk into it, using a predetermined and very precise terminology. It is, in fact, speculated that the future may see us ending up with two languages, one a precise scientific one for this and similar types of communication, plus the current colloquial English which is used on the social level.

It is also speculated, even planned now in some cases, that future spaceships will include "human organ banks" in which vital body parts are stored so that items lost through injury or disease can be replaced.

Some kind of "meteoroid shield" or "meteoroid force field deflector" will be necessary in true spaceships. If not a force field, it may be a magnetic field which deflects cosmic dust or small meteoroids via an opposite charge. Or it might consist of a probing Laser beam which deflects and/or destroys dust and small particles from the path of the ship.

The more involved everyone became in developing the design of the bridge, the placement of the controls, and the makeup of the various consoles, the more convinced Gene became that STAR TREK would require the services of a highly unusual special effects man. Here was yet another area of need that had to be filled; and prompted the following memo:

TO: Pato Guzman             DATE: August 25, 1964
FROM: Gene Roddenberry      SUBJECT: U.S.S. *Enterprise*
                            CONTROLS & INSTRU-
                            MENTATION

It seems to me likely that design of controls, dials, instruments, etc., aboard our spaceship, particularly the complex "three dimensional" ones which our scientist friends insist would be there, necessitates we locate some hopefully near-genius gadgeteer and electrician and jack-of-all-trades here at Desilu who can augment our speculation and sketching with some idea of what he can accomplish with batteries, lights, wires, plastic, etc.

For example, going on an instrument I saw yesterday at North American's Advanced Space Research Center, is there some way to construct a plain revolving globe on which flicker on and off various small lights, lighted path progressions, projected course lines, etc.? The point being, although neither you nor I may see this as possible or within our budget limits, a highly inventive and mechanically minded person may know of fairly simple ways to accomplish it.

In short, I think it's important to locate the best possible man here and, rather than wait for the more formal preproduction meetings, immediately include him in some of our speculating and discussions. If you agree, please call Jim Paisley. Have forwarded him a copy of this note.

                              Gene Roddenberry


In the meantime the studio began to complain about the amount of money Gene was spending on this research phase of STAR TREK.


THE STUDIO'S ATTITUDE WAS "COME ON BABY, WHAT'S SO DIFFICULT ABOUT DESIGNING A SPACESHIP? YOU TAKE A CIGAR SHAPE, PUT SOME WINDOWS ON IT, NOW THERE YOU'VE GOT IT. LET'S GET ON TO THE NEXT THING."

MY FEELING WAS THAT IF YOU DIDN'T BELIEVE IN THE SPACESHIP . . . IF YOU DIDN'T BELIEVE YOU WERE IN A VEHICLE TRAVELING THROUGH SPACE, A VEHICLE THAT MADE SENSE, WHOSE LAYOUT AND DESIGN MADE

SENSE . . . THEN YOU WOULDN'T BELIEVE IN
THE SERIES. IN DISCUSSING THE DESIGN OF
THE BRIDGE, THE STUDIO'S ATTITUDE WAS
WE SHOULD HAVE A LOT OF TRICKY LIGHTS
IN THE BACKGROUND SO THAT NO MATTER
WHICH WAY THE CAMERA WAS TURNED YOU
COULD ALWAYS SEE COLORED LIGHTS. OUR
ATTITUDE, ON THE OTHER HAND, WAS TO SIT
DOWN AND SAY TO OURSELVES, "WE ARE AC-
TUALLY   BUILDING   A   SPACESHIP.   HOW
SHOULD IT BE DESIGNED, WHERE WOULD THE
CAPTAIN BE, ETC.,?" FOR EXAMPLE, WE FELT
THE CAPTAIN SHOULD BE POSITIONED SO HE
COULD SWIVEL AROUND AND SEE EVERY
VITAL STATION. HIS PEOPLE SHOULD BE IN
CONTACT WITH HIM EASILY. THIS TYPE OF
APPROACH RESULTED IN THE DESIGN THAT
WE NOW HAVE.

TO THE STUDIO, THIS APPROACH SEEMED
TO BE AN ENORMOUS WASTE OF TIME AND
MONEY, WHEREAS WE FELT THAT THE AUDI-
ENCE ISN'T DUMB, AND THEREFORE IF IT WAS
DESIGNED RIGHT, IT WOULD "SMELL RIGHT"
EVEN   TO   AUNT   TESSIE   AND   THE   TAXI
DRIVER. DURING THOSE MONTHS I WAS
UNDER ENORMOUS PRESSURE FROM THE STU-
DIO TO QUIT SPENDING MONEY ON THIS SORT
OF THING. THEY KEPT SAYING, "BACK OFF,
YOU'VE GOT SOMETHING THAT WORKS. WHAT
ARE YOU, SOME KIND OF SCIENTIST? YOU'RE
A WRITER. WRITE THE SCRIPT. YOU'VE GOT
SOME CHAIRS AND SOME BLINKING LIGHTS,
PUT IN SOME PEOPLE AND LET'S GO." THE
WISDOM OF PERSEVERING, MAKING IT FUNC-
TIONAL AND, TO US, THE RIGHT WAY, IS
REFLECTED IN THE FACT THAT AMT CORPORA-
TION'S PLASTIC SCALE MODEL KIT OF THE
U.S.S. *ENTERPRISE* HAS BEEN ONE OF THE
LARGEST-SELLING HOBBY KITS TO EVER HIT
THE MARKET. AND I THINK IT HAS TO DO BA-

SICALLY WITH OUR INSISTENCE ON BELIEVA-
BILITY AND SCIENTIFIC ACCURACY.

On top of everything else, Roddenberry had still another
problem to solve: how to achieve the complex opticals he
was creating in the pilot script.

TO: Those Concerned         DATE: August 24, 1964
FROM: Gene Roddenberry      SUBJECT: STAR TREK
                            SPECIAL EFFECTS

Some comments on the list of special photographic
effects work in "The Cage":

Let me say first, I am delighted Anderson * and others find the project interesting and fascinating. It will
take a lot of cooperation and creative thinking to bring
this in exciting and on budget.

It seems to me the scale of the miniature U.S.S. *Enterprise* is a little large. We anticipate a final design
might see the ship as 200 feet in length, and thus even a
1½-inch scale would give us quite a huge miniature.

I think we can safely forget the animated beam of
light from the transporter chamber to the planet surface.
It would be much cheaper and certainly handier from a
story point of view to simply "dematerialize" the passenger in the transporter chamber, "rematerialize" him on
the planet surface. We can also save the effect here of
the crew being transported down a light beam to the
planet.

There is some question whether the Griffith Park
Planetarium authentic slides of interstellar space will be
as effective as drawings. The enormous telescopic mag-
nification required in these slides may not give us the
undistorted dimensionalism our ship would encounter in
true outer space. Perhaps they can be used as a guide.
Either way, could we get an estimate of the cost of such

_____

* Howard A. Anderson Company. A Hollywood firm specializing in
opticals.

a drawn backdrop? At least I would like to see a comparison between the two.

Am wondering about the comparative costs and difficulties between split screen disappearance of our people as opposed to simply stopping the camera.

Of course, will be getting into all of this in detail later. Am delighted interested parties have begun to think and plan.

Gene Roddenberry

At the same time, work on the script had to be continued. By the end of September the final draft was ready to send to NBC. Scientific accuracy and general believability of the story were greatly enhanced by the generous technical advice given to Gene by a number of scientific consultants. The following exchange of letters between Gene Roddenberry and Harvey Lynn demonstrates the amount of effort expended to maintain scientific accuracy, within the limits of still telling an entertaining and dramatic story:

14 September 1964

Mr. Gene Roddenberry
Desilu Productions, Inc.
780 North Gower Street
Hollywood 38, California

Dear Gene,

Thanks for sending me a copy of "The Cage." It is highly exciting and hard to put down when you start to read it. I see right now that my association with you is going to cost me $400. For, when the series is shown, I'll just have to buy a color TV set.

Although I am enthusiastic about the script, I couldn't resist your invitation to make comments, and these are attached. These few suggestions are intended to be helpful, and you can use them or throw them in the wastebasket as you see fit. I hope that I have made myself clear, but if you have any questions, give me a call.

This week I'll send you a package of magazines for your office, as you requested. I still haven't heard from the North American people in Downey. I am checking to see if there is anything at Hughes Aircraft which warrants a tour—if so, I'll telephone you.

I'm ready to help in any way I can, and I'm looking forward to seeing you again soon.

Best regards,

Harvey P. Lynn, Jr.

## COMMENTS ON "THE CAGE"

| Page | Scene | Item and Comment |
| --- | --- | --- |
| 2 | 8 | *Docking*—From what I have read docking is likely to occur by having the large ship ahead of the space shuttle or taxi. As the *Enterprise* slows down, the taxi nears it from the rear. To accommodate smaller shuttles, taxis, and tugs, I visualize the *Enterprise* having something like a bomb bay. When a ship is to be docked, the doors open, and a ring, two or three feet in diameter, is lowered. Upon this ring, pointed to the rear, is an intense beam of light. As the shuttle nears, a hook is extended above the smaller ship, and upon this hook is something like a photoelectric cell. The cell directs the hook to the ring as it "rides the beam." When the hook is automatically locked on the ring, a hoist lifts the shuttle into the "docking bay," doors close, valves are opened to let air into the area, and we have our shirt-sleeve atmosphere. *Voilà!* |

| Page | Scene | Item and Comment |
| --- | --- | --- |
| 2 | 6 | |

*Antares*—Antares is just not a good choice of a name here. It is a super-giant star, or sun, with a diameter of about 370,000,000 miles—just not the sort of heavenly body for humans. I suggest you choose a more vague name—Tycho, Fabricus, Lynnicus! Or I have another suggestion (I imagine that you receive unsought suggestions on scripts from scores of people each day). The shuttle or taxi could be from another ship, similar to the *Enterprise*, which has recently left the Earth. This would tie in well with the appearance of José and Yeoman Colt.

7    14    *"edge of the galaxy"*—I suggest that this is *too* far out, and it isn't really necessary to the plot. After all, the galaxy is over 100,000 light-years across. In fact, at this point, I think it would be a good idea to use some real names to show that you have given the matter some thought.

There are three star groups, fairly close together, which could be habitable. These are Sigma Draconis, Eta Cassiopeiae, and HR 8832. Thus, at this point, Number one could say:

> We have no ships or Earth colonies in that sector, sir. It's listed as TALOS IV in Eta Cassiopeiae, a binary system with eleven planets, spectral class F9.

7    15    "disappeared in that *quadrant*"—quadrant signifies one-fourth of something. How about substituting "region"?

8    15    *Epsilon VII and Orion*—Suggest substituting Draconis and HR 8832.

| Page | Scene | Item and Comment |
|------|-------|------------------|
| 10   | 19    | *dual-sun system*—Here, a quotation from A. C. Clarke's *The Exploration of Space* may be helpful: ... |

(There followed a long quote from Clarke on the appearance, configuration, and movement of a double star system.)

| | | |
|------|-------|------------------|
| 10 | 21 | *Gravity 1.3 of Earth*—Over on page 16 you describe the Talosians as small and slim with elongated heads. This is not consistent with a gravity of 1.3, but it is consistent with a gravity of less than that of the Earth. Why not substitute "0.85," "Point 85," or "85%"? |
| 11 | 21 | *Astroscientist*—Suggest substituting "Geologist," as done on page 11. This would aid the viewer in identifying exactly what the guy will do, whereas "Astroscientist" is rather vague and covers a lot of territory. |
| 16 | 36 | *solar batteries and directional beams*—These two have no connection with each other. Also the survivors would be more likely to send out a broadcast beam, inasmuch as the directional beam would be much less likely to be intercepted. I suggest something like: |

> After we could no longer use the ship's power, we switched to atomic batteries and started praying.

I prefer atomic to solar batteries for two reasons: (1) they are more powerful, allowing a signal to be sent farther, (2) a solar-powered radio would require the presence of a fairly large array of solar cells at the site of the crash to catch the rays of the sun (by fairly large, I mean

| Page | Scene | Item and Comment |
|------|-------|------------------|

something, say, six feet by ten feet). A much more powerful atomic battery could be in something the size of a suitcase.

As far as set design is concerned, I doubt if it makes any difference, as you'll probably show the transmitting equipment rather than the batteries, or cells, anyway.

19    45    *Laser guns*—Don't forget to have a connection between the guns and the "power belt." I visualize the belt looking something like a waist-type life preserver, having individual power units, say, three inches by six inches. These units can be replaced, just as bullets in a gun can be replaced.

Another thought occurs to me here. LASER stands for Light Amplification Stimulation Emission Radiation—the M in MASER stands for Microwave. Now, your guns (and the big gun used later on) are highly advanced pieces of hardware. Don't you think it is likely that they will have a *new* name? After all, LASER and MASER are only five or six years old. A new name would also serve to silence critics who will contend that a Laser cannon will not whip up dust and will not need to be dug-in.

Some possible candidates for a new name might be: HEAT gun (High Energy Amplification Transport); BEE gun (Beam of Electromagnetic Energy); ACE gun (Amplified Coherent Energy); CLEB gun (Coherent Light Energy Beam).

23    57    *"at the other end of this galaxy*—I still drag my heels at getting *this* far out. Could you substitute: ". . . from a small planet named Earth far away in this galaxy."

| Page | Scene | Item and Comment |
|------|-------|------------------|
| 40 | 81 | *Rigel 113*—Rigel is mighty far away. How about Vega 113? For the same reason, I would suggest Centaurian traders to Orion traders on page 47. |
| 59 | 117 | *"Switch to impulse rockets"*—In a sense, all rockets are impulse rockets. How about, "Switch to rocket power," or, "Switch to emergency power"? |

*The Transporter*—I have one final comment, which is also out of my bailiwick. Supposedly, anyone can operate the Transporter at will, even though he may be on a planet (or else the people in the ship would not be surprised to see Yeoman Colt, Number One, and Captain April suddenly reappear from the Transporter Room). Do you really want to give him this capability?

My reason for asking is this. Let's say that in a future story April is in some kind of real, not illusionary, danger. In this script, you are setting the precedent for him to just thumb his nose at the danger and hightail it back to the *Enterprise*. What kind of fun is that? Where is the suspense? Or have I missed the point entirely?

September 16, 1964

Mr. Harvey P. Lynn, Jr.
3218 Colby Avenue
Los Angeles 66, California

Dear Harvey:
Have your comments on "The Cage" and find them very thoughtful and helpful. Am already making script changes which reflect them.

Reference the binary sun, am a little at a loss here on exactly what it should look like. Maybe when we get together next you can sketch out what it would look like from the planet surface. Of course, if it is too bizarre or confusing to the audience, we'll probably have to go back to a single sun.

Hoped to see you this week, but will be out of town from Thursday through Saturday. Will call you early next week.

Many thanks again.

> Warmest regards,
>
> Gene Roddenberry

The following is a short note from Harvey Lynn to Gene Roddenberry, posing a problem, the solution, and the humor in the serious business of research:

Photographic Laboratory.
Have a photo lab on the *Enterprise*. Rapid development of pictures.
Idea—film shows objects invisible to eye.
Idea—scientists analyzing photo find invisible, dense "photoplasmas" which act as wall to Captain April. Gun no good, because hole is filled by other photoplasmas immediately. After discovery through use of film, chemistry lab makes special spray to kill mean old plasmas. Everybody happy.

September 24, 1964

Mr. Harvey P. Lynn, Jr.
3218 Colby Avenue
Los Angeles 66, California

Dear Harvey:
Enclosed the revised draft of the STAR TREK pilot.

Reference your comments on September 14, you'll note we've taken out the whole "docking" procedure. Will hold your suggestion here for future stories which involve it. This also eliminates the use of Antares as a colony reference.

Most of your other suggestions are reflected in this new version. There are some exceptions, however. For one thing, would like in the pilot to use the names of stars which are fairly familiar to the audience. This is why I've avoided such terms as "HR8832," etc. Also, trying to maintain other points identifiable to the audience, have decided to keep "Laser" as the description of the gun.

Reference the continuing use of the stars Rigel and Orion, these can still be substituted in the final shooting version with names like Vega which may be equally familiar and would not be so wrong from a scientific point of view.

Again, many thanks for your comments and would much appreciate further comments on this new version. Any point you feel strongly about, please feel free to continue arguing.

Warmest regards,

Gene Roddenberry

30 September 1964

Mr. Gene Roddenberry
Desilu Productions, Inc.
780 North Gower Street
Hollywood 38, California

Dear Gene,
Here are the slides I promised to send to you. If you already have a set, or if you do not plan to use them, please return them to me as I would value them highly—I think that they are magnificent!
As for the revised script, my criticisms are trifling. But as Arthur Balfour so profoundly remarked, "Society, dead

or alive, can have no charm without intimacy and no intimacy without an interest in trifles."

### Page 4 April—"Any oxygen planets"?

I missed this the first time around. Technically, a planet could have oxygen and still be unsuitable to sustain life for many other reasons. If you liked, you could substitute "suitable," "likely," or "habitable" for oxygen. On the other hand, oxygen certainly gets the right idea across.

### Page 5 José—"Course is computed and on the board."

Would "on the screen" be better? Incidentally, can you use the idea of a screen display I sent you last week? I found a quotation by Salvador Dali which, I think, applies to complicated things like the screen display: "For myself, le more complicated things for this reason, like it best today: le nuclear microphysics and mathematics because no understand, myself no understand nothing of these. Is tremendous attraction for understand something in this way."

### Page 17 Insert—Knoll

If you are going to use Laser beams, it is likely that there will be some time involved in ripping away the rock. It can be visualized as something akin to cutting a piece of metal with an acetylene torch—only faster. I'd say on the order of seconds. Can you spare the time?

### Page 47 Number One—"We've pinpointed static . . ."

Another trifle, one I also missed the last time. "Static" implies that the generators are similar to those we have today. How about substituting "disturbance"? A disturbance could be electrical, seismic, acoustic, or even something we know nothing about today.

To repeat a Cleopatra pun, "I am not prone to argue" about these points of mine which you did not choose to accept, for three good reasons. First, you are in the entertainment business and you are not making a pilot to show off scientific knowledge. If you have to bend sci-

ence a little to make the story understandable and exciting, then by all means bend it. Second, my Air Force
career conditioned me to give as good advice as possible
to a superior officer. But if he chose another course of
action or if he chose to use only part of my advice, that
was his privilege. And, thirdly, I'm quite satisfied with
the batting average I have, as far as suggestions to you
are concerned!

What else can I do for you? How is the set coming
along?

Best regards,

Harvey Lynn

The last week in September Gene submitted the proposed
shooting script to NBC. Their reaction was better than he
had expected. The principal objection voiced by the network
centered around a proposed dream sequence which Gene had
written into the script. NBC cautioned against overemphasiz-
ing this dream sequence, fearing that the message concerning
what is reality would be lost on the viewer. A number of
other, minor changes were also requested, but in essence the
network gave its approval to shoot the pilot.

Now it was time for the acid test.

Chapter 7

## Voyage One

I first became aware of the series when Gene told me he was going to do a science fiction pilot called STAR TREK. I said, "Marvelous, whatever the hell that is."

Morris Chapnick, Paramount
studio executive and former
assistant to Gene Roddenberry

Talent will show up a lot faster in television than it will in feature motion pictures.

It's "do or die" in television. Production requirements, limited budgets, and limited time allow no margin for error. If you can't "cut it," it becomes painfully obvious in short order. The conditions under which personnel must work are sometimes close to frightening.

Producing a one-hour series like STAR TREK is like producing one-half of a motion picture every week. You must create forty-six to forty-eight minutes of actual air time per show, every six days. In comparison, the average motion picture feature may take three months or more to make only eighty to one hundred minutes.

The contrast in costs is equally dramatic. A medium-quality feature picture will have a budget of a million dollars or better. A television episode budget runs about $160,000 to $180,000, or an average of $340,000 for the same number of minutes as a feature picture. Compared to television, features seem to have unlimited time and unlimited money.

In early October, 1964, as he began preparations to shoot the pilot, Gene Roddenberry was not unaware of the problems he faced.

One of the people who joined the STAR TREK staff about that time was a young man named Morris Chapnick. Morris is a thin man, of medium height, with wide, peering eyes set behind black horn-rimmed glasses. He has a thoughtfully serious nature, a blunt, straightforward sense of humor, and is rapidly developing into a talented writer in his own right. Morris had worked as Gene's administrative assistant on "The Lieutenant," and in October Gene hired him as his assistant on STAR TREK.

Morris recounts his introduction to STAR TREK with candor:

> I read the series format and suddenly it was like a whole new world, it was fantastic. The stars and the whole schmeer. I have to say in front of this thing [the ever-present Whitfield tape recorder] that I don't know from science fiction. I am sure there are many other worlds out in the sky somewhere, but I don't think in those terms. I can give you a Brave New World because that is something I can see, but some of the stuff Gene does on the show—I don't understand it. When they do "people stories," then I'm all for it. The situation may be nothing that I've ever seen or anyone has ever seen, but you can understand it, relate to it, if you can believe the people in it. Anyway, I read this thing, and I don't know anything about outer space, but the wagon train of the stars—that I understand.

As STAR TREK registered another addition to its staff, the show was also registering its first casualty. Pato Guzman. Homesick for his native country, Pato returned to Chile* and was subsequently replaced by Franz Bachelin, a man with the unusual background of having been a German fighter pilot in World War I.

Casualties or no, the set designs had to be completed before the sets themselves could be built. As ideas went down on paper, they were sent to technical consultants for verification or modification. Everyone contacted verified the validity of the basic approach to the *Enterprise*. (Assuming the solution of three basic requirements—motive power, environmental

---

* Pato remained in Chile for about a year, designing several resort hotels, and then returned to Hollywood, where his exceptional talents are again being utilized, at another studio.

support system, and artificial gravity—any type of spaceship is possible. With those three conditions met, the *Enterprise* could in fact be built. All that is necessary is to place the materials in orbit and assemble the ship in space.)

The final development of the vessel's bridge turned out to be Matt Jefferies' baby:

The split-level bridge was not part of the original idea. I did not like it, and in many ways I do not now. There is much to be said for it pictorially, in terms of people movement and picture composition. But it's had a great many difficult ramifications for me. The split-level design limits the type of camera shot you can do, for example. For any close-ups of people on the bridge, you have to jack the camera up off the floor. Another problem that resulted from the split-level design is the high noise level in the bridge. The original bridge was built in eight "wild" [separate] sections.* These sections have a tendency to squeak a great deal because they weaken and loosen from daily usage, being pulled in and out and moved around.

Franz and I worked out how many people would be on the bridge and what their functions would be. Then Franz proceeded with the design of the rest of the sets for the pilot and left me alone with the bridge. The first thing I did was to work out the size of the units and the shapes of the consoles and screens at each station. I then made a full-size cut-out of each screen, pinned it up on a wall, and sat back in a chair in front of it in order to check the feel of the thing, and how high the screens were to look at. When that checked out properly, I set to work drawing full-size layouts for every button, panel, screen, console, and the eight instruments on each of the eight sections. The full-size drawings were then sent to the construction department so that they could begin building the actual sets. At the same time, I called

---

* Prior to STAR TREK's first season, the bridge was modified, and now has ten movable sections. Also, by that time, Bachelin had departed for another assignment and Matt Jefferies had been promoted to art director.

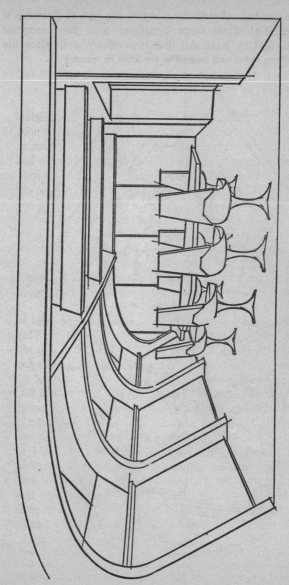

**EARLY SKETCH OF
BRIEFING ROOM**

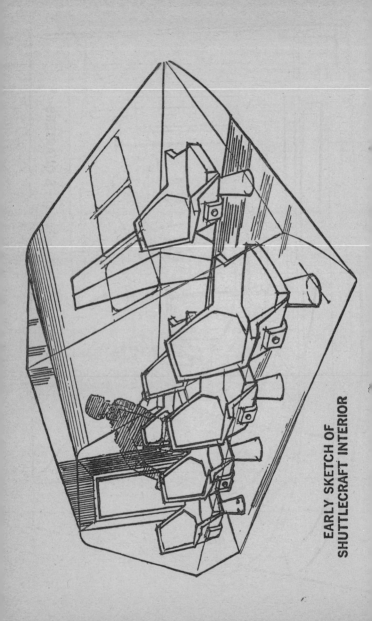

EARLY SKETCH OF
SHUTTLECRAFT INTERIOR

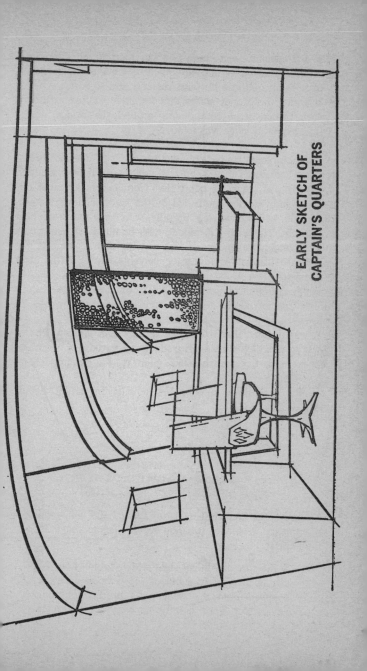

EARLY SKETCH OF
CAPTAIN'S QUARTERS

in the special effects man and got him started building the electrical boxes and equipment that would be needed to light all of those buttons, screens, and so forth. After choosing the proper colors that I wanted for the various view screens and components around the bridge, the final assembly stage was relatively easy.

The completed bridge contains hundreds of electrically automated sequential instruments, switches, and light indicators. All instruments can be controlled from a central panel offstage or individually controlled by the actors at their stations on the set. Miles of wiring, literally, were required to connect everything. The wiring job alone took hundreds of man hours to complete. Twelve translucent viewing screens around the bridge provide data of every conceivable nature to the crew of the *Enterprise*.

From design-development to final completion, the vessel's bridge interior alone required approximately six weeks to construct and a total cost approaching $60,000.

It was decided that the bridge would be in the top area of the saucer, which would also contain a variety of laboratories, the sick bay, the officers' quarters, the briefing room, and so forth.

In the meantime, smaller but equally important details were being attended to.

TO: Franz Bachelin  DATE: October 14, 1964
FROM: Gene Roddenberry  SUBJECT: LASER HAND GUN

Whatever the final design of our Laser hand gun, I think practicality in such a weapon would dictate the following items:

a. Some sort of optical sight which could either be swung up or raised out of the weapon itself, or snapped onto the weapon—a precision aiming device for very careful or very long-distance use.

b. In addition to the basic hand grip, some sort of grip near the fore part of the weapon (also either swung out from the weapon itself or snapped on) which allows a two-handed shooting stance for extreme precision firing.

Obviously, none of this is necessary in our present story, but the design should certainly include this kind of planning for possible needs in future stories.

Gene Roddenberry

By the time November rolled around, the sets were ready to be constructed. The entire STAR TREK production crew was moved south to Desilu's Culver City studio, where they took up residence on Stages 14, 15, and 16. Predictably, the move created a fresh set of problems.

Foremost among the problems were the sound stages themselves. The particular stages assigned to STAR TREK had been constructed during the days of silent movies. Consequently, no provision had been made for soundproofing. (This presented many problems during the actual shooting of the pilot.)

For some mysterious reason there is a three-foot drop from one end of Stage 15 all the way across, through, and into the other side of Stage 16. When the large doors separating the two stages are opened up, you have the effect of one long, sloping ramp. This meant that everything had to be built on platforms in order to keep the floor of the set level. The result was more time lost, and extra money spent in the process.

Looking at the antiquated facilities in which they had to work, and remembering the somewhat better facilities back at Desilu's Gower Street facility, Gene and his small staff began to have the feeling they were being unnecessarily put upon.

More fuel was added to the fire as the sets began to take shape. As one individual close to the situation at the time related:

Desilu, of course, provided the construction people to build the sets. Some of them were built so close together that you couldn't get lamps in between them. You had to tear out pieces of the sets in order to get your lamps in just to light the set for shooting. Any production head with any experience in this business could have taken one look at the sets and known immediately that men and equipment could not get between them. Another example had to do with the bridge. Instead of a double platform being built in the base of the bridge to absorb normal noises of people moving around, they only put in one layer. This played havoc with our sound track.

The sets were built right next to the men's room.

Since the sound stages had been built with no provision for soundproofing, problems naturally ensued. Whenever anyone would go the the men's room, the water would flow through the pipes, and the noise would be picked up on the sound track, thereby ruining that particular take. Gene had to finally order the men's room shut down, and a guard posted outside the door to prevent its use.

Another staff member, recalling the incident, states:

When you develop a certain hostility toward someone, a suspicion that they are doing you wrong, you begin to read into the situation things that are not necessarily so. Nevertheless, I think the old-guard studio people could have helped us a hell of a lot more than they did. They made it very difficult for us.

The fact that the pilot was shot in spite of such problems is a credit to the character of the STAR TREK staff. They are the kind of people who will fight back. They're not afraid to battle The Establishment. Fortunately, Herb Solow was on STAR TREK's side, and he too is a man who loves a good fight. Herb's job was to insure that Gene could make the best pilot possible.

WE SPENT MORE ON THOSE SETS THAN ANY STUDIO IN TELEVISION HAD EVER SPENT BEFORE IN BUILDING A COMPARABLE THING. I THINK PROBABLY WE SPENT MORE THAN EVEN ANY MOTION PICTURE HAD EVER SPENT IN BUILDING A SPACESHIP UP UNTIL THAT TIME. ON SEVERAL OCCASIONS THE STUDIO GOT VERY UPSET ABOUT THE MOUNTING COSTS, BUT FORTUNATELY HERB SOLOW, WHO WAS IN CHARGE OF TELEVISION PRODUCTION AT THE STUDIO, WENT TO BAT FOR US. ALTHOUGH HE MAY NOT ALWAYS HAVE AGREED WITH US, HE BELIEVED IN US AND BACKED US, AND THAT WAS A GREAT HELP.

YOU MUST MAKE UP YOUR MIND WHEN YOU'RE IN A PROJECT OF THIS SORT THAT EITHER YOU ARE GOING TO DO IT YOUR WAY OR YOU'RE GOING TO DO IT THEIR WAY. AND IF YOU ARE GOING TO SLAVISHLY DO IT THEIR WAY, YOU MIGHT AS WELL WALK OFF AND LET THEM DO IT ALL. BUT IF YOU DECIDE YOU'RE GOING TO DO IT YOUR WAY, STICK WITH IT, REGARDLESS OF THE CONSEQUENCES. YOU MUST BELIEVE IN YOURSELF. IF YOU'RE WRONG AND GET SHOT DOWN IN FLAMES, YOU SAY TO YOURSELF, "OKAY BABY, I WAS WRONG, I TAKE THE BLAME." BUT TO GET SHOT DOWN BECAUSE YOU DON'T HAVE THE COURAGE OF YOUR OWN CONVICTIONS—THAT'S INEXCUSABLE. IT CAN GET TOUGH—YOU DO BEGIN TO DOUBT YOURSELF WHEN EVERYONE AROUND YOU BEGINS TO TELL YOU THAT YOU ARE WRONG. THEN YOU GO HOME AT NIGHT AND TOSS IN YOUR BED AND SAY TO YOURSELF, "COME ON NOW, ARE YOU CLAIMING YOU'RE INFALLIBLE? ARE YOU SAYING YOU ARE SUCH A GENIUS AND EVERYONE'S OUT OF STEP BUT YOU?" YOU HAVE THESE MOMENTS OF TERRIBLE DOUBT AND, I

SUPPOSE, INSECURITY. I THINK THIS IS PART
OF THE DIFFERENCE BETWEEN THE CREATOR
AND THE NONCREATOR.

(At the time Gene told me this, I asked him if his philosophy wasn't akin to the Spartans, who lived by the creed, "Live
each day like a lion rather than like a mouse." Gene grinned
and replied: "It's more often the case of live each day like a
lion and shake in bed each night like a mouse.")

Amid the rising furor over mounting costs, Gene plunged
ahead.

TO: Mr. Franz Bachelin,     DATE: December 10, 1964
     Art Department          SUBJECT: RIGEL
FROM: Gene Roddenberry                FORTRESS

We should see the following is done on our back lot
Rigel Fortress set.

  (a) Put fangs, long ears, etc., on the Chinese dog.
  Anything you can do to get and convey an unearth-
  liness.
  (b) Paint some arches, colonnades, etc., a weath-
  ering bright blue. In other words, an unusual color
  range. It should be seen from the outside of the
  fortress and used again on the inside of the fortress
  to give "alien" unity to the whole set.
  (c) The eagles over the courtyard arch are much
  too earthlike. We should remember this and find new
  heads to put on them.

Byron Haskin has discussed all aspects of this with me,
so feel free to work with him on them. Any job you have
in shape and would like me to inspect I am at your service.

                              Gene Roddenberry

Except for the part of Captain April,* casting the pilot was no problem at all. But then, the lead is usually always a problem when casting a new show. It's primarily a matter of availability. There are only so many acceptable leading men available who fit a particular part. Normally there are several things you look for in a leading man. First of all, he should be attractive, and physically appealing to the audience. Secondly, he must be able to project a great deal of warmth, because you want the viewer to like him. Thirdly, he must be believable in the part. And finally, he must be acceptable to the network, the studio, and the sponsors.

By the time STAR TREK began casting for the lead, there were so many other series in production that there were just not that many actors available. Those who were could afford to be choosy about what part they took. One of the actors Gene was interested in was Jeff Hunter, who eventually agreed to play the part of Captain April.

By that time, the rest of the cast had already been chosen. Leonard Nimoy would play the part of Mr. Spock. Ever since his appearance on an episode of "The Lieutenant," Roddenberry had always wanted to cast Leonard in the role of an alien. Majel Barrett was to play Number One, the ship's Executive Officer.† Peter Duryea (Dan Duryea's son) was cast as the Navigator, José Tyler. Dr. Philip Boyce was played by John Hoyt. The part of Yeoman J. M. Colt was played by Laurel Goodwin. The guest star role of Vina was played by Susan Oliver. Ed Madden was cast in the part of the geologist. In the lesser roles, a mixture of racial types was featured.

The decision to have an obvious mixture of races in the cast caused a lot of raised eyebrows. Integration was not commonplace in television at that time.

A number of people expressed concern that the viewer might reject the concept of different races, particularly Negro and white, working side by side. Others voiced the opinion

---

* The name "Captain April" was changed to "Captain Winter" and then to "Captain Christopher Pike" just before the pilot was shot. When recasting for the second STAR TREK pilot, "Pike" became "Captain James T. Kirk."

† The series format called for a woman in this role.

that segregationist elements would cause the show to be banned in certain areas of the country. Others were worried about the vessel's designation *United Space Ship Enterprise* . . . suggesting that this "one world" concept would be unpopular. Why couldn't it be a good, safe patriotic *United States* spaceship?

Gene stood his ground, gambling on his belief in the television audience, determined to carry out his plan of presenting subject matter and situations on STAR TREK that would challenge and stimulate the thinking of the viewer. He insisted everything about the show must be a logical projection into the future. He believed that a peaceful, harmonious, *unified* Earth must be the result of a natural and logical evolution of society, if society is to survive.

THIS APPROACH EXPRESSES THE "MESSAGE" BASIC TO THE SERIES: WE MUST LEARN TO LIVE TOGETHER OR MOST CERTAINLY WE WILL SOON ALL DIE TOGETHER. ALTHOUGH STAR TREK HAD TO ENTERTAIN OR GO OFF THE AIR, WE BELIEVED OUR FORMAT WAS UNIQUE ENOUGH TO ALLOW US TO CHALLENGE AND STIMULATE THE AUDIENCE. MAKING STAR TREK HAPPEN WAS A BONE-CRUSHER, AND UNLESS IT ALSO "SAID SOMETHING" AND WE CHALLENGED OUR VIEWER TO THINK AND REACT, THEN IT WASN'T WORTH ALL WE HAD PUT INTO THE SHOW.

When a television show becomes a success, many people tend to attribute that success solely to the ability and personal quality of the actors and actresses in the cast. And STAR TREK's acting talent certainly proved to be among the best in the industry. But a more realistic appraisal of what makes a successful show must include the production staff and crew members, who have the initial and primary responsibility for the end result seen on the home viewing screen.

It is therefore not surprising that Gene devoted quite a bit of effort toward acquiring the talent necessary to ramrod the production. One of the first people Gene hired, as assistant director, was Bob Justman.* Bob arrived at STAR TREK fresh from a successful stint on "Outer Limits." His ruddy complexion is dominated by a large, bushy handlebar moustache. He forever looks as though he needs a haircut, and this impression is enhanced even more by the fact that his hair is in a perpetual state of disarray. An exceptionally fine talent, Bob is a very funny guy and has a tremendous sense of humor.

Another addition to the staff was Jerry Finnerman,† who was hired as the camera operator for the pilot. The addition of makeup artist Fred Philips swelled the ranks of the talented staff even further.

Although the situation was beginning to shape up pretty well, and despite the numerous problems that had continually plagued STAR TREK, at least one major hurdle remained.

Spock's ears.

Gene had had several crude pairs of ears made, but promptly discarded them as being unsatisfactory. Then, when Fred Philips joined the staff seven or eight days before shooting was scheduled to commence, Gene called him and described what he had in mind. Fred immediately set to work making the molds from Leonard's ears, and from those original molds, fashioning the pointed ears that Gene wanted.

WE HAD TO TRY A LOT OF DIFFERENT TYPES OF EARS ON LEONARD TO GET THE RIGHT ONES, ONES THAT LOOKED REAL. WE HAD THEM TOO BIG, TOO FLAT, TOO POINTED, AND SO FORTH. SO LEONARD CAME IN FOUR OR FIVE DAYS IN A ROW AND TRIED ON THESE DIFFERENT KINDS OF EARS. WE WOULD THEN SHOOT TEST FOOTAGE AND VIEW THEM THE NEXT DAY IN THE PROJECTION ROOM.

---

* Bob performed so well that he was later promoted to associate producer, and then in early 1968 he moved up to co-producer of the series.

† A measure of Jerry's talent is the fact that he was later moved up to cinematographer for the series.

AS ALWAYS HAPPENS WITH A HIGH-SPIR-
ITED CREW, THEY BEGAN MAKING JOKES
ABOUT "PIXIE" AND "JACKRABBIT." NOW,
LEONARD IS A VERY SERIOUS ACTOR, AND
THESE REMARKS FINALLY BEGAN TO GET
TO HIM. SO ONE DAY LEONARD CAME INTO
MY OFFICE, SAT DOWN, AND BEGAN TO EX-
PRESS HIS DOUBTS ABOUT THE "POINTED
EARS" ROLE. HE EXPLAINED HIS DESIRE TO BE
KNOWN AS A SERIOUS ACTOR, THE HOPES
AND DREAMS HE HAD FOR HIS FUTURE. THIS
SPOCK PART WAS BEGINNING TO LOOK TO
HIM LIKE HE'D BE PLAYING A FREAK WITH
EARS. HE WOUND UP BY SAYING, "I'VE DE-
CIDED I DON'T WANT THE PART."

WELL, AFTER ALL THAT WE HAD GONE
THROUGH, AND WITH ONLY A FEW DAYS
LEFT BEFORE SHOOTING, AND I'M CERTAIN
SPOCK CAN BE A MEANINGFUL AND CHAL-
LENGING ROLE, NOW COMES THE PROBLEM
OF TALKING LEONARD OUT OF THIS. WE
MUST HAVE ARGUED FOR AT LEAST HALF AN
HOUR. I WAS DESPERATELY TRYING TO CON-
VINCE LEONARD THAT THERE IS DIGNITY IN
SPOCK AND FOR THE ACTOR PORTRAYING
HIM. BUT THERE HAD BEEN TOO MANY COM-
MENTS AND REMARKS ABOUT THE POINTED
EARS—NIMOY WAS UNCONVINCED. FINALLY
THE ONLY THING I COULD THINK OF TO SAY
TO HIM WAS, "LEONARD, LOOK, BELIEVE ME. I
MAKE THIS PLEDGE TO YOU. IF BY THE THIR-
TEENTH SHOW YOU STILL DON'T LIKE THE
EARS, I WILL PERSONALLY WRITE A SCRIPT IN
WHICH YOU WILL GET AN EAR JOB AND GO
BACK TO NORMAL." HE LOOKED AT ME FOR A
MINUTE AND THEN PRACTICALLY FELL
DOWN ON THE FLOOR LAUGHING. SUDDENLY
THE EARS HAD BEEN PUT BACK IN PROPER
PERSPECTIVE, AND THAT WAS THE END OF
THAT PROBLEM.

An interesting footnote to the ear problem came up following the end of STAR TREK's first season, and was the result of a bit of playacting on the part of Bob Justman:

You know, wearing the ears is a strain. It's painful, tiring, uncomfortable, and it takes an hour and a half to get into them every morning. Before we started the second season, I put Leonard on, telling him I could solve the ear problem for the whole second season. I said, "Leonard, I think I've come up with the answer to the ear problem. You're going to be able to save all that time in makeup. No more being uncomfortable, no more pain, no more problems. You can just get regular makeup and everything will be perfect." And he says, "Yeah, what is it, Bob?" And I said, "We're going to send you to a plastic surgeon and we're going to point your ears. When the series is finished, we'll pay to have them put back to normal!" I almost had Leonard convinced that it would be much easier, much less painful. The more I talked, the more he began to listen and sort of nod his head. You could almost hear the thought going through his mind, "You know . . . it would possibly be much better. . . ." At that point I couldn't keep a straight face any longer and broke up. That's when Leonard realized that I was putting him on, and he cracked up, too.

There is an old saying that if you stick with something long enough you will eventually make it. Apparently it's true, because despite seemingly insurmountable problems, on December 12, 1964, shooting began on the STAR TREK pilot "The Menagerie." *

A normal hour pilot will generally take from eight to ten days to shoot. Since there was nothing "normal" about STAR TREK, the pilot took twelve days.

_____

* Gene had changed the title "The Cage" to "The Menagerie" because he felt the new title more closely described the situation in which Captain Pike (now renamed) found himself during the course of the story.

Gene and his staff are quick to admit they do not think of everything:

THE TRUTH IS, NOT ONLY DO WE MISS, BUT WE HAVE ALSO CHEATED A BIT IN CERTAIN AREAS. WE'VE DONE SO BECAUSE THERE ARE CERTAIN THINGS THAT ARE DRAMATICALLY NECESSARY IN A SHOW. FOR INSTANCE, A SPACESHIP TRAVELING THROUGH SPACE, WHERE THERE IS NO ATMOSPHERE, DOES NOT MAKE A SOUND AS IT PASSES. WHEN WE DID THE ORIGINAL TITLES * FOR THE PILOT, WHERE WE HAVE THE SHIP ZOOM PAST THE CAMERA AT SEEMINGLY GREAT SPEEDS, WE HAD NO SOUND . . . JUST THE VISUAL MOVEMENT OF THE SHIP. AS A RESULT, THAT SEQUENCE WAS LITERALLY DEAD. IT HAD NO FEELING OF SPEED OR EXCITEMENT ABOUT IT AT ALL. SO WE ADDED A "SWISH" SOUND AS THE SHIP PASSED BY, AND SUDDENLY IT CAME ALIVE. WE ARE STILL EARTHBOUND CREATURES, AND WE ARE USED TO SOMETHING GOING THAT FAST MAKING A SOUND AS IT GOES BY. WE HAD TO PUT IT IN EVEN THOUGH WE KNOW THAT SCIENTIFICALLY IT WOULDN'T HAPPEN.

WHEN AN EXPLOSION HAPPENS IN SPACE, AS LONG AS THE EXPLOSION DOESN'T HIT THE SHIP, THE VESSEL WOULDN'T BE ROCKED BACK AND FORTH. IF WE ADHERED TO THE SCIENTIFIC REALITY IN THIS CASE, PICTURE WHAT WOULD HAPPEN: A KLINGON WARSHIP IS ATTACKING US WITH PHOTON BOLTS, AND THERE ARE NEAR MISSES GOING ON ALL AROUND US . . . . EXPLOSIONS. AND WE ARE SITTING THERE IN OUR CHAIRS WITH NOT A HAIR ON OUR HEADS DISTURBED. AGAIN, A "DEAD" SCENE WITH NO DRAMA, NO EXCITE-

---

* "Titles" include the name of the series, episode name, cast list, and other screen credits.

MENT. WE FOUND THAT WE HAD TO MAKE
THE SHIP ROCK IN SUCH SITUATIONS. WE HAD
TO HAVE OUR PEOPLE KNOCKED OUT OF
THEIR CHAIRS. IT JUST HAD TO BE DONE.
OTHERWISE AN EARTHBOUND AUDIENCE SIM-
PLY CANNOT RELATE EMOTIONALLY TO THE
JEOPARDY GOING ON.

SCIENTISTS HAVE TOLD US THAT AT HYPER-
LIGHT SPEEDS OF OUR SHIP THE STARS WILL
NOT SEEM TO PASS AS WE SEE THEM ON THE
SCREEN. RATHER, THE WHOLE UNIVERSE
WILL SEEM FORESHORTENED AND WILL SEEM
TO ACCUMULATE INTO A GREAT MASS IN
FRONT OF US, WITH DARKNESS ALL AROUND
IT. AGAIN, THERE WOULD BE SIMPLY NO
FEELING IN THE AUDIENCE OF GOING SOME-
WHERE. WE ARE ACCUSTOMED TO THE FEEL-
ING THAT IF YOU ARE GOING FAST, THINGS
GO BY YOU. IT IS SELF-DEFEATING TO USE
SCIENTIFIC ACCURACY TO THE POINT THAT
ALL OF THE SENSORY AND EMOTIONAL
THINGS THAT MAKE THE SHOW ENTERTAIN-
ING ARE LOST.

Shooting was eventually completed without serious mishap.
Although that phase of production had been successfully concluded, Gene was still having problems with the opticals, as
indicated by the following series of memos:

SPECIAL EFFECTS SCREENING
COMMENTS

12-28-64

1. APPEARANCES AND DISAPPEARANCES OF CREW:
    Eliminate the thick line around the crew members as
    they are transported.
    Have a subtle suggestion of sparkle rather than the
    Peter Pan sparkle presently being used.

Get rid of the colored outline. Have crew members *slowly* dissolve. Maintain whole image with slight flickering of color instead of present solid color.

2. STARS:
   There should be no movement of the stars as the U.S.S. *Enterprise* crosses into the screen and then exits.

3. ARRIVING ON THE PLANET SURFACE:
   All the actors should have the same color effect instead of the present individual assortment of colors.

4. TITLES:
   Have titles change colors.


TO: Those Concerned    DATE: January 5, 1965
FROM: Gene Roddenberry SUBJECT: TRANSITION
                                OF BACKGROUNDS OR
                                PERSONS IN ILLUSION
                                SEQUENCES


The illusion transitions which occur in STAR TREK are of two types:

a. The background shifts and the person finds himself in a new setting.
b. The person is made to appear or disappear.


Both of the above will be accomplished via a "rapid shimmer" effect. In other words, a wave-like changing of plane and focus similar to what showed on the viewing screen of the U.S.S. *Enterprise* bridge, but in this case illusion occurring with much shorter and more rapid waves. It should happen almost with the speed of what happens when one jars a heavily tinseled Christmas tree. The following points are worth attention:

a. The "shimmer" effect is *not* wiped onto or off the screen but rather fades into existence and fades off when the transition is completed.

b. There should never be a hard line between the area of shimmer and matted non-shimmer. For example, in the case of the background shimmering and changing—the shimmer progressively gets less in the area of the matted figure, eliminating the feeling there is a matte there.

c. In the case of it being a human figure which is intransition (as happens to Vina in Scene 74 at the end of Act I), her figure shimmers and disappears. Whether *only* her figure should shimmer or whether it should include some of the surrounding area is probably worth a quick test.

d. The effect should be short, probably not over eight feet in total.

e. Please note the shimmer effect accompanies *every* illusion transition and hopefully will become familiar to the audience as something signaling illusion. Please double-check that you are planning such an effect in the case of every illusion in the script.

Gene Roddenberry


TO: Those Concerned    DATE: January 5, 1965
FROM: Gene Roddenberry  SUBJECT: LASER CANNON
                                 EFFECT

The following should be the sequence of the Laser cannon blasting Talos IV rocky knoll, Scenes 67 through 73:

a. The glowing and flashing red and white lights emanating from the cannon are seen *only* preliminary to shooting. Consider this effect the "warming up" of the cannon. Once the cannon fires, this glowing red and white light effect is stopped and is seen no more.

b. When the cannon fires, the "beam" effect begins about the same transparency and intensity as in the test strip seen today. As the firing continues (and as Number One calls for more power), the effect becomes deeper and stronger.

c. The explosion of rock takes place *immediately* upon the rocky knoll being touched by the blue beam from the cannon. There will be only one explosion. We will combine the two previous explosions into one long explosion effect, joining them via the device of cutting away to crew members' reactions in between. In other words, the Laser cannon creates a long continuous blast of rock away from the metal elevator shaft, persisting until all loose rock is blasted away from the metallic door. At that time, the explosions tail off.

d. The Laser cannon beam continues without interruption, now being absorbed by the metallic door which begins to glow dully red, then brighter and brighter red, finally becoming white-hot.

e. During the above (d), at which time Number One requests an increase of power, the blue beam is seen to get stronger and more intense. In other words, after the beam has blasted away all the loose, intervening rock, it heats the metal up somewhat, possibly to a dull red. Then power is increased and the stronger and more intense blue beam achieves the heating of the metal to white-hot. At this time, however, Mr. Spock has advised Number One the circuits are beginning to heat and it becomes necessary to shut off the Laser cannon.

f. When the Laser cannon is shut off and the blue beam stops, we see the metallic door quickly cool from white-hot down through red to its original dull metallic color.

Gene Roddenberry

TO: Those Concerned    DATE: January 13, 1965
FROM: Gene Roddenberry SUBJECT: GREEN FILTERS

Just a reminder that during production when viewing dailies we decided with Darrell Anderson that scenes on the surface of Talos IV could safely be printed with a slight green filter—enough to get the sky green as planned without causing the skin to go green at all. Darrell Anderson already has experimented with this, and we selected a filter which seemed to do the job.

In fact, we thought we might vary the filter slightly in some long scenes where we are more conscious of the sky, thereby creating a green impression which will stay over the other scenes.

Just a reminder so that we can plan accordingly.

Gene Roddenberry

By the time the pilot had been completed in every respect, the production cost had soared to $630,000.

YES, IT WAS AN ABNORMAL AMOUNT TO SPEND FOR A PILOT. BUT WE HAD TO REALIZE THAT WE WERE BUILDING THE INTERIOR OF A SPACESHIP, DOING COMPLEX OPTICALS OF SHIPS IN FLIGHT AND TRANSPORTER EFFECTS AND SO FORTH, ALL PROPS HAD TO BE BUILT FROM SCRATCH, ALL COSTUMES HAD TO BE DE-

SIGNED FROM SCRATCH. TO BE QUITE HON-
EST, I DON'T THINK THE "POWERS THAT BE"
AT THE STUDIO WERE AWARE OF HOW MUCH
WE WERE SPENDING UNTIL AFTER IT WAS
SPENT. BUT WE SPENT IT MAKING A GOOD
PRODUCT.

In February, 1965, almost ten months after NBC had first
expressed interest in STAR TREK, the completed pilot was delivered to the network for their evaluation. In due time the
results of that evaluation were made known.

NBC rejected the pilot.

Chapter 8

## The Second Time Around

They plant the seed in the womb. The seed is their creative ideas, the womb is the studio. They give birth to their child, which is STAR TREK, and now they raise the child with all the aggravation, joy, sorrow, and triumph that go with it. Then one day the parent has to go to the graduation exercises. They sit there, and then somebody sitting there beside them says, "You know, that's a hell of a good show." It's a temporary thing, but it's a lovely, lovely thing.

Morris Chapnick

There is no question but that NBC liked the first pilot. The premiere screening of the pilot took place in NBC's executive offices in New York City. Among those present were Mort Werner, Vice President in Charge of Television Programming, and Grant Tinker, Vice President in Charge of West Coast Operations. It was a long pilot . . . most hour pilots run perhaps fifty minutes, a little over airing length, but "The Menagerie" ran sixty-five minutes. Herb Solow, who was present during that first screening, recalls that when the lights went out and the show began, Mort Werner's first reaction was that he really *believed* these people were out there in deep space in a starship. This was crucial because one of Werner's doubts from the beginning was whether Roddenberry's concept of science fiction could ever project the high believability so necessary in attracting television's mass audiences.

When the first screening was over, the general reaction from the people in the room was, "This is the most fantastic thing we've ever seen." A quote commonly used in the television industry is, "It's too good for TV," which it was. It was beautiful. Nor did this reaction wear off with subsequent screenings. No matter how often the pilot was screened, the reaction was always highly favorable. In spite of this response to the pilot, NBC nevertheless rejected it.

The overall reason given for the rejection was that the pilot was just "too cerebral." NBC felt the show would go over the heads of most of the viewers, that it required too much thought on the part of the viewer in order to understand it.

Although NBC chose to fall back on a vague, generalized statement as the reason for rejecting the pilot, they did in fact have a number of specific objections. They felt the story line was too involved, too literate, and dwelt too much upon intangibles. The basic premise of the story dealt with members of the *Enterprise* being captured by thought control, which isn't the easiest thing to try to sell to sponsors. Basically, they felt there just wasn't enough action in the show.

LOOKING BACK, THEY PROBABLY FELT THAT I HAD BROKEN MY WORD. IN THE SERIES FORMAT I HAD PROMISED TO DELIVER A "WAGON TRAIN TO THE STARS" . . . ACTION-ADVENTURE, SCIENCE-FICTION STYLE. BUT INSTEAD, "THE MENAGERIE" WAS A BEAUTIFUL STORY, IN THE OPINION OF MANY THE BEST SCIENCE FICTION FILM EVER MADE UP TO THAT TIME. BUT IT WASN'T ACTION-ADVENTURE. IT WASN'T WHAT I HAD PROMISED IT WOULD BE.

CLEARLY, THE PROBLEM WITH THE FIRST PILOT WAS EASILY TRACED BACK TO ME. I GOT TOO CLOSE TO IT AND LOST PERSPECTIVE. I HAD KNOWN THE ONLY WAY TO SELL STAR TREK WAS WITH AN ACTION-ADVENTURE PLOT. BUT I FORGOT MY PLAN AND TRIED FOR SOMETHING PROUD.

Additionally, the network did not like some of the casting. Some of the character types were wrong, and some of the character relationships were wrong.

And most of all, the network did not like the alien, Mr. Spock.

NBC had expressed doubt about the use of pointed ears, prior to shooting the pilot. Now, after seeing Spock on film, Gene was admonished with statements like, "Remember, we have a big religious group in this country, and those pointed ears look too much like the devil."

THEY WERE NERVOUS ABOUT SPOCK AS A CHARACTER. THEY WERE AFRAID HIS SATANIC APPEARANCE WOULD REPULSE PEOPLE. THEY WERE SURE NO ONE WOULD EVER IDENTIFY WITH A PERSON FROM ANOTHER WORLD.

MY OWN IDEA ON THAT WAS, IN A VERY REAL SENSE, WE ARE ALL ALIENS ON A STRANGE PLANET. WE SPEND MOST OF OUR LIVES REACHING OUT AND TRYING TO COMMUNICATE. IF DURING OUR WHOLE LIFETIME WE COULD REACH OUT AND REALLY COMMUNICATE WITH JUST TWO PEOPLE, WE ARE INDEED VERY FORTUNATE; AND THIS IS EXACTLY WHAT SPOCK IS TRYING TO DO. LITERALLY TENS OF THOUSANDS OF LETTERS HAVE COME IN TO SPOCK, SAYING, "YES, I UNDERSTAND, I'VE HAD THE SAME PROBLEM ALL MY LIVE."

ALSO, THERE IS ANOTHER LITTLE SIDE OF SPOCK, JUST A HINT OR SUGGESTION, THAT PULLS TOWARD EVIL, À LA EVE, THE SNAKE, AND THE APPLE. I THEREFORE FELT HIS SLIGHTLY SATANIC APPEARANCE WOULD HAVE A GREAT FEMALE ATTRACTION.

(This insight was further reinforced by the compulsive fascination for Spock which women visitors displayed on the pilot set. They were drawn to him like a magnet. It was really weird to watch it happen.)

When the dust had finally settled and everyone had had a chance to have their say, the network officials were faced

with one significant conclusion: Gene Roddenberry and Desilu had proved that it could be done. A series like STAR
TREK could be made, and made well. The network officials
also reached the conclusion that much of what was wrong
with the pilot was directly traceable back to an earlier NBC
decision. They had simply chosen the wrong story among the
three that Gene had submitted prior to developing the
script.*

Thus NBC shattered all television precedent and asked for
a second pilot. This caused quite a stir within the industry,
because up until that time no network had ever asked for a
second pilot. This time, however, the network officials were
somewhat more specific in their requirements.

THEY REJECTED MOST OF THE CAST AND
ASKED THAT SPOCK BE DROPPED, TOO. IN
FACT, THEY PARTICULARLY ASKED THAT
SPOCK BE DROPPED. THIS IS ONE OF THOSE
CASES WHERE YOU GO HOME AT NIGHT,
POUND YOUR HEAD AGAINST THE WALL, AND
SAY, "HOW COME I AM THE ONLY ONE IN THE
WORLD THAT BELIEVES IT?" BUT I SAID I
WOULD NOT DO A SECOND PILOT WITHOUT
SPOCK BECAUSE I FELT WE HAD TO HAVE
HIM, FOR MANY REASONS. I FELT WE
COULDN'T DO A SPACE SHOW WITHOUT AT
LEAST ONE PERSON ON BOARD WHO CON-
STANTLY REMINDED YOU THAT YOU ARE
OUT IN SPACE AND IN A WORLD OF THE FU-
TURE. NBC FINALLY AGREED TO DO THE SEC-
OND PILOT WITH SPOCK IN IT, SAYING, "WELL,
KIND OF KEEP HIM IN THE BACKGROUND."

EVENTUALLY, WHEN NBC BOUGHT THE SE-
RIES, THEIR SALES DEPARTMENT PREPARED
BROCHURES AND ADS ON STAR TREK IN
WHICH THEY AIRBRUSHED OUT LEONARD'S

---

* Gene's personal feelings about "The Menagerie" were vindicated
when, about a year later, this rejected first pilot film was expanded
into a two-parter, it won science fiction's coveted Hugo Award.

POINTED EARS AND GAVE HIM ROUNDED EYEBROWS.

LATER, AFTER ABOUT EIGHT EPISODES HAD BEEN AIRED, HERB SOLOW AND I WERE CALLED OVER TO NBC'S BURBANK OFFICE, WHERE WE WERE QUESTIONED BY ONE OF THE NETWORK'S NEW PROGRAM EXECUTIVES. THIS FELLOW SAID, "LISTEN HERE, WE WANT TO KNOW WHY YOU'RE KEEPING SPOCK IN THE BACKGROUND. WHY AREN'T YOU HAVING MORE STORIES ABOUT HIM?"

HERB LAUGHED, AND I REPLIED I HAD BEEN PUSHING SPOCK AS MUCH AS I COULD, BUT THAT I HAD BEEN WARNED THERE WOULD BE GRAVE TROUBLE FROM NBC IF I PUSHED HIM TOO FAR. THE EXECUTIVE SAID, "COME ON NOW, YOU'RE OUT OF YOUR HEAD. WHO EVER SAID THAT? EVERYBODY KNOWS SPOCK IS TERRIBLY POPULAR." I ASKED HIM TO HAVE HIS SECRETARY BRING IN THE BROCHURE ON STAR TREK. HE LOOKED AT WHAT THEY HAD DONE WITH THE AIRBRUSHES, AND THEN HE LOOKED UP AND SAID, "I'M SICK AT MY STOMACH."

A word of caution (not an ultimatum) was expressed once more regarding the plans for an integrated crew aboard the *Enterprise*. There were still those who were afraid of the consequences, from a strictly dollar-and-cents point of view. By putting a Negro in the crew they might lose the Southern states, by putting a Mexican in the crew they might lose Texas, Arizona, and parts of California, and so forth. The overseas sales representatives were also greatly concerned about the matter. A Chinese crew member could lose sales for the show in Indonesia, etc., etc., etc. Gene began to realize that if he listened to all these people, the *Enterprise* would end up with an all-white, Protestant, Caucasian crew. This could then rebound with the same result in a great many foreign countries, because why should they believe that 200 years from now such a ship will be manned by an all-

American crew? So many different people became embroiled in so much controversy that they ended up leaving Gene alone to do it the way he wanted to!

Anxious that too cerebral a story be avoided this time, NBC asked that three complete scripts be submitted for their review. They would then choose one of the three as the script for the second pilot. Desilu and Roddenberry agreed.

The first order of business was to get the scripts under way. Roddenberry met with studio and network people, and two free-lance writers were selected: Sam Peeples and Stephen Kandel. The characters established in the first pilot, as well as their relationships to each other, were thoroughly discussed and analyzed. As a result, several fundamental changes were made in the crew concept.

NBC recommended eliminating the character of Number One from the series. Gene agreed. He had thought it might be an interesting situation to have a female with important command responsibilities. Also, it was hoped this would help draw the female audience to the show. Although portrayed by an excellent actress, it hadn't worked out that way. Audience tests of this character, after viewing the pilot, ranged from resentment to disbelief. Yet, audience questionnaires stated they liked the actress. There was a seeming inconsistency in the audience reaction.

The answer, once it became clear, contained a valuable principle. Although STAR TREK was a show about the 23rd century, it was being viewed by a 20th century audience—who resented the idea of a tough, strong-willed woman ("too domineering") as second-in-command.

I DECIDED TO WAIT FOR A 23RD CENTURY AUDIENCE BEFORE I WENT THAT FAR AGAIN. BUT AUDIENCE REACTION TO THE ACTRESS WAS SUCH THAT WE LATER MADE HER A SEMI-PERMANENT CHARACTER ON THE SHOW IN ANOTHER ROLE (NURSE CHRISTINE CHAPEL).

Although the part of Number One was eliminated, the ship still needed a second-in-command. And certain personality traits of Number One still held interesting possibilities. The logical (if you will pardon the expression) solution was to add the cold, computer-like personality of Number One to that of Mr. Spock. The alien was already something of a mystery man, and the addition of these personality traits to his character would serve to strengthen the identity of Spock and add to his air of mystique.

The change effected in Spock's character can easily be seen by comparing his actions in both pilots. In the first pilot he displays almost as much emotion as a normal human being. In the second pilot he is what is now his typical unemotional Vulcan self. Also, in the first pilot Mr. Spock ranked about fourth in importance among the characters. In the second pilot he was in the now-familiar position of second-in-command. (An interesting change occurred midway through the first season. Mr. Spock began the second pilot with the clearly defined rank of Lieutenant Commander and was subsequently "promoted" to full Commander.)

Once having established the primary character changes, work commenced on the story outlines that were later expanded into the three scripts requested by NBC.

Neither Desilu nor NBC wanted to pay for another $600,000 pilot. A budget of slightly under $300,000 was established, taking into consideration the fact that many of the sets required for the interior of the spaceship had already been built for the first pilot. It was assumed that additional set construction costs would be in the area of refinements to the existing ship's interior. In an effort to insure meeting the budget, and in order to avoid unexpected expenditures not previously budgeted for, Gene periodically circulated memos such as the following:

TO: All Department Heads   DATE: May 3, 1965
FROM: Gene Roddenberry    SUBJECT: STAR TREK
                          SHIP SET, PROPS,
                          ETC.

Again I would like to solicit heads and members of all departments involved in the STAR TREK pilot to submit

early recommendations for any improvements, econo-
mies, or other changes in our basic STAR TREK ship,
equipment, and so on. I appreciate the fact some are already at work changing the panel board lighting, simpli-
fying it and increasing the intensity. Some other things
obviously need changing, too. A couple which come to
mind are an improvement in the Laser gun, more entries
from the ship's bridge upper deck to the lower section,
plus carpeting or some other ways of reducing footstep
sounds in the ship areas. I am sure there are others,
some of which might not only be inexpensive but, in
fact, save us money in the end. Will be glad to set up
any screenings or conferences you think necessary. Let
me know if there is anything else I can do to help.

                                        Gene Roddenberry

The constant concern over production costs was justified
time and again in the months that followed.

Everyone knew that even a second STAR TREK pilot would
be difficult and expensive to produce. While they realized that
a certain number of things must be built for any show, they
did not realize the total number of new and unusual items
that would have to be newly designed and specially built for
STAR TREK. A normal contemporary show can rent much of
what is needed. STAR TREK needed things that were not even
invented yet. There was no place alien planet vegetation, costumes, starship decor, weapons, medical instruments, etc.,
could be rented. In order to avoid piling up enormous costs,
everyone had to develop new ways of doing things. They
found themselves having to be ingenious not only as writers
and story creators but as businessmen as well.

The problem was further compounded by the inability of
studio workmen to adapt to STAR TREK needs. For instance,
studios are equipped with special effects shops wherein the
workmen create all sorts of things in wood, plastic, etc. These
people are usually pretty talented in their area, but they are
not locked into the 23rd century. A man who can make a

fairly good replica of a Colt .45 can't necessarily design and make a phaser intended for use in the 23rd century.

The hand weapon is, in fact, a good case in point. Eight of them were required and with normal breakage should have carried STAR TREK through its first year of production. The weapons were built by the studio, cost nearly $7,000, and when delivered, were unusable. They had no imaginative surface detail—just plain, flat surfaces. They were good-looking toys, but they weren't believable as 23rd century weapons. An outside company had to be hired, at high additional cost, in order to make them believable. That one project alone almost wrecked the whole special equipment budget in one shot.

The specialized (and extremely expensive) opticals required for STAR TREK continued to threaten frightening cost consequences. Most television series do not use too many opticals. An average television episode might use one optical every other week. STAR TREK estimated fifteen or twenty opticals per show.

The old, comparatively slow, and costly way of making opticals, which grew up in the motion picture industry, was impossible for STAR TREK. Cost factors aside, the series simply could not afford to wait ten to fifteen weeks for each episode's opticals to be completed and delivered. Roddenberry and his staff out of sheer necessity found themselves becoming innovators in opticals, which is a vast and complex field. They found themselves going into optical houses and suggesting certain ways to create the effects they needed. Frequently they were met with an attitude of "Who the hell are you? A man spends twenty-five or thirty years in this business and just begins to learn it. And you're telling us what to do?"

THE FACT NEW AND CHEAPER METHODS WERE DEVELOPED TO IMPROVE UPON SOMETHING THAT HAD BEEN DONE A CERTAIN WAY FOR 20 OR 30 YEARS IS A DEFINITE TRIBUTE TO THE UNUSUAL GROUP OF PEOPLE WE HAVE AT STAR TREK. STAR TREK IS PROBABLY, PHYSICALLY, THE MOST DIFFICULT TELEVISION SERIES THAT'S EVER BEEN DONE.

WHILE I BOW LOW AND SMILE WHEN PEOPLE COMPLIMENT ME, THE UNSUNG HEROES OF THE SHOW ARE PEOPLE LIKE BOB JUSTMAN WITH HIS INTIMATE KNOWLEDGE OF SETS, COSTS, PRODUCTION FACILITIES, AND SO ON; MATT JEFFERIES WITH HIS UNCANNY TALENT FOR BRINGING IN IMPOSSIBLE SETS ON IMPOSSIBLE BUDGETS, EVERY TIME; AND EDDIE MILKIS,* WHO IS AN ABSOLUTE WHIZ IN THE POST-PRODUCTION AREA, PRACTICALLY WITH OPTICALS; BILL THEISS WHO IS A GENIUS AT COSTUME DESIGN; IN FACT, VIRTUALLY EVERY MEMBER OF THE PRODUCTION CREW. THESE ARE THE PEOPLE WHO HAVE MADE STAR TREK WHAT IT IS. THESE ARE THE PEOPLE WHO KEEP US IN BUSINESS. TELEVISION IS NOT ONLY A CREATIVE ART (WE DIGNIFY IT WITH THAT TERM) BUT IT'S ALSO A VERY, VERY TOUGH BUSINESS.

While the three scripts were being developed, other details were being attended to.

TO: Kellam De Forest     DATE: May 18, 1965
FROM: Gene Roddenberry     SUBJECT: NAME CLEARANCE—STAR TREK CHARACTERS

The following are the last names we are considering for the Captain in STAR TREK. I would appreciate your checking them out for any clearance problem or conflict.

> January
> Flagg
> Drake
> Christopher

---

* Eddie Milkis joined STAR TREK's staff, as post-production supervisor, In August, 1966, and was promoted to associate producer in early 1968.

Thorpe
Richard
Patrick
Raintree
Boone
Hudson
Timber
Hamilton
Hannibal
Neville
Kirk
North

Thank you.

Gene Roddenberry

Necessity (sometimes meaning desperation) very often was the reason why certain terms, ideas, or items of equipment were created. This was certainly the case with the term "sensors." The more complex the *Enterprise* became, the easier it was for the characters to get wrapped up in technical dialogue. The characters were in danger of having such a vast assortment of terminology (however clever and scientifically correct) that the audience would never be able to follow what they were saying.

It's easier to use the generic term "sensor." It senses things, tells you if life is out there, analyzes chemical components, and does practically anything. Scientifically, the term sensor is a colloquial expression applied to many different items having similar functions. Even today our language is full of these expressions. We tend to say "gun." We don't say "rifle," "repeating rifle," "semi-automatic rifle with eight-inch barrel," and so forth. We simply say "gun," a general term applied to many different items having similar functions.

WE WERE FORCED INTO USING TERMS LIKE "SENSOR" BY THE REALIZATION THAT UNLESS WE LIMITED TERMINOLOGY TO SIMPLE GE-

NERIC TERMS, NO ONE, INCLUDING OUR-
SELVES, WOULD UNDERSTAND OUR SCRIPTS.

The original series format called for a crew complement of
203 persons. Overall length of the *Enterprise* was originally
estimated at approximately 200 feet. Now, however, with the
*Enterprise* design firmly established, it became obvious these
two points were no longer valid. According to Matt Jefferies'
calculations, the full-size *Enterprise* would measure 947 feet
overall. With that much room to play with, the crew complement was boosted to 430.

By the first week in June the three scripts had been submitted to NBC. They were "Omega Glory" by Gene Roddenberry, "Mudd's Women" by Stephen Kandel, and "Where No
Man Has Gone Before" by Samuel A. Peeples. Roddenberry
was taking no chances on a "cerebral" script this time—all
three represented strong action-adventure plots. No matter
which one NBC chose, STAR TREK would be in good shape.

It was not long before network officials made their choice
known—"Where No Man Has Gone Before." The network
had been quite pleased with all three scripts, making their
final selection simply on the basis of which one contained the
most science-fiction "flavor." *

Roddenberry now had a production to get under way.
Shooting was scheduled to commence on July 5, 1965.


TO:   Herb Solow     DATE:   June 11, 1965
FROM:   Gene Roddenberry     SUBJECT: STAR TREK
                                            EPISODE 2

Proceeding full speed into casting and preparation.
And with enthusiasm. Our aim is to make an episode
which will sell STAR TREK.

Among our first steps will be the preparation of a *production revision* of the current script. By this we mean a
quick rewrite aimed to bring photographic effects, spe-

---

* Both "Omega Glory" and "Mudd's Women" later became STAR TREK
episodes.

cial effects, sets, and shooting time into something that approaches practicality from a production time and budget point of view. We've already had a meeting with Darrell Anderson and slashed deeply there; we'll be meeting with other departments immediately—and we certainly invite further comments from all affected departments at this early stage.

While there will be some dramatic revisions, too, we feel it necessary to get the production revisions into mimeo as soon as possible, hopefully next week.

Meanwhile, associate producer Bob Justman has detailed information on which first pilot sets, effects, etc., we will be keeping and which we are discarding. He is, of course, making himself available for discussions on this.

Gene Roddenberry

While everyone began preproduction planning in earnest, Roddenberry's insistence on believability continued unabated.

TO: Matt Jefferies    DATE: June 18, 1965
FROM: Gene Roddenberry    SUBJECT: STAR TREK
EPISODE 2
HOSPITAL BED

I'm sure you've already thought of this, but I think we should be medically accurate on which instruments we decide to show on the bed, and then very carefully *label* each of them so the audience can easily read it and know *exactly* what these gizmos are doing.

Gene Roddenberry

Leonard Nimoy was, of course, set in the role of Mr. Spock. Jeff Hunter as the Ship's Captain was making a motion

picture and was unavailable. A long and difficult search for a
new series lead was cut short when William Shatner accepted
the role, by now renamed Captain Kirk. James Doohan was
cast in the role of Engineering Officer Scott. George Takei
was well-known to both Gene Roddenberry and Herb Solow,
and was cast as Sulu. Interestingly enough, in the second pilot
Sulu was a physicist. Later, when the series actually went on
the air, his function was changed to Helmsman. Pilot guest
stars were Gary Lockwood as Lieutenant Commander Gary
Mitchell and Sally Kellerman as Dr. Elizabeth Dehner. Other
guest roles were Paul Carr as Lieutenant Lee Kelso, Paul Fix
as Dr. Piper, Andrea Dromm as Yeoman Smith, and Lloyd
Haynes as Communications Officer Alden.

The shooting date was moved back to July 21st.

There were problems with the script. Although the script
had gone through several rewrites, it still indicated a show
that would run over budget. Part of the agreement on this
second pilot was that it be done on budget and on time—to
prove to NBC it *could* be done. A number of changes were
considered; some were made; and some changes were later
reinstated.

TO:     Bob Justman              DATE:    June 18, 1965
FROM:   Gene Roddenberry         SUBJECT: STAR TREK
                                          EPISODE 2
                                          SETS

Reference scenes 5 through 7 in the Captain's cabin,
would like your opinion on something. You may remember we once discussed the possibility of the ship's briefing room being a part of the corridor, either widened
out or as part of a corridor that runs through the briefing room. However we do it, I'd like your opinion on the
shooting time and set savings we would effect if the
Kirk-Spock chess game is going on in that briefing room
area—i.e., we can assume it's being used at this moment
for a lounge recreation room, possibly some of our
extras standing and watching what is something of
a "battle of chess giants," perhaps giving even greater

meaning to the moment and the warmth we hope to build into Kirk and Spock from the start.

In other words, approximately the same dialogue and situation, then an Alarm Signal (see previous memo on Optical Effects) and the Captain and Spock hurry down the corridor as we have it in succeeding scenes.

Gene Roddenberry


There were problems and disappointments, but there were also lucky breaks. James Goldstone, for instance. Roddenberry considered him one of television's top directors and had worked with him on "The Lieutenant." Goldstone read the script, liked it, and was signed immediately.


TO:   James Goldstone        DATE:    June 29, 1965
FROM: Gene Roddenberry       SUBJECT: STAR TREK
                                      BRIEFING
                                      ROOM
                                      SEQUENCE

Subject scenes 99 through 103, the briefing room sequence which closes Act 2, in an effort to simplify production I rewrote the scene limiting it to three people after Kelso leaves—Captain, Spock, and Elizabeth Dehner. The assumption is, of course, that three people require less coverage and would make the scene go faster. However, upon reading it in this new version, I get a definite feeling that the scene loses something by not having a full group there—i.e., the department heads, ship's scientist, etc. Their discussion is something of immense importance to everyone. What happens if we put a number of these people back? How does this affect your covering the scene and how much more time will it take?

Gene Roddenberry

The network continuity people (censors) expressed a few doubts of their own about the script. A few of their comments were:

Page 2, Scene 5: The sexual connotation of the word "frigid" precludes its use with reference to Elizabeth. It is suggested that another word conveying her chilly exterior be found.

Page 3, Scene 5: In line with the above, please delete the underlined from Mr. Spock's speech, "The human mechanism is capable of generating a surprising amount of energic heat—depending on the skill of the operator."

Page 51, Scene 128: As indicated in prior comments, please exercise extreme caution when showing the three dead men. Keep in mind that portion of the NAB Code which states, "The use of visual or aural effects which would shock or alarm the viewer . . . are not permissible."

The script was still loaded with opticals, each of which represented a considerable amount of money. Further efforts were made to eliminate a few more of them, if at all possible.

TO:   Matt Jefferies          DATE:   July 7, 1965
FROM: Gene Roddenberry   SUBJECT: SHIPS RECORD-
                                             ER—SCENE 29

The ship's recorder which materializes in the *Enterprise* transporter chamber should have some sort of *antenna* on it.

Is it possible to devise a folded antenna arrangement which on the Captain's "Q-signal" order and the subsequent beeping signal, could be extended out via wires from above or some other arrangement? If this could be done at low cost (and in post-production) then it would be possible to eliminate the Beam Effect which Anderson Company will have to animate down from the ceiling. Let's ask Bob Justman to compare the cost of that

Beam Effect with what you estimate some simplified un-folding antenna would cost.

Alternate possibility for Justman to investigate with you—the use of a *darkened* transporter chamber at this point, then utilizing a highly directional light from above which bathes the recorder in pulsating colors which suggest something happening—i.e., single transmission. We can always throw in a faint beeping sound similar to what Spock hears in the next scene at his listening panel.

Gene Roddenberry

Opticals were not the only problem. For maximum excitement and believability, Gene considered every element of the production to be of paramount importance. This included the way in which the sound was handled. His concern was plainly evident in the following excerpt from a memo he wrote on the subject:

Can we get Joe Sorokin pulled free to devote some time to STAR TREK now? Have intended to bring the subject up to you several times, but there's always something else that interferes.

The most important point of all this being the dailies seem to indicate probably even more creative sound work on this episode than on the original pilot. When you start counting the buttons which are pushed and the various force field effects, instrument sounds, ad infinitum, it begins to look a little hairy. Is that your impression, too? I think we really need some early planning and working on this—perhaps even on a reel-by-reel basis as Foley gets them anywhere approaching first cut.

The second pilot was to be shot in familiar surroundings —Stages 15 and 16 at Desilu's Culver City facility.

A television show is an amazingly complex operation. There are so many different activities all going on at the same time that it seems impossible to keep track of them. Successful completion of a show is by no means an accident. It is based on a phenomenal amount of detailed advanced planning. Every step is broken down into minute detail . . . every word, every move, bush, light, tree, etc . . . and planned out in advance.

Once the script is completed, a detailed show budget is prepared. This is a thoroughly detailed estimate of all anticipated costs that will be incurred from the first official day of preproduction, all the way through until the show has been completed and delivered to its final destination (the network). All departments at the studio are asked for their estimates, and these are compiled into the overall budget. Once established, the budget becomes the bible for all activities and costs that follow. Most show budgets begin with an estimate of expenses that will be incurred during the preproduction phase. Pilot Number 2's estimate looked like this:

|  | SHOW BUDGET |
|---|---|
| PRODUCTION | |
| Producer, Writer, and Associates | $ 20,000 |
| Associate Producer | 2,030 |
| Director | 5,000 |
| Casting or Dialogue Director | 400 |
| Secretaries | 4,000 |
| Screen Directors Guild Pension | 250 |
| Miscellaneous | 1,650 |
| TOTAL | 33,330 |
| MUSIC | |
| American Federation of Musicians | 3,500 |
| TOTAL | 3,500 |
| STORY | |
| Writers Guild Pension | 127 |
| Mimeographing | 300 |
| TOTAL | 427 |
| CAST | |
| Regular | 13,750 |

| | | |
|---|---|---:|
| Supporting .......................... | $ | 4,500 |
| Extras & Standins ................... | | 3,954 |
| Casting Fee ........................ | | 1,146 |
| Guest Artists: | | |
| One @ $5,000 | | |
| One @ $2,500 ................... | | 7,500 |
| Screen Actors Guild Pension .......... | | 1,038 |
| TOTAL | | 31,888 |

**OTHER**

| | |
|---|---:|
| TV Alliance Fee .................... | 185 |
| Desilu Service Fee | |
| 15% of $73,330 .................. | 11,000 |
| TOTAL | 11,185 |

**PAYROLL TAXES**

| | |
|---|---:|
| Payroll Charges ..................... | 4,000 |
| GRAND TOTAL $ | 84,330 |

Putting all of the other estimated costs together, Pilot Number 2's total budget looked like this:

## PRODUCTION BUDGET

PRODUCTION:  STAR TREK — PILOT NUMBER 2
SHOW TITLE:  "Where No Man Has Gone Before"

| PRODUCTION/DIRECTION | SHOW BUDGET |
|---|---:|
| Production & Direction ............... | $ 33,330 |
| Music ............................. | 3,500 |
| Story ............................. | 427 |
| Cast .............................. | 31,888 |
| Other ............................. | 11,185 |
| Payroll Taxes ...................... | 4,000 |
| TOTAL | 84,330 |

**PRODUCTION COSTS**

| | |
|---|---:|
| Production Staff ..................... | 5,523 |
| Camera ............................ | 5,812 |
| Sound Recording .................... | 3,152 |

| | |
|---|---:|
| Art Department | $ 2,809 |
| Set Construction | 20,100 |
| Greens | 1,156 |
| Grips & Standby | 6,899 |
| Electrical | 11,973 |
| Wardrobe | 3,890 |
| Set Dressing | 5,078 |
| Props | 3,679 |
| Makeup | 3,092 |
| 35MM Film Neg. & Process | 9,714 |
| Special Effects | 5,372 |
| Transportation | 2,494 |
| Studio Facilities | 7,200 |
| Payroll Taxes | 12,192 |
| TOTAL PRODUCTION COSTS | 110,135 |

POST-PRODUCTION COSTS

| | |
|---|---:|
| Titles-Prints-Dupes, Etc. | 25,466 |
| Cutting & Editing | 8,905 |
| Stock & Matte Shots | 15,000 |
| Scoring & Recording | 6,554 |
| Payroll Taxes | 1,529 |
| TOTAL POST-PRODUCTION COSTS | 57,454 |

OTHER COSTS

| | |
|---|---:|
| Insurance | 745 |
| Production Overhead | 1,715 |
| Audience & Publicity | 490 |
| Indirect Expenses | 28,128 |
| TOTAL OTHER COSTS | 31,078 |

INSURANCE ADJUSTMENTS

| | |
|---|---:|
| TOTAL | 198,667 |

AMORTIZATIONS

| | |
|---|---:|
| Preparation | 11,819 |
| Layoff | 5,158 |
| TOTAL AMORTIZATIONS | 16,977 |
| TOTAL COSTS EXCLUDING OVERAGES | 215,644 |
| ADJUSTED TOTAL COSTS INCLUDING OVERAGES | $299,974 |

Estimating costs is one thing. Controlling them is something else again.

The production phase is probably the one most susceptible to unforeseen expenses, and therefore a number of tight control procedures are established in an effort to maintain the budget. Even so, the production phase on Pilot Number 2 ran $12,000 over.

Had it not been for something called the "shooting schedule," costs probably would have been much higher. The shooting schedule is a step-by-step blueprint of the production phase, beginning with the first day of shooting and ending with the last day of shooting. During the preproduction phase, the script is broken down, scene by scene. The scenes are then rearranged in an order that will allow shooting to progress as quickly, efficiently, and economically as possible. (I was quite surprised to learn this. I had always assumed that a show is filmed in the order in which you see it on the air.)

For example, suppose we have three scenes to shoot. The first one takes place on the bridge, the second in the transporter room, and the third back on the bridge again. For the scene on the bridge, we have to set up the camera in its proper position, arrange as many as twenty or thirty different lights in their proper places, make sure the bridge itself is properly prepared, have the property master bring out the necessary props that will be used in the scenes, and attend to a host of other details that are necessary in order to shoot the scene. All this preparation takes time and may involve as many as twenty-five or thirty different people. At an average cost of roughly $200 per minute, it's a very expensive operation.

We shoot the scene on the bridge and move over to the transporter room set. Not only do we have to move a lot of equipment from the first set over to the second set, but we also have to go through the entire preparation procedure again in order to shoot the scene in the transporter room.

After we are through shooting Scene 2, we move all the equipment and all the people back to the bridge, for Scene 3. Again we go through the detailed preparations necessary.

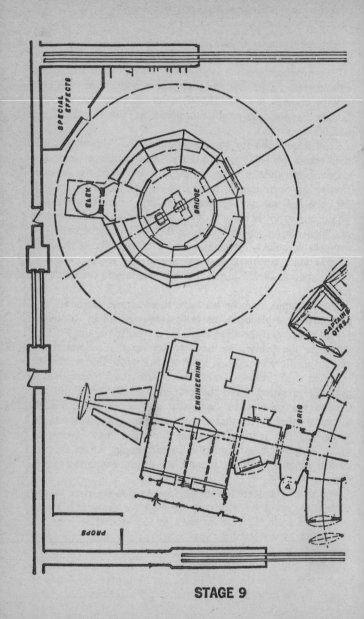

**STAGE 9**

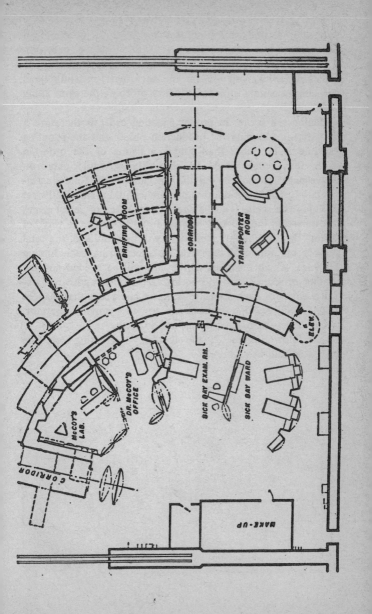

Only now we find we are doing the same kinds of things all over again that we did in Scene 1. In this instance, television is no different from any other business. If you have to do something twice, you are (at the very least) wasting time. You simply cannot afford the luxury of doing the same thing twice.

Placing the scenes in proper shooting order is therefore a vital step in planning the production phase. But the shooting schedule is far more than simply a listing of the order in which the scenes should be shot. The schedule may run twelve pages or more in length, and includes the following information: the scene number or numbers, the name of the set in which the scene is to be shot, the number of script pages encompassing the scene or scenes, an indication as to whether or not "day" or "night" conditions will be simulated, the total number of individual scenes to be shot during each filming sequence, which members of the cast will be needed and the number of scenes they will be involved in, the number of extras needed for each scene, a listing of any props that may be needed, and specific instructions for the camera operator, special-effects man, electricians, and so forth.

For Pilot Number 2, the first day's shooting schedule looked as follows:

"STAR TREK"

## SHOOTING SCHEDULE

"WHERE NO MAN HAS GONE BEFORE"

PRODUCTION #5149-2

PRODUCER: GENE RODDENBERRY

ASSOC. PRODUCER: ROBERT H. JUSTMAN

DIRECTOR: JAMES GOLDSTONE

PROD. MGR: JAMES PAISLEY

| SET, SCENE NUMBERS & DESCRIPTION | PGS. | D/N | SCS. | CAST & REQUIREMENTS |
|---|---|---|---|---|

FIRST DAY, MONDAY, 7/19/65
LOCATION: DESILU CULVER, STAGE 15

---

**(4) INT. BRIEFING ROOM (MATTE)** — 1 7/8 — D — 3

Sc. 5-6-A7-7A ~ Outerstellar space on
Monitor Screen as Kirk & Spock play
chess ~ Crewmembers watch ~ Kelso appears
on Screen & everybody cuts out.

NOTES: TIEDOWN FOR MATTE ON SCREEN.
OPTICAL REP. ON STAGE

1-Kirk
2-Spock

EXTRAS: 2 Male S.I.
1 Crewwoman (Play-
clothes)
1 Crewman (Playclothes)
2 Crewmen
1 Officer

CONST. & EFX
Stencil Cutout for Alert Signal
on Monitor Screen - Sc. 7A

PROPS
3 Dimensional Chess
Set, Kirk's watch

ELECTRIC: Flashing
Red Lite works on cue
behind Monitor Screen

---

**(27) INT. BRIEFING ROOM** — 5 7/8 — D — 4

Sc. 99-100-103-103A-FADE OUT — Kelso
displays damaged Terminator Connection —
Liz enters — Kirk & Spock question her —
Kirk dismisses all except Spock — argues
with him — orders course set for Delta-Vega.

1-Kirk
2-Spock
4-Elizabeth
5-Kelso
6-Piper
7-Scott
10-Sulu

ELECTRIC: Color Filters on
lamps lighting backing behind
translucent set walls (Also for
other sequence in this set)

PROPS
Damaged Terminator
Connection, Folders,
Reports, Metal clip-
boards

EXTRAS: 2 S.I.
(Covered)
1 Female S.I.
2 Male S.I.

---

**(7) INT. SHIP'S CORRIDOR** — 3/8 — D — 1

Sc. 8 - Mitchell crosses thru - crewmembers
react favorably, especially Yeoman Smith.

3-Mitchell
8-Yeoman Smith
7-Scott

CONST. & EFX
Wild signs as per discussion.
Varied Dressing in rooms.
Wild F.G. Pieces as per
discussion.

PROPS
Clever props for
crew, Kirk's watch

EXTRAS: As B4 PLUS:
1 Crewman
2 Crewwomen
3 Officers
1 Transporter Techn.

SPECIAL EQUIPMENT
Arriflex
18mm Lens for BNC

---

**(8) INT. ANOTHER SHIP'S CORRIDOR** — 2/8 — D — 1

Sc. 9 - Kelso's voice over as Kirk &
Spock hurry along the corridor.

1-Kirk
2-Spock
10-Sulu

EXTRAS: (Covered)

CONST. & EFX: As B4

PROPS: As B4

| (9) INT. CORRIDOR INTERSECTION | 2/8 | D | 1 | 1-Kirk |
|---|---|---|---|---|

Sc. 10 - Mitchell joins Kirk & Spock
in the elevator just as the doors close.

2-Spock
3-Mitchell

EXTRAS: (Covered)

| CONST. & EFX | PROPS |
|---|---|
| Wild Grating to shoot down thru. Elevator Doors work on cue. | As B4 |

SPECIAL EQUIPMENT
Arriflex & Pod
18mm Lens for BNC

- - - - - - - - - - - - - - - - - - - - - - - - - - - - - -

| (33) INT. TRANSPORTER ROOM | 1 1/8 | D | 4 | 1-Kirk |
|---|---|---|---|---|

Sc. 112-113-114-11: Kirk & Spock
supporting the groggy Mitchell, enter
followed by Elizabeth Mitchell starts
to revive a gal strength they restrain
him while Piper gives his another hypo -
group enters the Transporter Chamber & is
dematerialized for the trip down to surface.

NOTES: TIEDOWN FOR DEMATERIALIZATION EFFECTS.
OPTICAL REP. ON STAGE.

2-Spock
3-Mitchell (EYES)
4-Elizabeth
6-Piper
7-Scott

EXTRAS: S.I. (Covered)
1 Transporter Tech-
nician (Covered)

ELECTRIC: Top &
Bottom Transporter
Chamber Lights to be
on Dimmers & work
on cue.

| CONST. & EFX. | PROPS |
|---|---|
| Rig & run Electronic Gear | Hypo Gun, Doctor's kit, Communicators, Phaser pistols? |

- - - - - - - - - - - - - - - - - - - - - - - - - - - - - -

| (15) INT. TRANSPORTER ROOM | 1 5/8 | D | 5 | 1-Kirk |
|---|---|---|---|---|

Sc. A8-B8-C8-D8-E8: Damaged Ship's
Recorder Device materializes in
Transporter Chamber Kirk orders "Q"
signal pulsating spotlight effect hits
the Recorder & its antennae move out &
click into position Kirk exits.

NOTES: TIEDOWN FOR MATERIALIZATION EFFECTS.
OPTICAL REP. ON STAGE..

2-Spock
7-Scott

EXTRAS: S.I. (Covered)
1 Transporter Tech-
nician (Covered)

ELECTRIC: Top &
Bottom Transporter
Chamber Lights to be
on Dimmers & work on
cue.
Snooted Lamp on
Dimmer to hit Record-
er Device on cue &
pulsate.

| CONST. & EFX | PROPS |
|---|---|
| Rig & run Electronic Gear. Rig Recorder Antennae to extend out into position. | Ship's Recorder Device, Kirk's watch |

- - - - - - - - - - - - - - - - - - - - - - - - - - - - - -

| (4A) RECORD KELSO'S V.O. DIALOGUE | 5-Kelso |
|---|---|

Sc. 6 - 8 - 9 - Record V.O. Dialogue for
dubbing into these scenes.

END OF FIRST DAY - TOTAL PAGES: 11 3/8

Desilu Productions, Inc.

CALL SHEET

NO. 5140-2

SERIES "STAR TREK"
PRODUCER G. Roddenberry
DIRECTOR J. Goldstone
ASST. DIR. R. Justman/G. Peters
LOCATION DESILU-CULVER

| SET | SCENES | | D or N | PAGES | CAST NO. | NIGHT |
|---|---|---|---|---|---|---|
| INT. BRIEFING ROOM (MATTE) | 5-6-X7-7A | | | 1-2-3 | | 15 |
| INT. BRIEFING ROOM | 99-100-101-103-103A | | D | 4 6/8 | 1-2-4-5-6-7-10 | 15 |
| RECORD KELSO'S V.O. DIALOGUE | 6-8-9 | | | | 5 | 15 |
| INT. SHIP'S CORRIDORS | 8-9 | | D | 5/8 | 1-2-3-7-8-10-X | 15 |
| INT. CORRIDOR INTERSECTION | 10 | | D | 2/8 | 1-2-3-X | 15 |
| INT. TRANSPORTER ROOM | 112 thru 115 | | D | 1 1/8 | 1-2-3-4-6-7-X | 15 |
| INT. TRANSPORTER ROOM | A8-B8-C8-D8-E8 | | D | 1 4/8 | 1-2-7-X | 15 |

| CAST AND DAY PLAYERS | PART OF | MAKEUP | SET CALL | REMARKS |
|---|---|---|---|---|
| 1. William Shatner | Capt. Kirk | 7:00am | 8:00am | Breakfast Furnished |
| 2. Leonard Nimoy | Mr. Spock | 6:30am | 8:00am | Breakfast Furnished |
| 3. Gary Lockwood | Mitchell | 11:00am | 11:30am | |
| 4. Sally Kellerman | Elizabeth | 7:30am | 9:00am | |
| 5. Paul Carr (New) | Kelso | 8:30am | 9:00am | |
| 6. Paul Fix (New) | Dr. Piper | 8:30am | 9:00am | |
| 6. James Doohan (New) | Scott | 8:15am | 9:00am | |
| 7. ~~XXXXXXXXXXXXXX~~ (New) | | | | |
| 8. Andrea Dromm (New) | Yeoman Smith | 10:00am | 11:30am | |
| 10. George Takei (New) | Sulu | 8:30am | 9:00am | (No Makeup - Wdbe. Only) |

| ATMOSPHERE AND STANDING | SPECIAL INSTRUCTIONS |
|---|---|
| 4 Male S.i. @ 7am; 1 female S.i. @ 9am | NOTE: DOORS BETWEEN STAGES 15 & 16 TO BE |
| 3 Men as Crewmen @ 7:15am; 1 Woman as Crew @ 7:15am | CLOSED & FASTENED BEFORE 7am. |
| 2 Men as Crewmen @ 11am; 3 Men as Officers @ 11am | ALL DEPTS. PLEASE CHECK SHOOTING SCHEDULE |
| 2 Women as Crew @ 11am | CAREFULLY FOR ALL DAILY REQUIREMENTS. |
| 1 Man as Transporter Technician @ 11am | |
| NOTES: ALL MALE EXTRAS TO BE YOUNG, CLEANCUT & | |
| APPROX. 5'10" - TECH. MAKEUP | |

**ADVANCE SCHEDULE: TUESDAY, 7/20/65 — DESTINI CULVER, STAGE 15**

## CAMERA / CONSTRUCTION / MAKEUP

| No. | ITEM | TIME |
|---|---|---|
| | **CAMERA** | |
| 1 | Cameraman | 7am |
| 1 | Operator | 7:30am |
| 1 | Assistant | 7am |
| 1 | Assistant | 7am |
| 1 | Extra Camera Arriflex | |
| | Extra Operator | |
| | Extra Assistant | |
| | **CONSTRUCTION** | |
| 1 | Stillman | 9am |
| 1 | Key Grip | 7am |
| 1 | 2nd Grip | 7am |
| X/1 | Extra Grips | 7am |
| 1 | Crab Dolly Grip | 7am |
| X 1 | Craft Service Men 7 | |
| | Greensman | |
| 1 | Painter | 7am |
| | Prop Makers | |
| | Plumber | |
| 3 | Spec. Effects Men | 7am |
| X | Ward. Check Rm. | |
| X | Benches for 20 people | |
| | Submariners | |
| | Knockdown Sch. Rms. | |
| 2 | Knockdown Dr. Rms. Stg. 15 | |
| 8 | Portable Dr. Rms. Stg. 16 | |
| | **MAKEUP** | |
| 1 | Makeup Men | 6:30am |
| 1 | Extra Makeup Men | 6:48am |
| 1 | Hair Stylist | 7:24pm |
| 1 | Extra Hair Stylists | |
| | Body Makeup Women | |

## SOUND / ELECTRICAL / MUSIC / PROCESS

| No. | ITEM | TIME |
|---|---|---|
| | **SOUND** | |
| 1 | Sound Mixer | 7:30am |
| 1 | Sound Recorder | 7:24am |
| 1 | Mike Men | 7am |
| 1 | Extra Cable Men | 7am |
| | Playback Mach. & Op. | |
| | Acetate Rec'der & Op. | |
| | P.A. System | |
| | **ELECTRICAL** | |
| 1 | Gaffer | 7am |
| 1 | Best Boy | 7am |
| 7 | Lamp Operator | 7am |
| X | Hook-up Dr. Rms. | 6:30am |
| | Operate Generator | |
| X | Operate Wind Mach. | |
| | Heat Stage | |
| X | Portable Telephone Stg. 15 | |
| X | Siren/Wig Wag 14-15-16 | |
| | Work Lights | |
| | Gas Generator | |
| | **MUSIC** | |
| | Process Elec. | |
| | Music Representative | |
| | PIANO | |
| | Practical-Dummy-Tone | |
| | Music Tracks & Cutter | |
| | Sideline Orchestra | |
| | Singers | |
| | **PROCESS** | |
| | Process Camera | |
| | Process Camera | |
| 1 | Prop. Mach. & Op. | |
| 1 | Stereo Mach. & Op. | |
| | Plates | |

## PROPERTY / OPERATIONS-TRANSPORTATION

| No. | ITEM | TIME |
|---|---|---|
| | **PROPERTY** | |
| 1 | Property Men | 7am |
| 1 | Asst. Prop. Men | 7am |
| 1 | Set Dresser | 7am |
| | Drapery Men | |
| X | Wardrobe Rack's In KD's | |
| X | Makeup Tables Stg. 15 | |
| X | Hair Dr. Tables Stg. 15 | |
| | Animals & Handlers | |
| | **OPERATIONS/TRANSPORTATION** | |
| | Camera Truck | |
| | Insert Car | |
| 1 | Standby Driver | 7am |
| | Busses | |
| | Picture Cars | |
| | Trucks | |
| | Schoolroom Trailers | |
| | Dressing Rm. Trailers | |
| | A.H.A. Man | |
| | Wranglers | |
| | Wagons, etc. | |

## WARDROBE / POLICE / CATERER / MISCELLANEOUS / PHOTO EFF / FIRE

| No. | ITEM | TIME |
|---|---|---|
| | **WARDROBE** | |
| 2 | Costumer (Men) | 6:30am |
| 2 | Costumer (Women) | 6:42am |
| | Extra Cost. (Men) | |
| | Extra Cost. (Women) | |
| | Checkers | |
| | Doorman | |
| | **POLICE** | |
| | Watchmen | |
| | City Police | |
| | Studio Police | |
| | Motorcycle Police | |
| | Police Permits | |
| | **CATERER** | |
| | Hot Lunches | |
| | Box Lunches | |
| | Dinners | |
| | Gals. Coffee | |
| | Gals. Chocolate | |
| | Doz. Doughnuts | |
| | **MISCELLANEOUS** | |
| | Extra Asst. Dir. | |
| 1 | 2nd Asst. Dir. | 6:30am |
| 1 | Script Supervisor | 7:30am |
| X | First AMON LOT | 6:30am |
| | Dialogue Coach | |
| | Movible Machine | |
| | Projectionist | |
| X | Film COLOR | |
| | **PHOTO EFF** | |
| 1 | Dept. Representative | 7:15am |
| 1 | Camera (ANDERSON) | |
| | Tiedemann | |
| | **FIRE** | |
| | Firemen | |
| | Fire Warden | |

INT. ELEVATOR & BRIDGE — D — Sq. 11; INT. BRIDGE — D — Sq. 12-15, A16, A17, A18; 32,35,36,41.
42,43,44,45,46,47,48,52,53,A54,A55,56,59,60,61,63,64.

# DESILU PRODUCTIONS, INC.

## PRODUCTION REPORT

Prod. No: 5149-2 Series Title "STAR TREK"
Date: MON. 7-19-65 "WHERE NO MAN HAS GONE BEFORE"

Producer: GENE RODDENBERRY Prod. Mgr: JAMES PAISLEY
Director: JAMES GOLDSTONE Cameraman: ERNEST HALLER
Asst. Dir: ROBERT H. JUSTMAN Asst: CAMERON MC CULLOCH

Set Description & Location: START SHOOTING - DESILU CULVER STAGE 15
INT. BRIEFING ROOM DESILU CULVER STAGE 15
INT. SHIP'S CORRIDORS INT. TRANSPORTER ROOM
INT. SHIP CORRIDOR INTERSECTION

| Company Time | | No. Days on Pict. | | Shooting Schedule | |
|---|---|---|---|---|---|
| Crew Call | 7:00A | Worked | 1 | Start DARKMK REH. 7/15/65 | |
| Shooting Call | 8:00A | RKMX REH. | 2 | Finish Location REH. 7/16/65 | |
| Started | 8:00A | Holidays | | | |
| Finished | 6:55PM | Travel | | Start Studio 7/19/65 | |
| | | Total | 3 | Finish Studio 7/27/65 | |

| | Setups | Scenes | Time | Pages | SCENE NUMBERS SHOT |
|---|---|---|---|---|---|
| | | | | | 5,6,A7,7A,6,9,10,99 |
| Shot Prev. | | | | | 100,102,10A,112,113,214 |
| Shot Today | 27 | 18 | 7:20" | 9 7/8 | 115,A8,C8,E8 |
| Shot To Date | | | | | |

| NEGATIVE | B.&F.Mil./I.P Film | EXPOSED TODAY | E & W Color I.P Film | CRAFT SERVICE TO CABLE |
|---|---|---|---|---|
| Bal. O.H | 18,960 | Gbod Footage | 3,120 | RATE- CABLEMAN TO MIKE |
| Rec. Today | | N.G. Footage | 1,010 | RATE 1 - SEAMSTRESS FOR |
| Exp. Today | 4,440 | Waste Footage | 310 | WARDROBE ARRIFLEX |
| O.H. Tonite | 14,520 | Total Today | 4,440 | BREAKFAST FOR 3 COSTUMES |
| | | Total To Date | 4,440 | & 2 MAKEUP MEN |
| | | | | COLOR CONSULTANT ON SET. |
| Meals | Out | in | no. Served | 3 SPECIAL EFFECTS MEN |
| | 1:30H | | | Extra ARRIFLEX |
| 2ND ASST. CAMERA 1P | 1P | | | *GIVEN 6 AM CALL BY ROY LONG |
| CAST & CREW | 2P | | | 2ND ASST. CAMERAMAN TO 1ST ASST. |
| | | | | ARRIFLEX |

## CAST AND DAY PLAYERS

| | M/U Wdb Call | Set Call | Lv. Stu. | Arr. Loc. | Fin. Loc. | Lv. Loc. | Arr. Stu. | Fin. Stu. | Start Date | Fin. Date | Meals Lun. Din. |
|---|---|---|---|---|---|---|---|---|---|---|---|
| WILLIAM SHATNER | 7A | 8A | | BRKF. | SERVED | | | 6:50P | 7-15 | | 1P-2P |
| LEONARD NIMOY | 6:30A | 8A | | BRKF. | SERVED | | | 6:35P | 7-15 | | 1P-2P |
| GARY LOCKWOOD | 11:00A | 11:30A | | | | | | 6P | 7-15 | | 12:45-1:45 |
| SALLY KELLERMAN | 7:30A | 9A | | | | | | 6P | 7-15 | | 1P-2P |
| PAUL CARR (NEW) | 7:30A | 9A | | | | | | 5P | 7-19 | | 12:45-1:45 |
| PAUL FIX (NEW) | 8:30A | 9A | | | | | | 6P | 7-19 | | 12:45-1:45 |
| JAMES DOOHAN (NEW) | 8:15A | 9A | | | | | | 6:55P | 7-19 | | 12:45-1:45 |
| ANDREA DROMM (NEW) | 10A | 11:30A | | | | | | 5P | 7-19 | | 12:45-1:45 |
| GEORGE TAKEI (NEW) | 8:30A | 9A | | | | | 5:35P | | 7-19 | | 12:45-1:45 |

## EXTRAS - STANDINS

| No. | Rate | Call | Dismissed Location | Dismissed Studio | Meals | O.T. | T.T. | Adjustments |
|---|---|---|---|---|---|---|---|---|
| 1 | 23.59 | 7:00A | | 6:05P | 12:30-1:30 1/2 | | | UP TO EXTRA 25.47 |
| 1 | 23.59 | 7:00A | | 6:50P | 12:30-1:30 1/2 | | | UP TO " 25.47 |
| 1 | 23.59 | 7:00A | | 5:55P | 12:30-1:30 1/2 | | | UP TO 25.47 PLUS26.25 |
| 1 | 25.47 | 7:15A | | 4:50P | 12:30-1:30 1/2 | | | |
| 1 | 25.47 | 7:15A | | 4:50P | 12:30-1:30 1/2 | | | PLUS 17.50 |
| 1 | 25.47 | 9:00A | | 6:05P | 1P-2P 1/2 | | | |
| 4 | 25.47 | 1A | | 4:50P | 12:45P-:45 | | | |
| 1 | 25.47 | 1A | | 4:50P | 12:45P-:45 | | | PLUS 17.50 |
| 1 | 25.47 | 1A | | 6:50P | 12:45P-:45 | | | SILENT BIT 70.63 |
| 1 | 25.47 | 1A | | 6:50P | -- | | | |

1 1:45P

NOTE: 2- 25.47

FLOYD HOLLY ) DISMISSED FROM SET
JOHN HERMAN ) AS THEY WERE TOO TALL TO FIT INTO COSTUMES
INDEPENDANT CASTING TO TAKE CARE OF CHECKS.

And now, to compare with the shooting schedule, here is the first group of scenes as they appeared in the script:

5   INT. BRIEFING ROOM—CLOSE ON MONITOR SCREEN (INSIDE MONITOR FRAME—MATTE OF SCENE A4 STAR B.G.)

ESTABLISH, then at end of narration OPTICAL ZOOM BACK to reveal we have been looking at the monitor screen. Briefing Room is now dressed and being used as a lounge. Ship's Captain JAMES KIRK sits across a table from Science Officer MISTER SPOCK, a three-dimensional chess game between them. Several n.d. crewmen (including one female) are watching the game interestedly. At the moment Kirk is turned toward the monitor screen watching the thinning stellar groups MOVE TOWARD US AND PAST CAMERA. Mister Spock has looked up toward Kirk, showing a bit of impatience.

MISTER SPOCK
Your move, Captain.

Kirk turns from the screen TOWARD CAMERA and Spock, examines the chessboard.

6   ANOTHER ANGLE—MONITOR SCREEN O.S.
Captain Kirk looks at his watch.

KIRK
The bridge said they'd call. We should be intercepting this object . . .

MISTER SPOCK
(nods, finishing sentence)
. . . any minute now. I'll have you checkmated your next move.

> KIRK
> (*looks up at
> Spock*)
>
> Have I ever mentioned you play very
> irritating chess, Mister Spock?

> MISTER SPOCK
>
> Irritating? Oh, yes ... one of your
> Earth emotions.

But Kirk has seen an opportunity, pounces on a chess
piece and moves it. Reaction from the onlookers at this
play. And reaction from Mister Spock, who inspects the
chessboard and realizes he is in trouble. Kirk watches
him a moment, then dryly:

> KIRK
>
> Certain you don't know what
> irritation is?

> MISTER SPOCK
> (*frowning at board*)
>
> The fact one of my ancestors
> married a human female ...

> KIRK
> (*interrupting*)
>
> Terrible ... having bad blood
> like that.
> (*smiles*)
>
> But you may learn to enjoy
> it someday.

> KELSO'S VOICE
> (*filtered*)
>
> Bridge to Briefing Lounge.
> Object is now within tractor
> beam range.

A7  PAST KIRK AND MISTER SPOCK—ONTO MONITOR  A7
    SCREEN (SCENE 5 SET-UP)

as Kirk and Spock turn toward the monitor screen,
where we see MATTE REPEAT of the thin star
background drifting in and past us.

                    KIRK
                (*toward screen*)
            No visual contact, Mister Kelso?

On monitor, the MATTE OF STAR B.G. IS RE-
PLACED BY MEDIUM SHOT OF KELSO ON
BRIDGE as his image turns toward us and Kirk,
puzzled.

                    KELSO
                (*filtered*)
            No sir. Can't be a vessel.
            Reads only about one meter
            in diameter.


                    MISTER SPOCK
            Not large enough even for a
            lifeboat.


                    KELSO
                (*filtered*)
            Small enough to bring it
            aboard ... if you want to
            risk it.


                    KIRK
                (*hesitates, then
                    nods*)
            Lock onto it, Mister Kelso.
7A  ANOTHER ANGLE (MONITOR SCREEN O.S.)                7A
    as Kirk and Spock stand and exit.

The day before shooting begins, something known as a call sheet is prepared and distributed. The call sheet is a daily reminder to all concerned as to what will be required for the next day's shooting. It alerts each member of the cast as to what time they are expected at the studio the next day, reaffirms the number of extras needed, and establishes the time of day at which they are to report on the set, indicates to all departments concerned the number of men and the type of equipment that will be needed the next day, as well as any other specific instructions that may be necessary.

What follows is the call sheet that was prepared for Pilot Number 2's first day of shooting, and the subsequent production report.

Use of the shooting schedule and the call sheet is an effective way to help insure efficient, economical production. Unfortunately, these two documents are nothing more than guides to what is *supposed* to happen. To find out what *actually* happened, a production report is prepared.

The production report is prepared at the end of each day's shooting and is a recap of the progress to date. Analysis of the production report will, among other things, reveal whether or not the show is running into trouble in any area. For example, the shooting schedule for the second pilot called for 11⅜ pages to be shot the first day. The production report, prepared at the end of that first day's shooting, revealed that only 9⅞ pages had been shot. Thus production fell behind on the very first day of shooting.

Shooting finished eight days after it began, a full day behind schedule. Reason for the delay was attributed to a number of minor problems and one "act of God." This latter was an incident referred to as the "battle of the wasps" and resulted in a significant delay in shooting.

Wasps have a habit of building nests high overhead in the maze of scaffolding attached to the ceiling of the sound stage. The problem has plagued most studios off and on for years. In the summertime the wasps become fairly active, and when shooting takes place on the stage, the wasps are attracted to the glare of the lights on the sets below.

On the fifth day shooting was progressing nicely when suddenly wasps began to appear everywhere. What followed was a minor panic situation. There were a number of quick casualties as the invading wasps piled up a string of "hits." The victims included two members of the cast—Sally Kellerman, who took a direct hit in the middle of her back, and Bill Shatner, who suffered the indignity of a sting on the eyelid. The remaining crew members who had not immediately fled before the onslaught of the attack were cleared from the stage, exterminators were called, and the whole place fumigated. That took care of the wasps, but several hours of valuable production time were lost in the process.

The only fortunate aspect of the incident was that it had occurred on a Friday. Shatner's eyelid grew to immense proportions and was not at all suitable for filming. Until the swelling could be reduced, he would be out of the production. By the time the following Monday rolled around, Shatner's eyelid had shrunk back to reasonable proportions, and shooting continued without further delay.

If the production phase of the second pilot had its share of problems, the post-production phase that followed was something else again. Almost seven full months were required to complete the pilot and ship it off to NBC in New York.

First, enormous problems were encountered in creating the opticals needed for the pilot. The fact that these problems were eventually overcome is a credit to the ingenuity (and grim determination) of Gene Roddenberry, Bob Justman, and the optical house with whom they were working.

Second, completion of the pilot was severely hampered by the fact that Gene could not devote his full attention to it. During the month of August he was called upon to produce a pilot for his proposed series, "Police Story." In September he was asked to produce still another pilot, "The Long Hunt Of April Savage." It was not until October that Gene could once again devote his full attention to completing STAR TREK'S second pilot. (With the fate of his new series hanging in the balance, I can imagine how terribly frustrated he must have felt at not being permitted to devote his full time to STAR TREK.)

Roddenberry is in many ways a perfectionist. Even the tiniest detail does not escape his attention. This was perhaps another reason it took so long to complete the pilot. Not only was he driven by his perfectionist nature, he was also acutely aware that this second pilot represented now or never. If NBC did not like it, STAR TREK would be dead forever. As a result, Gene felt his personal attention was required at every step of the way. The score (music) was chosen and prepared almost note by note; the proper sound effects were selected and added to the film, foot by foot; the opticals were made, changed, and changed again. Step by step, Roddenberry supervised the creation of the individual elements that would ultimately result in a completed film.

It is during this process that a man's creative genius becomes apparent. A certain sound effect, added at just the right place on a piece of film, can make all the difference in the world in heightening the dramatic effect of that particular scene; in a moment that is obviously filled with tension, the use of quick cuts to show close-ups of the players' faces heightens still further the feeling of tension. All of these things are part and parcel of the creative process, and Gene Roddenberry has many times since proved his skill at using them.

October became November, and November rolled into December. By this time, the studio heads had become exceedingly restless and had begun to pressure him more and more to finish the pilot and ship it to New York. But he was still not satisfied, tried to ignore the pressures, and continued to perfect the elements of his creation.

In January, 1966, the film was judged ready. The second pilot had taken almost ten months to produce and had cost $330,000. The STAR TREK pilot episode "Where No Man Has Gone Before" was shipped to New York the end of January, and everyone held their breath.

The waiting period that follows the submission of a pilot is emotionally rough on everyone at the studio. Literally blood, sweat, and tears go into the making of just about any pilot, and people get deeply and emotionally involved in it. To sit around for weeks or months, waiting for a decision to be rendered by a group of strangers 3,000 miles away, becomes almost unbearable.

The waiting period is made worse still by the knowledge that a show is not always judged on its own merit alone. A hundred different intangibles can affect the final decision rendered by the judges. Often it will depend upon how the decision makers happen to feel on the morning they view the show. They may be suffering from a hangover, or they may simply be in a bad mood. The sound system in the projection room could be a little off that particular day. The film could split at a crucial moment, thus breaking the focus of attention. Available time slots, other pilots being considered, competition from rival networks . . . all these factors contribute to the sale of a show. It's a strange system, but it's the only system that television has at the moment.

The period of waiting stretched from days into weeks, and then, in the middle of February, the waiting came to an end. The decision had been made. A new series, known as STAR TREK, would make its debut on television the following September.

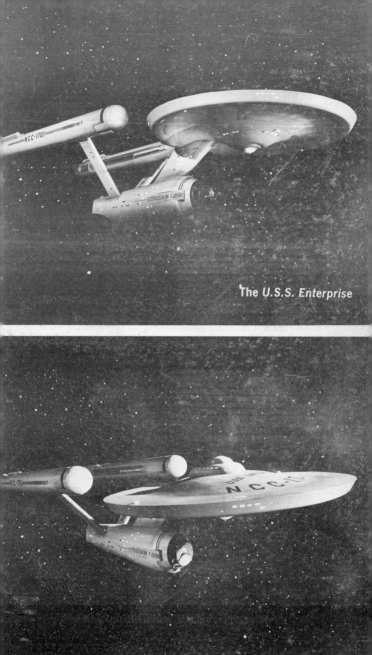

The *U.S.S. Enterprise*

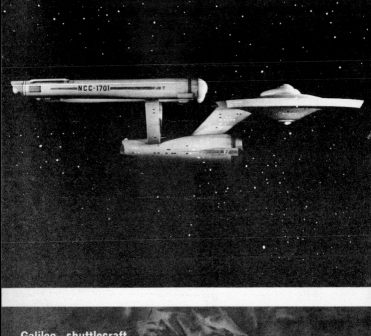

Galileo—shuttlecraft

**Gene Roddenberry—Producer**

**William Shatner—Captain James T. Kirk**

**Leonard Nimoy—Mr. Spock (First Officer)**

**DeForest Kelley—Dr. Leonard McCoy**

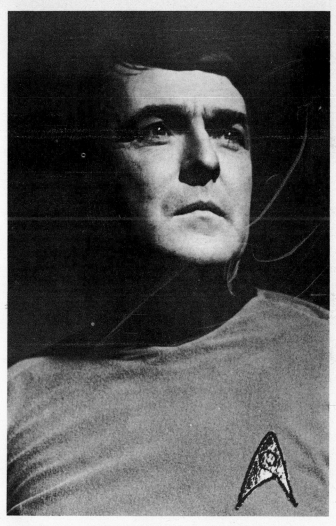

**James Doohan—Montgomery Scott (Chief Engineer)**

**George Takei—Sulu (Helmsman)**

**Nichelle Nichols—Lt. Uhura (Communications)**

**Majel Barrett—Nurse Christine Chapel**

**Walter Koenig—Ensign Chekov**

**Spock's station on the Bridge**

**Captain's station looking toward Main View Screen**

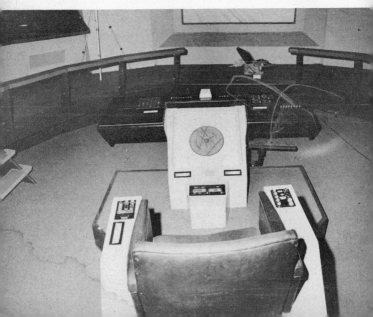

**Corridor of _Enterprise_**

**Sickbay**

**Diagnostic Bed**

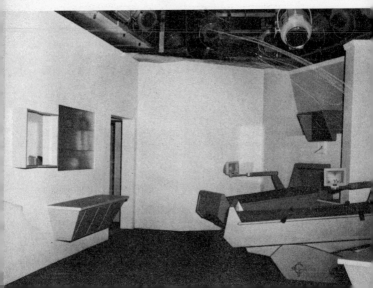

**Briefing Room**

**Recreation Room**

**Three dimensional chess**

The "Jeffries Tube"—much of ship's critical engine
circuitry is in this area

**Main Engineering Control Panel in Engineering Section**

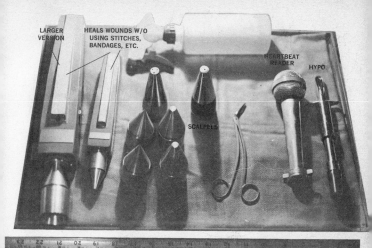

LARGER VERSION

HEALS WOUNDS W/O USING STITCHES, BANDAGES, ETC.

HEARTBEAT READER

HYPO

SCALPELS

MEDICAL POUCH

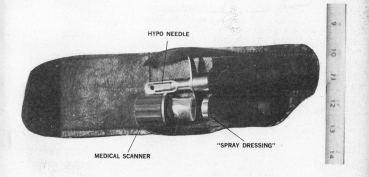

HYPO NEEDLE

MEDICAL SCANNER

"SPRAY DRESSING"

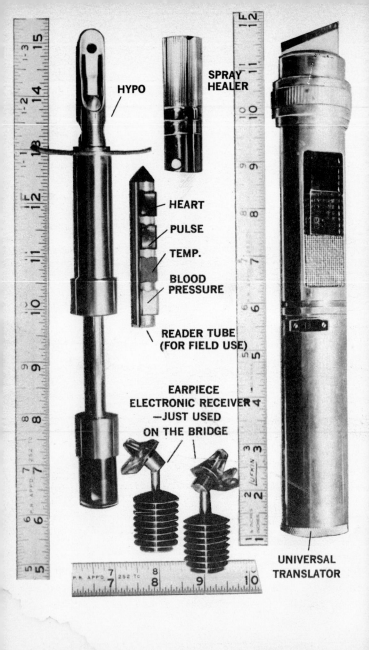

HYPO

SPRAY HEALER

HEART

PULSE

TEMP.

BLOOD PRESSURE

READER TUBE
(FOR FIELD USE)

EARPIECE
ELECTRONIC RECEIVER
—JUST USED
ON THE BRIDGE

UNIVERSAL
TRANSLATOR

GENIUS AT WORK

PHASER
UNIT

HAND PHASER

INSIDE
DETAIL OF
PHASER

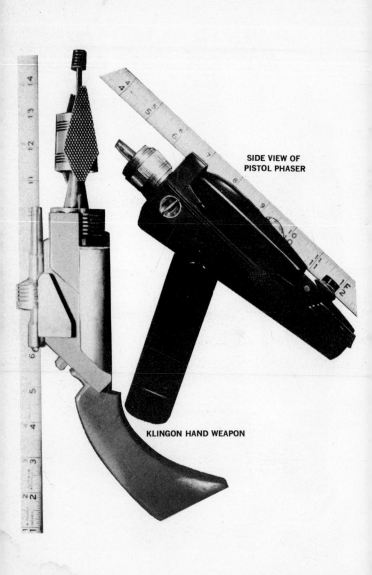

SIDE VIEW OF
PISTOL PHASER

KLINGON HAND WEAPON

(SPOCK BUILT)
RAY GENERATOR AND
ENERGY NEUTRALIZER

OFFENSIVE/DEFENSIVE
RAY GUN EMITS
A LIGHT BEAM

**TRICORDER**

**COMMUNICATOR**

"Opticals" sequence—getting zapped by a phaser
Courtesy Westheimer Co.

**Bolt of lightning**

**Lightning hitting man**

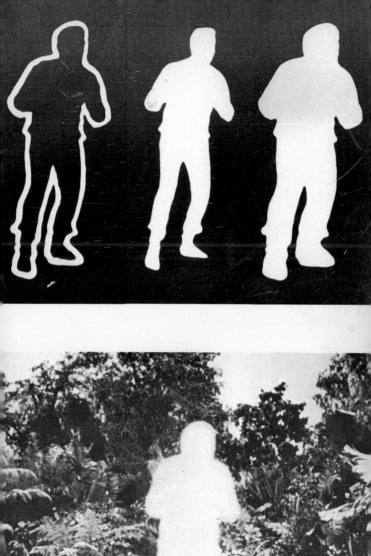

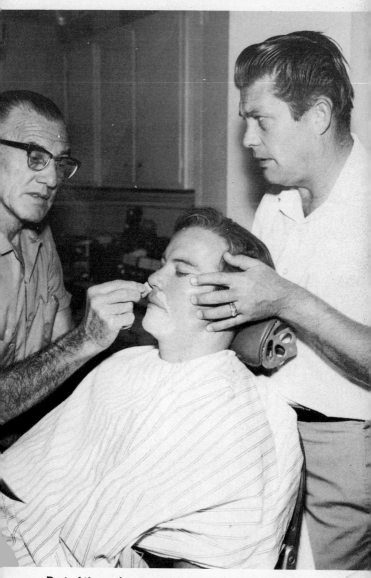

Part of the make-up sequence involved in "aging."

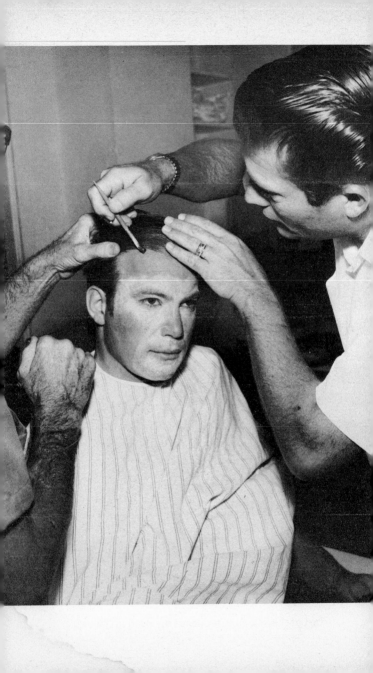

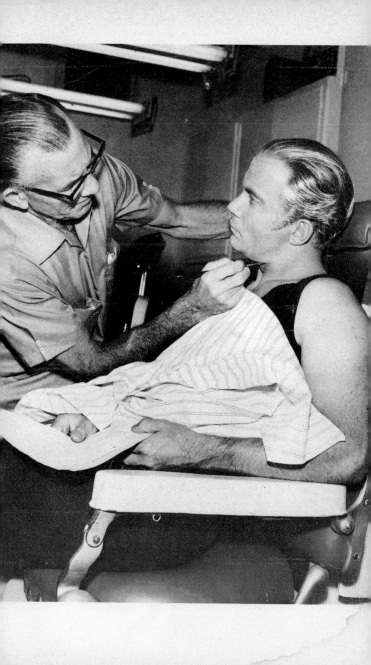

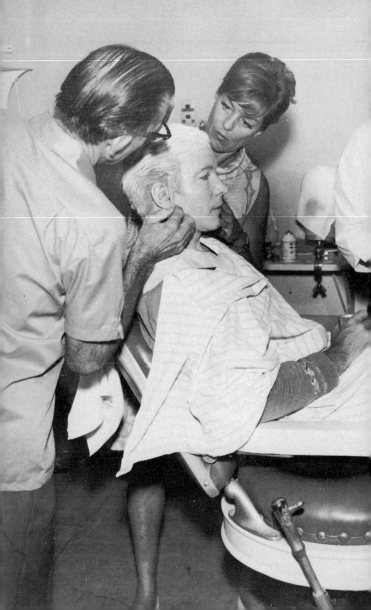

REHEARSAL

**The final result—Kirk, McCoy and Scotty.**

Part II

# AN OFFICIAL BIOGRAPHY
# OF A SHIP AND ITS CREW

Chapter 1

## Prelude

LET'S FACE IT, IF WE HAD TRIED TO THINK
OUT AND PRESENT EVERY POSSIBLE DETAIL
OF STAR TREK, IT WOULD HAVE TAKEN
TWENTY YEARS OF RESEARCH AND STUDY TO
GET FIFTY PERCENT ACCURACY. WE DIDN'T
WANT TO PUT STAR TREK ON THE AIR IN 1980,
OUR CONTRACT CALLED FOR THE SHOW TO
START IN SEPTEMBER, 1966.

Gene Roddenberry

The second pilot represented an accumulation of detail
never attempted in television. It was a combination of speculation, inspiration, and (within the limits of practicality) verification with scientific sources. Literally thousands of questions were asked, covering even the tiniest of details.

As production began, an incredible amount of detail was
still being filled in. This process continues even today. An example:

| | | | |
|---|---|---|---|
| TO: | Gene Roddenberry | DATE: | August 8, 1967 |
| FROM: | D. C. Fontana | SUBJECT: | STAR FLEET— |
| | | | 12 STARSHIPS |

Dear Gene:

We have, in the course of a season and a half, established that Star Fleet includes 12 ships of the starship
class. We are frequently called upon to name one or the
other of them, and no one has kept track of who's
where. The following is a list of suggested names and

some international alternates which we may wish to establish as the starships of the Fleet. Would like you and Bob J. to indicate preference for names, put it in the STAR TREK Guide and use it . . . if this seems feasible.

*Enterprise*
*Exeter*
*Essex*
*Excalibur*
*Lexington*
*Yorktown*
*Endeavor*
*El Dorado*
*Excelsior*
*Saratoga*
*Constellation* (destroyed in "Doomsday Machine."
            Presume she would be replaced by Star
            Fleet.)

Alternates include the names of some famous fighting ships of the past, plus a couple of international variations we might consider, Star Fleet being composed of a united service.

*Hornet*
*Wasp*
*Farragut* (mentioned as destroyed in "Obsession")
*Hood*
*Bonhomme Richard*
*Monitor* or *Merrimac,* depending upon your loyalties
*Tori* (bird)
*Lafayette*
*Ari* (lion)
*Krieger* (warrior)

                    Please consider.

                                    D. C. Fontana

cc: Bob Justman

TO:  Gene Roddenberry     DATE: August 9, 1967
FROM:  Bob Justman        SUBJECT: STAR FLEET—
                                    STARSHIPS

Dear Gene:

I am in receipt of a memo from someone using the pseudonym of D. C. Fontana. This character suggests that we establish the names of the 12 ships of the Enterprise Starship Class.

Of the names that D. C. Fontana mentions, I prefer the following:

*Enterprise*
*Essex*
*Excalibur*
*Lexington*
*Yorktown*
*Endeavor*
*Eagle*
*Constellation*
*Hornet*
*Wasp*
*Lafayette*

I think there would be several other candidates, such as *Saratoga* and perhaps another English Carrier, a French Carrier, a Russian Carrier and certainly a Japanese Carrier. In addition, I think a name ought to be made up that would be of Vulcan origin.

Bob

cc: D. C. Fontana

The following names have been established for starships: *Enterprise, Exeter, Excalibur, Lexington, Yorktown, Potemkin, Republic, Hood, Constitution, Kongo, Constellation, Farragut, Valiant,* and *Intrepid.* The latter four are listed as destroyed in various episodes.

Sometimes additional information was required simply because a writer had brought up a new point in a script. A number of early changes were simply an effort to keep STAR TREK's technology ahead of present-day scientific developments. This was the reason Gene reversed himself on an earlier decision in the "planning" stage and discarded the term "Laser," substituting the term "Phaser."

WE WERE TWO DAYS INTO FILMING ON THE SECOND PILOT WHEN WE REALIZED THAT LASERS MIGHT VERY WELL BECOME COMMONPLACE BY THE TIME THE SHOW GOT ON THE AIR, OR AT LEAST WITHIN THE NEXT COUPLE OF YEARS. RATHER THAN RUN THE RISK OF BEING OUTDATED, WE DECIDED TO SAY "PHASER" INSTEAD. THE REASON WE PICKED PHASER IS THE "PHASING" PRINCIPLE IN PHYSICS BY WHICH POWER CAN BE INCREASED. IT WAS LOGICAL, AND IT SOUNDED GOOD, SO WE USED IT. WE DIDN'T WANT PEOPLE SAYING TO US THREE YEARS FROM NOW, "OH, COME ON NOW, LASERS CAN'T DO THAT."

A number of the changes that have been made are the direct result of Gene's insistence that everything be believable. In a memo he wrote prior to going into production for the season, Gene said, "This U. S. S. *Enterprise* is terribly important to us—if the audience does not believe it, they are not going to believe a multimillion-dollar series investment."

The desire for believability extended to subtle touches:

TO: Robert Justman    DATE: August 17, 1966
FROM: Gene Roddenberry SUBJECT: RE YOUR MEMO
                              —MATTE SHOTS
                              ON PLANETS

Salient points missed:

1. The door or entrance we materialize against, the one built to match the planet matte, should be highly identifiable in both shape and color if possible—so that this high identifiability can be painted into the

matte also, catch the eye, lock us in exactly to where we are.

2. Where possible, we should have *movement* of these bushes, or possibly some dust sifting through scene, or etc., depending on how creative we are—the idea being to give us a cue and reason to dub in planet wind sounds or so on.

Perhaps there are other ways also. Let's explore them, let's keep looking for every possible way, perhaps even some use of light and shadow, to help keep the planet exterior alive and *believe* we are on an alien world.

> Regards,
> Gene Roddenberry

Again, on the point of subtleties, Gene later wrote the art director:

TO:  Matt Jefferies        DATE:  December 12, 1966
FROM:  Gene Roddenberry SUBJECT:   SPACE
                                                    SYMBOLS

Dear Matt:

Would like to see a greater use of symbols, some design of significant form and color, used to identify and tie together particular planet cultures, alien vessels, other Earth vessels, organizations, etc.

As always, would appreciate you coordinating with costume, property, etc.

A handy example: In "Return of the Archons," the law-givers and the Society of Landru could have been characterized by a symbol, say an unusual triangle-circle, which then could have given us unity by allowing it to appear on their rugs, possibly on their staffs, certainly on the walls of Landru's palace. As we discovered in the past, this trick has a way of *unifying* things, gives it a sense of *greater* reality, gives the director things to play to, and furnishes guide posts for the audience. For example, an upcoming one is the other vessel in "Space Seed." Can we do anything here?

Gene Roddenberry

Every member of STAR TREK's staff and crew are encouraged to participate in the creative process:

TO: All Concerned          DATE: June 15, 1966
FROM: STAR TREK Office ·  SUBJECT: CREATIVE
                                           BUDGETING

From time to time in the future, various departments will see in script descriptions of items or methods concerning them the term "(MEASURE)."

This term "(MEASURE)" is to indicate that our minds are by no means made up as to how we shall actually handle that set, or that special effect, or that item of wardrobe, or etc. This term will be a kind of personal code to all of us to put on our thinking caps. Is it too costly? Is there a better way, more effective, more believable, simpler and faster?

"(MEASURE)" means we're not sure about this item: We're inviting you to be inventive and creative—and practical.

Hopefully, you will either show us a way to handle various budget problems, or else you will come up with alternative suggestions that will be much, much cheaper and much, much better to boot.

Gene Roddenberry

Occasionally something new will be added as an outgrowth
of an attempt to solve a particular problem:

TO:  R. H. Justman          DATE:  April 14, 1966
FROM:  Gene Roddenberry     SUBJECT:  CAPTAIN'S
                                      YEOMAN

While trying to work out additional duties for the
Captain's Yeoman, fill out her role a bit, plus give her
some landing party duties where we need her on a planet. It has been suggested that she carry as part of her
regular equipment (and she's got some pretty good
equipment already) some sort of neat, over-the-shoulder
recorder-electronic camera via which she can take log
entries from the Captain at any time, make electronic
moving photos of things, places, etc. Haven't given
much creative thought to what this would look like, but
it seems like it could also be a potential toy item for fe-
male-type children.

    Any comments?

                                    Gene Roddenberry

The problem Roddenberry posed was how to increase the
importance of the role of the Yeoman. Solving that problem
led to the STAR TREK device now known as *The Tricorder*
(which became not only a most interesting piece of equipment but vital to story and believability for ship's landing
parties).

In sharp contrast with the highly detailed background development for the show is the fact that virtually none of it is
explained to the viewer. Technology is discussed only when it
is absolutely essential to the story. Normally, though, they
never stop to explain phaser weapons, the transporter, Warp
Factors, sub-space radio, or any of the other technology they
use.

BELIEVABILITY IS THE TEST. WHAT DO REAL
PEOPLE DO AND SAY? WHEN A POLICEMAN

PICKS UP HIS .38, DOES HE EXPLAIN HOW IT WORKS? DO YOU KNOW HOW THE TRIGGER LEVERS WORK THE FIRING PIN, THE NATURE OF THE PRIMER, THE CHEMICALS IN THE POWDER, AND SO ON? ALL YOU NEED OR REALLY CARE TO KNOW IS THAT WHEN HE USES IT, YOU SEE IT WORK, AND YOU ACCEPT IT. SO WHY SHOULD THE CAPTAIN EXPLAIN A PHASER WHEN HE PICKS IT UP? IS THE PHASER SCIENTIFICALLY ACCURATE? MY SCIENTIST ACQUAINTANCES ARE PRETTY CERTAIN THEY'LL HAVE SOMETHING LIKE A PHASER WELL BEFORE THE 23RD CENTURY. THEY ESTIMATE THE SAME WAY WE ESTIMATE—IF MAN NEEDS A DEVICE THAT CAN DO CERTAIN THINGS, HE'LL INVENT IT. HE ALWAYS HAS. ASSUMING HE DOESN'T DECIDE IT'S MORE IMPORTANT IN THE MEANTIME TO DESTROY HIMSELF.

Chapter 2

## The U.S.S. *Enterprise*

The *Enterprise* is the largest man-made vessel in space. It is 947 feet long, 417 feet wide overall, and has a maximum gross weight of 190,000 tons (compared to a displacement of 59,650 tons of our aircraft carrier, the U. S. S. *Forrestal*). It is divided into three main sections: the saucer-shaped primary hull, the cigar-shaped secondary (engineering) hull, and the twin engine pods.

The unit components were built at the Star Fleet Division of what is still called the San Francisco Navy Yards, and the vessel was assembled in space. The *Enterprise* is not designed to enter the atmosphere of a planet and never lands on a planet surface. When assignment takes the ship to a particular planet, it enters a standard orbit around the planet, which can range from 1,000 to 7,000 miles away, depending on planet size and gravity, atmospheric envelope, size and proximity of sun (s) and moon(s), and other factors.

The primary hull is 417 feet in diameter and is eleven decks thick through the middle. Designed to operate separately from the rest of the ship, the saucer therefore contains all elements necessary for independent operation.

Propulsion for the primary hull is provided by impulse power. The impulse engine section is located at the bottom rear end of the saucer. Headquarters for the engineering division is also located in this same area, as are main engineering control facilities plus sufficient repair, storage, and other facilities to service the primary section when detached from the star-drive sections of the vessel.

The bulge atop the center of the "saucer" is deck one, and houses the bridge. The circular-shaped bridge is the nerve center of the *Enterprise*, and it is here that Captain Kirk presides over the entire ship's complex operation. He sits in his command chair in the inner, lower elevation, facing the large bridge viewing screen. Directly in front of him, also facing the viewing screen, sit the Navigator and the Helmsman, at their combined console. In the outer raised circular elevation of the bridge are eight individual stations.

From the turbo lift doors, and numbered counterclockwise, these stations are:

1. Communications—manned by Lieutenant Uhura.
2. Library-Computer—manned by Mr. Spock.
3. Navigational Subsystems Checkout—normally unmanned, this station provides information and readings on all navigational instruments and subsystems.
4. Weapons Subsystems Checkout—normally unmanned, this station provides data on the operation of all subsystems within the ship's weapons system.

From the turbo lift, and numbered clockwise:

1. Engineering—usually manned by Lieutenant Commander Scott.
2. Environmental Systems—normally unmanned, this station provides data on the functioning of all components of the ship's environmental systems. Manual adjustments can be made at this station to affect ship's gravity, air supply and composition, temperature, etc.
3. Engineering Subsystems Checkout—normally unmanned, this station provides information and readings on all engineering subsystems.
4. Defensive Systems Monitor—normally unmanned, this station continually monitors the status of all defensive systems, deflector screens, etc.

Tied into Kirk's command position are the main controls for the vessel's vast computer complex which automates and affects every system aboard the vessel. The computer complex is the "duotronic" type, invented by Dr. Richard Daystrom 25 years ago (STAR TREK time). At Spock's station and tied into his viewers and screens are the more detailed cross-circuit regulating controls plus visual and audio information on the status of all systems and activities. Thus Kirk's second-in-command can independently report on or override any ship function or condition in case of trouble or emergency.

The vessel's computer system contains voice-recognition circuits and self-programming that permit it to respond to verbal orders; it, in turn, can reply through a vocorder. It uses a feminine voice, a familiar occurrence, even today. The pre-take-off computer systems used on today's F-105 Fighter, for example, speak to the pilots in a female voice because it has been discovered that the feminine voice penetrates noise better and results in improved response by men (and women).

Spock's primary bridge function is handling all of the ship's vast and varied sensor systems fed into his station. As indicated, "sensor" applies to any equipment aboard the ship capable of sensing or reading almost any sort of information. They include mass detection of energy waves, radiation, heat, energy, and any other known force. They are also capable of detecting the presence of life.

Spock's secondary bridge function is main control of the vessel's library-computer. It contains computer memory banks that hold a vast correlated mass of data, history, arts, sciences, philosophy, plus all known information on other known solar systems, colonies, alien cultures, a registry of all space vessels, complete information on nearly all personnel in the Starfleet, and all other information that can be recorded, stored, and used by a starship. (Such a storehouse of information would be highly desirable, and perhaps even vitally necessary, for a successful STAR TREK-type mission into the unknown.)

The ship's library-computer can be channeled to any intercom station or viewing screen anywhere on the ship, and will (verbally or visually) analyze any known information in a matter of seconds. The computer, however, deals only in fact. If an ambiguous question is asked, the computer will so inform the questioner. It will also reject known lies, misinformation, and so forth, and is used effectively in official hearings of all types.

In emergencies, the ship's computer system is capable of controlling the entire operation of the ship. As with its 20th century forebears, it can operate to an independent conclusion, based upon its programming. Its capabilities include some that are rather exotic. Unless specifically "overridden" by a senior officer with known voice patterns, it automatically prevents navigational, weaponry, or other functions that appear dangerous or in error.

As is true with other systems of critical nature, the ship's computer system has an emergency back-up system, complete with identical memory banks, in case the primary system should fail. Switchover is automatic and instantaneous.

The "tricorder," always carried by one or more landing party members, is a combination portable sensor-computer-recorder device that resembles many of today's smaller portable tape recorders but includes a tiny viewscreen. The tricorder can measure, analyze, and keep records on almost any required subject.

One of STAR TREK's most necessary and useful devices has been the communicator. These cigarette pack-size transceivers are used for communications between landing party members on a planet or between ship and planet. When in use, the communicators serve the additional purpose of a transporter-locater device. This allows the transporter to locate, lock-on, and "beam aboard" any crewman within range.

Proceeding down through the interior of the saucer, Decks 2 and 3 are primarily research labs, work areas for various technicians, and related duty stations. Decks 4, 5, and 6 are primarily crew quarters, with some provision for passenger quarters. There are no duty stations on these decks, since the ship is big enough not to need action stations on the decks containing the crew quarters. The Captain's quarters, as well as those of Mr. Spock, Dr. McCoy, and Scotty, are located on Deck 5. Senior officers are assigned quarters on an individual basis, and are not normally required to share their quarters. Their accommodations consist of a two-room complex, evenly divided between an outer work room and inner bedroom/living area.

Junior officers are assigned similar accommodations, but usually are required to share them with one other fellow officer. The bedroom/living area therefore is correspondingly larger, while the outer work area is somewhat smaller.

The central section of the seventh deck level includes the office of the ship's Surgeon, the entire sick bay complex, and all labs and related functions falling under the jurisdiction of the medical department. The outer section is a "protective shell" complex of water and other bulk storage.

At the very center of the seventh deck, and extending down to the eighth deck, is the core of the ship's main computer system, its memory banks and primary controls.

Roddenberry has learned from experience that developing background detail for STAR TREK sometimes has interesting repercussions. He likes to tell the following story regarding the ship's sick bay:

WE KNEW WE NEEDED A SICK BAY AND MEDICAL DEPARTMENT ON THE SHIP. SO WE SAT DOWN AND THOUGHT TO OURSELVES, "WHAT WILL A SICK BAY LOOK LIKE IN THE FUTURE?" ONE OF THE FIRST THINGS THAT OCCURRED TO US WAS THE REALLY PRIMITIVE NATURE OF MANY ASPECTS OF MEDICAL SCIENCE TODAY. . . . TAKING A PERSON'S TEMPERATURE BY STICKING A THERMOMETER IN HIS MOUTH, OR WHEREVER, WRAPPING THE ARM IN ORDER TO CHECK BLOOD PRESSURE, INSERTING A NEEDLE IN A VEIN IN ORDER TO DRAW BLOOD TO BE EXAMINED, ETC. SO WE ASKED OURSELVES, "WHAT ARE THE MORE EFFICIENT THINGS MAN NEEDS IN A SICK BAY OF THE FUTURE?"

LOGICALLY, ALMOST NECESSARILY, WE SOON MUST HAVE BEDS IN WHICH PATIENTS ARE BEING CONTINUALLY SCANNED BY SENSOR DEVICES. THESE DEVICES WILL MAINTAIN A CONSTANT PHYSIOLOGICAL RECORD OF EVERY FUNCTION AND ACTIVITY GOING ON WITHIN THE BODY. THE CONCEPT, AS A LOGICAL EXTENSION OF TODAY'S MEDICAL SCIENCE, WAS VERIFIED BY SOURCES IN THE SCIENTIFIC COMMUNITY, AND WAS MADE AN INTEGRAL PART OF OUR MEDICAL DEPART-

MENT ABOARD THE *ENTERPRISE*. THE CON-
CEPT TOOK THE FORM OF BUILT-IN BED
POSITIONS WITH A DIAGNOSTIC PANEL ABOVE
EACH. WITHOUT ATTACHING ANYTHING TO
THE BODY OF THE PATIENT, A MEDICAL
"PROBE" CONTINUALLY SCANS THE PATIENT,
TAKES READINGS, RECORDS THEM THROUGH
THE DIAGNOSTIC PANEL, AND REGISTERS
THEM THERE VISUALLY WHEN DESIRED BY
DOCTOR OR NURSE.

STAR TREK HAD NOT BEEN ON THE AIR
VERY LONG BEFORE WE WERE CONTACTED
BY NO LESS THAN THREE SEPARATE RE-
SEARCH ORGANIZATIONS, ALL OF WHOM DE-
MANDED TO KNOW HOW WE HAD OBTAINED
THE INFORMATION ON THE SAME DEVICES
THEY HAD UNDER DEVELOPMENT!

Suprisingly enough, as "futuristic" as we may think STAR
TREK's concepts, are, the show finds it extremely difficult to
stay three hundred years ahead of today's technology!

At least one element in the sick bay, far from being well-
thought-out in advance, was a pure accident.

IN THE VERY FIRST SHOW* OF OUR FIRST
SEASON ("THE MAN TRAP" BY GEORGE C.
JOHNSON) WE NEEDED SOME SALT SHAKERS
BECAUSE WE HAD A CREATURE THAT
CRAVED SALT, WE HAD A STORY POINT
WHICH REQUIRED THE CREATURE (DIS-
GUISED IN HUMAN FORM) TO GIVE HIMSELF
AWAY WHEN SOMEONE PASSED WITH A SALT
SHAKER ON A TRAY. THIS POSED A PROBLEM.
WHAT WILL A SALT SHAKER LOOK LIKE
THREE HUNDRED YEARS FROM NOW? OUR
PROPERTY MASTER, IRVING FEINBERG, WENT
OUT AND BOUGHT A SELECTION OF VERY EX-
OTIC-LOOKING SALT SHAKERS. IT WAS NOT

---

* Although the first episode aired, "Man Trap" was actually the *fifth*
episode filmed.

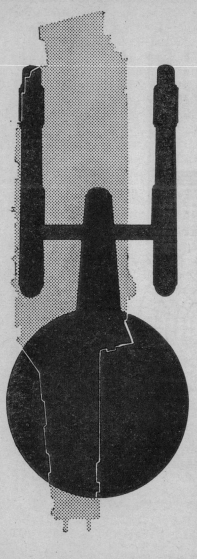

STARSHIP U.S.S. ENTERPRISE (BLACK)

US NAVY AIRCRAFT CARRIER CVA-65 ENTERPRISE (GRAY)

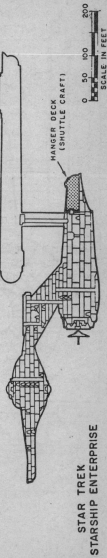

HANGER DECK
(SHUTTLE CRAFT)

SCALE IN FEET

0    50    100    200

STAR TREK
STARSHIP ENTERPRISE

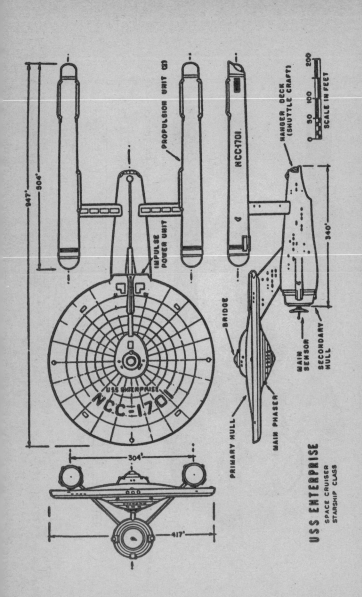

947'

506'

PROPULSION UNIT (2)

NCC-1701.

HANGER DECK
(SHUTTLE CRAFT)

200

100

50

SCALE IN FEET

IMPULSE
POWER UNIT

340'

BRIDGE

MAIN
SENSOR

SECONDARY
HULL

USS ENTERPRISE

NCC-1701

PRIMARY HULL

MAIN PHASER

304'

417'

**USS ENTERPRISE**

SPACE CRUISER
STARSHIP CLASS

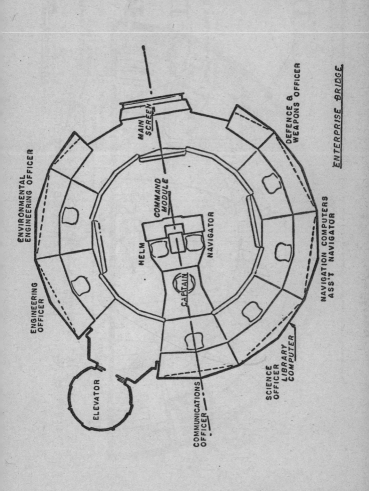

ENTERPRISE BRIDGE

ENVIRONMENTAL
ENGINEERING OFFICER

ENGINEERING
OFFICER

ELEVATOR

COMMUNICATIONS
OFFICER

SCIENCE
OFFICER
LIBRARY
COMPUTER

NAVIGATION COMPUTERS
ASS'T NAVIGATOR

DEFENCE &
WEAPONS OFFICER

MAIN
SCREEN

COMMAND
MODULE

HELM

NAVIGATOR

CAPTAIN

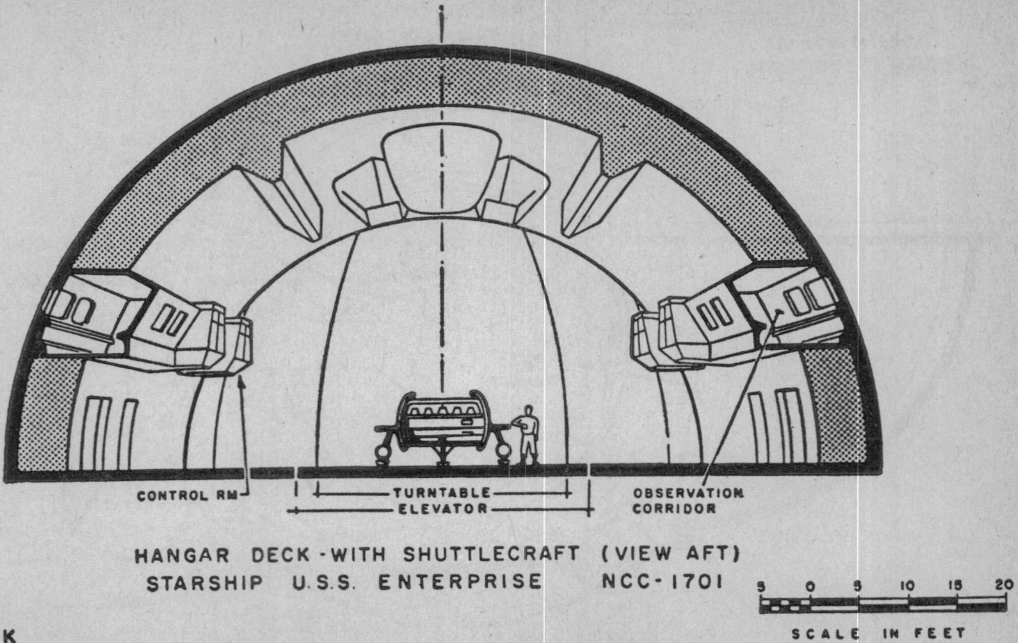

CONTROL RM.

TURNTABLE ELEVATOR

OBSERVATION CORRIDOR

HANGAR DECK · WITH SHUTTLECRAFT (VIEW AFT)
STARSHIP U.S.S. ENTERPRISE NCC-1701

SCALE IN FEET

5  0  5  10  15  20

STAR TREK

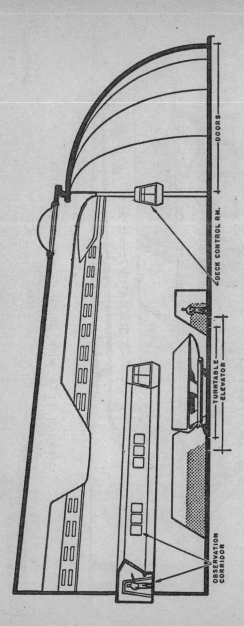

SECTION AT CL HANGAR DECK WITH SHUTTLECRAFT
STARSHIP U.S.S. ENTERPRISE NCC-1701

DOORS

DECK CONTROL RM.

TURNTABLE-ELEVATOR

OBSERVATION CORRIDOR

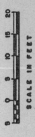

0  5  10  15  20
SCALE IN FEET

STAR TREK

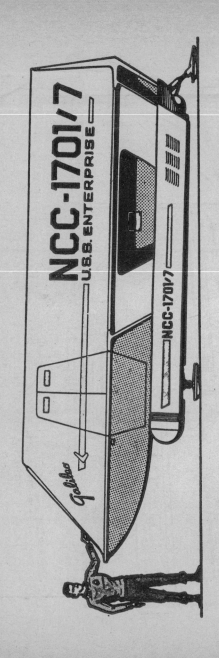

NCC-1701/7

U.S.S. ENTERPRISE

Galileo

NCC-1701/7

0 1 2 3 4 5

SCALE IN FEET

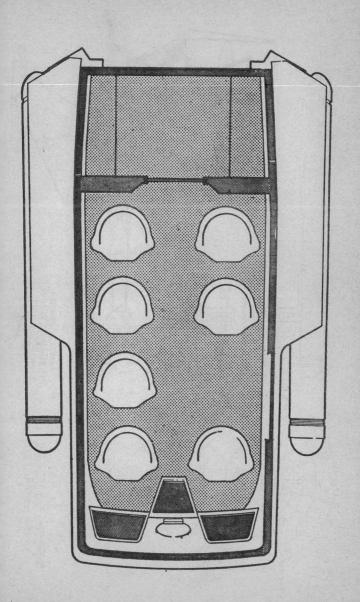

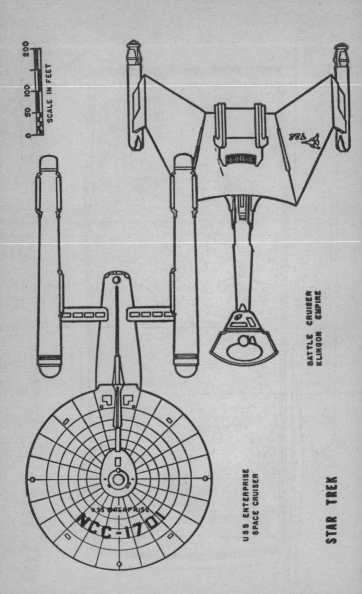

SCALE IN FEET

0  50  100  200

U S S ENTERPRISE

NCC-1701

USS ENTERPRISE
SPACE CRUISER

BATTLE CRUISER
KLINGON EMPIRE

STAR TREK

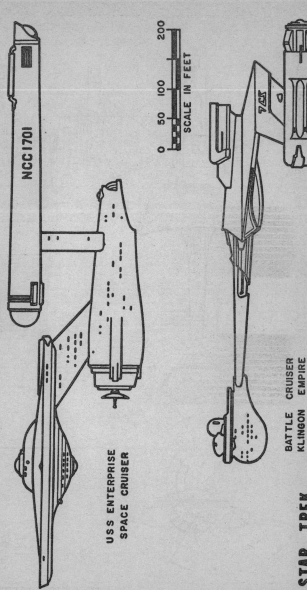

NCC 1701

USS ENTERPRISE
SPACE CRUISER

SCALE IN FEET
0    50    100    200

BATTLE CRUISER
KLINGON EMPIRE

STAR TREK

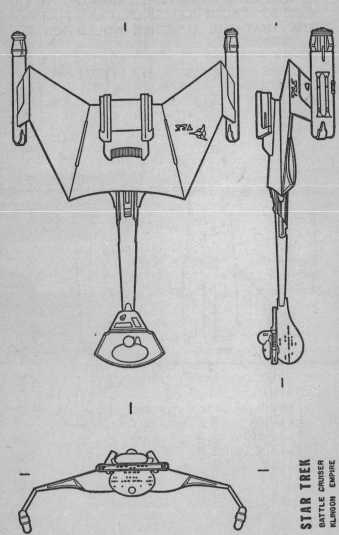

**STAR TREK**
BATTLE CRUISER
KLINGON EMPIRE

UNTIL AFTER HE BROUGHT THEM IN AND
SHOWED THEM TO ME THAT I REALIZED THEY
WERE SO BEAUTIFULLY SHAPED AND FUTUR-
ISTIC THAT THE AUDIENCE WOULD NEVER
RECOGNIZE THEM AS SALT SHAKERS. I WOULD
EITHER HAVE TO USE 20TH CENTURY SALT
SHAKERS OR ELSE I WOULD HAVE TO HAVE A
CHARACTER SAY, "SEE, THIS IS A SALT
SHAKER." SO I TOLD IRVING TO GO DOWN TO
THE STUDIO COMMISSARY AND BRING ME SEV-
ERAL OF THEIR SALT SHAKERS, AND AS HE
TURNED TO GO, I SAID, "HOWEVER, THOSE
EIGHT DEVICES YOU HAVE THERE WILL BE-
COME DR. MC COY'S OPERATING INSTRU-
MENTS."

FOR TWO YEARS NOW THE MAJORITY OF
MC COY'S INSTRUMENTS IN SICK BAY HAVE
BEEN A SELECTION OF EXOTIC SALT SHAKERS,
AND WE KNOW THEY WORK, BECAUSE WE'VE
SEEN THEM WORK. NOT ONLY HAS HE SAVED
MANY A LIFE WITH THEM* BUT IT'S HELPED
KEEP HAND PROP BUDGET COSTS LOW.

(I must admit I was more than a little embarrassed when
Gene told me about McCoy's operating instruments. I had
examined them closely on a number of occasions, and not
once did it ever occur to me they were salt shakers. As a
matter of fact, they always looked like pretty nifty surgical
instruments.)

The primary hull's eighth deck level contains four major
facilities: a large recreation area, the main food preparation
area (similar to the galley aboard our ships today), ship's
laundry, and a rather exotic entertainment center. Although
this recreation area has never been shown in any past

---

* Part of the trick is effective use of sound, plus fragments of "throw-
away," but accurate, future medical terminology as the instruments are
requested from the surgical nurse. STAR TREK has received a number of
letters from physicians who comment on the practicality of McCoy's
instruments and indicate that such instruments are quite possible.

STAR TREK episodes. This set has now been built and will be seen in the third season. Gene describes it this way:

MEN AND WOMEN ON A STARSHIP, SO LONG OUT OF CONTACT WITH EARTH AND SO LONG AWAY FROM OTHER PLANETS, TOO, WILL REQUIRE A FEELING OF FRESH AIR AND SKY AND WIND AND SCENTS. BECAUSE WE ARE, IN MANY RESPECTS, STILL ANIMALS, OUR MENTAL AND EMOTIONAL EQUILIBRIUM WILL REQUIRE THE FAMILIARITY OF THIS. MAN HAS BEEN TOO LONG A PART OF EARTH TO BE TOO LONG SEPARATED. THEREFORE WE INTEND TO BUILD A SIMULATED "OUTDOOR" RECREATION AREA WHICH GIVES A REALISTIC FEELING OF SKY, BREEZES, PLANTS, FOUNTAINS, AND SO FORTH.

ONE OF THE REASONS FOR MAKING A STARSHIP SO LARGE WOULD BE TO HAVE SOMETHING LIKE THIS—IN FACT TO CREATE A WHOLE "COMMUNITY" SO NECESSARY TO A SOCIAL ANIMAL. AN AUTOMATED STARSHIP LIKE OURS COULD PROBABLY BE OPERATED BY TEN PEOPLE IF NECESSARY, BUT IT WOULD BE A TERRIBLY LIMITED, UNHEALTHY, MISERABLE LIFE.

The food preparation galley is also highly automated. No chefs in white hats here. The mechanical functions of measuring and mixing spices, sauces, stews, and so forth have been transferred to the computer tape. The art of cooking today will be translated into computer programming in the future. Although there may be ten thousand "best ways" to make a certain type of sauce, a computer can record and duplicate each more efficiently than a dozen chefs. You simply program the computer and a mechanical unit makes it. The enormous sophistication of computers aboard the *Enterprise* makes possible the producing of the thousand best menus of the thousand best restaurants in all the alien planets of the Federation. Crew members can select an infinite variety of food—they simply press the button. From the central food preparation area, the selection is transferred via a small turbo lift that connects the several dining and recreation areas scattered throughout the ship. This concept is in direct contrast to the belief held by many science-fiction writers, that men of the future will take nourishment via pills. (But discrepancies to this overall thinking have crept into at least two shows, one in which disparaging remarks were made about "reconstituted" food by McCoy, and another where the Captain rather apologetically requests the galley to make fake Thanksgiving turkey out of meat loaf. . . . Considering the pressure under which the series is produced, it is surprising there are not more serious inconsistencies.)

MY ATTITUDE WAS, WHY SHOULD MAN GIVE UP THE JOY OF HAM AND EGGS IF THE FOOD PRESERVATION TECHNOLOGY OF THE PERIOD WOULD PERMIT HIM TO HAVE IT? BOTH TRADITION AND TASTE WILL KEEP ROAST TOM TURKEY POPULAR FOR THANKS-GIVING DINNER. IN FACT, THERE WILL PROBABLY BE A BLENDING OF DELICACIES FROM MANY PLANETS—A MUCH GREATER RANGE OF FOOD AND CULINARY ARTISTRY THAN WE CAN EVEN CONCEIVE NOW. JUST AS IN AMERICAN RESTAURANTS TODAY WE HAVE MENUS BORROWED FROM GERMANY, SPAIN, SOUTH AMERICA, JAPAN, ALL COUNTRIES. IT'S THE SAME WAY IN OUR *ENTERPRISE* GALLEY, ONLY MORE SO.

In order to support this food preparation capability, the *Enterprise* has extensive food storage areas with preservation techniques that maintain food in "garden-fresh condition" over extended periods of time. Hydroponic food growing is not necessary and would use a disproportionate amount of manpower. There are, of course, hydroponics tanks aboard that are part of the botany laboratories. There is also a section where crew members can prepare individual dishes if they wish—an activity that comes under the heading of "rec-reaction."

Ship's laundry bears little resemblance to its 20th century ancestor. Primarily because garments are reconvertible. It is simply easier to put a garment into the processing machine, reduce it to its original chemical fibers, take out the dirt, and then recreate a "new" garment back into its original form. Aboard the *Enterprise*, since it is a self-contained unit, out of sheer practicality nothing is ever lost.

The fourth major facility on the eighth deck level is the entertainment center. Certainly man of the future will require entertainment as much as we enjoy motion pictures and tele-vision today. Probably entertainment will be three-dimen-sional in nature and perhaps will even go further, in that you will sit in the room and the story will take place all around you. In other words, a sophisticated extension of holography.

This technique will also have its effect on the traditional "mail call." Instead of receiving a letter, a man can sit in the room and, via tape, actually "see" the person sending the correspondence. As the tape is projected, the images will form in the air in front of him, so he will be able to see how his child looks, what's happening to the house, and how great his grandmother looked that day. It will be just as if he were standing there with them. Having used the "projecting unit," he can then use the "photographing unit," do a similar thing himself, and send it home. To a certain extent, we are doing this even today through the practice of corresponding by tape and tape recorder.

Decks 9 and 10 are primarily devoted to freight and cargo carrying space, some technicians' repair shops, and other mis-cellaneous activities. The ship's phaser banks are located on the underside of the saucer-shaped hull, and therefore deck 11 contains the ship's phaser controls and other related equipment and facilities. Phasers can also be fired from an area atop the saucer-shaped hull, in an area surrounding the bridge, but primary control facilities and equipment are lo-cated on deck 11.

The cigar-shaped secondary hull is 340 feet long, 112 feet in diameter, and is connected to the saucer by means of a large access pylon. The secondary hull is often referred to as the engineering hull, as much of the facilities and activities conducted in this area are devoted to that department. A number of the deck levels (there are sixteen of them) are also devoted to fuel, supply, main repair centers, water and waste reconversion, and interplanet freight. Minimal crew quarters are located in this hull, used by duty engineers and by the star-drive crew when the saucer section has detached and is operating separately.

The starship's main sensor-deflector (a parabolic sensor antenna and asteroid-deflector) is located at the front end of the secondary hull. The ship's hangar deck area, where the vessel's shuttlecraft are stored, is located at the aft end. Huge hangar doors, 60 feet wide and 30 feet high, provide egress and entrance for the six shuttlecraft. Designed to carry a crew of seven, the shuttlecraft are used on limited exploratory patrols away from the *Enterprise* and are capable of entering the atmosphere of a planet on its surface.

The two long nacelles, atop the ship and attached to the engineering hull by slender pylons, house the main starship engines. The engines are each 504 feet long, 60 feet in diameter, operate via controlled fusion of matter and anti-matter, creating the fantastic power required to run the *Enterprise* and drive it at faster-than-light speeds.

The speed of light, 186,000 miles per second (about 700,000,000 miles per hour), is in itself a speed with which much of the audience has difficulty relating. Even greater problems result when it becomes necessary to express a speed many times faster than the speed of light. STAR TREK dialogue solves the problem by measuring all faster-than-light speeds in terms of "Warp Factors." Warp Factor One is the speed of light. Warp Factor Three is 24 times the speed of light. Maximum safe cruising speed of the *Enterprise* is Warp Factor Six, or 216 times the speed of light. At Warp Factor Eight (512 times the speed of light) the ship's structure begins to show considerable strain, due to the inability of the ship's field mechanisms to compensate. Warp Factor Six is therefore exceeded only in instances of extreme emergency.

(By way of contrast, the impulse engines can drive the ship only at sub-light speeds, and can be continuously operated for about a month before exhausting impulse power fuel. The entire vessel can operate on battery power alone at sub-light speed for about a week, depending on velocity required.)

The matter-anti-matter engines were not fully settled upon until after the series was already on the air. Originally the *Enterprise* was said to be powered by something loosely called a "space warp." As episode after episode went into production, it became increasingly obvious that this point would have to be tied down.

Discussions with scientific consultants had already ruled out atomic power as inefficient and inadequate for achieving hyper-light speeds. Ion drive was ruled out for the same reasons.

Finally, the conclusion reached was that the only power source conceivably large enough to do the job would be the energy released by the sheer annihilation of matter and anti-matter. This has already been achieved on a minute scale by several research laboratories. Theoretical release of such power, on STAR TREK's scale, compares to nuclear energy as an H-bomb compares to a kitchen match!

The transporter room embodies a concept that has long been discussed by the scientific community. It is a device for converting matter temporarily into energy, beaming that energy to a predetermined point, and reconverting it back to its original pattern and structure. No receiver is needed. Its range is about 16,000 miles, it can reach out to pick objects out of space, and is used to transport personnel from ship to ship or between ship and planet surface. A maximum of six people can be beamed by the main operational transporters at any one time. These transporter rooms are circular in shape, and are controlled from a nearby console by a transporter officer and a technician. There are eleven personnel and cargo transporter stations aboard the vessel. Four are the familiar main operational stations, two are cargo transporters, five are emergency personnel transporters which can handle twenty-two people each but involve a risk factor at such power loads and are limited to use in ship-abandoning emergencies.

Obviously, efficient movement about such a large vessel requires mechanical assistance. This is provided by the ship's turbo-elevators. These high-speed lifts run both horizontally and vertically. Television story needs first made the turbo-elevators necessary. An action-adventure television show must move at a fast dramatic pace. And it became obvious in the first few episodes that this could be no mere "elevator"—our characters had to get places horizontally just as fast. Once again story needs resulted in a concept that was not only logical but necessary in a vessel of this size.

The turbo-elevators operate in a way similar to huge pneumatic tubes, each elevator independently turbine-driven, controlled by computer-activated relays in the shaft that control and direct the air pressure created by the turbines.

## WEAPONRY

The hand-carried weapons, called "phasers," are pure energy weapons (as are all offensive weapons in the ship's arsenal). All phasers emit a beam of energy similar to the light beam emitted by a Laser, but of a pulsating nature that can be "phased" to interfere or interact with the wave pattern of any molecular form. Phaser beams can be fired steadily, in one long burst, or in intermittent "squirts" or "phased" energy. They can be set to *dematerialize* (converting matter into energy), *disrupt* (breaking down cohesion), *heat* (increasing molecular velocity), or *stun* (neural impact).

There are three types of hand-carried phasers. The first and smallest is not much larger than a pack of cigarettes and is worn concealed on a belt under the uniform shirt. It is limited in range, power, and energy charge, and is primarily used when a landing party does not want to be conspicuously armed. For example, during a "friendly call" on a planet.

The second type of phaser is a combination of the small phaser snapped into a pistol mount. The handle of the mount is a power pack that increases the range, power, and energy available. This type of phaser is worn visibly, hanging from a weapons belt at the waist.

The third type is a more powerful phaser rifle, providing even greater range and effectiveness.

The hand phasers' variety of power settings include a wide

range of choices that permit the phaser to be used as a cutting torch, welding device, and similar hand tool needs.

Phasers can also be set to "overload," and can be used in emergencies as a time bomb. This setting causes the power source to build to the point where it explodes. Detonation will destroy the phaser and most natural physical objects within a fifty-yard radius. There is a safety device built into each phaser that emits a characteristic sound as the phaser enters overload condition.

The arsenal of the *Enterprise* itself includes a battery of ship-mounted phasers, which derive their enormous power directly from the ship's engines. Multiple units, called phaser banks, are titanic versions of the hand phasers. They are capable of demolishing matter over vast distances.

The *Enterprise* is equipped with a second type of offensive weapon, called photon torpedos, which are energy pods of matter and anti-matter contained and held temporarily separated in a magno-photon force field. These can be used as torpedos or depth charges, and can be set with electrochemical, proximity, and a variety of other fuses. Photon torpedos can be fired directly at a target, laid out as a mine field, or scattered in an attacker's path as depth charges.

The Helmsman is also the ship's Weapons Officer and coordinates phaser fire, using the ship's navigational aids to scan, track, lock-on, and fire on the Captain's order.

## DEFLECTORS

The *Enterprise* is equipped with several types of deflectors, one of which is employed as a defensive weapon. This deflector shield does the same thing that steel plating does for a modern-day battleship. It is, in effect, an invisible force barrier around the *Enterprise,* protecting the vessel from anything but the most sophisticated and powerful of weapons. It is automatically activated by the ship's sensors and computers when an unknown danger approaches. If the vessel should come under attack, the power of the deflector shield can be increased considerably, but at a commensurate loss to the ship's power. At optimum setting, shielding can be maintained for only twenty hours. When the deflector shield (or "screen," as it is sometimes called) is operating, the ship's transporters cannot be used, because the force-field barrier completely envelopes the ship.

The *Enterprise* is also equipped with navigational deflector beams which, triggered by navigational scanners, sweep far ahead of the vessel's path through space. Reason—at hyperlight speeds, striking even a particle of space dust would pierce the skin of the vessel. The navigational sensors sweep the path ahead of the ship at distances so great that minimal deflector power is required to divert space debris and other objects from the ship's path. The vessel's computers constantly monitor this, and should too large an asteroid or other object be sensed, the ship will be automatically diverted from a collision course.

While not classified as a weapon, the tractor beam can be used as one. It operates on the reverse principle of the deflector. It is a beam that grabs and pulls, rather than deflecting away. The tractor beam has a maximum range of about 100,000 miles. It can be used to hold a firm position alongside another vessel, pull a smaller vessel toward the *Enterprise,* or tow another ship out of danger. It can also be used to pull small objects within transporter range, whereupon they can be beamed aboard.

Since space knows no north or south, and no "up" or "down," directions are given in two planes rather than one. For example, the position of an unidentified object would be expressed as, "unidentified object ahead on a bearing of 37 mark 211." The "space horizon" is a plane bisecting the galaxy at its widest point, and "zero" horizon is the line from Earth to the center of the galaxy. The vertical plane, "up" and "down," is at right angles to the galaxy "horizon," and "zero" on this plane is an imaginary line from the center of the galaxy through its thinnest point to a distant galaxy dubbed Polaris II. Thus the "unidentified object" mentioned previously would be 37 degrees "up" on a vertical plane and 211 degrees "out" on a horizontal plane. It is therefore very much like having two compass circles through the galaxy, one through the thick "horizontal" plane and the other circle through the thin "vertical" plane. The word "mark" is simply a means of separating the first statement in degrees from the second statement in degrees.

When questioned on this point, Gene said:

WHY USE THE WORD "MARK"? WELL, I GUESS IT SOUNDED SEMIMILITARY AND SEMI-NAVIGATIONAL. AS A MATTER OF FACT, YOU'RE THE FIRST PERSON WHO'S EVER QUESTIONED ME ON THAT. EVERYONE ELSE HAS JUST ACCEPTED IT AS THE WAY WE DO IT. YOU'RE BEGINNING TO SHAKE ME UP—IT'S HARD ENOUGH TO THINK UP SOME OF THESE THINGS, MUST LESS HAVING TO EXPLAIN THEM.

Measuring great distances is handled in this fashion:

MEASUREMENTS

We use the metric system for most close and small measurements, such as distance of another vessel lying alongside, its size, etc. For long measurements, such as distance between stars, we use light-year measurements. For example, the closest star to Earth is Proxima Centauri, which is 4.2 light years away. Other stars in our galaxy are hundreds or thousands of light years away. NOTE: *The writer need not trouble himself with computing or studying such terms—we have excellent technical advisers who review all scripts.*

For those who are interested, the term PARSEC is also used in measuring vast distances—PARSEC is 3.26 light years, or 19.2 trillion miles—206,265 times the radius of the Earth's orbit. *(Parallax* of one *second.)*

However, the writer should keep in mind that the audience often needs more understandable measurements, and we often vary the above statements, such as: "That alien ship is more than a mile in diameter!" Or, "That ship is a million miles away, and we're still being probed by its sensors!" Generally, we use the more precise scientific measuring terms in giving and answering bridge commands, go to the less scientific but more understandable "audience terminology" in exclamations and in private conversations. Present-day example—the weaponry control officers of a modern-day naval vessel will always be very precise in giving aiming orders, but might remark conversationally to the man next to them, "They're still a mile out of range."

Excerpt from STAR TREK Guide

In order to avoid problems in communicating over these vast distances, Roddenberry decided on the term "subspace radio." It is explained as follows:

SUBSPACE RADIO

Lieutenant Uhura, Communications Officer, sits at this control station. We use the term "subspace" since it is necessary that communications from the *Enterprise* to its bases are a "space warp" effect which travels at speeds far exceeding even that of the *Enterprise*. If we did not have such "subspace" or "space warp" communications, obviously the *Enterprise* could warp off to a base and return faster than a message could be sent there.

Excerpt from STAR TREK Guide

Another problem involved in deep space travel is time. How do you express time when there is no point of reference to make it mean anything, such as we have here on Earth? Our own time on Earth is based on months and years, which are strictly terrestrial cycles tied to the sun and moon. At the other end of the galaxy the cycle doesn't mean a thing. As a matter of fact, the cycle changes from planet to planet, let alone from solar system to solar system!

It seems logical, therefore, that some sort of time-keeping system would be established in order to solve the problem. Such a system would undoubtedly have to be based on a highly scientific and mathematically complex formula.

Not so, with STAR TREK's "Star Date."

IN THE BEGINNING, I INVENTED THE TERM "STAR DATE" SIMPLY TO KEEP FROM TYPING OURSELVES DOWN TO 2265 A.D., OR SHOULD IT BE 2312 A.D.? I WANTED US WELL IN THE FUTURE BUT WITHOUT ARGUING APPROXIMATELY WHICH CENTURY THIS OR THAT WOULD HAVE BEEN INVENTED OR SUPERSEDED. WHEN WE BEGAN MAKING EPISODES, WE WOULD USE A STAR DATE SUCH AS 2317 ONE WEEK, AND THEN A WEEK LATER WHEN WE MADE THE NEXT EPISODE WE WOULD MOVE THE STAR DATE UP TO 2942, AND SO ON. UNFORTUNATELY, HOWEVER, THE EPISODES ARE NOT AIRED IN THE SAME ORDER IN WHICH WE FILM THEM. SO WE BEGAN TO GET COMPLAINTS FROM THE VIEWERS, ASKING, "HOW COME ONE WEEK THE STAR DATE IS 2891, THE NEXT WEEK IT'S 2337, AND THEN THE WEEK AFTER IT'S 3414?"

IN ANSWERING THESE QUESTIONS, I CAME UP WITH THE STATEMENT THAT "THIS TIME SYSTEM ADJUSTS FOR SHIFTS IN RELATIVE TIME WHICH OCCUR DUE TO THE VESSEL'S SPEED AND SPACE WARP CAPABILITY. IT HAS LITTLE RELATIONSHIP TO EARTH'S TIME AS WE KNOW IT. ONE HOUR ABOARD THE U.S.S. *ENTERPRISE* AT DIFFERENT TIMES MAY EQUAL AS LITTLE AS THREE EARTH HOURS. THE STAR DATE SPECIFIED IN THE LOG ENTRY MUST BE COMPUTED AGAINST THE SPEED OF THE VESSEL, THE SPACE WARP, AND ITS POSITION WITHIN OUR GALAXY, IN ORDER TO GIVE A MEANINGFUL READING." THEREFORE STAR DATE WOULD BE ONE THING AT ONE POINT IN THE GALAXY AND SOMETHING ELSE AGAIN AT ANOTHER POINT IN THE GALAXY.

I'M NOT QUITE SURE WHAT I MEANT BY THAT EXPLANATION, BUT A LOT OF PEOPLE HAVE INDICATED IT MAKES SENSE. IF SO, I'VE BEEN LUCKY AGAIN, AND I'D JUST AS

SOON FORGET THE WHOLE THING BEFORE I'M
ASKED ANY FURTHER QUESTIONS ABOUT IT.

The history of the making of STAR TREK is full of examples of things being invented for the show and later cropping
up again in real life in some form or another.

One example involves the "alert" sound made by the communicators. The sound, which was picked because it cut
through most other sounds and immediately caught everyone's attention, is used as a dramatic device to alert people.
Not long ago the studio received a call from a research group
at a hospital, inquiring about STAR TREK's "marvelous beeping sound." It seems they were designing a new cardiac-arrest
ward and needed a sound that would cut through all other
noises and alert a doctor when a patient is in trouble. The
sound "invented" as a dramatic device for STAR TREK was exactly what they were looking for! The hospital was sent a
tape recording of the sound with STAR TREK's compliments.

A slightly different example involves the universal translator
device used to translate alien languages into English. The concept was analyzed, and when investigation proved that it is, in
fact, theoretically possible to make such an instrument, one
was created for use on the ship. About seven months later the
STAR TREK staff read that the United States Government is
working on such a device.

On another occasion a man wrote:

> I am an apartment complex builder in Santa Barbara,
> and I continue to attempt to add amenities and upgrade
> my units as best I can.
>
> For some time I have wanted to install in our new
> units an electrically controlled pocket-panel door, and I
> have done some research in this area. Our basic problem
> has been that we can't get the door to open or close fast
> enough.
>
> How do you get your damn doors to open and close so
> fast?
>
> I would appreciate any information you might be able
> to supply. I would like to know in particular the creator's
> name or the builder's name of any information you your-

self might be able to offer regarding the basic operating characteristics of the doors.

If, in effect, the sliding doors in the spacecraft in your STAR TREK series are special effects, then, of course, you can be of no help to me.

STAR TREK couldn't be much help. The ship's doors are *manually* operated by a man on the set, hidden from view.

QUITE OFTEN WE HEAR INDIVIDUALS WHO ARE HEAVILY INVOLVED IN OUR NATION'S SPACE PROGRAMS EXPRESS THE FEELING THAT STAR TREK IS HELPING PREPARE THE PUBLIC (AND MEMBERS OF CONGRESS, WHOM THEY DEPEND UPON FOR THEIR BUDGETS) FOR AN EVENTUAL MARS SHOT, AND BEYOND. THIS IS GRATIFYING TO US.

WE HOPE WE ARE HELPING TO FORM THE CONCEPT THAT PRESENT SPACE ATTEMPTS ARE NOT WASTED MONEY—OR THAT FUTURE INTERPLANETARY SPACE TRAVEL IS NOT JUST "WILD FICTION." IT WILL BE AS IMPORTANT TO MANKIND TOMORROW AS THE DISCOVERY OF AMERICA WAS IN ITS DAY.

AS MAN REACHES OUT INTO SPACE, HE WILL ACQUIRE NEW DRUGS, FOODS, MINERALS, AND KNOWLEDGE WHICH HE CANNOT CONCEIVE OF NOW. JUST AS EUROPE ACQUIRED UNIMAGINED BENEFITS THROUGH THE DISCOVERY OF THE NEW WORLD. MUCH OF THE EUROPEAN DIET TODAY DID NOT EXIST PRIOR TO THE DISCOVERY OF AMERICA. CORN, POTATOES, TOMATOES . . . ALL WERE INTRODUCED FROM THE NEW WORLD. LATER THE COLONISTS DEVELOPED NEW VITALITY AND NEW IDEAS WHICH HELPED CHANGE MANKIND'S WHOLE DIRECTION. ONLY HOPE WE'LL BE WISER WHEN WE MEET THE "AZTECS" OR "MAYANS" OF ANOTHER PLANET.

IN THE INFINITE POSSIBILITIES "OUT THERE,"
IF WE ACT LIKE SAVAGES, WE MAY FIND
SOMEONE QUITE CAPABLE OF TREATING US AS
SAVAGES.

Chapter 3

## Mission and Men

To explore strange new worlds, to seek out new civilizations, to boldly go where no man has gone before.

Not too many years ago, anyone who publicly expressed a belief in life "out there" was automatically labeled a crackpot. Times certainly do change. Today our scientists frequently state it would be highly unusual if this planet were the only spot in all the universe where intelligent life existed. They tell us our universe is so vast it contains *millions* of planets similar to our own. Assuming they are right, life forms and civilizations must exist, ranging from primitive all the way to intelligence far surpassing our own. Unless our science, mathematics, and laws of probability are all wrong, infinite space promises just as much life and adventure as our own oceans and land masses here on Earth.

Consider.

The Rand Corporation recently speculated that there could be 640,000,000 planets in this galaxy alone where you could open the door of a spaceship, step out on the planet surface, and breathe fresh air. Just as bold men once discovered and subdued new continents here on Earth, bold men will someday venture into the fantastic unknowns of space.

Rule number one for a television action-adventure series is: tense, exciting, action-packed episodes every week. This is the reason Gene invented the "mission" assigned to the *Enterprise* and its crew. The mission requires our adventurers to remain on patrol and out of direct contact with their home base for at least five years. With millions of inhabited planets out there, they're bound to run into trouble. That seemed to solve the problem of rule number one.

Unfortunately, it wasn't that simple. A great deal of background had to be invented, just to support the mission and make it seem believable to the audience. Assigned to operate in a far-off sector of the galaxy, the ship's duties include: scientific investigation and reconnaissance of previously unexplored worlds, providing aid and supplies for Earth colonies, diplomatic courtesy calls on alien planets, and the enforcement of laws regulating commerce between Federation members. Except under orders from a higher authority, the *Enterprise* never leaves its assigned area.

When you consider it, the *Enterprise* is doing the same kind of job naval vessels used to do several hundred years ago. In those days ships of the major powers were assigned to patrol specific areas of the world's oceans. They represented their governments in those areas and protected the national interests of their respective countries. Out of contact with the admiralty office back home for long periods of time, the captains of these ships had very broad discretionary powers. These included regulating trade, fighting bush wars, putting down slave traders, lending aid to scientific expeditions, conducting exploration on a broad scale, engaging in diplomatic exchanges and affairs, and even becoming involved in such minor matters as searching for lost explorers or helping down-and-out travelers return to their homes.

(The missions may be similar in theory, but there's a big, big difference in practice. Our ancestors didn't have to worry about getting zapped by some alien monster!)

The *Enterprise* is a member of the Starship Class (there are twelve of them) Registry Number NCC-1701. Starship Class vessels are the largest and most powerful man-made ships in space. Their mere presence commands a healthy respect. Although the assigned mission is for a five-year period, the ship itself has a self-sustaining travel range of eighteen years.

The story of STAR TREK is partially a story of the opening up of the galaxy. STAR TREK's era is a period of exploration and discovery—ninety percent of the galaxy has not yet been explored. The *Enterprise*-class starships have been in existence for about forty years and are now capable of surveying and exploring the uncharted remainder of the galaxy.

On the surface, it would seem the starships could do a lot of exploring in a very short time. But it is not so when you consider the size of the galaxy and the fact that there are only twelve starships in service. Suppose there are only three million Class M (Earth-type) planets. Divide by twelve starships. Even if they could visit a planet every month, the STAR TREK series could go on forever!

IN ADDITION TO THE TWELVE STARSHIPS, THERE ARE LESSER CLASSES OF VESSELS, CAPABLE OF OPERATING OVER MUCH MORE LIMITED DISTANCES. THEY ARE INVOLVED IN COMMERCIAL VENTURES, SURVEY WORK, ARCHAEOLOGICAL EXPEDITIONS, MEDICAL RESEARCH, AND SO ON. THE STARSHIPS ARE THE HEAVY CRUISERS, THE ONES WHICH CAN BEST DEFEND THEMSELVES AS THEY PROBE FARTHER AND FARTHER OUT, OPENING NEW AREAS . . . AND THEN THE OTHERS FOLLOW.

The *Enterprise* operates at the outer end of a chain-of-command. Immediate higher headquarters is Star Base Command. There are seventeen star bases scattered across the small known portion of the galaxy. Star bases, commanded by an officer with the rank of commodore, provide repair and resupply facilities, replacement of personnel, and so forth. Next higher authority is Star Fleet Command, operating from a central point in the explored portion of the galaxy. Under normal conditions, the *Enterprise* operates far away and virtually out of touch with higher authority.

THIS IS INTENTIONAL, BECAUSE IT GIVES US A GREAT STORY ADVANTAGE. IN MANY OF OUR EPISODES OUR SHIP GOES BEYOND WHERE ANY SHIP HAS EVER GONE BEFORE. I SHOULD LIKE TO MAINTAIN THE FEELING THERE IS STILL MUCH WE HAVEN'T SEEN AND DON'T KNOW ABOUT. WE DON'T WANT OUR GALAXY IN STAR TREK BECOMING TOO TRAVELED AND TOO FAMILIAR. THIS TAKES AWAY THE MYSTERY AND REDUCES STORY OPPORTUNITIES. IT'S HARDER TO CREATE SITUA-

# TIONS OF HIGH JEOPARDY AMONG FAMILIAR SURROUNDINGS.

The 430-man crew (approximately one third are females) is completely international and multiracial in makeup. There are even crew members from other planets. Although Mr. Spock is the only alien crew member introduced so far, there are others who will make their appearance on future shows. The crew of each starship is predominantly of one type. The crew of some of these vessels is primarily human, others primarily Vulcan, and others perhaps something else. Each ship has a small percentage of aliens aboard, but the majority of the crew are usually of one type.

The reasoning is simple. Since the majority of the crew would have more in common with one another, they would work more smoothly together. They would be able to have the same environment without problems in adjustment and would enjoy similar food, sleeping and waking intervals, etc. Being mentally and physically alike, it would be easier to maintain the ship. Aboard the *Enterprise* it has been established that the majority of the crew are Earth-type humans. On the other hand, in at least one episode reference was made to another Starship whose crew was composed entirely of Vulcans. There is complete equality between members of the crew, between sexes and races, as well as between humans and aliens.

Organizationally, the crew members are assigned to one of the three principal operating divisions: Science, Engineering and Ships Services, and Command.

Such a large vessel, even though highly automated, would need a fairly large crew to handle the complexity of the ship, as well as to enable it to carry out all of its many and varied duty assignments. In addition, having both men and women as crew members would make the voyage more enjoyable and bearable. There are also the realities of television to face. A large crew would provide more flexibility for story lines in future episodes. A coeducational crew would, hopefully, have greater appeal to a wider television audience.

"All those people" are needed for other, very practical reasons. The *Enterprise* occasionally will leave a small group of people behind on some planet, for a variety of purposes. It could be for scientific investigation, teaching the local inhabitants, survey work, etc. These specialists are then picked up at a later date, by the *Enterprise* or one of her sister ships. This is a very necessary capability for a ship's mission, which includes exploration and scientific investigation. It dictates a crew complement large enough to withstand these temporary losses of personnel and still continue normal operations.

ONE OF THE REASONS FOR HAVING THIS MANY CREWMEN ON BOARD WAS TO KEEP MAN ESSENTIALLY THE SAME AS HE IS NOW. I BELIEVE THAT MAN IS AND ALWAYS WILL BE A "SOCIAL ANIMAL." I THEREFORE FELT WE HAD TO PROVIDE WIDELY VARYING TYPES AND WIDELY VARYING OPPORTUNITIES FOR INTERPLAY IN HUMAN RELATIONSHIPS. IT IS GOOD TO HAVE PEOPLE ABOARD AND AVAILABLE TO LEND THEIR CREATIVE TOUCH WHEN AUTOMATED MACHINERY GOES WRONG. BUT THIS WASN'T THE PRIMARY REASON, SINCE WE MIGHT EASILY HYPOTHESIZE THAT BY THIS FUTURE CENTURY EQUIPMENT WOULD HAVE THE ABILITY TO REPAIR ITS OWN DAMAGE, OR BYPASS DAMAGED PARTS AND LET AUXILIARY PARTS TAKE OVER THE JOB. INDEED, WE HAVE ALREADY BUILT SUCH CAPABILITY INTO EQUIPMENT LANDING ON THE MOON.

YOU CAN'T DIVORCE MAN FROM MEN. AND YOU CAN'T DIVORCE MAN FROM THE THINGS HUMAN RELATIONSHIPS CAN GIVE HIM.

Man-plus-woman-plus-time very often equals babies. It would be a trifle awkward having a bunch of toddlers around a Starship, and it is therefore natural to assume that some type of birth control will be required. This point has never been discussed in the series, since the censors won't allow it. But if the subject could be discussed, the consensus is that birth control would closely parallel the military practices of today.

Birth control would be mandatory for unmarried females, voluntary for married females. In keeping with the advanced state of the medical arts as practiced aboard the *Enterprise*, a single, monthly* injection would be administered. A woman found to be pregnant would be given her choice of a medical discharge or rotation to a shore base for the remainder of her pregnancy.

In the final analysis, science recognizes that the known, as well as the unknown, difficulties of pregnancy and birth in space make the practice of birth control in some form completely necessary. The alternative would seem to be all-male or all-female crews. (I suspect that neither gender would be in favor of this sort of arrangement, nor would it be healthy for them.)

Near the end of the first season Gene received a letter from a viewer who wanted to know why STAR TREK showed so many human-appearing aliens. In part, Gene replied:

WE DEPICT MANY HUMANOID ALIENS BE-CAUSE WE (ALONG WITH CAL TECH STUDIES AND OTHERS) DO BELIEVE PARALLEL EVOLU-TION IS A DISTINCT PROBABILITY. NATURAL LAWS UNDOUBTEDLY GOVERN LIFE DEVELOP-MENT JUST AS OTHER NATURAL LAWS GOV-ERN TIME, SPACE, AND ATOMS.

The term "human" refers to descendants from Earth. All other "human-appearing" aliens are called "humanoids"— Vulcans are humanoids. Frankly, STAR TREK has no choice but to use humanoid aliens. The actors playing these humanoids are human. It's the same old story. You have to use what's available. This is also why the *Enterprise* confines most of her travels to Class M worlds, those closely approximating the size and conditions of Earth.

YES, WE DO HOPE TO SHOW RADICALLY DIF-FERENT LIFE FORMS IN FUTURE EPISODES. IN

---

* Medical science at present states that to go beyond this point would risk interfering with metabolic cycles fundamental to the life-form itself.

OUR FIRST TWO SEASONS WE HAD SO MANY PROBLEMS TO SOLVE JUST USING HUMANOIDS THAT WE HAD LITTLE TIME, MONEY, AND CREATIVE ENERGY LEFT OVER. UNFORTUNATELY, WE HAVE TO DO THESE THINGS WITHIN THE LIMITS OF OUR BUDGETS. WE ARE ALSO LIMITED BY THE AMOUNT OF TIME WE CAN TAKE TO MAKE UP SOMEONE AS A RADICALLY DIFFERENT ALIEN, OR TO CREATE THE SPECIAL COSTUME NEEDED. PROBABLY THE ONLY WAY WE WILL BE ABLE TO DO IT IS BY CHEATING A LITTLE.

SUPPOSE WE ARE DOING A STORY ABOUT A PLANET WITH LITTLE FURRY THREE-FOOT-TALL WIDE ROUND THINGS WITH BIG GORGEOUS PLUMAGE. THE PRACTICALITIES OF TV MEAN WE WILL HARDLY BE ABLE TO GO TO THAT PLANET. WE SIMPLY DON'T HAVE ENOUGH MAKEUP MEN AVAILABLE TO CREATE A PLANET FULL OF THOSE CREATURES. WE CAN'T EVEN AFFORD TO PURCHASE ALL THE FEATHERS THAT WOULD BE REQUIRED! WHAT WE WILL PROBABLY DO IS INVENT SOME REASON FOR JUST *ONE* SUCH CREATURE TO COME ABOARD OUR VESSEL.

THE TRICK OF DRAMA, OF COURSE, IS TO CREATE THE ILLUSION THAT SUCH THINGS DO EXIST—TO ALMOST BE ABLE TO SEE THEM IN YOUR MIND'S EYE. AS THIS FURRY THING COMES ABOARD AND TALKS ABOUT HIS PLANET, IN THE MIND'S EYE OF THE AUDIENCE WE CAN CREATE A PLANET FULL OF THESE CREATURES ALMOST AS IF THEY HAD ACTUALLY BEEN SEEN. IN RADIO YOU CREATE MENTAL IMAGES IN THE MINDS OF THE LISTENER WITH SOMETHING AS SIMPLE AS THE SLAMMING OF A DOOR. TV, WITHIN ITS LIMITATIONS, HAS TO DO ESSENTIALLY THE SAME THING.

STAR TREK is probably inaccurate in the way it portrays the crew members aboard the *Enterprise*. If we project humanity three centuries ahead, we might find humanity has undergone some rather drastic changes. STAR TREK'S characters, however, are played essentially as 20th century men, rather than 23rd century men. This is another compromise forced by the needs of television. If STAR TREK had portrayed man's nature as significantly changed, the audience might have had great difficulty in identifying with them.

Perhaps this is also an expression of Gene's own hope for the future: Man won't allow himself to change that much. Perhaps he will reach a point where he will begin to resist the dehumanizing influences that rob him of his individuality. Perhaps he will resist attempts to make him nothing more than a cell of a larger organism. Perhaps he will even risk a certain amount of friction between himself and his fellow man, because he will realize different ideas and attitudes are precious and stimulating differences. It's quite possible that man of the future, if he realizes the danger in time, may be much more individualistic than man of today. (I must admit I rather like the idea. At least it's an optimistic analysis of man's future.)

Although the *Enterprise* is a military vessel, its organization is only semimilitary. The "enlisted men" category does not exist. STAR TREK goes on the assumption that every man and woman aboard the U.S.S. *Enterprise* is the equivalent of a qualified astronaut, therefore an officer.

Reference is occasionally made to "the crew," in which case it is a generalized statement meant to include everyone aboard the ship. A reference to "senior officers" would refer to a much smaller, specific group of the crew members.

RANK, WHEN PROPERLY USED, CAN BE A PLEASANT WAY OF ACKNOWLEDGING SENIORITY—OF SHOWING RESPECT TO A MAN, NOT ONLY FOR HIS LENGTH OF TIME IN SERVICE, BUT ALSO THE REPUTATION ACHIEVED IN HIS FIELD OR SPECIAL ABILITY. I THINK MAN WILL ALWAYS WANT THIS TYPE OF THING. IN OUR OPTIMISTIC ERA, ON OUR

STARSHIPS, WE ENJOY THE USE OF THESE COURTESIES. IF THE CREWMEN STAND WHEN OUR CAPTAIN ENTERS A ROOM, IT IS NOT BECAUSE THEY ARE BEING SUBSERVIENT. THEY ARE, IN EFFECT, SAYING, "HERE IS A MAN WHO HAS ACHIEVED GREAT THINGS, HAS BEEN AWARDED HIGH HONORS, AND HAS EARNED HIGH ACCLAIM." WHAT A PLEASANT WAY TO SAY, WHEN HE COMES IN, "CONGRATULATIONS." AND THIS IS, IN ESSENCE, WHAT IT AMOUNTS TO. AND YOU NEED NOT BE MILITARY TO DO IT. YOU AND I DO THIS WHEN OUR FATHERS ENTER THE ROOM, OR WHEN WE APPLAUD THE APPEARANCE OF AN ADMIRED STATESMAN.

However, many of the traditions, titles, and much of the terminology of the past have been maintained. Just as our Navy today has leftovers from the time of Drake.

The crew operates at all times in a shirt-sleeve, controlled-gravity environment, thanks to the life support systems aboard ship. These life support systems not only control the physical environment necessary for human life; they also play an important role in the psychological environment equally necessary to human life.

Science tells us man must have the proper balance between physical and psychological surroundings if he is to survive in space. His mental health is as important as his physical health. To this end, the life support systems are programmed for several functions that are purely psychological. For instance, subliminal sounds (below the conscious level of awareness) are continually broadcast throughout the ship. These sounds, directed to the subconscious level, include bird calls, the sound of falling water, the rustle of wind through the trees, and other sounds native to the crewman's home planet. He is not consciously aware he is hearing these sounds, but he is affected by them nonetheless. This helps prevent him from getting too lonely, even subconsciously, for his homeland.

Additionally, familiar odors are introduced into the environmental systems. The crew can actually smell the earth, fresh air, and even that distinctive smell that water has, in connection with trees and things that grow and are alive. This process is very subtle, but its impact is immensely significant all the same. The harmonious blending of colors used in the various rooms and corridors throughout the ship is yet another extension of this principle. These methods and techniques are being experimented with today aboard our Polaris submarines, where men are in confined areas for long periods of time. Even today science understands the importance of the proper environment in which man must work. Man's surroundings must be more than merely functional . . . they must be pleasant as well.

Relating to this (and referred to in several STAR TREK episodes) is the use of a "psychological profile." The implication is that everyone, even the Captain, continually undergoes a form of psychological testing. The purpose is to detect any aberrations that might be developing within the individual and to take the appropriate action, whether it be treatment or transfer. Science today realizes the importance of a continual monitoring program designed to maintain the highest level of mental fitness. STAR TREK merely applies the same principle.

WE TRY TO CREATE ABOARD THE STARSHIP, AS NEARLY AS POSSIBLE, THE NEEDS MAN HAS DEVELOPED FROM LIVING SO MANY CENTURIES ON EARTH. THERE ARE MANY SUBTLE EXAMPLES OF THIS. FOR INSTANCE, MAN HAS LIVED SO MANY THOUSANDS OF CENTURIES ON A DAY-NIGHT ROUTINE THAT ON OUR STARSHIP WE DECIDED WE WOULD DARKEN THE CORRIDORS SLIGHTLY FOR EIGHT OUT OF EVERY TWENTY-FOUR HOURS. YOU HAVE THE FEELING NIGHT HAS COME AND THEN LATER DAWN. WE MAINTAIN THERE IS A CLOCK INSIDE US THAT EVEN IN STAR TREK'S TIME WE WOULDN'T WANT TO DISTURB. EVEN IF WE COULD, IT'S A PLEASANT CLOCK—WHY MESS AROUND WITH IT? IT IS PARTLY THE REASON WHY MAN NEEDS A FEELING EVE-

NING HAS COME, THAT FOR SOME OF US THE
DAY'S DUTY IS OVER AND IT'S TIME TO REST.
SO LET US ADJOURN TO THE RECREATION
ROOM AND HAVE A DRINK AND LISTEN TO
MR. SPOCK PLAY HIS WEIRD VULCAN HARP.

Requirements were also established for clothing worn by
the crew:

### CLOTHING AND RELATED GEAR

Except in exceptional circumstances necessary to story,
our crew is always dressed in "Standard Uniform" or
"Dress Uniform." Unless an important story point, let us
provide "fatigues" and leisure wear as our budget permits.

Never have members of the crew putting things into
pockets; there are no pockets. When equipment is
needed, it is attached to special belts (as in the case of
the communicator and phaser).

We do not have space suits for hostile planet surfaces.
These may be obtained for special scripts, but keep in
mind that we generally restrict our missions to Class M
planets (approximating Earth conditions).

Excerpt from STAR TREK Guide

One subject STAR TREK avoids completely is the problem
of aging in space.

Accepted theory now is that any spaceship traveling at any
significant fraction of the speed of light would encounter
some frightening problems regarding the relative passage of
time on Earth and on the spaceship. You could go from
Earth to some distant star, and on your return find you'd
aged only one year, while your contemporaries were dead
and gone. Presumably, if you went at faster-than-light
speeds, when you got back to Earth you might meet your
great-great-grandchildren. STAR TREK avoids this problem entirely. On this point the show is inaccurate, and of necessity it
must be so, in order to entertain. STAR TREK stays scientifically accurate in those things that have true meaning. It stays

dramatically accurate in those things that create action, adventure, fun, entertainment, and thought-provoking statements. (The show cannot constantly be all things to all men; otherwise it would be giving scientific papers every week, instead of entertaining millions of viewers.)

In the original format Kirk's age was established as appearing to be in the early thirties. Gene is not at all sure, though, that the life span of people in STAR TREK's century may not be 130 years.

The way medical science is progressing today, it seems reasonable to assume men will live longer. They will remain young and virile for a longer period of time. It wasn't too many years ago that if you were a man of forty-six, you should be dead. If you weren't dead at forty-six, you probably would be trying to retire. Today forty-six-year-old men are riding surfboards, motorcycles, and perhaps next week are planning to take up sky diving.

Three hundred years from now, who knows?

# Chapter 4

## The Ship's Captain

STAR TREK IS BLESSED WITH THE FINEST GROUP OF PROFESSIONAL ACTORS I'VE EVER WORKED WITH. I'LL NEVER FORGET BILL SHATNER COMING INTO MY OFFICE HOLDING A COPY OF OUR FIRST SCRIPT, SAYING HE HAD SOME SUGGESTIONS. I WAS UNDERSTANDABLY APPREHENSIVE—I HAD NEVER WORKED WITH BILL BEFORE AND WONDERED IF THIS WOULD BE AN EGO-CENTERED LIST OF SELFISH DEMANDS. I WAS DELIGHTED, PLEASED, THEN ADMIRING, WHEN HIS OBSERVATIONS TURNED OUT TO BE SHREWD DRAMATIC POINTS WHICH IMPROVED THE WHOLE STORY IMMEASURABLY.

LEONARD NIMOY, SAME COMMENTS. ALTHOUGH I CREATED THE BASIC SPOCK, THE FINAL FLESHING OUT OF THE CHARACTER WAS A JOINT ENDEAVOR IN WHICH LEONARD AND I WORKED AS CO-CREATORS. NIMOY IS ACTUALLY A BIT LIKE SPOCK IN REAL LIFE; HE'S A DIGNIFIED GENTLEMAN WITH SOCIAL ATTITUDES AND PHILOSOPHIES WHICH I ADMIRE GREATLY. ONE DAY LEONARD (LIKE SHATNER) WILL ALMOST CERTAINLY BECOME A TOP FILM DIRECTOR OR PRODUCER.

DE FOREST KELLEY, LONG A CLOSE FRIEND, IS ONE OF THE MOST ACCOMPLISHED ACTORS I'VE EVER KNOWN. FOR YEARS I WAS MYSTIFIED TO SEE THE INDUSTRY USING ONLY A SMALL PART OF HIS ENORMOUS RANGE AND TALENT. ONE OF MY PRINCIPAL DELIGHTS IN STAR TREK HAS BEEN THE OPPORTUNITY TO

SHOWCASE THAT TALENT IN A SMALL WAY, KNOWING THAT NOW HIS CAREER CAN ONLY ZOOM UPWARD. HE'LL WIN AN OSCAR ONE DAY AND I HOPE I CAN BE THERE APPLAUDING WHEN HE PICKS IT UP.

I COULD SPEAK FOR A HALF HOUR ON THE TALENTS AND MY PERSONAL ADMIRATION FOR EACH OF THE OTHERS TOO. STAR TREK, AMONG ALL TELEVISION SHOWS, IS UNIQUE IN THIS COLLECTION OF TALENT, OF WHICH, WITHOUT THE ALL TOO USUAL EXCEPTION, EVERY ONE OF THEM IS AN ADMIRABLE GENTLEMAN OR A FINE LADY. THE GROUP HAS BECOME A "ONCE IN A LIFETIME" COLLECTION OF FRIENDS.

Gene Roddenberry

Every ship must have a man at the helm. STAR TREK's man is James T. Kirk, serial number SC 937-0176 CEC. He holds the service rank of Captain, his official position is Starship Commander, and his current assignment is the U.S.S. *Enterprise*.

The normal mission of a starship places the vessel out of communication with Earth and Star Fleet Base for long periods of time. A starship captain therefore has unusually broad powers over both the lives and welfare of his crew, as well as extensive jurisdiction over people and activities encountered during the course of the vessel's mission. He also functions as an Earth ambassador both to known alien societies in his sector of the galaxy. The loneliness and the enormous responsibilities of this position place an extreme burden on the man who holds it. Only an extraordinary man can rise to this position.

Captain Kirk is such a man. He appears to be about thirty-four years old and was born in a small town in the State of Iowa. He entered the Space Academy as a midshipman at the age of seventeen, the minimum age allowed. He attended the Academy and finished in the top five percent. Kirk rose very rapidly through the ranks and received his first command (the equivalent of a destroyer-class spaceship) while still quite young.

Kirk has been in command of the *Enterprise* for more than four years and was the youngest Academy graduate ever to have been assigned as a Starship Command Captain.

Although Kirk has never been married, he does have relatives back on Earth. His father is dead, but his mother is still living, as is a nephew. Kirk's only brother, Sam, and Sam's wife were killed in a planetary disaster.

James T. Kirk is an idealist, rather sensitive, with a strong, complex personality. Constantly on trial within himself, he feels acutely the responsibility of his position and is therefore fully capable of letting the worry and the frustration lead him into error. Ignoring the fact that he is also capable of fatigue, Kirk is often inclined to push himself beyond human limits. When he must give in to fatigue, he then condemns himself because he is not superhuman. The crew respect him, some almost to the point of adoration. High regard for their Captain notwithstanding, no senior officer aboard is fearful of using his own intelligence in questioning Kirk's orders, and will be strongly articulate up to the point that Kirk signifies his decision has been made. The young Captain is definitely a man of decision and decisive action.

In many respects Kirk resembles the captain of an 18th century ship of the line—Captain Horatio Hornblower. Anyone familiar with C. S. Forrester's famous Hornblower series will quickly recognize similarities in the personalities of both men. It should not be surprising to learn that Gene Roddenberry rates Captain Horatio Hornblower as one of the all-time great adventure characters in fiction.

Recognizing the value of specialists aboard, Kirk often solicits information and estimates from his principal division officers before making his decision. In the final analysis, however, Kirk will make the decision. He is a veteran of hundreds of planet landings and space emergencies. He has a broad and highly mature perspective toward aliens, their customs and civilizations (however strange or repugnant they may seem when measured against Earth standards).

The loneliness of command is intensified for Kirk by his continuing struggle within himself to preserve in the eyes of his crew the image he feels necessary. Because he sets impossibly high standards for himself, there are few aboard ship with whom he can talk without fear of showing what he fears may be construed as a weakness. He has therefore placed himself in a form of self-imposed exile from the rest of the crew.

There are only two people to whom Kirk allows himself to unbend at all. One is Mr. Spock. The Science Officer's friendship with the Captain is based on logic, high mutual respect, and his strong Vulcan loyalty to a commander. When a Vulcan takes an oath, it would be against all honor and tradition to break it, and death would be preferable. (If such a thing were to happen, it would seem like the "logical" thing to do.)

Kirk must necessarily confide in the ship's surgeon, Dr. McCoy, who has a medical responsibility constantly to be aware of the state of the Captain's mind, emotions, and physical body. The relationship that exists between Kirk and McCoy is quite different from that which exists between Kirk and Spock. The Captain and the Doctor are actually close friends, in the true sense of the word. Although Spock feels the same way, for a Vulcan to admit such emotion would be a declaration of weakness.

Long ago Captain Kirk consciously ruled out any possibility of any romantic interest while aboard the ship. It is an involvement he feels he simply could never risk. In a very real sense he is "married" to his ship and his responsibilities as Captain of her.

There have been three significant romances in Kirk's past, prior to his assuming Starship Command. While still a midshipman at the Academy, he became intensely involved with a young woman named Ruth. As often happens in the military service, he went into the Space Service and then somehow didn't manage to get back in time, and Ruth married someone else.

The second woman was a Lieutenant Commander Areel Shaw. Although their relationship had meant a great deal to them both, differences in life philosophy caused a breakup, and they subsequently went separate ways.

The third woman was a Dr. Janet Wallace. She and Kirk were very much drawn to each other and were seriously discussing marriage. Unfortunately, Janet was as dedicated to science as Kirk was to the Space Service. She could not give up her scientific career, and Kirk would not resign from the Space Service. It was an impasse that could not be resolved.

The impossibility of a romantic interest aboard ship does not necessarily preclude enjoyments ashore. Away from the confines of self-imposed discipline, Kirk is inclined to play pretty hard, almost compulsively so. It is at least a partial release from the severe regimen he imposes upon himself while aboard ship.

Kirk has very few recreational outlets to compensate for the loneliness of command. He does play chess with Spock and finds the games stimulating. He forces himself to be athletic, spends much leisure time working out in the gym. He also has quite an extensive library of books in his quarters and derives a great deal of pleasure from reading classics in literature.

A legend is beginning to grow about Captain Kirk within the Star Fleet Service. Certainly his crew holds him in a certain amount of awe, and with justifiable reason. Not only is he the youngest captain in the service—Kirk has distinguished himself far beyond his years in action both in space and on strange worlds. His commendations include Palm Leaf of Axanar Peace Mission; Grankite Order of Tactic, Class of Excellence; Prentaries Ribbon of Commendation, Classes First and Second. His Awards of Valor include the Medal of Honor; Silver Palm, with Cluster. Star Fleet Citation for Gallantry; Karagite Order of Heroism; three times wounded, honor roll. Inwardly, Kirk is pleased with his record of achievements, but outwardly dismisses them as being of no consequence.

Captain Kirk is expertly portrayed by handsome thirty-eight-year-old William Shatner. The Canadian-born actor attended McGill University, where he was particularly active in campus theatrical productions. During his senior year Shatner produced the school's nationally famous campus variety show. He spent his summer vacations throughout his college days acting with a summer stock company, The Mount Royal Playhouse.

When he was graduated in 1952 with a B.A., he was already a well-known voice on Canadian airwaves, having done numerous shows to augment his experience. The next phase found him working with the National Repertory Theater of Ottawa, where he earned untold dollars' worth of experience, although his actual income was roughly thirty-one Canadian dollars a week.

Bill Shatner reacts rather badly when hearing the two words "fruit salad."

Shatner isn't really peculiar. It's just that the very mention of fruit salad takes him back several years when he was a fledgling actor with the Repertory Theater. In order to have a roof over his head and clean clothes to wear, Shatner had to economize somewhere. He did it in his selection of food.

He says, "Daily, and sometimes twice a day, I shelled out twenty-seven cents for a plate of fruit salad at Kresge's lunch counter in Ottawa. It helped make my budget work, but to this day I not only can't bear the sight of the stuff—I react somewhat violently at its very mention."

None of Shatner's fellow actors in the repertory company fared much better financially. "They even had to make their own booze. I was their official taster—which is pretty funny, as I'm a nondrinker. When I keeled over from the mixture, they knew it was ready for imbibing."

To many, Shatner's early days of struggle might sound somewhat romantic. Shatner says, "They were hell. I got through them because in front of me was a dream. I hoped to become as fine an actor as Laurence Olivier."

Shatner took a giant step forward when he joined the famous Stratford, Ontario, Shakespeare Festival as an understudy. He started with walk-on and bit parts and eventually graduated to co-starring roles in *The Merchant of Venice*, *Henry V*, and others. That year he won the "Most Promising Actor" award.

Shorly thereafter, Shatner opened to rave reviews in New York in *Tamburlaine*. He was immediately offered a seven-year contract by 20th Century-Fox at $500 a week. He turned it down and returned to star in a TV play in Toronto

—a play he had written. ("I still had the idealistic dream of being an Olivier-type star. I didn't want to be a Hollywood actor.")

During rehearsals he met a young Canadian actress, Gloria Rand. "Rehearsing a scene with Gloria called for a long kiss, and by the time it was over, I knew this was the girl for me," he recalls happily. Several months later they were married and spent their honeymoon in Scotland, where Shatner played a feature role in the Edinburgh Festival production of *Henry V*.

Returning to New York, Shatner became one of live TV's busiest actors, starring in such important dramatic shows as Goodyear Playhouse, Philco Playhouse, Studio One, Circle Theater, and Omnibus. A co-starring role with veteran actor Ralph Bellamy in a two-part production of "The Defenders" led to his movie debut in *The Brothers Karamazov*. He was headlined with such distinguished actors as Yul Brynner, Maria Schell, Claire Bloom, and Lee J. Cobb.

Hollywood film-making also offered him the chance to act in Westerns, and the Shakespearean-trained Shatner learned to rope, shoot, and ride bareback.

Returning to New York for a memorable role in "No Deadly Medicine" on Studio One, Shatner was offered the starring role in the Broadway production of *The World of Suzie Wong*, a hit that ran for two years and garnered even more critical acclaim for him. He followed this with *A Shot in the Dark*, in which he co-starred with Julie Harris, and then moved on to the hit comedy *L'Idiote*, which ran for over a year.

At this point Shatner came to a decision. "Time enough after I achieved financial security to go back to the classics and be an artist. I returned to Hollywood after 'Suzie' and worked in many films and television series, always trying to have integrity about the roles I chose. But even that went by the board after a while. In order to survive, I had to work in anything that would pay me. Once I made that decision, I stuck to it. To everyone's surprise, I turned down starring roles in *Romeo and Juliet* and *King John* at Stratford, just to remain in Hollywood and keep my name in front of the Hierarchy.

"When I say I decided it was time to grow up, I mean I recognized the fact that great parts come rarely to an actor. Most of the time it's slugging away in run-of-the-mill endeavors. You do the best you can with all your resources. You work to make a living and to support your family."

When STAR TREK was offered to Shatner, he was intrigued with the challenges both in the concept and in his lead role. "I could have done equally well financially had I decided not to do a TV series in favor of guest shots and movies. But I believed in the potential of this show. We have the opportunity to do something truly worthwhile. Science fiction can be an art form. Ray Bradbury has proved this."

Shatner is also a writer and finds the combination valuable.

I've learned a great deal about acting from writing. An actor interprets a writer's work just as a musician interprets a composer's work. The criterion of a good actor is how well he interprets the work of the writer. Even the writer may not know exactly what he has written—this is the nebulous area in which the actor works.

I get up at six A.M. and seldom get home before nine or ten P.M. But I'm having a ball. Usually after some three or four months of such a schedule, performers carrying a heavy load get tired. But I'm still enthusiastic. I'm still having fun.

When I'm having fun, I know that all the elements that make up the show—the producer, the director, the players, the scripts—are working well. I hope this comes across on the screen. I hope STAR TREK can be as exciting to the audience as it is to me.

A television star's time is not always his own.

There are increasing demands on my time. I have spent maybe five lunch hours in which I haven't worked in some fashion or other, particularly publicity interviews. I enjoy the interview; I prefer to talk about other things than myself, but this is part of the job, part of the publicity attached to it. I feel after many years as an actor that this series is a very successful thing, and I want to be very sure, very careful that I do as much to grasp this opportunity as I can.

Shatner often offers suggestions on the set during shooting.

I know my parts, and I know what I am capable of in many areas. I have to be very careful that I don't alienate the other people. I am in the peculiar position of being the star of the show, and many of the things that go on reflect directly on me. So if something is bad, I am involved, and it's for me to correct it if I can.

Now, if I were to take advantage of this, there would be a great deal of trouble, but there has never been any difficulty. Far from it, we all bend over backwards to work together. In many instances I have been able to help in the rewriting of the script.

I sometimes have an idea that a director can use, and we have become so friendly with the directors that it has become a marvelous give-and-take relationship. In television the star of the series has much more power, to use a bad term, than is ordinarily given an actor. It's equivalent, I would think, to the power that a star—a big star —in a film has, and it takes a very strong, powerful director to curb that star. That power can corrupt, I am sure, but at this point I don't feel it has. If it does happen, I hope someone stops me fast.

And what if STAR TREK is a huge five-year TV hit?

That would suit me fine. It's what I've worked for. Although I've compromised my dreams, I haven't given them up entirely. If STAR TREK is a long-running success, it will mean in five or six years I can go back to the stage and do what I choose. If the series isn't successful, I'll just begin slugging it out again. They say fruit salad is healthy for a fellow.

Chapter 5

## Mr. Spock

The phenomenon that is Mr. Spock ranks unique in the annals of television.

Until the advent of STAR TREK, the viewing audience had never been confronted with a series "regular" in the form of an alien. Especially one with alien features which add up to a decidedly satanic appearance.

Yet the public reaction to STAR TREK's green-blooded Vulcan has been astounding.

"I Grok Spock" buttons are in evidence everywhere. Mr. Spock Fan Clubs have mushroomed in cities and towns all across the country. The sheer weight of Spock fan mail received each week is staggering. Unless extreme measures are taken beforehand, Leonard (Mr. Spock) Nimoy's public appearances rapidly assume the proportions of a full-scale riot.

In a society that preaches conformity, a society in which being "different" is frowned upon, this success story is remarkable.

I FRANKLY NEVER EVEN THOUGHT ABOUT SPOCK'S BACKGROUND WHEN I FIRST CREATED THE CHARACTER. ALL I WANTED AT FIRST WAS POINTED EARS AND A FAINTLY SATANIC LOOK. ONLY AFTER THE SERIES WAS WELL UNDER WAY DID I REALIZE THAT WE WOULD NECESSARILY HAVE TO TALK ABOUT HIS HOME PLANET. AT THAT POINT I BEGAN TO WORK BACKWARDS IN AN ATTEMPT TO JUSTIFY WHAT I HAD CREATED. I DECIDED THAT BECAUSE HE HAD LARGE EARS, ONE OF THE POSSIBLE REASONS FOR THIS IS AN ATMOSPHERE THAT IS THINNER THAN EARTH'S. HAVING ESTABLISHED CERTAIN SUPERHUMAN CHARACTERISTICS, I HAD TO WORK

BACKWARDS ON THAT, TOO. I DECIDED THE
REASON FOR HIS GREATER STRENGTH IS THAT
HIS PLANET WOULD HAVE TO BE SLIGHTLY
LARGER THAN EARTH, WITH A GREATER
GRAVITY, THUS REQUIRING GREATER
STRENGTH. AND SO BY WORKING BACK-
WARDS, SPOCK'S BACKGROUND SLOWLY DE-
VELOPED. BY NOW IT'S PRETTY EXTENSIVE,
AND AN AMAZING ASSORTMENT OF PEOPLE
HAVE CONTRIBUTED TO IT.

Mr. Spock is the ship's Science Officer, in charge of all
scientific departments aboard the *Enterprise*. As such, he is
the ship's number two ranking officer. His bridge position is
at the Library-Computer Station, which he operates with uncanny skill. He can extract and interpret complex information with great rapidity and can even read memory bank
"bleeps" direct, without the voice-translation needed by his
fellow crew members (something like "reading" the noise
made by a teletype machine!).

Spock is the product of an interplanetary marriage between
his mother, a native of Earth, and his father, a native of the
planet Vulcan. While such marriages are not unknown, they
are nonetheless quite rare, as the personalities of Vulcans and
Terrans are not normally compatible.

He has inherited characteristics from both parents, but his
Vulcan side is definitely the stronger, and he thinks of himself
as a Vulcan.

The alien influence is most obviously represented by his
stoic temperament, upswept eyebrows, mildly slanted eyes,
yellowish complexion, and somewhat enlarged, pointed ears.
His hair style is in the Vulcan mode.

Spock's physical characteristics are the evolutionary result
of the environmental conditions on planet Vulcan. It has a
hot, dry climate, a relatively small amount of surface water,
and an exceptionally thin atmosphere. The enlarged, pointed
ears result from the need to "cup" the tenuous sound waves
more efficiently in the thin atmosphere.

All of Spock's sensory organs are slightly better-developed
than those of Terrans. He can withstand higher tempera-

tures, go for longer periods of time without water, and can tolerate a higher level of pain. He can also exercise complete voluntary control over his consciousness and over pain. Control is so total that, at the extreme level, his physical appearance would closely resemble the cataleptic state.

A basic tenet of the Vulcan philosophy is nonviolence. Vulcans do not believe in killing in any form. They may hunt for the skill involved in tracking but eons ago ceased to kill the animal they are tracking. As a vegetarian, the mere idea of eating animal carcasses, cooked or not, is revolting to Spock. Even his vegetable diet is limited to the simplest of vegetable life forms.

Spock himself admits, however, that Vulcans are not totally incapable of killing. If given sufficient reason, a Vulcan will kill quite efficiently, but it must be a very logical reason. Normally, however, they will kill only in self-defense, and then only after first having expended all other means available to avoid it. It is a matter of record that Vulcans in the Space Service must occasionally be ordered to kill, if they do not think the situation logically justifies it.

This does not mean that Spock will not resort to physical violence of a lesser degree, again if logical. He has become quite famous for the "Spock Pinch." Applied with the fingers of his right hand to the area on the top of the right shoulder, near the base of the neck, it blocks blood and nerve responses to the brain and produces instant unconsciousness.

Spock's stoic temperament, his refusal to say anything or do anything not based solely on logic, is also a reflection of his Vulcan heritage. Complete adherence to logic is the primary motivating factor in the Vulcan mental process. Of necessity, complete suppression of emotions is required, lest logic be influenced in any way.

Over a period of many centuries, the Vulcans have practiced both total concentration and complete suppression of emotions. From the time of his birth, a Vulcan child is taught that to show emotion is highly improper, that it is considered an extreme breach of good taste.

The reason for suppressing emotions should be obvious. Emotion gets in the way of order and tranquility. It is undeniably true that emotion has killed more people on Earth than any other cause. Vulcans long ago concluded that emotion was dangerous, set about to repress it and replace it with logic. Century after century, through practice and custom, they repressed emotion until they became almost incapable of it. Logic became breath, sensation, as uplifting and delightful as the emotion it replaced.

In many ways logic made the planet Vulcan superior to Earth. Its last ten centuries have been much more peaceful than Earth's past eras.*

Because of his mother's origin, however, Spock does have a human side to his personality. A human side with emotions. The result is a continual struggle within himself to suppress his feelings. But his Vulcan half is normally in control. Conditioned since childhood not only to deny but also to be ashamed of emotion, Spock thrusts feelings aside and finds a "logical" rationalization to explain it.

WHICH IS ONE OF THE REASONS WHY SPOCK IS AN INTERESTING CHARACTER: THE TURMOIL AND CONFLICT WITHIN. AS HALF-HUMAN AND HALF-VULCAN, HE IS CONTINUALLY AT WAR WITHIN HIMSELF. FOR SOME REASON THIS MAKES HIM PARTICULARLY DELIGHTFUL TO OUR FEMALE VIEWERS, AND OF ALL AGES. I GUESS THEY KNOW THAT SOMEWHERE INSIDE HIM THERE IS A STRONG, EMOTIONAL EARTH MAN TRYING TO COME OUT. AND THEY WOULD LOVE TO HELP.

There is a price that the Vulcans pay for their repression of emotion. At certain times in their lives the Vulcan male is overcome with the mating urge. (It is very much like a "rutting season.") Having withheld emotion for so long, they must succumb to a period of time sufficient to get it totally

---

* STAR TREK's third season will emphasize the Vulcan philosophy of universal brotherhood via an unusually shaped medallion Mr. Spock will receive from "home" and begin to wear. Its design reflects the Vulcan belief that the greatest joy in all creation is in the infinite ways that infinitely diverse things can join together to create meaning and beauty.

out of their systems. Their behavior is based on a combination of Vulcan law, tradition, and instinct. When the time comes, in that time and in that place, it is entirely logical and entirely proper.

The specific time interval between these occurrences varies from male to male and by other circumstances. The average is about once every seven Earth years when a Vulcan is separated from his people as is Spock, more often if living among his own kind. It is possible that Spock might not follow the usual Vulcan pattern, since he has the human half influencing him as well.

Another unique Vulcan ability exhibited by Spock is a type of ESP that the Vulcans refer to as "mind-melding." He can merge his mind with that of another intelligence and read its thoughts. While he will use this ability when circumstances make it absolutely necessary, he dislikes doing so because the process requires emotional contact as well, thus robbing him of his stoic mask and revealing too much of his inner self. The physical cost of this process is also quite high.

Thus, while Spock is classified as a Vulcan, he is in reality neither Vulcan nor Terran. He is biologically, emotionally, and even intellectually a half-breed.

Mr. Spock's father, Sarek, is a Vulcan ambassador and prior to entering the diplomatic service was a highly esteemed physicist on Vulcan. Sarek's father, too, was a Vulcan ambassador, and Spock therefore has a distinguished Vulcan family heritage behind him. Sarek is 102 years old, or about middle-aged, in terms of Vulcan years (the Vulcan life span is about 250 years).

Amanda, Spock's mother, was a schoolteacher when she met and married Sarek. She is 58, also about middle-aged, in terms of Earth years, and has been Sarek's only wife. (Dorothy Fontana, our former Story Consultant, chose the name Amanda because it means "worthy of being loved," and Amanda must have been, for a Vulcan, who finds it almost impossible to express the emotion of love, to marry her.)

Tradition bound, Sarek had logically expected Spock to follow in his footsteps, first by going to the Vulcan Science Academy, and after that, by serving his race as a scientist. Spock also wanted to be a Vulcan scientist, but as he grew older, he had begun to realize the full impact of his mixed background. A half-Vulcan half-Terran was out of place on either Vulcan or Earth (something his father, a full Vulcan, could not understand). This realization was what led him into the Space Service. Because of its makeup, the Service was likely to accept him on the basis of his talent and ability and ignore his mixed parentage. Thus, within his own frame of reference, Spock's decision was logical.

Spock enrolled in the Space Academy and, following his graduation eight years later, entered the Space Service. In doing so, he ran completely counter to his father's sense of logic and to Vulcan tradition. this act alienated Sarek and Spock, and for 18 years they did not speak as father and son. The heavy weight of Vulcan tradition had created a barrier through which neither could pass.

It was only after both father and son were thrown together in a desperate situation involving the life or death of Sarek that the barrier was broken. There is at last a measure of understanding between them, and Sarek now comprehends the terrible loneliness of the world in which his half-Vulcan son must dwell.

Mr. Spock has served aboard the U.S.S. *Enterprise* for 13 years, the first nine of them under Captain Christopher Pike, the last four under Captain James Kirk. Spock is intensely loyal to Kirk and friendship exists between them, although the Science Officer would be quick to deny any "affection." He "logically" contends that his interest in Kirk is based solely on the fact that Kirk is an unusually good commander and the odds are against getting a better replacement.

His relationship with the Captain, as is his relationship with all other persons on board, is strictly formal. He never calls the Captain by his first name, except when placed under extreme emotional stress. He usually addresses Kirk as "Captain" or "Sir." He never calls the Doctor anything but "Doctor," or "Dr. McCoy." Even the Doctor's nurse, Miss Christine Chapel (whom he knows to be in love with him), is always addressed as "Nurse," or "Miss Chapel."

Something akin to a feud exists, on the surface, between Dr. McCoy and Mr. Spock. Superficially, Spock regards McCoy as an archaic, bumbling country doctor, usually achieving cures through sheer luck rather than applied skill. In return, McCoy regards Spock as little more than a sometimes useful piece of computer equipment. There is a continuing verbal exchange between them in which Spock attempts to penetrate the Doctor's mask of cynicism with sword strokes of logic, while McCoy attempts to reach Spock's emotional inner self with the surgically sharp barbs of a master cynic. Both are often successful in their efforts. Underneath it all, each respects the other for the talent he possesses, but there seems to be some sort of unspoken agreement between them that neither will ever openly admit this mutual respect.

Dr. McCoy regards Spock as somewhat of a medical phenomenon and is continually worried about treating him should he become ill. This concern stems from Spock's internal physiology, which is quite different from that of Terrans. His heart is located in the lower right area of his chest, approximately where the human liver would be. He has green blood, of a different composition from human blood, and a pulse rate of 242 beats per minute.

SPOCK'S BLOOD IS GREEN BECAUSE OF TRACES OF COPPER AND NICKEL WHICH OUR BLOOD DOES NOT HAVE. HOWEVER, CONCEPTION AND PREGNANCY WHEN PROPERLY PLANNED AND CONTROLLED BY TECHNICIANS OF THE HIGHLY ADVANCED VULCAN SCHOOL OF MEDICINE CAN BE BROUGHT TO FULL TERM. THERE IS ACTUALLY NO INCONSISTENCY IN HAVING A PULSE RATE OF 242 BEATS PER MINUTE AND PRACTICALLY NO BLOOD PRESSURE BY OUR STANDARDS. THE AVERAGE DIAMETER OF HIS ARTERIES IS LARGER THAN TERRANS', MORE EFFICIENT, AND THE FASTER, LOWER-PRESSURED HYDRAULIC ACTION OF HIS "SLIGHTLY DIFFERENT" HEART RESULTS IN ABOUT THE SAME VOLUME DELIVERED AS OUR SLOWER, HIGHER-PRESSURED SYSTEM.

Mr. Spock is by nature extremely precise in everything he

does. Even if forced by circumstance to state an approximation, he will try to locate any data at all that will increase the accuracy of his statement.

There are no other Vulcans aboard the *Enterprise*, and Spock's loneliness is increased by the fact that a Vulcan does not make the most interesting social company for humans. He does engage in three-dimensional chess, using the ship's computer as his opponent. Also, he sometimes plays an unusual Vulcan harp. As a computer expert, his primary interest lies in logic and abstract mathematics, and he spends a great deal of his leisure time engaged in pure research. This may be a form of escape for Spock, but it is also unquestionably a source of genuine enjoyment.

From the very earliest concepts of STAR TREK as a potential television series, Gene Roddenberry has insisted that Mr. Spock is a vital element. Not only because a science-fiction series should logically include an alien character, but also because Spock enables the series to make interesting social comments on the human race. Spock's alien perspective permits unusually barbed and interesting statements of the fallibility of both human customs and institutions. He allows us "to see ourselves as other see us."

Mr. Spock's popularity may give Leonard Nimoy immense pleasure, but the Vulcan's pointed ears very often give Leonard immense pain.

The ears are created from carefully molded, delicate pieces of rubber that fit tightly over Nimoy's own ears. But no matter how carefully they are fitted and adjusted, there is some small amount of movement when he talks and moves his head. The result is the same exquisite agony every woman has encountered from a pair of too-tight earrings.

The pain notwithstanding, Leonard was more than a little concerned in the beginning about viewer acceptance of the series. The closer the show came to its premier date, the more concerned he became that the show should be taken seriously by the viewers. Above all, he did not want to see STAR TREK classified as just another "kiddie science-fiction" serial. His concern is mirrored by the following comments:

Shortly before the show went on the air, Bill [Shatner] and I had been interviewed by a group of TV writers flown in from newspapers around the country to look over the season's new shows. And they were asking, "This is another 'Lost In Space'—right?" That was their attitude . . . some were indifferent and others openly hostile to a space show. They simply assumed that STAR TREK was going to be only a slightly more elaborate example of space hokum. Some comments were: "What's the idea of the pointed ears . . . what kind of gimmick is that?"

Bill and I had gone to great pains to explain how scientifically oriented the show was going to be, how dimensional the scripts were going to be, and how the level of writing was really going to be superior, with a minimum of dependence on action or violence and a maximum of thoughtful material. I don't know how well it went down, because a lot of them were openly skeptical.

Anyway, that was on a weekend. During the following week the group was brought out to the studio as guests. They were brought on the set, to watch us shoot the last scene of the day, after which we were supposed to break, and attend a cocktail party planned for them.

So here we are, shooting the scene, with about thirty or forty of the nation's top TV and newspaper writers watching. The scene takes place in the sick bay. I'm lying on one of the diagnostic beds, and Dr. McCoy is treating a wound in my head. The wound is oozing green blood. In rushes Captain Kirk, who says, "What happened?"

My line is, "Captain, the monster attacked me!"

We were all quite embarrassed about the situation, because, taken out of context, it would indicate the lowest level of gimmickry, space adventure, and violence. It was ridiculous, you know . . . a guy with pointed ears, bleeding green blood, and attacked by a monster! It was embarrassing and nobody found it particularly funny, but looking back on it, it was pretty hilarious.

What is the secret of Mr. Spock's success?

One of the theories advanced to explain Mr. Spock's popularity is that he's so "cool." "Cool" seems to be "in" today. Others, noting Spock's large female following, attribute his attraction to the "great animal magnetism" he seems to exude.

In discussing his strong appeal to the younger viewers, Leonard says, "I don't quite understand it all, but I suspect that the character's remote quality—a sort of loneliness because he is different from the rest of the Earthling crew—makes the kids react. I think they see some of their own feelings in his loneliness and inability to be one of the group."

How has the scientific community reacted to Mr. Spock?

In March, 1967, the National Space Club invited Leonard Nimoy to be their honored guest on an extensive tour of the Goddard Space Flight Center, followed by a dinner, attended by 1,500 club members, at which the principal speaker was Vice-President Humphrey.

Perhaps the following letter, written by Leonard upon his return from Washington, will serve as an indication:

March 28, 1967

Mr. Gene Roddenberry
Desilu Studios
780 N. Gower Street
Hollywood, California 90038

Dear Gene:

I would like to outline some of the thoughts that are still fresh in my mind resulting from a very exciting trip to Washington, where, as you know, I represented STAR TREK as a guest of honor for the National Space Club.

The trip broke down into two major areas: One was a very extensive tour through the Goddard Space Flight Center; second was the Goddard memorial dinner, which was attended by 1,500 members of the National Space Club, and at which the principal speaker was Vice-President Humphrey.

I must start by telling you that I felt somewhat ill at ease. As an actor in a TV drama, dealing with people who are involved in the reality of the space program, I had no way of knowing what the scientific community attitude toward our show would be. I was met at the airport by Mrs. Alberta Moran, who is the Executive Secretary to Dr. Clark, head of the Center, and was driven to the Sheraton Plaza Hotel where, even while checking in, I was besieged by fans with questions about the show, and specifically its future life on NBC.

The next morning my wife and I were driven to Goddard Center and, upon arriving, discovered that a major part of the population, secretaries and scientists alike, having learned that we were coming, were waiting to greet us at the front door. This was the first real taste that I had of the NASA attitude toward STAR TREK.

I do not overstate the fact when I tell you that the interest in the show is so intense that it would almost seem they feel we are a dramatization of the future of their space program, and they have completely taken us to heart—particularly since you and the rest of the production staff of STAR TREK have taken such great pains in the area of scientific detail on our show. They are, in fact, proud of the show as though in some way it represents them.

The trip through Goddard was very exciting, and I found them constantly pointing out equipment and procedural activities as they are specifically related to equipment and procedures on our show. In the communications room, for example, comments were made, such as, "This is the equivalent of the communications panel on the bridge on your ship." The lunch period was spent in the executive dining room with the top scientists and executives working at Goddard, all of whom were extremely responsive and friendly, and the two major subjects of conversation were, one, U.F.O.'s and, two, the possibility of life on other planets. On the first subject, the attitude most generally expressed was that U.F.O.'s are most probably scientifically explainable phenomena; and on the second subject, the attitude seemed to be that it would be surprising if there were no life on other planets, since there are so many solar systems and therefore, mathematically, so many possibilities.

At the reception prior to the dinner, I was introduced to John Glenn and the other men who were to sit on the dais at the dinner. They were all most cordial, many of them wanting autographs and pictures for themselves and their children.

During this time I encountered representatives of various important engineering, scientific, and electronic firms, who were in Washington specifically for this dinner, and who are providing in some way materials or information for the space program. They were most interested in the show as a vehicle through which they might promote their theories in order to popularize them and thereby gain acceptance at the real scientific level. Ion propulsion for the *Enterprise*, for example, was one of the theories most strongly put forth.

In general, there is a very strong interest in the scientific possibility as expressed by science fiction writers and STAR TREK, since these ideas stimulate the thinking of the more pragmatic scientists whose job it then becomes to implement these theories. They readily accept the need for such thinking and are, in fact, excited by it. I am very pleased to report that we have had several other invitations to other scientific installations, and these contacts should prove extremely valuable for research and promotion in the future.

In short, it was an exciting privilege to be able to represent the show in that environment.

Sincerely,

Leonard Nimoy

Leonard Nimoy finds Spock an intriguing role as well as an interesting personality. "Spock is fun to portray, because, underneath, he really does have emotions. If Spock didn't have any emotions, he wouldn't be interesting. Actually,

Spock has a considerable amount of compassion, though he won't allow himself to believe that."

The emotion-curtailed behavior that Nimoy must display as Mr. Spock has been achieved the hard way, over a considerable period of time.

When I first started as an actor, my work was over-emotional. I considered acting an opportunity to express emotions, and I took advantage of every opportunity I got. It took me a long time to discover that restraint can be admirable.

The thing that irks me is the lack of emotion trying to pass for restraint. Lack of emotion is pathological: restraint is civilized. Actors, for instance, try to be so cool that they become emotionless. Cool is an admirable trait under certain conditions, but there comes a point where you have to become human and make a choice and say, "No, I *feel* this is right—or wrong." Feelings and emotions can never and must never be replaced. We must never do away with man's humanity.

Leonard is quick to point out that he values and respects the power of the mind, and says, "We are heading into an era where calculated, cool logic is very important. The astronauts are almost computer-like, in the good sense of the word. That's necessary because science is so complex."

In preparing for his TV role, Leonard's reading habits underwent a decided change, as he normally leans toward Salinger, Steinbeck, and Shakespeare.

I started reading science fiction to get the feel of the concept and found that science fiction can be intelligent and entertaining. I also read current events about space flights, astronauts, flying saucers, and so forth. I must have looked at hundreds of pictures of these same things. As I became tuned in to these things in my daily life, they began to affect the character of Spock. He started to evolve, unconsciously.

Another thing was his speech. We had decided that his manner would be suggestive of an educated speech.

Spock probably learned English through formal instruction. To achieve this kind of speech pattern I listened to recordings of Somerset Maugham reading his own short stories.

Many people have wondered how Gene Roddenberry chose the name "Spock." It has no connection with the famed baby-book Dr. Spock, and in fact at the time Gene had not heard of him. What he wanted was a one-syllable name that sounded strong, implied strength. Spock sounded strong, so that's what he decided to use. It was not until later that someone told him about Dr. Spock.

Like most serious actors, Leonard attempts to give the character he plays more depth than a pair of pointed ears and slanted eyebrows might indicate. "I don't want to play a creature or a computer. Spock gives me a chance to say some things about the human race. Plus the fact that I'm having a ball. This is the first steady job I've had in seventeen years!"

Those jobs, while waiting for the big acting break to open up, included jerking sodas, delivering newspapers, selling vacuum cleaners, servicing vending machines, working in a pet shop, ushering in movie theaters, and driving a cab.

With no show business experience in his Boston background, Leonard decided to become an actor when he was only eight years old. That was when he played Hansel in an Elizabeth Peabody Playhouse production of *Hansel and Gretel*. He continued appearing in Playhouse productions for the next twelve years.

Leonard attended the drama school of Boston College and then, in 1949, went to Hollywood, where he enrolled in the Pasadena Playhouse. He also met a young actress, Sandra Zober, whom he married in 1954. By that time he had been drafted, and with the new Mrs. Nimoy he spent the next eighteen months in Georgia. Stationed at Fort McPherson, he was assigned to Special Services, writing, narrating, and emceeing GI shows. In his spare time he worked with the Atlanta Theater Guild. His first child, Julie, was born in Atlanta in 1955. When the second child, Adam, arrived a year later, the Nimoys were back in Los Angeles.

There, while holding down a variety of "existence" jobs, he

continued to study acting and after a while taught acting. He began to get better and better parts in such TV programs as "Rawhide," "The Virginian," "Dr. Kildare," "Outer Limits," and "Profiles in Courage." He also appeared in the movies *Seven Days in May* and Genet's *The Balcony*.

For the past six years the Nimoys and their two children have lived in a modest Mediterranean-style home in West Los Angeles. The walls are covered with modern paintings, most of them by their own friends. In the living room is a chess board which Leonard rarely uses ("I don't know enough people who are bad enough for me to play with"). He plays the guitar and sings folk songs to his own satisfaction ("If I'd kept studying, I'd now be playing bad classical guitar instead of fair folk").

Except for the Spock haircut, which he does not alter off screen, Nimoy does not look like an actor. He is a quiet, serious man, with a warm personality and a flashing smile. He wears shell-rimmed glasses, which not only correct his far-sightedness but also hide the half-shaved eyebrows necessary for the makeup process. On the set, where nicknames are commonplace, he is always addressed as Leonard, which may be something of a tribute to the dignity he brings to the character he plays.

His leisure hours are spent with his family, or in his workshop building cabinets and other furniture for his home. He enjoys reading a variety of literature and likes nearly all forms of music, from jazz to classical.

Leonard maintains that he has no trouble adjusting to the personality of Spock when the day's filming gets under way:

No, I don't find it difficult at all. To me, that's part of my craft . . . in the same way that a plumber walks into my house and in no time at all can fix a leaky faucet that has been frustrating my attempts for weeks. But that's his craft, I pay him money to do that, and I expect him to be able to do that. And if he were a fumbler and it took him hours to do it, I would probably get myself another craftsman for the job.

I am a craftsman in that sense . . . this is what I am trained to do . . . and I trained at it for a long, long time. I am supposed to be good at my craft, and that includes adopting another person's mannerisms and personality traits.

Now, on the other hand, Spock does affect me—there is no question about that. He has affected me in various ways right from the start. Not so much emotionally as philosophically, because constantly thinking for Spock ten, twelve hours a day, five days a week, and putting myself in his philosophical position all the time . . . I cannot help but become affected and eventually find myself identifying with and living through some of the philosophies that Spock speaks.

I must say, too, that before the show started my philosophies in general were pretty much what Spock talks about. I am essentially peaceful, I hate bombs and killing and war, and I am a curious guy, like Spock. But I think my philosophy has been sharpened considerably as a result of thinking for Spock. And I think, more specifically, I have become a better and perhaps more sophisticated observer of human nature, because that is Spock's nature . . . to observe human nature almost as a hobby . . . almost like, as Spock would say, "Those creatures, those fascinating creatures. . . ."

Chapter 6

## Chief Medical Officer

Dr. "Bones" McCoy is Senior Ship's Surgeon of the U.S.S. *Enterprise* and head of the Medical Department. As such, he is medically responsible for the physical and emotional health of the crew of the *Enterprise*. He also has broad medical science responsibilities in areas of space exploration.

As Senior Ship's Surgeon, "Bones" McCoy is one man who can approach Captain Kirk on the most intimate personal levels relating to the Captain's physical, mental, and emotional well being. Indeed, he has the absolute *duty* to constantly keep abreast of the Captain's condition and speak out openly to Kirk on this matter. He is probably the only person aboard who could talk back to Kirk, say something sharp or argumentative, and get away with it. Part of this stems from the relationship between himself and his Captain and part from his own crusty personality.

McCoy is something of a future-day H. L. Mencken, a very outspoken character, with more than a little cynical bite in his attitudes and observations on life. He has an acid wit which, under close scrutiny, carries more than a grain of truth about medicine, man, and society. Like most cynics, Dr. McCoy is at heart a bleeding humanist, but he attempts to hide his sensitive humanitarian feelings with the brusqueness of his personality.

Of all aboard the *Enterprise*, McCoy is the least military. He is filled with idiosyncrasies, which have become his trademark, and is regarded by the other crew members as something of an eccentric. McCoy has been put down by Kirk on occasion for speaking out in his straightforward manner. Usually the Doctor can get away with it because of his privileged medical status. Star Fleet regulations give him broad areas of responsibility, including the right to demand medical examinations of his Captain's physical and emotional fitness.

In many medical areas he can overrule Kirk's orders. In extreme emergencies he can certify the Captain as unfit for duty.

McCoy has an inbred distrust of machines, as evidenced by his loathing for the transporter system used for "beaming" personnel from the ship to planet surfaces. He often protests that he does not care to have his molecules scrambled and beamed around as if he were a mere radio message.

"Bones" is highly practical in the old general practitioner sense. He hates pills except when they are vitally needed, does not feel machines are the best way to treat people, and sincerely believes a little suffering is good for the soul and maturity of the individual. He has a great fear that computerized medicine and advanced tranquilizers and pain-killers may rob man of his individuality and his divine right to wrestle a bit with life. McCoy is a superb physician and surgeon —and often seems to be treating the wrong ailment, but usually is proved right in the end.

Dr. McCoy is 45 years old, was born in Georgia in the United States, and never wanted to be anything but a doctor. A student of the "old school," he received his medical training as a general practitioner.

He was married once, but the details are a mystery to all in the Space Service. What is known is that the marriage ended unhappily in a divorce. However, he has a twenty-one-year-old daughter named Joanna, from that marriage. McCoy has properly provided for her well-being, hears from her as often as interstellar communications permits, but his duty aboard the *Enterprise* keeps them apart. Ordinarily, a general practitioner would be of little practical value aboard a starship, but McCoy's unhappy marriage and subsequent divorce made him long for an escape from familiar and painful surroundings. He therefore plunged into intensive courses in Space Medicine and then volunteered for Star Fleet. Dr. McCoy, like many a man before him, has taken up wandering in order to get away from painful memories.

Quite attractive to the ladies, he has retained, in spite of past unhappiness, an active and healthy interest in the opposite sex and is usually something of the gallant Southern gen-

tleman in social life. (On those occasions, his Georgia accent
is most noticeable.) While outwardly he seems to have buried
his life in his work, he is nevertheless a human being capable
of needs and wants and is in reality, although somewhat gin-
gerly, searching for female companionship. He is a little
afraid of it because of the time it didn't work out.

IN A FUTURE STORY WE WILL BRING MC COY'S
DAUGHTER JOANNA ABOARD. SHE WILL BE
A LOVELY GIRL, AND CAPTAIN KIRK, OF
COURSE, IS GOING TO BE INVOLVED WITH
HER. DR. MC COY IS SUDDENLY GOING TO DIS-
COVER HE IS A FATHER VIEWING KIRK FROM
A FATHER'S PERSPECTIVE. AN INTERESTING
AND SOMETIMES ANGRY NEW MC COY-KIRK
RELATIONSHIP WILL BE SEEN.

McCoy's great interest in people and his compassion for
them account for his added role of counselor-at-large to the
crew members who consult with him on a variety of problems.

De Forest Kelley, who plays the part of Dr. McCoy, was
once described as a sinister character—because of his numerous roles on television, stage, and screen as villain.

De Forest was born in Atlanta, Georgia, where he graduated from high school at the age of sixteen. At seventeen he
made his first trip outside the state, visiting an uncle in Long
Beach, California. He went for two weeks and stayed a year.
Returning home, Kelley told his mother, "I have a terrible
shock for you. I am going to go and live in California."

This decision did not set well with his parents. His interest
in entertainment was foreign to the understanding of his father, a Baptist minister. But his mother encouraged rather
than discouraged his artistic talents. She realized the limitations of Atlanta for the son of a Baptist minister and had earlier cleared the way for him to sing in the church choir. For
a period of time he did solo work and eventually sang on a
program on radio station WSB in Atlanta. For this he won an

engagement at the Atlanta Paramount Theater, singing with Lew Forbes and his orchestra.

His subsequent move to Long Beach, California, changed his entire future. Joining the Long Beach Theater Group, he formed a radio group with his friend, Barney Girard. Barney wrote the plays, and the rest of the group put them on at the local radio station. Off the air, Kelley earned his living as an elevator operator.

During the war Kelley was spotted in a Navy training film by a Paramount talent scout. The result was a screen test and a contract. He remained with the studio two and one-half years. In 1948 he went east to New York, gaining experience in stock, stage, and television. Upon returning to California, he discovered Hollywood has a short memory. But many of the people he had known in New York were now working on the West Coast. His friend Barney Girard, writing for the "You Are There" TV series, helped De Forest reestablish himself in the film capital.

Numerous TV appearances followed, including roles on "Schlitz Theater," "Playhouse 90," "Gunsmoke," "You Are There," "Navy Log," "Zane Grey Theater," "Rawhide," and "Bonanza." Among his motion picture credits are *Tension at Table Rock*, *Gunfight at the O.K. Corral*, *Raintree County*, *The Law and Jake Wade*, *Warlock*, and *Where Love Has Gone*.

De Forest married Carolyn Dowling on September 7, 1945. They met while appearing together at the Long Beach Theater Group. Carolyn has since given up the theater, and the pair reside in Sherman Oaks, California. The only member of the family is Cheers!, a "Schnoodle" (schnauser and poodle).

Although De Forest plays the part of a highly skilled doctor, his personal background contains no training in medicine. He has always had, however, a strong interest in medicine and at one time was asked by his parents to consider a career as a doctor. Had it not been for his move to California, he might have gone into medical school.

De Forest feels much of McCoy's personality is a reflection of his own personal feelings—probably because he has developed much of McCoy's character himself. (This is another example of Gene Roddenberry's uncanny ability in casting the right person for the right role.)

Away from the TV camera, De Forest paints, enjoys swimming and working around the house.

# Chapter 7

## Engineering Officer Scott

Lieutenant Montgomery Scott is the *Enterprise*'s indefatigable Engineering Officer. He is affectionately known as "Scotty" by all those aboard. Of Scottish descent, he speaks with a brogue that is heavy with the heather and highlands of his native Scotland.

Scotty came up through the ranks, acquiring his knowledge the hard (and practical) way. He probably knows more about Spaceship engineering than anyone else in the Service. Several of his books on the subject have become standard texts at the Space Academy.

Scotty has knocked around space more than any other man aboard. At one time or another he has served aboard passenger vessels, merchant marine-type vessels, freighters, and a variety of military-type vessels, acquiring a valuable broad-based knowledge of engines and engineering.

As the ship's Engineering Officer, Scotty is recognized as the third-in-command and assumes charge of the vessel when Kirk and Spock are absent. As one of the senior officers aboard, he has significantly influenced the outcome of many an adventure involving the *Enterprise* and its crew.

Adventure seems to be in his blood. He comes from a long line of adventuring men—there were Scotts in clipper ships, in early aviation, at Flanders in World War I, in the RAF in World War II, a Scott was on the first large expedition to the Moon.

Engineering also seems to run in his blood. He is an engineer by nature as much as by trade. During off-duty hours he would rather tinker around in the engineering department than join in recreation activities. Engineering is an emotion to Scotty; beauty is a perfect engine, perfectly maintained, perfectly operating.

He considers the Engineering Department his own private

domain and is likely to view anyone entering his department (even the Captain) as an intruder. He considers the U.S.S. *Enterprise* to be owned by himself, subconsciously thinks of the Captain as simply the "driver." Where his precious vessel is concerned, he is fiercely defensive. Let anyone say anything less than complimentary about the *Enterprise* and they immediately find themselves facing his considerable wrath.

Scotty is intensely loyal to Captain Kirk and Mr. Spock. His relationship with Dr. McCoy, on the other hand, is a different one entirely. Scotty and McCoy are extremely close friends. They enjoy drinking together and are more alike as characters than either Kirk or Spock.

Scotty has no desire to command a space vessel. He is much happier as Engineering Officer, which he considers an assignment really more important and certainly more enjoyable than that of Captain.

In view of Scotty's roving nature, perhaps it is a good thing that he has few family ties. Although his mother and father are still living, he has no brothers or sisters. Although he enjoys children, he has never been married. He is a hellraiser while on shore leave, and his escapades usually involve women, the more exotic the better.

Aboard ship, however, he's completely another man. There the ship's engines are his all-consuming passion. Where Kirk is "married" to the vessel out of his command responsibilities, Scotty's attachment to the vessel comes out of deep love.

Engineering Officer Scott is played by James "Jimmy" Doohan, one time "bad boy" of the Royal Canadian Air Force. (Scotty was named Montgomery Scott at Jimmy's request, because his middle name is Montgomery and one of his sons is named Montgomery.) A native of Vancouver, British Columbia, Doohan earned the eccentric title when flying an artillery observation plane during World War II. Doohan says, "I guess they thought I was crazy because I used to fly my plane on a slalom course between telephone poles."

A veteran radio performer with over 3,500 shows to his credit, Jimmy first came to the United States in 1946, remaining here until 1953. He spent three of those years teaching techniques of acting at the Neighborhood Playhouse in

New York. He returned to the States again in 1961, working in television, radio, motion pictures, and on the stage.

Prior to becoming a regular on STAR TREK, Doohan had made more than 350 television appearances. His credits include roles on "Bonanza," "Blue Light," "Gunsmoke," "The FBI," "The Virginian," "Ben Casey," "Bewitched," "Hazel," and "Peyton Place."

Among his numerous motion picture credits are *The Wheeler Dealers*, *The Satan Bug* and *Bus Riley's Back in Town*. He has also appeared in several films produced by the National Film Board of Canada.

His theatrical appearances number more than one hundred and include roles in *King Lear* and *Macbeth*. He says his ultimate goal in the theater is to play Lear at the age of fifty-five.

An expert dialectician, Jimmy is as much at home in his role of a Scotsman as he would be if called upon to portray a Scandinavian or a Southern gentleman.

An excellent marksman and sportsman, he lists his hobbies as riding, skiing, swimming, and mountain climbing.

Jimmy Doohan resides in Hollywood with his lovely dark-haired wife, Anita. He has two daughters and a set of twin boys by a previous marriage.

Chapter 8

## Other Star Trek Regulars

The remaining members of STAR TREK's cast of regulars are: Sulu, Chekov, Uhuru, and Nurse Christine Chapel.

### SULU

Sulu, despite mixed Asian ancestry, is definitely not an inscrutable Oriental. He changes hobbies about once a week, and whatever he is currently involved in, he lets you know all about it. Biology, fencing, and physical exercise have all been kicks of his at one time or another. Although he goes from one new hobby to another, an interest in space biology has been somewhat consistent.

Although of mixed Oriental and Filipino background, Sulu's cultural heritage is mainly Japanese, and he finds himself drawn to the samurai concept as a philosophy. Despite this, he is a rather "hip" character and has an excellent sense of humor.

Sulu is a career officer, a most efficient Helmsman, and is also considered highly proficient in his secondary duty of *Enterprise* Weapons Officer. He usually is the one who handles the firing of phasers or torpedoes as needed.

George Takei plays the part of Sulu and in real life is a man with great curiosity concerning new places and people. George's wanderlust has taken him on camping expeditions to the rugged Rocky Mountains, a foray into the Alaskan panhandle, numerous trips into Baja California, and an extensive tour of Europe.

George was born in the Boyle Heights district of Los Angeles and lived there until World War II, when his family moved to Arkansas. He began his college education as an architecture student at the University of California at Berkeley. He later transferred to the Los Angeles campus of the university, majoring in theater arts with a minor in Latin American Studies. In 1960 he was graduated with a Bachelor of Arts degree. While a student at UCLA, George made his professional debut in a "Playhouse 90" production. Concurrent with his studies, he furthered his training as an actor at the Desilu Workshop.

In 1962 George traveled to New York for what he describes as "the time-honored actor's ritual of existence in cold water flats, off-Broadway plays, odd jobs, an occasional live TV appearance, but mostly stark, unadulterated experience."

The following year he went to Europe. During his "leisure time" George racked up credits on such television shows as "Perry Mason," "Hawaiian Eye," "The Islanders," "Alcoa Premiere," "Checkmate," "Mr. Novak," "The Wackiest Ship in the Army," "I Spy," "The John Forsythe Show," and many more. His motion picture credits include *Ice Palace, A Majority of One, Red Line 7000, From Hell to Eternity, An American Dream, Walk, Don't Run,* and the soon to be released *Green Berets.*

George resides in Hollywood and lists his hobbies as hiking, camping, swimming, reading, cycling, and painting.

On the subject of Sulu, Gene Roddenberry recalls a letter he received about halfway through the first season:

IT WAS FROM THE ORIENTAL PROTECTIVE ASSOCIATION, WHICH IS LIKE THE NAACP. THE LETTER FIRMLY CHASTISED US BECAUSE THESE PEOPLE HAD WATCHED A NUMBER OF THE SHOWS AND HAD NOTICED IT WAS THE OCCIDENTALS WHO ALWAYS ENDED UP WITH THE GIRLS. THEY THREATENED TO BOYCOTT THE SHOW IF WE DIDN'T GIVE THEM A SATISFACTORY ANSWER.

SO, WITH GEORGE'S PERMISSION, I WROTE THEM BACK SAYING THAT OUR CONTRACT WITH MR. TAKEI WAS BASED ON THE KELLOGG-BRIAND TREATY OF 1925 IN WHICH JAPAN GOT THREE BATTLESHIPS FOR EVERY FIVE THAT GREAT BRITAIN AND THE UNITED STATES GOT. I PROMISED THEN THAT ON

THAT BASIS MR. TAKEI WOULD RECEIVE
THREE GIRLS FOR EVERY FIVE THAT KIRK
AND MC COY GOT. IT MUST HAVE SEEMED
LIKE A REASONABLE ANSWER BECAUSE WE
NEVER HEARD FROM THEM AGAIN!

One incident occurred with George that points out the unexpected problems that can arise, simply in writing ideas into
a script. During the rewrite session on "The Naked Time" by
John D. F. Black (a story in which a disease is brought
aboard the ship—a disease that strips away inhibitions and
reveals the "core" of each person), someone suggested it
would be funny if Sulu, as an Oriental, secretly wanted to
be the French swordsman, D'Artagnan. Gene thought it was
a wild idea, so it was written into the script.

Little did anyone suspect that Oriental George Takei really
*did* want to be a French swordsman! During the six days of
filming, George continually wandered around the sets, lung-
ing and parrying with his sword. The crew ultimately threatened to quit, en masse, if anyone ever gave Takei a sword
again!

## ENSIGN CHEKOV

The part of Chekov was the result of two things. First, a
desire on Roddenberry's part to strengthen the show's appeal
to the teen-age audience:

TO: Joe D'Agosta          DATE: September 22, 1966
FROM: Gene Roddenberry    SUBJECT: NEEDED
                                   CREW TYPE

Keeping our teen-age audience in mind, also keeping
aware of current trends, let's watch for a young, irrever-
ent, English-accent Beatle type to try on the show, possibly with an eye to him reoccurring. Like the smallish
fellow who looks to be a hit on "The Monkees." Person-

ally I find this type spirited and refreshing, and I think our episodes could use that kind of lift. Let's discuss.

Gene Roddenberry

Second, a criticism by the youth edition of the Russian newspaper *Pravda*. In an official article the newspaper mentioned STAR TREK favorably but complained about the lack of a Russian crew member aboard the *Enterprise*. They felt Russians had been more than a little important in space exploration and should be so recognized.

THE CHEKOV THING WAS A MAJOR ERROR ON OUR PART, AND I'M STILL EMBARRASSED BY THE FACT WE DIDN'T INCLUDE A RUSSIAN RIGHT FROM THE BEGINNING. HOWEVER, NOW IT'S RUSSIA'S TURN TO BE EMBARRASSED. AFTER WE WROTE CHEKOV INTO THE SHOW, WE SENT A LONG, POLITE LETTER TO THE MINISTER OF CULTURAL AFFAIRS IN MOSCOW, APOLOGIZING FOR THE ERROR AND TELLING HIM ABOUT CHEKOV. THAT WAS OVER A YEAR AGO, AND THEY STILL HAVEN'T ANSWERED US. SO WE'RE SQUARE.

The character of Chekov is played with all the impetuousness of youth. All Ensigns seem universally twenty-two years old, but he is portrayed as being reliable and dependable, with a good head on his shoulders in spite of his youth.

This is his first space assignment. Officially, he's a Navigator, but he's also able to be assigned to various points around the ship. If he is ultimately going to be a Command Officer, he has to have a working knowledge of the ship. He may be transferred down into Engineering at some point, or take over the helm, and very frequently takes over Spock's Library-computer if Spock is not there. He may prove to have a logical, analytical enough mind to qualify in that area. Possibly he would move up to Science Officer someday. Spock feels that Chekov is good material to work with and has potential, but they are not pals or buddies.

He was born in Russia, near Moscow. Chekov comes from a middle-class family. Pavel is his first name, which means Paul in Russian.

He is a nice, normal young man, with the normal strong twenty-two-year-old urge for young ladies. Still, he is nowhere near ready to settle down yet. He probably will make a career of the Space Service, is a dedicated young officer who is believed by Captain Kirk to have the potential of being a future starship commander.

Ensign Chekov is portrayed by Walter Koenig, an unusually likeable young man and a highly talented actor. Interestingly enough, both his parents were born in Russia.

He grew up in New York in the Inwood area of Manhattan. He went to public school—P.S. 52 and P.S. 98—through the sixth grade. All secondary education was accomplished at Fieldston High School of the Ethical Culture School System in Riverdale, New York. Walter's first acting was done there when he played the title role in his sophomore year production of *Peer Gynt* and again in his senior year production of Shaw's *Devil's Disciple*.

During the summer months he worked in camps for underprivileged children in upstate New York. There he instituted a theater program, which was, in truth, a thinly disguised psycho-drama for disturbed and overaggressive youngsters. Later he incorporated this same program into the camps' parent settlement house in the Lower East Side of New York. To his knowledge, it is today still a valuable adjunct on the settlement house community itinerary.

Walter spent his first two years of college at Grinnell College in Iowa as a pre-med major, while at the same time doing stock during summers in Vermont. With the passing of his father and brother, he moved to the West Coast and completed his education at UCLA. He graduated from there with a B.A. in psychology, but with the encouragement of Professor Arthur Friedman, whose class was the only theater arts course he took in college, he returned to New York. With Professor Friedman's recommendation he was enrolled at the Neighborhood Playhouse. His second year at the Playhouse was rewarded by a scholarship offer from the school's regents.

During this period money was scarce, and for six months, at 98 cents per hour, he lived on $75 a month. After a couple of years off Broadway, he returned to L.A. to play a variety of interesting roles on the local stage and television. His first television lead was in actuality only his second filmed television part. He played a Russian student defecting from behind the Iron Curtain on the "Mr. Novak" series. Since then he has played an Armenian grape picker on "Great Adventure," a Swedish businessman on "Gidget," an Arabian rock and roll singer on "I Spy," and a French resistance fighter on "Jericho." Koenig also appeared in a "Lieutenant" episode, in which he gave an excellent performance.

On the stage he played three roles in the highly acclaimed theater group production of *The Deputy*: a Jewish refugee, a Nazi sergeant, and a Catholic monk. His most recent theater experience was as the Welsh psychopathic murderer in the Angels Theater production of *Night Must Fall*. For this performance Walter received rave reviews from the Los Angeles *Times* and *Daily Variety*.

Walter has been married two years, and his wife, Judy Levitt, is an accomplished actress in her own right.


## UHURA

Communications Officer Uhura is an African, a citizen of the Bantu Nation of United Africa of the 23rd century. Since childhood she had been interested in communications and was already a highly proficient communications professional at eighteen years of age when her sense of adventure led her into the Space Service. She is a desirable and attractive young lady, and a highly able starship officer, considered by Captain Kirk fully as capable and reliable as any lieutenant aboard.

Uhura is torn between the idea of someday becoming a wife and mother, and a desire to remain in the service as a career officer. Her life at present is a battle between her female need for the pleasant routine of Earthbound home and family versus the personal challenge of starship life and continued new worlds to conquer.

Proud of her heritage, she wears African dress off duty and when relaxing. Her life philosophy, nowhere near as Westernized as Sulu's, reflects the warm, nonaggressive "man-nature-oneness" culture of the 23rd century Bantu nation which became Earth's best example of blending advanced technology with a naturalistic agrarian philosophy.

Uhura (feminine for the Swahili word for "freedom") frequently figures prominently in STAR TREK adventures. She is well-liked by the entire crew, and during off-duty hours in the ship's recreation areas is in demand for her song ballads, ranging from traditional Earth tunes to favorites from a dozen other planets (making use of the actress's background as a professional songstress).

Nichelle Nichols is featured as Communications Officer Uhura.

A brilliant dancer as well as a fine singer, Miss Nichols had demonstrated her ability as an actress, twice being nominated for the Sara Siddons Award as best actress of the year. Her first nomination was for her portrayal of Hazel Sharp in *Kicks and Co.*, the second for her performance in the hit play *The Blacks*.

Nichelle was born and raised in Chicago and studied there, in Los Angeles, and in New York. During her time in New York she appeared at the famed Blue Angel and the Playboy Club. Between appearances at the clubs, she doubled as standby to the lead in the Broadway musical *No Strings*.

She appeared in the title role of a Chicago stock company production of *Carmen Jones*.

On the West Coast Nichelle has appeared in *The Roar of the Greasepaint, The Smell of the Crowd, For My People,* and won high critical acclaim for her performance in the James Baldwin play, *Blues for Mister Charlie*.

As vocalist with the Duke Ellington and Lionel Hampton bands, Miss Nichols toured throughout the United States, Canada, and Europe.

A relatively new face on TV, Nichelle appeared on "CBS Repertory Theater," followed by a guest star role on "The Lieutenant."

Movie audiences will soon see Nichelle in featured roles in

the forthcoming feature films *Mister Buddwing* and *Three for the Wedding*.

During her leisure hours Nichelle enjoys oil painting and designing her own clothes, and says she is "mad" for sports cars. In a desire to further her artistic abilities, she is currently taking lessons in sculpting.

Nichelle lives in Los Angeles, sharing her home with her two Siamese cats.

## NURSE CHRISTINE CHAPEL

Nurse Christine Chapel is Dr. McCoy's chief medical assistant. She was engaged at one time, but her fiancé, a well-known scientist, was lost on an expedition. She entered the Service, hoping against hope that possibly in her travels as a nurse with the Starship she would find some indication that he was still alive. She eventually discovered he had found a civilization which had perfected androids to the point that they were almost "human." Her fiancé was alive only in the sense that his mind had been deposited in an android body that looked precisely like him. In that adventure he ultimately died.

Like many women aboard, Christine is desperately in love with Mr. Spock, but it is an unrewarding relationship. Mr. Spock is not insensitive to her feelings, but knows that it can never work out. He tries to spare her as much as possible by remaining totally unemotional and detached toward her.

Dr. McCoy knows how Nurse Chapel feels toward Mr. Spock, but he never chides her for it. He knows it can't go anywhere but sympathizes because she is not only his most efficient assistant, but he feels fatherly affection for her. She is certainly an efficient nurse. The loss of her fiancé has broken all emotional ties with Earth. Now she is totally dedicated to the Service. Christine Chapel is well-educated for her task, with a doctorate of her own in Bio-Research. Her rank is Lieutenant, and she will probably move up in Star Fleet medical service.

The part of Nurse Christine Chapel is played by the lovely Majel Barrett. Her list of acting credentials is impressive.

Prior to her role in STAR TREK, she appeared in no less than sixteen plays, both on and off Broadway; ten motion pictures, and has played numerous parts in seventeen different television shows.

A partial listing of her TV appearances includes: "Dr. Kildare," "I Love Lucy," "Bonanza," "The Untouchables," "Sunset Strip," and "Westinghouse Playhouse."

Miss Barrett is a resident of Hollywood, and lists her leisure time activities as music, reading, swimming, and indulging the whims of her pet French poodle, "Fang."

Chapter 9

## The Bad Guys

Every action-adventure story must have conflict. Although this can be achieved in many ways, the type of story almost necessarily requires some combination of "bad guys" in opposition to the "good guys." STAR TREK's "bad guys" are of two types: the Romulans and the Klingons.

## THE ROMULANS

The Romulans are members of the Romulan Star Empire, which is located on the outskirts of the galaxy. While little is known of the Empire as a whole, we do know that it encompasses several solar systems. The Romulans are an off-shoot of the Vulcan race, but lost contact with the Vulcans in the distant past. The two races are physically almost identical, and it is extremely difficult to tell them apart, even with sensor readings.

Romulans are highly militaristic, aggressive by nature, ruthless in warfare, and do not take captives. The Star Empire is a dictatorship, with some similarities to the warrior-stoic philosophies of Earth's ancient Roman Empire. Their equivalent of a starship captain carries the title "Sub-Commander." The generic title of all Romulan Officers translates into English approximately as "Centurion." A "Commander" is one who commands an entire fleet.

There is complete equality between the sexes; women are as often found in command of a ship as are men.

Due to a recent alliance, the Romulans are primarily armed and equipped with Klingon weapons, ships, matériel, etc. The combination is posing a serious security problem to STAR TREK's United Federation of Planets.

An uneasy peace exists between the Star Empire and the

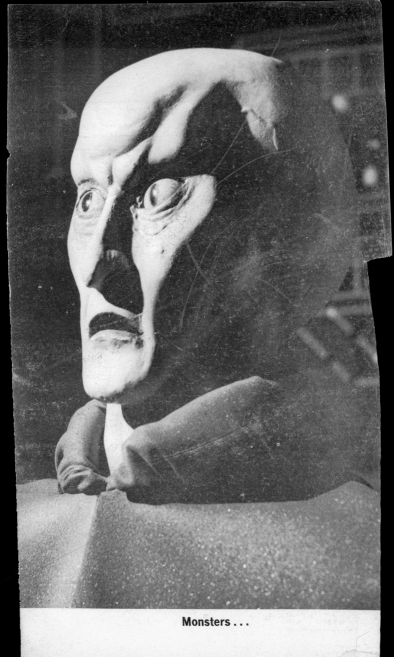

**Monsters . . .**

. . . and Damsels.

Vulcan ruler

**Sarak and Amanda, Spock's parents**

**Captain Kirk in the Transporter Room**

**Spock with tricorder**

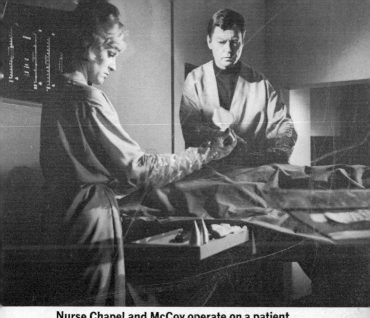

**Nurse Chapel and McCoy operate on a patient**

**Kirk and McCoy—"The Apple"**

**"Amok Time"**

"Who Mourns for Adonis"

"Space Seed"

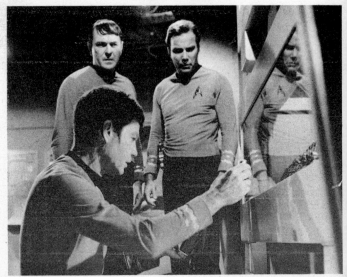

**"Journey to Babel"**

**Second Pilot—"Where No Man Has Gone Before":** Note style of shirt, sideburns, and gold braid on sleeve

**Spock and Kirk (Earth clothes) "Assignment Earth"**

**Kirk in action—"Who Mourns for Adonis"**

**Set—"Who Mourns for Adonis"**

Spock with Vulcan harp

**Bill Shatner studies script**

**Leonard Nimoy with Bill Theiss**

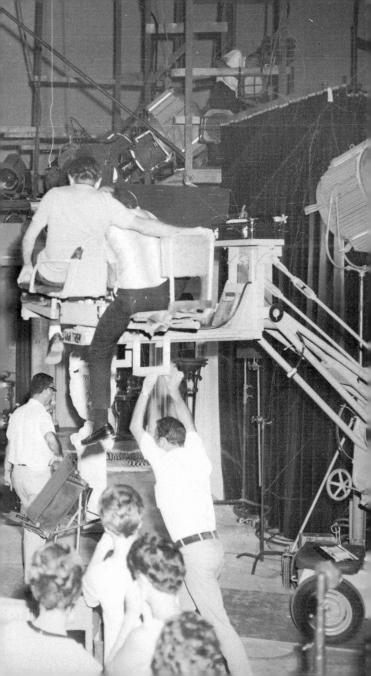

**Briefing Room**

**Technicians at work on Bridge**

**Gene Roddenberry, Jimmy Doohan and DeForest Kelly at NASA**

**Triple Head Printer (Courtesy Westheimer Co.)**

D. C. FONTANA

**Joe Pevney, Director**

Federation and is based on a prolonged war which occurred about 100 years ago. The conflict was inconclusive, and eventually both sides decided to put an end to hostilities. A peace treaty was negotiated (entirely by sub-space radio—there was no physical contact during the negotiations), and a neutral zone established between the two combatants. Entry into the neutral zone is considered an act of war. The treaty has remained unbroken, except for one major incident depicted in an episode titled "Balance of Terror."

It is hard to hate the Romulans completely, as they often display enormous courage. Although members of a warrior society in which the strong alone survive, they live their beliefs with great integrity.

## THE KLINGONS

The number-one adversary of the Federation is the Klingon Empire. More powerful than the Romulans, the Klingons are less admirable characters. Their only rule of life is that rules are made to be broken by shrewdness, deceit, or power. Cruelty is something admirable; honor is a despicable trait. They will go out of their way to provoke an incident with the Federation.

The Klingon Empire is, in many areas, in close proximity to Federation territory. A specific border separates the two, but it is continually being violated by the Klingons.

Rule is by absolute dictatorship, and assassination is common. Their society is totally devoted to personal gain by the cleverest, strongest, or most treacherous. As a result, their vessels often operate much like "privateers," and warlike acts are a way of life. Life on all levels is completely supervised, and extensive use is made of "snooping devices" (again, on all levels) to help maintain total control.

Physically, the Klingons are slightly oriental looking, dark complexioned, with bushy eyebrows that arch up at both ends. The men, without exception, are bearded. They have no patience with women, even their own, and treat them as sometime useful animals.

About two years ago, both the Klingons and the Federation

were preparing for an all-out war. In fact, a Klingon battle fleet was already in space, bound for an attack. The war never materialized, however, as it was averted by superior beings from the planet Organia.* Quite arbitrarily, these beings disarmed both fleets simultaneously, and declared the war over before it had begun.

A treaty was imposed on both sides, and is now known as the Organian Peace Treaty. Terms are very specific: neither side may fight. In cases of dispute over a newly discovered planet, the Organians arbitrate the matter, awarding the planet to whichever side can develop it more efficiently.

The treaty remains in effect, but there have been numerous minor incidents and encounters, usually provoked by the Klingons.

In terms of weaponry, the Klingons are armed with Sonic Disrupter Pistols. Their ships are comparable in power and capability to the starships, although design-wise the difference between the two classes of vessels is startling.

All in all, the Klingons appear to have little (by our standards) in the way of redeeming qualities.

---

* Shown in the Episode "Errand of Mercy," by Gene L. Coon.

Part III

# FROM THEN UNTIL NOW

Chapter 1

## Putting the Show on the Road

JUST MAKING AN HOUR TV SHOW (AND MAKING IT WELL) HAS BECOME AN ALMOST IMPOSSIBLE TASK, PHYSICALLY, FOR THE PRODUCTION TEAM. FOR AN "AVERAGE" TV SHOW, THEY FIND THEMSELVES WORKING TWELVE TO FOURTEEN HOURS A DAY. COMPARE THAT TO THE SITUATION WE FOUND OURSELVES IN, WITH A COMPLEX SHOW LIKE STAR TREK. IT BEGAN TO APPEAR THAT EVEN IF WE COULD WORK TWENTY-SEVEN HOURS A DAY, SEVEN DAYS A WEEK, WE COULDN'T QUITE CUT IT. IT WAS A BITCH OF A FIRST YEAR.

Gene Roddenberry

NBC's decision, in February, 1966, to put STAR TREK on the air* the following September set off an immediate flurry of activity. Desilu quickly placed STAR TREK on an "In Production" status and requested Gene to begin production activities at once. Shooting was tentatively scheduled to begin the first of June. At that time this was a very early start for an hour TV show, but the STAR TREK staff foresaw many difficulties ahead (they were so right) and wanted to get as early a start as possible.

Suddenly there were a million details to be taken care of simultaneously. The production crew had to be hired, story consultant and other staff vacancies filled, writers selected, directors lined up, office space acquired. There was also the problem of moving the sets. STAR TREK would be produced

---

* At that point, the Network's commitment was for sixteen episodes. This was enough to carry the show through the first half of the new season. This is typical of the networks, and is their way of hedging the bet. They can always cancel at the end of the sixteen, if the show's Nielsen's ratings aren't impressive enough.

at Desilu's Gower Street facility, and all the sets that had been built at the Culver City facility had to be torn down, moved, and rebuilt at Desilu Gower. Moving the complex ship's bridge interior was a major task in itself. Although it had been modified from the first pilot, additional changes were planned. (It's still undergoing improvements today . . . they are always adding new things to that bridge.)

Bill Theiss was immediately put to work redesigning the costumes. It had been decided that instead of slacks, the women would wear the short mini-skirt uniforms they now wear. A design change was also contemplated for the men's shirts, as well as modifications to their trousers.

From the beginning there was a tremendous amount of work to be done. There was also a tremendous amount of money at stake. At roughly $180,000 per episode, Desilu (and NBC) had committed itself to an expenditure of about $2,340,000 for the first thirteen episodes.

Gene quickly began pulling together the nucleus of his production staff. Bob Justman was officially named series associate producer on STAR TREK the same day the go-ahead had come from NBC. Matt Jefferies was (fortunately) still available and joined the staff as art director.

A short time later Gregg Peters was hired as first assistant director* for the series. Gregg is a tall, heavyset fellow and bears a faint resemblance to Yul Brynner. Although his job is one production headache after another, Gregg has one of the most cheerful personalities I've ever seen. He also has a tremendous sense of humor.

Preproduction began in earnest, as evidenced by the following memo, typical of the many such memos circulated at the time:

TO:  Robert H. Justman     DATE:  March 22, 1966
FROM:  Gene Roddenberry  SUBJECT:  PLANNING STAR
                                                          TREK

---

* At the beginning of the second season Gregg was promoted to unit production manager, and in early 1968 was promoted to associate producer.

Reviewing some notes from our budget meeting, just wanted to make certain you would follow up at the proper time on:

a. Greens and greensmen. We want one man assigned from Walter Allen to service us constantly, someone who becomes trained in our methods and needs. And, probably leaning on Matt Jefferies for some advice on this, we probably should develop some alternate sources of supply. I always get nervous when everyone at the budget meeting seems to feel there is *only one place* which is best for our needs.

b. Someone promised us some figures on rental prices on the back lots of other studios.

c. We should have a meeting soon on revisions in the spaceship interiors already constructed.

d. We should have a meeting soon, possibly at the same time of the above, on anticipated new interiors and a general critique on what they should be like in order to plan for greatest flexibility, for maximum contrast between various ship sections, etc.

e. We should have a meeting soon on revisions of the U.S.S. *Enterprise* models.

f. Also needed is a meeting on additional stock footage shooting—this get-together coming some time after we've got enough outlines in to make a reasonable projection. *Important*, we should also at this meeting review how we liked past stock footage and plan to revise and correct wherever we feel it is indicated. For example, in STAR TREK #2 on some of the U.S.S. *Enterprise* approaching planet footage, I felt the time-speed-distance perspective was considerably off.

g.  Also, we should press Editorial Department to develop a broader, more inventive and creative survey of existing footage stock sources, including Air Force, NASA, and similar programs. I think we have a file on such information which Dorothy has been keeping up-to-date over the last year or so.

Gene Roddenberry

While planning for the impending start of production, Gene was also looking far ahead into the future (his foresight later proved to be well-founded), as can be seen from the following excerpt from a memo written March 22nd:

The expansion of "The Menagerie" into a two-parter for television—the use of it for this purpose could become imperative as a means of making all our NBC episode delivery dates. Even if we are successful, as we hope to be, in beginning photography of our first episode by May 24, the anticipated extra post-production time involved in optics and etc. will have us down pretty close to the wire by the time we have reached our twentieth to twenty-fourth episode. And, of course, any delays occasioned by crew illness or other unforeseen circumstances could result in this two-parter becoming a lifesaver. STAR TREK associate producer Robert Justman has these dates pretty well figured out and estimated by now, and it might be very much worthwhile to go over this with him when any further discussions of that are contemplated.

As story outlines began to come in from various writers, Gene distributed them to all departments for comment. He was determined to avoid production problems later by "plugging in" at the earliest possible moment all those concerned.

TO: All Concerned    DATE: April 4, 1966
FROM: Gene Roddenberry    SUBJECT: STAR TREK
                               OUTLINES

You will shortly begin receiving mimeographed STAR TREK outlines for your information and aid in preplanning our episodes.

The purpose of this broad distribution is to solicit from Desilu departments early general comment and suggestions bearing on cost, time, sets, locations, wardrobe or transportation problems, any and all factors which should be considered in planning to photograph the story. At this prescript stage many changes and switches are possible, and now is the time to flash us so we can discuss them with the writer.

For those who have not worked with writer outlines before, I wish to *strongly emphasize* that a television story at this stage is often rough, leaving many things to be worked out in the many drafts of the script, and should be treated as "confidential" material.

                              Gene Roddenberry

TO: All concerned    DATE: April 11, 1966
FROM: Gene Roddenberry    SUBJECT: STAR TREK
                               OUTLINES

Reference the STAR TREK story outlines you are now receiving and will continue to get, we need the following:

  a.  We need comments as early as possible. Please keep in mind that writers can be sent to first draft of the script in a matter of days after you get your copy of their outline.

  b.  We need *written* comment so that it can

be appended to our file on that outline, alerting us to cover this point with the writer, seek a less expensive or less difficult method if required. Working with dozens of writers, plus with our principal emphasis at this time on drama and entertainment, it is impossible for us to keep literally hundreds of technical and budget comments sorted out in our minds.

c.  These comments can be brief. If secretarial assistance is unavailable to shop or to a department assistant who is working on this outline, we will try to make our STAR TREK secretaries available to you for this task—and they can, if necessary, be handled in brief dictation over the phone to them.

Gene Roddenberry

In the meantime, Bob Justman (who has an unbelievable genius for figuring out shooting schedules and anticipating production problems) had developed a tentative production plan for the series. The first STAR TREK episode would be allotted seven days for shooting. Thereafter, six production days would be allotted to each succeeding episode. There would be a one-day gap in between each show to be used for either a cast rehearsal day and/or a seventh shooting day, if needed. Privately, Bob conceded most shows would probably take seven days to shoot. In order to make up the lost time, if a particular show would shoot for only six days, production would commence on the following day for the next episode (known as shooting "back-to-back").

In discussing his proposed shooting schedule, Bob reminded all concerned that NBC would undoubtedly expect final prints to be shipped two weeks prior to the episode's scheduled air date. He cautioned that while this requirement could be met in the beginning, the further along the show got in production, the more impossible it would become to ship episodes that early. All hands were thus alerted that production schedules had to be met at all costs.

Bob Justman is one of the most amazing production men in the business. He can flip through a script and in fifteen minutes tell you how long it will take to shoot it, and almost to the penny how much it will cost. He has a complete grasp of every facet of production, right down to how many cups of coffee the man should make every morning on the stage.

Bob is a sort of Mr. Spock within the production area, although a somewhat pessimistic Mr. Spock. During the first season he would walk into Gene's office every morning and announce, "We can't make it. There's no way we can make it." But the beauty of the man is that you can tell him, "Let's keep going!" and he will.

For instance—there was a little creature they needed to build for one of the shows. Bob announced that only $535 remained in the budget, and the creature couldn't be built for less than $5,000. Roddenberry replied, "We'll expect you to come in by five P.M. this evening with a way to build it for $535." Great ranting, great raving, great threats to quit, great tearing of his bushy moustache. At 5:00 P.M. that evening he came in with a way to do it for $535. A genuine character.

With an increasing number of story outlines and first-draft scripts being received, it was necessary to select a Script Consultant. A new addition to the staff was therefore made, in the person of Writers Guild Award winner John D. F. Black. His official title was Associate Producer (along with Bob Justman), but his primary function was dealing with writers, scripts, and rewrite.

Naturally, he had to be properly initiated. A put-on was arranged. John arrived at the studio fresh, bright, and enthusiastic to begin his new assignment. After being given enough time to get settled in his office, he was told Roddenberry had to be at a screening that morning, and would John please take care of an interview with an actress that Gene had inadvertently scheduled for the same time. He was asked simply to interview her, ask for some of her screen credits, and then terminate the interview with a polite "Don't call us, we'll call you" kind of statement.

John was very serious about his new job and very anxious

to make a good impression. He readily agreed to handle the interview. Promptly at 11:45 the actress appeared at his office, walked in, and closed the door. That was John's first mistake.

The girl, an attractive blonde, sat down in a chair in front of John's desk and in a thick honey magnolia accent began telling him, "Well, Mr. Black, sir, my experience is . . ." As she listed her credits, she slowly unbuttoned her dress. John's color rose with his alarm. He immediately began stammering objections. "Just a minute . . . ah . . . I don't quite understand . . . ah . . . you came here to be interviewed for a job. . . ." The girl, who was wearing a fringed bikini under her dress, was now almost out of her dress and cooing innocently, "A job? I thought that's what we were talking about."

By now John was gripping the sides of his desk so hard that his knuckles were turning white. At that moment the dress dropped to the floor (and before John could realize the undergarments were only a bikini), Gene Roddenberry, Bob Justman, Sylvia Smith (Bob's secretary), D. C. Fontana, and Morris Chapnick all began pounding on the door.

John's normally deep bass voice hit a high soprano note as he yelled, "Wait a minute!"

Ignoring his shout, the whole group burst into the room. Roddenberry pretended shock, demanded, "John! What *are* you doing?" Playing the part to the hilt, the actress was demurely pulling herself together. John was so shaken he was actually pale. Less than an hour on the job, and his new boss had caught him with a half-clad girl! At the same instant the telephone rang, and it was his wife calling! He later admitted that if his office hadn't been located on the second floor, he probably would have flung himself out the window. When everybody burst out laughing, he realized he had been had, and classically so!

John recovered from his ordeal and served STAR TREK ably and well. He acquired quite a reputation during his tenure on STAR TREK as a top rewrite man and a talented original writer as well. (John's original script, "The Naked Time," was one of the first STAR TREK episodes filmed.)

The practice of rewriting scripts is something to behold. STAR TREK will buy a completed script from a writer and then sometimes completely rewrite the whole thing. STAR TREK scripts often go through so many rewrites that a color coding system is employed, simply to keep track of the various revisions.

First draft scripts with relatively limited distribution are always in a yellow cover. The revised script is called a final (shooting) script and has a gray cover. It goes without saying that revisions are made to this final script, and the revised pages are printed on a succession of colored sheets, depending on the latest version of the revision. As incredible as it may seem, a "final draft" may be *completely* rewritten again! When this happens, a "revised final script" is issued, in a red cover. This script may also have "change pages" inserted later, being printed on either blue, pink, or succeeding paper colors, depending on the number of times a page is revised.

One of John D. F. Black's earliest assignments was to develop Captain Kirk's background more fully.

TO: John D. F. Black     DATE: April 23, 1965
FROM: Gene Roddenberry     SUBJECT: ANALYSIS OF CAPTAIN KIRK BY WILLIAM SHATNER

John, attached a number of pages on Captain Kirk written by Bill Shatner, based on conversations you and I had with him. I think it's a good start, but it will have to be much more interesting, more incisive, and in considerably more detail in certain areas to be of the most help to writers.

For example, I think we should spend much more time on Kirk's humanistic nature and background. You'll know what I mean, especially if you have read the Hornblower novel. We must make the inner conflict between humanist and military commander more evident to our writers, even if it means trimming down some on Kirk's mother and father.

Also I find missing here the small character flaws and weaknesses we need to fully round out the character. We need some comments on the self-doubts, the moments of pettiness, the attention to the materiality of his career, etc.

I think a couple of lines would suffice for the back story of his "lost love."

Do you like "United Celestial Service"? If you do, will keep it. But perhaps you have another suggestion.

I think we should make it clear that although the Yeoman might appeal to his sense of fun, his real mistress is the ship and he really doesn't have any fun with the Yeoman. In fact, he may very well have puritan instincts via which having a woman so close around his quarters (bedroom) makes him nervous and slightly irritable.

John, have discussed with Bill the fact his NBC audience profile on the pilot did not surge up the way and at the variations we and they would prefer to see. Although these tests are not infallible, there was a strong indication he is not showing the contrasting layers and flavors which we need. And so I think this basic character sketch on him which we should send to our writers soon may be of great help in establishing the multidimensional things, the occasional weaknesses, the idiosyncrasies and so on which give him something to play to.

Gene Roddenberry

For the second time, Gene found he had to recast characters. Some of the cast from the second pilot were simply no longer available. Also, discussions with NBC, as well as further analysis of the second pilot, indicated certain characters should be revised, which made previous actors physically wrong for the new concept.

One of the major roles recast was that of the ship's doctor. De Forest Kelley got the role, partly on the strength of his performance in the pilot "Police Story." Dee had played the crusty, eccentric police lab Chief and the characterization he had brought in to the role was precisely the quality Gene was looking for in the ship's doctor. Grace Lee Whitney, who also appeared in "Police Story," was cast in the role of the Captain's Yeoman.

The part of the Communications Officer was rewritten in order to have another female member in the cast, and Nichelle Nichols was subsequently signed to play the role of Uhura. The role of Nurse Christine Chapel was added, as Dr. McCoy's assistant, and Majel Barrett was cast in that part. Bill Shatner, Leonard Nimoy, Jimmy Doohan, and George Takei were all retained from the second pilot. Sulu was changed from astrophysicist to ship's Helmsman and Weapons Officer.

In producing the first two pilots, the only sets needed (aboard the *Enterprise*) were the bridge, briefing room, sick bay, transporter room, and a fairly simple corridor. However, as each new script was selected for production, the need for additional sets depicting other portions of the *Enterprise*'s interior became increasingly obvious.


TO: Matt Jefferies          DATE: May 24, 1966
FROM: Gene Roddenberry      SUBJECT: LARGE *EN-
                                     TERPRISE* IN-
                                     TERIOR

Much pleased with our *Enterprise* sets, Matt.

Now, however, we will shortly be getting two scripts which call for other *Enterprise* sets. Referring now specifically to the need for "engineering decks" or "engineering room," we should definitely think in terms of creating an illusion of a room of considerable *size*. We've got a huge ship, and I definitely feel the audience will be greatly disappointed if they are not taken occasionally into a set or sets with some feeling of vastness. Some areas of considerable spaciousness would be only logical within a vessel of these dimensions.

Perhaps some of this can be done in cohort with Anderson Company, letting them create the extra space with some form of optical matte. Let's discuss it ourselves, and then with them.

Also suggest we consider having somewhere on the ship a large port,* possibly overhead, which uses an Anderson painting or something, to give us a view of the ship's nacelles thousands of feet long and hundreds of feet over our heads.

Gene Roddenberry

A problem that had continually plagued Roddenberry from even before the shooting of the first pilot was the design of the weapons to be carried by the crew—now renamed phasers. With filming of the first episodes less than one month away, Gene was still attempting to finalize the design and construction of the phasers.

TO: Matt Jefferies  DATE: April 26, 1966
FROM: Gene Roddenberry  SUBJECT: PHASER
WEAPONS

Reference the mating of various components of the phaser weapons, the point I was trying to make in my original sketch (if you can call my scribbling "sketching") is that when the hand phaser is mated to the pistol, they should appear as *one weapon*. Same with the pistol mating into the future rifle. This not only has good dramatic logic behind it but would have much greater toy advantages that way, too.

Gene Roddenberry

One very talented fellow who got involved with the phasers at this point was Jimmy Rugg, the special effects man. Jimmy

---

* This idea was later dropped, in view of the theoretical size established for the *Enterprise*. It was also decided that such a "viewing port" would not be in keeping with the ship's technology, since a scanning device could project this on any one of the ship's viewing screens.

has a wiry, slender build and a sort of weather-beaten-type face and constantly wears a worried, serious expression. He is a great guy, and without doubt one of the most creative special effects men in the business. (No small indicator of his ability is the fact that he was nominated for an Emmy, television's highest award, for his special effects work on STAR TREK in the first season.)

As the hassle over the phasers continued, it was Jimmy Rugg who pointed out that "working phasers" (so constructed that they would actually emit a beam of light when the firing button was depressed) were not necessary. He pointed out that an actual light beam from the phaser was not needed since an optically created phaser beam was to be added later anyway. Besides, no one could seem to come up with a combination of light bulb and power supply that was both strong enough and small enough to fit inside the hand phaser and at the same time emit a beam of light strong enough to be detected under the bright lights on the set. (As it turned out, some authentic-looking dummy phasers were later built, and these are now used almost all the time. The expensive "working phasers" are not normally used any more. There are too many little pieces in them that get broken or out of adjustment when people play with them.)

Relentlessly days rolled by, bringing the first official day of shooting closer and closer. Apparently Bob Justman began to worry about meeting the schedule production date. A man with a keen sense of humor (some claim he must have once been held prisoner in a Chinese gag-writing factory), he has that singular ability to attack a problem with a combination of seriousness and flippancy.

TO: Gene Roddenberry
FROM: Bob Justman

DATE: April 25, 1966
SUBJECT: STAR     TREK
              PRODUCTION
              START

Gentlemen:

Today is Monday, April 25, 1966. Next Monday is May 2, 1966. Next Tuesday is May 3, 1966. Three weeks from Monday we start rehearsing our first show.

It looks to me as if we will have to decide which story we will go with first by this Friday, April 29, 1966. The reasons for this are as follows:

1. We need time to get specific sets ready for our first show, whichever story it is.
2. We need time to get any makeup design and appliances into work if there is a need for them.
3. We need time to get special props ready for the first show if there is any need for same.
4. We need to know where we are going if we are to plan intelligently.

The thought is frightening, but the reasoning is undeniable. Take two Miltowns and let's make a decision by the end of this week.

                                        Fearful

The following week he was totally absorbed by a new challenging problem. As a matter of fact, the problem was so challenging and stimulating that it caused a chain reaction that rippled through the studio for more than a week and involved a number of prominent studio personnel. The matter started innocently enough, with the following memo:

TO: Gene Roddenberry      DATE: May 3, 1966
FROM: Bob Justman         SUBJECT: STAR TREK
                                   PLANET VUL-
                                   CAN PROPER
                                   NAMES

Dear Gene:

I would like to suggest that all proper names for denizens of Mr. Spock's "PLANET VULCAN" follow a set routine.

To wit: all names begin with the letters "SP" and end with the letter "K." All names to have a total of five letters in them—no more and no less.

Therefore: Mr. Spock aptly fits this pattern. Other names would be as follows:

| | | | |
|---|---|---|---|
| Spook | Spenk | Spurk | Spakk |
| Spuck | Sponk | Spawk | Spekk |
| Spack | Spilk | Spauk | Spikk |
| Speek | Spalk | Speuk | Spokk |
| Spouk | Spelk | Spuik | Spukk |
| Spaak | Spolk | Spouk | Spark |
| Spilk | Spulk | Splak | Sperk |
| Spiak | Spirk | Splek | Spirk |
| Spunk | Spark | Splik | Spork |
| Spank | Spork | Splok | Spurk |
| Spink | Sperk | Spluk | Spxyx |

Hope that the suggestions are of immense help to you. I remain,

Your humble and obedient servant,

Robert H. Justman

to: Gene Roddenberry
from: Herb Solow

date: May 5, 1966
subject: PLANET VULCAN PROPER NAMES

Dear Gene:

In an industry that is founded on the uncontrollable appetite for creativity, it is indeed heartwarming for the management of a major studio to receive a copy of a memo that deals with such an intensely competitive and accurate discussion of proper names on the planet Vulcan.

However, what with time being of the essence, with our schedule calling for production of our series to commence in three very short weeks, I feel enough time

—rather more than enough time—has been spent devising names for Mr. Spock's relatives. With a deep respect for creativity, I feel we should go on to something of greater importance.

                                             H.F.S.

P.S.   Have you thought of the name Spiik? Or Sprik? Or Sprak? Or Sprok? Or Spruk? Or Spudk? Or Spidk? Or Spuck? Or Spisk? Or Spask? Or Spesk? Or Spask? Or any of the other seventy-eight I already devised?

P.P.S.   Please refer to Mr. Justman's May 3 memo and you will find that the fifth name in column one is the same as the sixth name in column three. I understand that you science fiction people with your technical jargon have a word to describe this happening. It is known as a "mistake."

P.P.P.S.   What do you say if all the people on the planet Vulcan are lawyers (interesting idea) and they all have a firm name like Spook, Speek, Spork, Splik, and Roddenberry? (The last name is necessary to keep the audience aware at all times that this relates to science fiction.)

P.P.P.P.S   Also note that in the May 3 memo the eighth name in column two is the same as the eighth name in column four. Also the tenth name in column two is the same as the ninth name in column four. There are probably others, but my time is too valuable to waste pointing out that the seventh name in column one is the same name as the third name in column two.


TO: Herb Solow              DATE: May 6, 1966
FROM: Bob Justman           SUBJECT: STAR TREK
                                     PLANET VUL-
                                     CAN PROPER
                                     NAMES

Dear Mr. Solow:

I refer to your memo, dated May 5, 1966. Any Vulcanite or science-fiction aficionado would know that the fifth name in column one (Spouk) is pronounced "Spook." Whereas the sixth name in column three (Spouk) is pronounced "Spowk."

The eighth name in column two (Spirk) is pronounced "Sperk." Whereas the eighth name in column four (Spirk) is pronounced "Speerk."

Also, the tenth name in column two (Spork) is pronounced "Spawrk." Whereas the ninth name in column four (Spork) is pronounced "Spohrk."

Also, the seventh name in column one (Spilk) is pronounced "Spilk." Whereas the third name in column two (Spilk) is pronounced "Speelk."

Consider yourself chastised.

Your Phrend,

Bahb

TO: Robert Justman
FROM: John D. F. Black

DATE: May 6, 1966
SUBJECT: YOUR MEMO TO H. SOLOW RE: STAR TREK PLANET VULCAN PROPER NAMES

Dear Bahb. . . .

I refer to your memo, dated May 6, 1966, regarding Mr. Solow's memo, dated May 5, 1966 . . . specifically pertaining to paragraph three of your note.

I certainly take no issue with your reference to the tenth name in column two (Spork) being pronounced "Spawrk." This, of course, is common knowledge.

However . . .

I am forced to raise some question in regard to your "whereas." By this I mean the ninth name in column four (Spork) as being pronounced "Spohrk." The proper pronunciation for the ninth name in column four (Spork) is, in fact, "Sphork" rather than "Spohrk."

. . . unless, of course, you are one of those infected
by the current trend toward excessive use of "jargon"
and "common usage."

I sincerely hope that you will take this slight criticism
in the spirit in which it is intended.

Sincerely yours,

John D. F.

TO: John D. F. Black          DATE: May 9, 1966
FROM: Herb Solow             SUBJECT: VULCAN
                                      PROPER
                                      NAMES

As you will learn, I make it a practice not to get involved in the private squabbles between members of a
particular production unit. However, I feel it necessary
to throw caution to the wind and strongly and publicly
take issue with your unkind criticism of our Bobby Justman. Our Bobby has been with this company for almost
a year. How someone who is new to our shores and who
uses Dorothy Fontana's initials between his two names
can rise up and publicly strike out at Our Bobby is beyond the realm of serious thought by the management
of this studio.

This is especially disastrous in that your reasoning for
taking to task Our Bobby is bad reasoning. Those of us
who have discarded our rose-colored glasses and who see
life as life is meant to be seen know, in fact, that the
proper pronunciation of the ninth name in column four
(Spork) is not "Spohrk" and is not "Spawrk," but is, in
fact, a throwback to a German company that manufactured Christmas cookies, and is pronounced with a silent
"f" and is spelled "Sfpork."

Sure, Bob Justman is wrong. If he doesn't understand
the "Sf" factor in Vulcan proper names, then he should
be publicly chastised, and I am surprised that you have
not taken it upon yourself to be slightly critical of
whatever-his-name-is. . . .

(Don't ask me how they still manage to get their work done. I've observed these people for almost two years now, and I still don't understand it.)

NBC's Broadcast Standards Department requires (as do the other networks) that all scripts for shows to be aired on NBC be cleared with their department prior to shooting. The people working in the Broadcast Standards Department are the ones commonly referred to as the "TV Censors." They can normally be expected to make a certain number of comments on every script submitted. Their comments are usually phrased in the form of "suggestions" and, of course, are mandatory.

In any event, at the same time that John D. F. Black was wrestling with the problem of "Planet Vulcan Proper Names," he was also becoming acquainted with NBC's Broadcast Standards Department.

TO: Gene Roddenberry          DATE: May 3, 1966
FROM: John D. F. Black          SUBJECT: "WHAT   ARE
                                                LITTLE GIRLS
                                                MADE OF?"

Gene . . .

Have just received two pages of remarks on "What Are Little Girls Made Of?" from NBC.

Holy (censored)!

Has anyone told them "Let's Pretend" has gone off the air?

I have a feeling we had better discuss this and lay hold of NBC in short order . . . by that I do not mean to imply "anything grotesque or shocking" . . . and, naturally, "embraces" are out.

Gently and nicely yours,

John D. F.

Although there does not seem to be any way to second-guess what the networks will object to in the way of dialogue or other aspects of a show, there *is* a way to orient writers as to how they should approach their scripts for the STAR TREK series. Every potential scriptwriter for a STAR TREK episode is issued a copy of the STAR TREK Guide. This is a document outlining the character traits, script requirements, standing sets available to use in various scenes, and a whole host of background information related to the STAR TREK series.

The following is an example of the type of guidance offered to aspiring STAR TREK scriptwriters:

IF YOU'RE A TV PROFESSIONAL, YOU ALREADY KNOW THE FOLLOWING SEVEN RULES:

I. Build your episode on an action-adventure framework. We must reach out, hold and *entertain* a mass audience of some 20,000,000 people or we simply don't stay on the air.

II. Tell your story about *people,* not about science and gadgetry. Joe Friday doesn't stop to explain the mechanics of his .38 before he uses it; Kildare never did a monologue about the theory of anesthetics; Matt Dillon never identifies and discusses the breed of his horse before he rides off on it.

III. Keep in mind that science fiction is not a separate field of literature with rules of its own, but, indeed, needs the same ingredients as any story—including a jeopardy of some type to someone we learn to care about, climactic build, sound motivation, you know the list.

IV. Then, with that firm foundation established, interweave in it any statement to be made about man, society, and so on. Yes, we want you to have something to say, but say it entertainingly as you do on any other show. We don't need essays, however brilliant.

V. Remember always that STAR TREK is never fantasy; whatever happens, no matter how unusual or bizarre, must have some basis in either fact or theory *and stay true to that premise* (don't give the enemy Starflight capability and then have them engage our vessel with grappling hooks and drawn swords).

VI. Don't try to tell a story about whole civilizations. We've never yet been able to get a usable story from a writer who began . . . "I see the strange civilization which . . ."

VII. Stop worrying about not being a scientist. How many cowboys, police officers, and doctors wrote Westerns, detective, and hospital shows?

THE STAR TREK SCRIPT FORMAT

THE TEASER. We open with action, always establishing a strong jeopardy, need, or other "hook." It is not necessary to establish all the back story in the teaser. Instead, we tantalize the audience with a promise of excitement to come. For example, it can be as simple as everyone tense on the bridge, hunting down a marauding enemy ship . . . then a tale-telling blip is sighted on the screen, and the Captain orders, "All hands to battle stations." Fade out, that's enough.

THE ACTS. Four acts in length. Act One usually begins with Captain's VOICE OVER, Captain Kirk dictating his log. Necessary back story should be laid in here, not in the teaser. The Captain's log should be succinct and crisp . . . in ship commander "log" language.

Opening Act One, we need some form of orbit, establishing, or other silent shot to give us time for both Captain's log and opening credits.

We *must* have a strong ending to Act Two, something that will keep the audience tuned to our channel.

STYLE. We maintain a fast pace . . . avoid long, philosophical exchanges or tedious explanations of equipment. And note that our cutting technique is to use the shortest possible time between idea and execution of it . . . like, for instance, Kirk decides that a landing party will transport down to a planet . . . HARD CUT

to lights blinking on the Transporter console, PULL
BACK to REVEAL the landing party stepping into the
Transporter.

PAGE COUNT. First drafts can run up to 70 pages, if you
intend to trim and tighten later. But for final polished
draft *absolutely no more than 65 pages, please.*

ANOTHER PLEASE. Cast and set lists with your draft.
Thank you.

Excerpt from STAR TREK Guide

Although the foregoing represents only one small portion
of the entire Guide, it should provide anyone with a pretty
good idea as to how they should approach a STAR TREK
script. If a writer adheres to the foregoing guide lines implic-
itly, the odds are that his script will be rewritten anyway. (See
Part IV).

When a script is scheduled for shooting, a production
meeting is called, attended by all departments involved in the
production. The purpose of the meeting is to discuss the requirements of the script so necessary preproduction planning
can begin as soon as possible. To illustrate the point, the following is a transcription of notes which I made during such a
production conference:

PRODUCTION    CONFERENCE—SCRIPT—"WOLF    IN    THE
FOLD" by Robert Bloch.

Those present—Bill Theiss, costumes. Irving Feinberg,
props. Joe Stone,* set decorator. Rusty Meek, assistant
director. Joe Pevney, director. Gregg Peters, production
manager. Jimmy Rugg, special effects. Matt Jefferies, art
director.
Meeting begins with discussion of props and set decorations needed. Pevney wants bowls of fruit. Question
—edible or not? Both.

---

* Joe Stone left STAR TREK midway through the second season in
1967 and was subsequently replaced by John Dwyer.

Script calls for flickering table lights (that planet's way of showing applause) in cafe scene. Flashlights are discussed. Pevney likes table lights that flash. Matt says people seated at tables will obscure at various points. Wiring problem. Overcome. Decision made to use flickering lights at tables, activated by individual buttons pressed at tables.

Problem over payment of check as Kirk and party leave. Decide to fake signing check on small device with lights on it. Kirk signs on this.

Knife—Irving says we need three. Real ones, rubber one for attack scene, one with short blade shown sticking in victims. Must be made. More money.

Scene-by-scene discussion continues.

Pevney wants scenery green outside doorways. Matt protests. No more money in budget—spent all on basic sets. Unresolved.

Discussion brings out defects in script. Some are simply corrected by altering an approach or requirement. Others are corrected by means of rewrite.

Meeting breaks up informally as those leave whose areas of discussion are over.

The foregoing is only one example of how even minor changes can come about in a script. Numerous other examples take place all the way through the production process, even to the last day of filming the last scene. The changes made as a result of this process insure a more entertaining show, but also greatly increase the high degree of believability so often expressed by STAR TREK's viewing audience.

WHAT MOST PEOPLE DON'T REALIZE IS THAT THE REASON FOR THIS BELIEVABILITY LIES IN THE ENORMOUS CREATIVE TIME AND ATTENTION WHICH GOES INTO EVERY SINGLE DETAIL OF EACH EPISODE. TO ILLUSTRATE THE POINT, SUPPOSE WE DECIDE THAT IN THE NEXT SHOW WE ARE GOING TO VISIT PLANET POLARIS IX.

SINCE THE SCRIPT WILL HAVE AT LEAST

SOME INDICATION OF HOW THE WRITER HAS VISUALIZED THE PLANET SURFACE, WE HAVE A DISCUSSION WITH OUR ART DIRECTOR, MATT JEFFERIES, AND DEVELOP THE APPEARANCE IN DETAIL. IN THIS CASE, WE ESTABLISH THE PLANET IS HOT, HUMID, AND COVERED WITH DENSE VEGETATION. THE HISTORY, GEOGRAPHY, TOPOGRAPHY, GRAVITATIONAL VARIATIONS, AND SO FORTH, ARE THOROUGHLY DISCUSSED. THIS ENTIRE DISCUSSION IS THEN REFLECTED IN THE SET MATT BUILDS: THE COLOR OF THE SKY, THE TYPE OF ROCK FORMATIONS, ETC.

HAVING DONE THIS, WE PROCEED TO COSTUMES. BIILL THEISS, OUR COSTUME DESIGNER, CAN'T SIMPLY GO DOWN TO THE LOCAL COSTUME RENTAL SHOP AND SAY, "I'D LIKE TO SEE THE RACK OF POLARIS IX CLOTHING, PLEASE." HE MUST START FROM SCRATCH, GUIDED BY OUR EARLIER DISCUSSIONS. THE TYPE OF CLOTHING DESIGNED MUST ACTUALLY BE SUITABLE FOR A HOT, HUMID PLANET WITH DENSE VEGETATION.

THE SAME APPROACH MUST BE TAKEN WITH THE SET DECORATIONS. DIFFERENT SOCIETIES WILL INVARIABLY HAVE DIFFERENT TYPES OF FURNISHINGS, FLOOR COVERINGS, ETC. WE ASK OURSELVES, "WHAT KIND OF SOCIETY ARE WE ESTABLISHING ON THIS TYPE OF PLANET, AND WHAT WOULD THEIR WORKS OF ART LOOK LIKE? WOULD THEY USE STATUETTES, PAINTINGS, TAPESTRIES, OR WHAT?" BASED ON THE CONCLUSIONS REACHED, THE ART OBJECTS AND FURNISHINGS ARE BUILT ACCORDINGLY.

HAIR STYLES, MAKE-UP—EVERY ASPECT OF THE SHOW IS APPROACHED IN THIS MANNER. BY THE TIME THE SHOW HAS BEEN SHOT, HUNDREDS OF HOURS HAVE BEEN SPENT IN ACHIEVING A REALISTIC EFFECT. THE SUM

TOTAL OF THIS EFFORT IS WHAT ENABLES
THE VIEWER, CONSCIOUSLY OR UNCON-
SCIOUSLY, TO SIT BACK AND SAY, "YES, I BE-
LIEVE IT. I REALLY AM ON PLANET POLARIS
IX."

Bob Justman's fears proved groundless, after all. STAR
TREK began its first day of shooting, on its first episode for its
first season, on schedule.

TO: All Concerned          DATE:    May 19, 1966
FROM: Bob Justman          SUBJECT:   GETTING
                                     STARTED ON
                                     THE RIGHT
                                     FOOT

Dear Friend:
   You are cordially invited to attend a little get-together Monday evening, May 23rd, at approximately
seven on the clock in the STAR TREK offices, "E" Building, Desilu-Gower.
   A small amount of Saurian brandy will be available;
not too much, as we start shooting the following morning, but sufficient to get a glow on.
   Hopefully, there will be many more of these yearly
affairs for all of us to enjoy.

                              Very truly yours,

                                 STAR TREK Gang

# Chapter 2

## These Are the Voyages . . .

All businesses have occupational diseases. For the crew, it's flat feet and varicose veins. Ulcers? Only the producers . . . we can't afford them.

A former Assistant Director

At last STAR TREK was officially in production. Two years had passed since NBC first expressed interest in the series. Two long years of trial and error, frustration, agonizing reappraisals, and finally—triumph. Gene Roddenberry, of all people involved, must surely have experienced a feeling of high exhilaration on that, his first official day of production. Now there was a show to get on the road.

The very same day production began, Gene issued a series of requests, by which he hoped to insure production would proceed in an efficient, orderly, and uncomplicated manner. His requests included a verbal report from the set twice a day to be delivered to him by the assistant director, a twice-daily visit to the set by executive script consultant John D. F. Black, immediate advisement of significant dialogue changes during the course of filming, and immediate notification from the set of any deviation from production planning or routine.

STAR TREK shifted into high gear.

Only a few days prior, however, Gene had been faced with a totally unexpected situation. STAR TREK's male actors had voiced their objections to having to wear their hair permanently cut in a futuristic style. Gene had asked them to adopt the new haircuts as a means of further relating to the viewing audience that *Enterprise* crewmen were, in fact, living in a futuristic time period. He also felt it was logical to assume man's haircut style would probably evolve to something different by the time he reached STAR TREK's time period. The actors objected, maintaining that off camera they had to live in the 20th century. A compromise was finally reached, wherin the actors would retain their own favored hairstyles, but would simply point the bottoms of their sideburns.

Although the STAR TREK staff recognized that serious production problems were appearing, they were not about to let them interfere with the humorous side of life. They promptly arranged a put-on (one of many, as time went by) for Gene Roddenberry.

Gene was lured out of his office on the pretext of having to resolve a problem on the set. While he was out of the office Gregg Peters brought in a mannequin that had to be straight out of the movie *Psycho*. It was a woman with a terribly cadaverous, rotted face, and in general the most hideously gruesome creature imaginable. Gregg set the cadaver just inside Gene's office door in such a manner that when he opened the door the thing would fall out on him.

A little while later Gene came barreling back into his office. Whenever he is going in or out of his office, he has a habit of just charging right through, as if his motor were forever set in high gear. As expected, he barreled through the outer office, flung open his door . . . and collided with the cadaver halfway through. He never uttered a sound, but he must have jumped backward at least three feet!

Several times after that the cadaver would be sneaked into Bob Justman's office and placed in such a position that anyone coming into Bob's office for a conference would not immediately notice it. Inevitably some poor fellow would come in, sit down in a chair, and there would be this thing looking over his shoulder. Eventually the guy would unconsciously "feel" it, turn around and suddenly find himself staring into the face of this hideous cadaver. The shock was always immediate. And it worked every time!

It was also shortly after production started that Gene acquired the title "Great Bird of the Galaxy." The expression was taken from a line of Sulu's in "The Man Trap" and was meant to be like a humorous blessing: "May the Great Bird of the Galaxy roost on your planet." Gene had written the line, it was picked up by the staff, and caught on as a slang expression. When Herb Solow called Gene "The Great Bird of the Galaxy" one day, it stuck immediately.

At any rate, the Great Bird of the Galaxy became a household word around the studio, and in some cases was even used in a threatening manner.

TO:  Matt Jefferies      DATE:  July 28, 1966
FROM:  Bob Justman     SUBJECT:  SET SKETCHES—
                                                  "MUDD'S WOMEN"

Dear Matt:

If I don't get those preliminary set sketches for "Mudd's Women," the Great Bird of the Galaxy is going to do something nasty on you.

Your former friend,

Bob Justman

When STAR TREK moved onto the Desilu Gower lot, the production was assigned two complete sound stages—Numbers 9 and 10. Stage 9 contains the primary sets used aboard the *Enterprise,* including the briefing room, sick bay, Captain Kirk's quarters, the bridge, engineering section, corridors, turbo-lifts, and transporter room (and other ship's interiors required from time to time). Stage 10, the larger of the two, was reserved for sets used to depict alien planet surfaces. It was hoped that almost any type of alien landscape imaginable could be constructed on this stage.

Actually, STAR TREK should have the use of a third sound stage. The need often will arise for additional sets, and there is no place to put them. Unlike most TV shows, STAR TREK can only rarely go on location and must therefore confine most of its shooting activities to the two stages available, severely limiting flexibility and arrangement of sets. With Stage 9 totally filled by the *Enterprise* interior sets alone, and with a planet surface constructed on Stage 10, the production company is usually out of luck on space for additional sets.

The term "stage" is really inaccurate. Inside, there is no elevated portion you would think of as a stage, no curtains you would draw across the front. A sound stage is a big building. It is perhaps seventy-five feet high on the outside, and (at least in the case of Stages 9 and 10) approximately one hundred feet square on the inside. Ten thousand square feet, unsupported, under one roof, is an awful lot of room. It's amazing how easily it can be filled to capacity.

Sound stages are built with super-thick walls, double airlock-type doors, and are theoretically soundproof. At the outside entrance, just above the door, is a flashing red light or rotating beacon. When this light is flashing, it means shooting is in progress inside, and one must not enter or the door noise will be picked up by the sensitive recording equipment. It would spoil a scene and is guaranteed to bring down the wrath of a lot of people about your head and shoulders in a great big hurry.

Inside, the red beacon light is connected to the sound mixer's* console. When shooting begins, the sound mixer presses a button that automatically turns on the red rotating beacon. At the same time, a gawdawful loud bell rings all over the room. When the bell rings, it is a signal for everyone inside the stage to remain absolutely quiet, for the cameras are about to roll.

My very first visit to Stage 9 (they were shooting on the bridge that day) produced the following notes:

Place is really jammed. Equipment scattered everywhere. Walls of different sets crowded together. Big lights on black stands all over floor, many electrical cables strewn everywhere. Watch step. Don't trip.

Much bustle of activity. People running everywhere. Stay out of way. Probably get run down.

Men on network of catwalks high overhead. Manning lights. Adjusting angles. So much crap hanging from

---

* Carl Daniels, a thoroughly delightful pixie-like man, is STAR TREK's sound mixer. He sits at a movable console and monitors the sounds picked up by the microphones on the set. He can adjust the volume on each one, as needed. His console is connected to the recording equipment, which is located in another building.

ceiling, amazed whole thing doesn't come crashing down.

Orders shouted by different people. "Move this prop!" "Light this one!" "Dampen that one!"

It seems like mass chaos. Wonder how they can possibly achieve quiet on the set for shooting.

Bizarre contrast.

Amid this confusion actors sit around seemingly oblivious. Some are reading the trade papers, some going over lines, some standing around smoking, in idle conversation with others around them.

Then the shout from the director. "Hold it quiet for rehearsal, please!" The bell rings. Suddenly you can hear a pin drop. The change is stark and dramatic.

Camera mounted on thing with wheels. Camera rolls in close to actors.

"Cut! Where's the activity? I want people moving!"

We begin again. Places. Interruptions. Finally the director is satisfied. One more rehearsal and then we shoot. A very dramatic take. Cameras rolling. Tension mounts. Camera on Kirk.

Beeping noise signals call on communicator. Kirk whips out communicator. Starts to speak into it. Communicator malfunctions. Grid won't stay up. Slowly flops down. Kirk stands there looking at it. Moves hand slightly, flips open grid. Watches it slowly flop down again. Cameras still rolling. Flips grid up again. Grid flops down again. Kirk smiles. Director yells, "Cut!"

They do it again.

The intensity of the lights used to illuminate a set is difficult to comprehend. Even to describe them as "intensely bright" would be inadequate. George Merhoff, the gaffer (lighting director), estimated that as much as 650,000 watts may be needed to properly light a STAR TREK set. Figuring an average home requires about 7,000 watts, that's enough to light a small subdivision. If a person were to look directly into an unfiltered set light, he could suffer eye damage. Very often you will hear a gaffer on set shouting, "Watch your eyes!" as a light is being adjusted.

Despite the seemingly chaotic conditions on a set, activities are actually progressing in an orderly, coherent fashion. (It's hard to believe, but it's true.)

Probably one of the most uncomfortable moments I've ever spent in my life occurred on a later visit to that same set. I casually strolled in one afternoon and had the great misfortune to get caught in a master shot.

Normally, a "take" runs about thirty to sixty seconds or perhaps maybe a minute and a half at the most, before the Director calls, "Cut!" But the master shot is the overall shot of a scene, and all the activity that goes on during that scene. A long master shot may run four or five minutes —sometimes ten! without stopping. When the bell rings, you have to freeze where you are, and not move at all while the camera is rolling.

There I was, the bell rang, and the master shot started rolling. It doesn't take long before the situation starts getting to you. Your breathing begins to sound like a bellow after a while, your throat starts to tickle, your foot starts itching, you get a cramp in your leg, but you don't dare move to get rid of the cramp in your leg for fear of making a noise. You begin to get this unbearable, uncontrollable urge to cough. But of course you can't cough, and you have to stifle it.

In a long take you see people going through all sorts of convulsions, trying to hold themselves quiet. Nobody wants to spoil a master shot, because the director likes to get it down in one continuous take. When the director yells, "Cut!" and the all-clear bell rings two short bursts, signaling that the take is over, you don't really believe it. It's like a new lease on life. I always try to avoid master shots.

The sound stages may be soundproofed against outside noises, but STAR TREK's production crew soon discovered *inside* noises were creating a problem. The sound department began to complain about picking up footsteps on their recording instruments. The footsteps, it turned out, were those of the cast as they moved about during the filming of the scenes. Corrective action was taken by adding additional sound-absorbing materials to the sets. No more complaints from the sound department.

As the weeks of production rolled by, personnel became

acquainted with STAR TREK's futuristic atmosphere and little by little began to regard the *Enterprise*'s equipment as more fact that fiction. People fell into the habit of referring to this or that piece of equipment in terms of how it actually operated or what its particular function was. Witness the following notice posted on Stage 9:

The red wall panel light (flanking the elevator entrance) is only to be used when the *Enterprise* is in a state of ALERT.

The small blinker located between the helm and navigator positions (on their common console unit) will serve as warning and alarm light (to notify the bridge of sensor probes, problems in the engine room, malfunction of the transporter, etc.).

Undoubtedly, this growing tendency to regard the equipment aboard the *Enterprise* as real certainly helped the cast to impart a greater believability in their respective roles. It did not, however, automatically insure that such equipment would appear believable to the viewing audience. Efforts to increase the Believability Factor continued unabated.

TO: Gregg Peters          DATE: August 16, 1966
FROM: Bob Justman          SUBJECT: ELEVATOR
                                         EFFECTS

Fellows:
It would be greatly appreciated that any time we have a shot in an elevator where we have a light effect to indicate movement and speed of movement, in addition to indicating the speed-up of movement as the elevator starts off, we also indicate a slowdown of movement before the elevator stops and the doors open. We have got to be able to give the Special Effects Man or the Electrician working the light effect a correct cue to start work-

ing that light effect, so that we can believe that the elevator is stopping prior to the opening of its doors.

Regards,

Bob Justman

While the STAR TREK production crew worried about believability, studio executives began to worry about STAR TREK falling behind schedule (it was), thereby incurring additional, unbudgeted costs.

TO:   Gene Roddenberry          DATE:   July 11, 1966
FROM:   Herb Solow              SUBJECT:   POST-PRO-
                                           DUCTION·

In looking over our post-production area and in discussions relating to post-production, I notice that the cutters on STAR TREK are taking a great deal of time getting their shows ready for dubbing. I recognize and understand the fact that these are the first shows and that they will necessarily take additional time. However, if the records I saw are correct, and I think they are, we are about past the "necessary time" point. As you know, we have music and effects cutters sitting idly by waiting for the cuts to get into their hands. What will make life worse is the fact that we shortly have to schedule the routine dubbing and scoring times. If the cuts are not ready to be scored, then we have to put our cutters on an overtime basis in order to get them ready and, of course, run into additional expense.

I agree one hundred percent that we should give the first shows in particular as much tender, loving care as possible. I think, however, we must set standards for ourselves and set schedules that by a certain day the film must be given up from the film editor to the music and effects people. After all, how can we improve on beauty?

Thank you.

---

As far as falling behind schedule was concerned, the problem was by no means limited to the post-production area. For some reason or other, there seemed to be an endless number of script problems, and Gene found himself in a perpetual state of rewrite. The situation became so tight that Gene was literally rewriting scenes the day before they were supposed to be shot on the set. He and his secretary often worked until three or four in the morning and even Saturdays and Sundays —feeding rewritten pages and acts to the mimeo company, so that scripts could be mimeographed and distributed.

Understandably, Bob Justman became frantic with the situation. In desperation, he walked into Gene Roddenberry's office, climbed up on top of his desk, and stood there loudly declaring he would not move one inch until Gene finished the rewrite on the scene. And he stood there until Gene finished. He then accepted the new scene with thanks, jumped off the desk, and walked out of the office.

For quite a while after that it was a common sight to see Bob Justman standing on top of Gene Roddenberry's desk waiting for him to finish rewriting a scene so he could hurry down to the set and give it to the director. Gene eventually countered Justman's tactic by having an electrically controlled lock installed on his door. The switch was hidden from view and could be operated only from the outside by his secretary. She, of course, was sworn on pain of death not to reveal the location of the switch.

Gene really isn't slow; it's simply that Justman is notorious for being fast. Bob has to have it *now*. He is a compulsive man who works twenty-four hours a day. Gene is a compulsive man who works twenty-three hours a day. It's that hour's difference that Bob Justman makes demands upon.

Bob Justman's relentless attention to even the tiniest of details developed into a legend. Whenever he spotted even a minor flaw, he would pounce upon it in typical Justman fashion! And with typical Justman humor.

TO:   John D. F. Black          DATE:  July 15, 1966
FROM: Bob Justman               SUBJECT:  STAR TREK
                                          SEMANTICS

Dear John:

Perhaps the following information might be of use to you and your host of talented writers. The prefix "tera" attached to a word denotes a number followed by 12 zeros. The prefix "mega" denotes a number followed by 6 zeros and the prefix "kilo" denotes a number followed by 3 zeros.

The prefix "decca" denotes a numeral on a record album.

Regards,

Bob

Another typically Justman habit is to protest loudly that a certain thing cannot be done. In *no way* can it be done. When such a situation arose, Gene (in typical Roddenberry fashion) countered with a long, involved statement, which translated into: "Let's find a way to do it."

TO:   Gene Roddenberry          DATE:  August 15, 1966
FROM: Bob Justman               SUBJECT:  MONEY

Dear Gene:

I had some conversations with Herb last week in which we discussed, among other things, the cost of making our various STAR TREK episodes. It is Herb's intention that should we get picked up for additional shows those *new* episodes should be brought in for $185,000.00, or less.

The only way we are going to be able to afford to do this is to write shows that are very tight and play mostly on board ship. Shows that do not have much optical special effects or the need for new set construction and expensive casts. Shows that can be shot in a maximum of six days. Shows that do not call for location work and all that that entails. Shows where the story is the thing and the gimmicks are unnecessary.

Yes, I know that NBC wants planet shows. But I feel strongly that if they want planet shows, then they should help bear the cost. We could make STAR TREK such a successful show that the Studio would never recover financially. And I am sure that is not your intention, from all our previous talks together.

                                        Bob Justman


TO: Robert Justman        DATE:  August 17, 1966
FROM: Gene Roddenberry    SUBJECT:  YOUR MEMO
                                    RE: MONEY

Yes, we will aim to bring the second batch of shows in for $185,000 or less.

Yes, we will try to find shipboard shows. The writers and stories being what they are, we will sometimes have to accept the bald practical fact that we must go for the best and most entertaining stories we can find, work from there.

I fully understand that new sets and local locations are expensive. At the same time, I have been a part of shows shot on local locations (even distant locations) and shows with differing sets which made out by creative use of what can be doubled over, stolen, and borrowed. They have been brought in for figures like this, even taking into account Desilu's high markup. I think we can do it too.

Now, what we need most at this particular time is

some farsighted thinking, some cautioning of what is impossibly expensive, some advice on what *can* be done, so Gene Coon and you and I can work with these writers and these scripts to make it possible.

What are the things we can *do*?

Gene Roddenberry

NBC's request for more planet shows, at no increase in budget, was not the only request emanating from them. As a matter of fact, the network's Broadcast Standards Department was just full of requests where STAR TREK's scripts were concerned.

Regarding "Dagger of the Mind," their comments included:

Page 5: Please try to find some other way for Van Gelder to subdue the Crewman, since the knee in the face would be considered brutal.

Page 17: McCoy's injection of Van Gelder must not be shown on camera if a needle-type hypodermic is used; if he uses his air-hiss injector, this restraint does not apply.

Page 45: Please delete the underlined in Janice's speech: "I'm a damned attractive female."

Re: the hypnotism sequences (pages 36-37 and page 57), I quote from the outline report dated May 20, 1966:

In accordance with our precautions to avoid hypnotizing a viewer, the act of hypnotizing must be either out of context or done off-camera. Further, since you are portraying hypnotism as a legitimate medical tool, Van Gelder should be hypnotized by *Dr.* McCoy rather than *Mr.* Spock unless *Mr.* Spock can be established as being qualified in the use of this technique.

For the episode entitled "Miri," their comments included:

Page 9: Restraint is necessary here so the sight of the boy creature will not alarm or shock the viewer; please avoid the objectionably grotesque in general appearance and makeup. This caution applies also to the sight of the girl creature noted on page 44.

Page 12: Caution on the sight of the dead boy creature; avoid seeing the open eyes.

Page 24: Please use restraint here and throughout the script to be sure the blemishes are not unnecessarily gruesome to the viewer.

Page 44: As above, caution on the sight of the dead girl creature.

Page 62: Caution here where Janice opens her uniform to check on the progress of the disease; avoid exposure which would embarrass or offend.

While NBC was wrestling with STAR TREK scripts, STAR TREK was also wrestling with STAR TREK scripts. To illustrate some of the problems that can arise with scripts received (even on assignment) at the STAR TREK office, consider a few of the following comments, made by the staff members, to each other, after their first reading:

In Scene 23, the script indicates Kirk is throwing cold water on his face. We have no provision for a bathroom or fire hydrant in Kirk's quarters.

On Page 16, Janice rushes for her door, "pulls it open." As you know, none of our doors pull open or have knobs on them or any such thing. There are a number of instances of this sort of action within this script.

South's speech in Scene 76 refers to available wood for the fire. Is there wood available, or would they be using cow patties?

It sure is lucky for our side that when South gets the drop on Kirk and shoots him, Kirk is only knocked unconscious by the phaser charge, instead of being killed outright.

On page 14, South looks at Janice's wristwatch. Does she wear a Timex or an Ingersol?

Could we discuss the "wallet" routine in Scene 73?

Kirk's reference to forgetting his wallet troubles me and makes me uneasy for some weird reason.

The last speech on Page 62 contains several ideas which sound like trouble to me. I find it hard to believe that Spock could get winded easily, and I am not sure about his reference to "integration."

Since there are a number of amazing coincidences in this script, I think we should take advantage of it and heighten our suspense. Therefore, I wish there was some way to have Kirk, Spock and Sulu in close proximity to each other in Scenes 44 through 46. And Kirk and Spock could miss discovering Sulu just by the very slimmest of margins. This ought to be enough to drive the audience out of its collective skull.

Page 14A caused me to become exceedingly cruel to my wife and children the other night. And it is only one-eighth of a page.

The writer has made the oft-repeated statement that this show will cost 98 cents to shoot. Please keep him out of my office. I know that he will try to convince me that this show will cost 98 cents to shoot. I can't afford to take the time to explain to him why it will cost more than 98 cents to shoot. I have been down this road with him before. Tell the writer that if he insists upon arguing budget with me, in the future I shall have to restrict him from my couch. He will no longer be allowed to sleep on my couch or to come in and stand on my desk.* I will have him taken away by the "Civil People." He will also be denied the right to eat any leaves off my secretary's plant. He shall have to find emotional nourishment elsewhere.

The foregoing are merely random examples of the detailed analysis that is made on every script submitted to STAR TREK. These analyses, written by the executive producer, producer, associate producer, and story consultant often run to five pages or more. In part, it is one reason why scripts are

---

* Apparently the writer in question had heard of Bob Justman's habit re: Gene Roddenberry.

so often rewritten. Perhaps it is also an indicator of why the rewrite seems to take such a long time to finish.

On September 3, 1966, Gene Roddenberry was an honored guest at the 24th Annual World Science Fiction Convention in Cleveland, Ohio. The Convention Committee had requested a special screening of "Where No Man Has Gone Before."

The response was fantastic! When the wildly approving tumult had subsided, Gene was pleased to accept a precedent-shattering award from the assembled delegates: "For Distinguished Contributions to Science Fiction."

A thoroughly delighted Gene Roddenberry sent the following telegram to Desilu's head of television:

> 756P PDT SEP 3 66 LB367 CTA271
>     CT CLB506 NL PD CLEVELAND OHIO 3
> HERB SOLOW, VP TV, DESILU
> STAR TREK HIT OF THE CONVENTION, VOTED
> BEST EVER. RECEIVED STANDING OVATION.
>     GENE R.

STAR TREK's television premiere was two weeks away.

Chapter 3

## Steady As She Goes

NOTHING WOULD PLEASE ME MORE THAN
TO TAKE CREDIT FOR THE WHOLE THING.
THERE ARE MANY ASPECTS OF IT THAT I
THOUGHT OUT INDEPENDENTLY, AND IT
PLEASES ME THAT THEY WORKED. BUT MUCH
OF THE CREATIVITY OF STAR TREK IS OF A
SUBTLE NATURE, INCLUDING MUCH WHICH
THE AUDIENCE NEVER REALIZES, AND FOR
WHICH AS EXECUTIVE PRODUCER I CANNOT
TAKE CREDIT. EIGHTY OTHER PEOPLE HELP
MAKE THE SHOW . . . THEY ARE THE ONES
WHO DESERVE A LION'S SHARE OF THE
CREDIT. WE'VE GOT GOOD PEOPLE AND WE
LET THEM DO THEIR JOB.

Gene Roddenberry

One of the things that has always impressed me about
STAR TREK is that every single member of the production
crew is personally concerned about the show. As an ex-Marine,
I am quite familiar with esprit de corps. What I have
observed goes far beyond that. I have never seen any group
of people anywhere function as a team the way the production
staff and crew does on STAR TREK. Every person strongly
feels they are *creatively* involved. They seem to feel each one
of them—the cameraman, the gaffer, the makeup man, the
script consultant, the grips—is, personally, the key factor in
the success of the production. And perhaps they are. Perhaps
without them there never could have been a STAR TREK.

THIS IS ONE OF THE THINGS WE ENCOUR-
AGE. THE JOB WAS SO HORRENDOUS, SO DIFFI-
CULT, WE REALIZED WE COULD NOT (AS IS

DONE ON SO MANY SHOWS) TOTALLY SEP-
ARATE EACH FUNCTION. IF BILL THEISS HAS
A GREAT IDEA ON SET DESIGNING OR ON
MAKEUP, IF FRED PHILIPS HAS A GREAT IDEA
ON COSTUMES, IF EDDIE MILKIS HAS A GREAT
IDEA FOR A DIALOGUE CHANGE . . . WE
WANT TO HEAR IT. WE'VE GOT SO MANY
PROBLEMS, SO MUCH TO FIGHT . . . IF WE
HAVE CREATIVITY IN ANY AREA, WE'D BET-
TER LISTEN TO IT!

Roddenberry felt it absolutely necessary to personally produce the first dozen episodes made. He had the second pilot
to show new writers, but that single film nailed down only a
fraction of the concepts he believed were vital to STAR
TREK's success.

For even a fairly ordinary television series, ten or twelve
episodes must be made before the style of the new series is
finally crystallized. During those early episodes actors and
producer must work closely together to evolve the characteri-
zations, the dozens of small strengths, flaws, gestures, and attitudes that see a Kirk, Spock, or McCoy begin to emerge
into someone the audience believes is *real*. Relationships between characters must also be worked out. In a series like
STAR TREK a familiar "family group" is essential to the
show's success.

Roddenberry knew also that many of his ideas about ship
technique, terminology, routine bridge practices, and so on
must be tested on film during early episodes. Too much complexity in early episodes would confuse the audience and turn
the viewers away. It was imperative that highly believable
ship and bridge techniques be quickly adopted and standardized.

A GOOD EXAMPLE WAS ONE OF THE EARLY
FIRST DRAFTS I RECEIVED FROM A WRITER.
AN IMPORTANT STORY POINT IN THE TEASER
WAS CAPTAIN KIRK REVERSING THE COURSE
OF THE VESSEL. THE WRITER GAVE US TWO
AND ONE HALF PAGES OF HIGHLY TECHNICAL,

SCIENTIFICALLY ACCURATE JARGON FROM KIRK IN ACCOMPLISHING THE MANEUVER. I THREW OUT THOSE PAGES, SUBSTITUTED IT WITH A ONE-LINE ORDER FROM KIRK: "RE-VERSE COURSE!"

STAR TREK was a formidable assignment to throw at any writer. It is difficult enough for a writer to come up with an acceptable, entertaining one-hour script about things he knows. But almost everything about STAR TREK was totally outside the writer's frame of reference. Experienced science-fiction writers create their *own* future civilization, habits, manners, morals, vessels, federations, and gimmicks. But in writing for STAR TREK they had to accept Roddenberry's concepts and ignore their own.

This reasoning made sense. STAR TREK was a television *serial* . . . in effect, a twenty-six-hour movie that would be aired in one-hour parts. Characters, ship techniques, and terminology had to be the same week to week. If the ship's sensors had certain limitations or abilities last week, they had to be the same this week. If Spock had certain mannerisms and speech patterns this week, they had to be the same the next week. It wasn't like writing a Western or a police script, where the writer could make a fair guess about something on the basis of his past experience and knowledge, historical research, or a phone call to his local police precinct. With STAR TREK at the beginning, there was only one source—Roddenberry.

It was only natural that some writers were confused by the sheer volume of ideas, terms, and techniques necessary. Others, including a few highly experienced science fiction pros with firm ideas of their own, resented being straitjacketed by another's concepts. They had ideas, too, often excellent ones, and insisted on incorporating them into their scripts.

THAT WAS ONE OF THE MOST DIFFICULT EXPERIENCES I HAVE EVER HAD. WORKING WITH A WRITER WHO WAS YOUR PEER, OR OFTEN YOUR SUPERIOR IN SCI-FI EXPERI-ENCE, AND HAVING TO INSIST HE THROW OUT

HIS OWN GOOD IDEAS AND USE YOUR CON-
CEPTS INSTEAD. BUT ONCE WE HAD A COUPLE
OF EPISODES ON FILM, FINISHED AND EN
ROUTE TO THE NETWORK, WE COULDN'T SUD-
DENLY CHANGE THINGS ALREADY ESTAB-
LISHED.

IT LOST ME THE AFFECTION OF SOME
WRITER FRIENDS BECAUSE THEY THOUGHT I
WAS SAYING NO ONE COULD HAVE A GOOD
IDEA BUT ME. YES, I WAS ARBITRARY. I *HAD*
TO BE. I COULDN'T SEND NBC TWELVE EPI-
SODES CONTAINING TWELVE DIFFERENT FOR-
MATS, A DOZEN DIFFERENT CONCEPTS OF MR.
SPOCK, AND SO ON. THE SERIES HAD TO HAVE
WEEK-TO-WEEK UNITY, EVEN THOUGH THAT
UNITY MIGHT TURN OUT TO BE THE UNITY
OF MY ERRORS.

Almost every writer's final draft during the first half of the
year was again completely rewritten by Roddenberry, to insure getting and keeping that unity. Budget problems also
made many of the rewrites necessary. Because of the complexity of the show, new sets, new opticals, etc., writers'
drafts would usually estimate out at far more money than the
studio would permit to be spent on one episode.

There were other reasons, too. NBC's requirements, for example.

A case in point involved Ted Sturgeon's excellent script
"Shore Leave." Sturgeon was on another assignment as shooting neared, and his script needed a rewrite to bring certain
scenes within budget possibility. Roddenberry had to leave
town for a week, and the rewrite was assigned to a new staff
member.

Unknown to the new man, NBC had been worried that
Sturgeon's story might seem to be "fantasy," and Roddenberry had pledged that the rewrite would emphasize reality.
Roddenberry's memo to the new man, detailing his agreement
with NBC, somehow got lost between their offices. The rewrit-
er saw a way to bring the episode within budget by empha-
sizing the fantasy aspects. Having no knowledge of the pledge

made to NBC, he revised the script to include those fantasy elements and sent it to mimeo.

Roddenberry returned to town the day before the show was to begin filming, read the script and realized he was in trouble.

The location chosen for filming was an area called "Africa U.S.A.," a huge thousand-acre ranch, complete with lions, tigers, elephants, lakes, etc. ("Cowboy in Africa" and "Daktari" often were filmed here). The entire STAR TREK production crew arrived and began preparations for shooting. Roddenberry sat down under a tree and began writing.

It was a case, literally, of writing the script as it was shot.

The concept of the show was wild to begin with, opening with Dr. McCoy encountering Alice and the White Rabbit— and going on from there. For some unknown reason, the rewrite mania hit everybody at the same time. As a result, almost everyone was improvising as they went along, throwing in new ideas here and there, whenever something new or different occurred to them. Under those conditions, the director, Bob Sparr, who was new to STAR TREK, must have been firmly convinced he really was on some alien planet, surrounded by a horde of wild-eyed maniacs.

At the end of the first day's shooting there was a round table rewrite session in the private room of a nearby restaurant which lasted till after midnight. Everyone there contributed wild ideas for the big climax scene at the end of the show—airplanes strafing the ground, samurai warriors charging through, tigers, elephants, etc.

The next day Gene Roddenberry made arrangements for the elephant. Normal cost was $300 for the elephant and $100 for the trainer. But because Gene was using so many other animals, too, he got a real bargain—one elephant for $150, with trainer thrown in. The elephant was promptly given to Gregg Peters, at the time still a First Assistant Director. Everyone asked him, as each day went by, when he was going to use his elephant. Gregg never did. They just ran out of time and never got around to it. (To this day, someone will occasionally ask Gregg, "Say—when do you get to use your elephant?")

The tiger, though, was something else again. Someone

came up with the idea that Bill Shatner should leap on the tiger and wrestle it down. Bill took to the idea right away, and no amount of pleading from Gene Roddenberry could make him change his mind. He was determined he was going to wrestle the tiger. Gene diplomatically tried to convince him a Starship Captain was great, but not that great. While the argument went on, the tiger just stood there, licking its chops.

Bill insisted on wrestling the tiger, until Leonard Nimoy finally said, "Bill, you don't have to wrestle the tiger. I'll just pinch him."

Later on in the day Bill and Leonard were trying to explain the "Spock pinch" to director Bob Sparr, who didn't know what it was all about. Bill explained, "Here, let me show you what it looks like." He walked over to Leonard and applied the Spock pinch. Leonard just stood there, smiling. Bill tried again. Nothing. Then Leonard said, "This is how it really works." He casually applied the Spock pinch to Bill Shatner, who promptly fell down unconscious. Sparr just stood there, incredulous.

STAR TREK is definitely not a show for new directors.

But somehow it all worked. The story had been returned to Sturgeon's original concept, it was finished on time and within budget . . . and strangest of all, became one of STAR TREK's most successful and talked-about episodes.

TO: Matt Jefferies          DATE:    October 21, 1966
FROM: Bob Justman          SUBJECT:    COMPUTER
                                       VOICE DEVICE

Matt:

We need some sort of device that will do something visual when the computer voice answers a question from the Captain. It should not be a blinking light device, as we have a surfeit of those. But it should be some sort of device that has some visual effect upon it. You might use light, but in a different manner than what we have done up to now. This is something that would come on when computer voice talks and go off when it stops talking, possibly. It would be insertable and portable, so that we could put it anywhere and it would not look as if it were something that was built by my eight-year-old son. Why don't you grab hold of Gene Roddenberry for a short talk about this device and then get to work on it?

Regards,

Bob

cc: Gene Roddenberry

TO: Matt Jefferies                    DATE: October 24, 1966
FROM: Gene Roddenberry            SUBJECT: COMPUTER
                                                          VOICE DEVICE

Dear Matt:

Think we *must* have something of this sort soon. The scenes where our people talk to a "disembodied" computer voice have not been nearly as good as those in "Mudd's Women," where we had the "computer voice" do something on a screen or with lights when the computer spoke back to someone.

Also, I would like to have someone write out for our various writers a computer voice format, specifying the exact terminology used in starting the machine, the type of phraseology used with it and from it, how to stop it, etc.

It's much better science fiction when the computer has a personality of its own, too.

Regards,

Gene Roddenberry

It did not take the production crew long to discover that even the smallest error made while shooting on the set could lead to definite problems later on. An example of this is a problem that came up in the post-production area of dubbing.

Due to improper timing in the shooting of some scenes, it sometimes became difficult to dub in certain sound effects, such as: the beep of the communicator, the hums and clicks of the library-computer just before its mechanical metallic voice answers, or the click of relays on the ship's turbo-elevator as it first begins to move.

In order to resolve the problem completely, it was suggested that it would be helpful to have someone offstage who could cue both the dubbing and the timing by actually saying, for example, "computer hum" or "elevator click, then turbo sound and movement begins." This could only be done, of course, in those situations where it would not interfere with or overlap dialogue going on during that particular take. Taking note of the fact that the problem needed a permanent solution, Roddenberry requested that production personnel establish a standardized timing system that would remain constant from show to show. This would enable dubbing personnel to use the same familiar sound effect from show to show. Here was yet another example of a subtle touch designed to increase believability and audience indentification with the show.

On October 5th, Desilu Studios received official notification from NBC that audience ratings on the early episodes had been satisfactory and thirteen additional episodes were being ordered. STAR TREK would continue for the second half of the season.

Again and again Gene Roddenberry impressed upon his staff the necessity for building the feeling of believability into every aspect of STAR TREK. The following memo demonstrates his continuing concern:

TO: Gene Coon          DATE:   October 24, 1966
FROM: Gene Roddenberry  SUBJECT: NECESSITY FOR
                                 WIDE ANGLE
                                 ESTABLISHING
                                 OF BRIDGE MAIN
                                 VIEWING SCREEN

Dear Gene:

Per our agreement on the above, am informing all involved people in this matter that it is *absolutely imperative* that every STAR TREK episode with a bridge scene be planned so that very early in the bridge scene we can use either stock wide angle establishing bridge main viewing screen, or such a tie-down shot must be made so that stars or planet can be matted on it.

The problem is that simply going to INSERT—MAIN VIEWING SCREEN is not enough to set up the geography of the bridge and tell the audience that there is a huge "windshield" there that shows our space travel and makes us *feel* we're inside a ship moving through space.

We have had some complaints lately that the audience simply did not understand where the main viewing screen was, its size, etc. Preferably, it can be shot over Mr. Sulu, a regular character. Or possibly over both helm and navigator's position if the angle and lighting are such that we cannot recognize the backs of the heads. Or it could be quartered from between Kirk's and Spock's positions so that it could serve as a point of view from either of them. If those receiving copies of this have other thoughts and suggestions, I trust they will send them along to you with appropriate comments.

Regards,

Gene Roddenberry

Nor was there any letup in the flow of comments on proposed scripts from NBC's Broadcast Standards Department. Regarding "The Squire of Gothos," NBC's B.S. department commented in part:

Page 54: Please delete the following speeches:
Kirk's line, "Bring back some of the suspense . . . the fun . . . of killing."
Kirk's line, "Here's your chance to see how exquisite real terror can be."
Pages 56 & 57: General caution to avoid unnecessarily

extending the physical conflict between Kirk and Trelane, and avoid the brutal. Further, it will be necessary for you to find some other device to establish Trelane's invulnerability in scene 84 as the passage of the saber through his body is not acceptable.

Page 59: Please deemphasize the movement of the saber point to Kirk's neck.

Page 61: Somewhere in the scene with the voices, would you please add a line which assures us that Trelane will be punished by his parents.

Comments on the "Space Seed" included:

Page 2: The Morse Code S.O.S. must not be audible. The distress signal is reserved for actual emergencies and may not be used on the air.

Page 25: Please minimize the use of the surgical instrument as McCoy is threatened.

Page 43: Caution on the embrace; avoid the open-mouth kiss.

At least NBC no longer objects to Mr. Spock's ears.

After all, it's quite possible they are every bit as curious about those ears as anyone else. I know I was curious about them and when Fred Philips invited me to sit in on a makeup session I jumped at the chance.

When I walked in the makeup room the next morning, Leonard was already there, sitting in a barber chair, waiting for the makeup process to begin. I dragged up a chair, behind Leonard and out of the way, and sat back to observe. The makeup room is a small, narrow area, and I had a good opportunity to watch Fred as he worked:

The foam rubber ears go on first. Since the ears have been made from molds of Leonard's own ears, there is no problem with the basic fit. Working very slowly and very carefully, Fred adjusts the position of the rubber ears over Leonard's own ears, making sure they are "seated" properly. Then, working with spirit gum as an adhesive, Fred begins the delicate operation of joining the wafer-thin edge of the false ear to Leonard's own ear. This is a critical part of the operation. No line of joint must show. The camera would pick up and record it immediately.

Working first on one ear and then on the other, Fred gradually smoothes out the thin edge of the foam rubber until it fits perfectly. Next, he places a small piece of double-faced tape behind Leonard's right ear and presses it against the side of his head, below the hairline. He then removes the tape, leaving a thin film of adhesive. The ear is pressed against this adhesive, which holds the ear flat against the side of Leonard's head. The same process is repeated for his left ear.

After this step is completed, yellowish body makeup is applied to the exposed areas behind the ears, as well as all skin surfaces inside the ears.

By now it is about 7:00 A.M. Charlie Washburn* comes in, and Leonard orders breakfast: orange juice, grapefruit, and an egg sandwich. Charlie departs for the studio commissary. A few minutes later De Forest Kelley comes in and sits down in one of the vacant barber chairs. Three actors are now being made up simultaneously. There is the normal amount of banter back and forth. Fred, meanwhile, continues to apply Spock's makeup.

He carefully shaves the eyebrows, removing the upper half on each side. This leaves a small tuft of hair on either side of the bridge of Leonard's nose. With an eyebrow pencil, Fred begins at the eyebrow tuft and draws in a line that swings outward and upward. This becomes the base line for Mr. Spock's slanted eyebrows. Spirit gum is carefully applied over the eyebrow pencil line. Fred brings out a long strand of hair (yak—from the belly) and starting at the outer, upper point of the eyebrow, he presses an eighth of an inch of hair on at one time, cutting it off from the long strand as it sticks to the spirit gum. Working downward, he repeats this process until the line of hair joins the eyebrow tuft. This procedure is repeated for the other eyebrow.

The wardrobe man (key costumer) comes in and asks Leonard if he's had his new shirt fitted yet. Leonard says no. The wardrobe man says he will leave the shirt in Leonard's

---

* At the time, Charlie was an apprentice assistant director, but since has been promoted to second assistant director.

dressing room and departs. The new eyebrows are trimmed with scissors and straightened with a comb. Fred touches up the edges with an eyebrow pencil.

Next, the face and neck are covered with a base coat of makeup. This provides the basic color to the face. Highlights and shadows are then worked in around the eyes, chin, nose, and cheekbones. This is necessary in order to give the appearance of a third dimension, since the camera sees flat. Finally, a coat of powder is applied all over the face. This sets the makeup in position and prevents it from shifting due to the action of body oils and the effect of the hot lights on the set.

George Takei comes in. It is now seven-thirty. Coffee is brought in by a makeup assistant. Leonard's hair is combed forward; the bangs are straightened and smoothed. Fred applies a good coat of hair spray to hold the hair in place.

Leonard's breakfast arrives. He eats while Fred applies the finishing touches to his makeup.

Kelley is now applying the finishing touches to his own makeup. I think to myself how strange it looks to see a man using a hand mirror and an eyelash curler.

Leonard says, "Okay." Fred replies, "I'm ready." Leonard stands up and leans in close to the wall mirror to examine the makeup job closely under the strong lights. He spots a defect on one ear and sits down again in the chair. In moments Fred has the problem corrected. Leonard gets up from the chair again and finishes the rest of his egg sandwich. He walks out, saying he'll be back. It's been one hour and fifteen minutes. Another actor immediately sits down in his place.

More people are now coming in and going out. Some take longer than others. These are extras.

Leonard is back in a few minutes with a cup of coffee. He begins to kid Dee about the red pants and white ducks he is wearing. He comments, "That takes guts!" Kelley, departing, smiles and says, "You got to be *tough* to wear these!"

The first assistant director comes in and asks for the man Fred is working on. Fred answers he's sorry, but he can't have him yet. A few minutes later someone else comes in and asks for a standby makeup man on the set. It's almost eight o'clock—time for the camera to roll. One of Fred's assistants immediately leaves, carrying a small black portable makeup case. I talk with Fred a few minutes longer, thank him again for letting me sit in on the makeup session, and wander out onto the set.

Eddie Milkis, the post-production supervisor, is just walking by, headed for the stage door. We exchange hellos, and he disappears around the corner of a set. Time to start another day of filming.

Looking back over the problems existing at STAR TREK in September and October, 1966, it is easy to understand why Eddie Milkis ranks high in Gene Roddenberry's eyes. In fact, Gene credits Eddie, to a great extent, for averting a near-disaster.

Every STAR TREK episode uses approximately fifteen to twenty opticals. After the tenth episode had been shot, it had become painfully obvious that the optical situation had reached the point of no return.

Once the completed opticals are delivered to the studio, they must be composited (added to the film). This is one of the last steps in post-production, before the film is completed and delivered to the network. So many problems were being encountered in creating the optical effects that they were delivered later and later. This held up completion of each episode. At the season's beginning, episodes were being delivered three to four weeks ahead of air date. By September the episodes, due to the optical problems, were being finished on Saturday night for airing the following Thursday!

Episodes began to back up, and it became a matter of survival, just getting one episode completed in time to make its scheduled air date. To make matters worse, there was just not enough manpower to handle the load. The backlog of opticals kept building up faster than they could be composited.

That being the case, the situation really was grim. If the opticals couldn't be composited, there would be no episodes to put on the air. Just when it looked as though STAR TREK were sinking fast, Gene was able to hire Eddie away from MGM and bring him in as post-production supervisor. Eddie came up with considerable genius and ability in the post-production area, and before long the backlog of opticals began to ease up.

A warm, friendly person by nature, Eddie is a genuine delight to work with. He has an infectious sense of humor and is often the instigator of many a put-on around the studio. He is a highly skilled, highly creative production man.

Prior to the start of production in May, 1966, Gene had written a memo in which he expressed the fear that as STAR TREK's first season got further and further along, circumstances would require the availability of an extra episode. Developments did not need to proceed beyond the middle of August to prove him correct. As problems with the opticals grew worse and worse, it became a distinct possibility that sooner or later an air date would be missed.

His idea for meeting such a contingency was to write what is known as an "envelope." This would be a script for a one-hour show, but one that would utilize all available footage from Pilot Number 1, "The Menagerie." As Gene saw it, the end result would be a two-part story, each an hour in length, and both based on the original Pilot Number 1. The task would certainly not be easy, as changes had been made in sets, and many members of the original cast were no longer available. But if he could pull it off, it would be a major coup.

By the end of September Gene had written the first draft of the proposed envelope for "The Menagerie" and had submitted it to NBC for approval. The letter that Gene later received, approving his first-draft script, contained a remark that the reader should find most interesting. The letter read, in part:

> As we discussed, Gene, this is a very creditable job of integrating the footage of our Pilot Number 1 with an original story by you, the screen results of which should make two exciting STAR TREK episodes. *We are very pleased that you have written in Mr. Spock as the primary character, since, as you know, he is emerging as one of the definite "pluses" in the series.**

As could be expected, NBC's B.S. Department had their own comments to make about the first draft. These included:

---

* Author's italics.

Page 4: Please delete McCoy's expletive, "Good Lord
. . ."
Page 4: Please make certain that the invalid Captain
Pike's appearance could not be considered unnecessarily
alarming or offensive to the viewer.

The first draft of the script was also submitted to Kellam
De Forest's research company for clearance, as is done with
every script. Kellam De Forest returned comments that read
in part:

### RESEARCH ON: "THE MENAGERIE" PART ONE

| CAST | COMMENT |
|---|---|
| Base Commodore José Mendez | No conflicts. |
| Capt. Christopher Pike | Cleared before. No conflicts. |
| Chief Humboldt | Source name: Alexander Humboldt 1769–1859 |
| Miss Piper | Source name: Henrietta Piper 1846–1906 |

| PAGE | SCENE | COMMENT |
|---|---|---|
| 4 | 6 | *Delta rays*—Fictional type of radiation. |
| 9 | 16 | Lieutenant Helen Johannson—no conflicts. |
| 15 | 28 | *They've tried to question him, but he's agitated himself almost into a* |

| PAGE | SCENE | COMMENT |
|------|-------|---------|
|      |       | *coma.* Medically the terminology would be "he's agitated himself almost into unconsciousness." |
| 24   | 49    | *Fuel down to 63.4.* When stating fuel supply, one usually indicates the term of measurement—e.g., gallons, liters, or the percentage. |
| 27   | 57    | *Blast you, anyway, you had no right to come along*—see 61/145. One would assume that Kirk and Mendez went to the shuttlecraft t o g e t h e r from Mendez' office, since time is so important. The replacement of the real Mendez by the creation of the Keeper begs explanation. |
| 29   | 65    | *Are you serving him pie and ice cream also?* Since these are American and contemporary delicacies, possibly in future others would have taken their place. |
| 32   | 70    | *a hearing on Lieutenant Commander Spock.* In "Court Martial" Spock's rank is established as full |

| PAGE | SCENE | COMMENT |
| --- | --- | --- |
| | | Commander, which is certainly the more suitable for the First Officer. |

Production was scheduled to commence on October 11th, with final shooting to be completed on the 18th. In signing Marc Daniels as the director, Gene was taking no chances. Marc is one of the best *creative* directors in the business and had directed a number of other STAR TREK episodes prior to his assignment on "The Menagerie."

With production dates set, and all major details tied down, Gene left on a much-needed vacation, leaving the following memo for Bob Justman:

TO: Bob Justman   DATE: October 7, 1966
FROM: Gene Roddenberry SUBJECT: THE ENVELOPE

As indication of my vast and sincere regard for you, I leave behind while I am on vacation in the High Desert some fifty or sixty pages of sheer genius. Read and weep as did Alexander when he beheld the glories of Egypt.

      Humbly,

      Gene Roddenberry

P.S. I also leave behind a new script just received by this office, which you may have equally strong feelings about.

The following memo, written after shooting had been completed, graphically illustrates the problem that still remained:

TO: Gene Roddenberry DATE: October 21, 1966
FROM: Bob Justman  SUBJECT: BELIEVE IT OR NOT

Dear Gene:

I would like to give you my impression of what needs to be done with regard to making air dates on Part I– Part II of "The Menagerie." What I am about to outline may sound improbable, but it is certainly not impossible. And if it is not impossible, why, then I am sure that you (the Great Bird of the Galaxy) and all us clever people can make our fondest dreams come true.

I do believe that the clever and energetic but highly overworked Mr. Swanson * may have a rough cut on Part I of "The Menagerie" ready sometime tomorrow. You will remember that we received the last of the dailies on this show yesterday. I know that it's tough having to wait two whole days for a rough cut after completion of principal photography, but that's the way it goes sometimes. Anyhow, we should see a rough cut sometime tomorrow.

Since we will have to dub Part I on Monday and Tuesday, October 31st and November 1st, it is imperative that we get a final cut as soon as possible. Working backwards from these two dubbing days, it would appear to make sense to me that we had better turn a final cut in for duping this coming Monday night, October 24th. This would get us dupes back sometime on Tuesday, October 25th, and thereupon our sound effects and music editors could start building up the reels for dubbing the following Monday.

To meet this sort of schedule, it is, of course, necessary that we condition ourselves to making editorial changes that are really inherently necessary in this film. I think we should discuss the broad, important areas with Bob Swanson and then give him the picture back and let him run like a thief with it. Undoubtedly, if we are not too finicky and adhere to the important things, Swanson can have us a final cut to see this coming Monday sometime.

Anyhow, that takes care of Part I. I have not yet said anything about opticals, but rather than try to detail everything that is being done in a memo, I am sure that

---

* Film Editor.

Eddie Milkis can fill you in and keep both of us straight.

Part II of "The Menagerie" will have to dub the following Monday and we hope to be able to get it dubbed in one full day, because it is already partially dubbed, as I have mentioned in a previous memo.

Anyhow, that's kind of the way things look from here. Every little piece in this puzzle of how to get "The Menagerie" on the air in time is an interlocking piece with some other piece. If one piece doesn't fit in at the right time, at the right place, I think we will never be able to complete the puzzle. If we bring the whole thing off, we can do anything. But I tell you now, oh, Great Bird, that this is a once-in-a-lifetime situation. I don't think any of us could stand sweating out a problem like this again without going completely crackers. As you know, most hour shows in color take between six and eight weeks of post-production time to complete. STAR TREK normally takes between fourteen and sixteen weeks of post-production time to complete. We are attempting to get Part I of "The Menagerie" out in a post-production time of approximately four weeks. Believe it or not!

> Regards,
>
> Bob

Believe it or not, the impossible was accomplished. Everything went fine. Gene somehow got the editorial changes he wanted, and Parts I and II of "The Menagerie" were completed on schedule.

It was this two-part show that went on to win Science Fiction's most coveted honor—the Hugo Award.

Part IV


# STAR TREK PRODUCTION—
# A CLOSER LOOK

# Chapter 1

## In the Beginning Was the Word

At the bottom of page thirteen, we establish the fact that Sulu shoots a police revolver six times. Later on in the script you will discover that Kirk, using the same pistol, fires at a mounted knight in armor five times. This would make the revolver an eleven-shooter. I can just see the letters we'll get from various members of the National Rifle Association when they see this show. Please have this discrepancy mended.

*Excerpt from script comment*

A former producer for STAR TREK often used to say that in order to write for this series you have to take a post-graduate course in the techniques of operating a starship. The fact that such a course does not exist may account for STAR TREK's difficulty in obtaining acceptable scripts.

And they do seem to have difficulties.

All STAR TREK scripts are written "on assignment only." Although the series receives a number of unsolicited manuscripts every month (as many as thirty) from recognized agents, to date only two have been purchased. (Those manuscripts received direct from individuals are not even opened, but are simply forwarded to the studio's legal department for return to the writer.) The primary reason scripts, even though properly submitted, are not accepted boils down to the fact that the writer is usually not familiar enough with the series. He has not read the series format, he has not read any of the back scripts, and he lacks an in-depth understanding of the real relationship of the characters to each other. Usually such a writer will create a story around one character, ignoring the rest of the series regulars. Or he will propose a story totally impractical in production terms, or lacking in believability, theme, and resemblance to a show called STAR TREK.

Dorothy Fontana emphasized the point even further:

> In reading some of the scripts prepared by novices— even some professionals—it's difficult to believe they've "done their homework"—that they've even watched the show. One of Gene's admonishments to professional writers in the earlier versions of the STAR TREK Guide was to avoid getting wrapped up in the "wonder of it all."
>
> Perhaps this is what happens to these young writers— they become too enchanted with gadgets, or one character, or with an exotic planet. The result is sixty pages of nice typing. It isn't a script.

At the beginning of every season, the producer will contact a number of writers and ask them to come in for an interview about possible script assignments. When the writer comes in, he will usually have developed several different ideas for scripts, and these are discussed and evaluated. The producer will select one idea among these and place the writer on assignment to develop it into a detailed story.

The following is a sample of the guidelines established for the writer, and contained in the STAR TREK Guide:

CAN YOU FIND THE MAJOR STAR TREK FORMAT ERROR IN THE FOLLOWING "TEASE" FROM A STORY OUTLINE?

The scene is the bridge of the U.S.S. (United States Spaceship) *Enterprise*. Captain Kirk is at his command position, his lovely but highly efficient female Yeoman at his side. Suddenly, and without provocation, our Starship is attacked by an alien space vessel. We try to warn the alien vessel off, but it ignores us and begins loosing bolts of photon energy-plasma at us.

The alien vessel's attack begins to weaken our deflectors. Mr. Spock reports to Captain Kirk that the next enemy bolt will probably break through and destroy the *Enterprise*. At this moment we look up to see that final energy-plasma bolt heading for us. There may be only four or five seconds of life left. Kirk puts his arms about his lovely Yeoman, comforting and embracing her as they wait for what seems certain death. FADE OUT. (END TEASER)

PLEASE CHECK ONE:

( ) *Inaccurate terminology.* The *Enterprise* is more correctly an international vessel, the United Spaceship *Enterprise.*

( ) *Scientifically incorrect.* Energy-plasma bolts could not be photon in nature.

( ) *Unbelievable.* The Captain would not hug a pretty Yeoman on the bridge of his vessel.

( ) *Concept weak.* This whole story opening reeks too much of "space pirate" or similar bad science fiction.

NO, WE'RE NOT JOKING. THE PRECEDING PAGE WAS A VERY REAL AND IMPORTANT TEST OF YOUR APPROACH TO SCIENCE FICTION. HERE'S WHY.

( ) *Inaccurate terminology.* Wrong, if you checked this one. Sure, the term "United States Spaceship" was incorrect, but it could have been fixed with a pencil slash. Although we do want directors, writers, actors, and others to use proper terminology, this error was certainly far from being the major STAR TREK format error.

( ) *Scientifically inaccurate.* Wrong again; beware if you checked this one. Although we do want to be scientifically accurate, we've found that selection of this item usually indicates a preoccupation with science and gadgetry over people and story.

( ) *Concept weak.* Wrong again. It is, in fact, much like the opening of one of our best episodes of last year. "Aliens," "enemy vessels," "sudden attack" and such things can range from "Buck Rogers" to classical literature, all depending on how it is handled (witness H. G. Wells' novels, Forrester's sea stories, and so on).

UNDERSTANDING THE RIGHT ANSWER TO THIS IS BASIC TO

UNDERSTANDING THE STAR TREK FORMAT. THIS WAS THE CORRECT ANSWER:

(x)    *Unbelievable.* Why the correct answer? Simply because we've learned during a full season of making visual science fiction that believability of characters, their actions and reactions, is our greatest need and is the most important angle factor. Let's explore that briefly.

NOW, TRY AGAIN. SAME BASIC STORY SITUATION, BUT AGAINST ANOTHER BACKGROUND.

The time is today. We're in Vietnam waters aboard the navy cruiser U.S.S. *Detroit.* Suddenly an enemy gunboat heads for us, our guns are unable to stop it, and we realize it's a suicide attack with an atomic warhead. Total destruction of our vessel and of all aboard appears probable. Would Captain E. L. Henderson, presently commanding the U.S.S. *Detroit,* turn and hug a comely female WAVE who happened to be on the ship's bridge?

As simple as that. This is our standard test that has led to STAR TREK believability. (It also suggests much of what has been wrong in filmed sf of the past.) *No, Captain Henderson wouldn't! Not if he's the kind of captain we hope is commanding any naval vessel of ours.* Nor would our Captain Kirk hug a female crewman in a moment of danger, not if he's to remain believable. (Some might *prefer* that Henderson were somewhere making love rather than shelling Asian ports, but that's a whole different story for a whole different network. Probably BBC.)

AND SO, IN EVERY SCENE OF OUR STAR TREK STORY . . . . . . translate it into a real life situation. Or, sometimes as useful, try it in your mind as a scene in "Gunsmoke," "Naked City," or some similar show. Would you believe the people and the scene if it happened there?

*If you're one of those who answers: "The character acts that way because it's science fiction," don't call us, we'll call you.*

The normal going price for a STAR TREK script is between $3,500 and $4,500, depending on the writer's qualifications. At the time the writer delivers the first draft of his story outline, he is paid a fee of $655. This is a partial payment, and pays for the development of the idea into a detailed story. The writer is also paid various amounts, based on contract requirements, when he delivers his first draft teleplay and revised teleplay. Total payments will amount to his agreed-upon price. A fully developed story usually runs between ten and fifteen pages.

When the writer submits his story, it is evaluated by the producer, associate producer, and script consultant. If it is found to be significantly lacking in certain areas, the writer is requested to submit a revised story, to which the series is entitled without further payment. If the revised story is totally unsatisfactory, the writer can usually be cut off at that point with no further obligation on the part of the show.

Assuming the story outline is accepted, it is then submitted to NBC's Program Management, as well as their Broadcast Standards Department. Once approval has been received from NBC, the writer is given the go-ahead into a teleplay.

When the writer submits the first draft of the script, it is then reviewed by the front office staff. They will try to determine whether the story satisfactorily meets a number of conditions, such as: Whether or not the story "hangs together" all the way through; whether or not the principal characters are properly portrayed; whether or not the dialogue is believable and fits the series format that has been established; whether or not the teaser and act endings are sufficiently strong to keep the audience interested so they will stay with the show during commercial breaks; whether there are problems in terms of budget, shooting practicality, sets, opticals, locations and so forth. The writer is called in for a discussion of these points and then requested to submit a revised draft. When the writer submits the revised draft, and it is accepted, that ends his obligations on the script, although he may make himself available for further polish. From assignment of story to submission of revised script usually takes six to ten weeks.

The script is then mimeographed and distributed to the various studio departments, NBC, and all other interested parties. As a result, changes of one sort or another are usually requested by a number of different people. For example, the actors receive advance copies of the script and might request changes. These changes are usually quite valid and stem from the actor's belief the character he portrays might not say some of the things indicated in that script.

And, of course, NBC's Broadcast Standards Department generally will request its strange changes. The following are typical examples:

McCoy's line, "Thank God for that fantastic strength of his . . ." must be delivered in a reverent manner.

Please add a line somewhere in the script to the effect that the stolen clothes were paid for or retribution received.

General caution here and later as Kirk and Edith embrace. Caution also as Kirk kisses her hard and she returns the kiss with equal decisiveness; avoid the open-mouth kiss.*

Please exercise restraint as Kartan charges at Spock with the axe.

Caution as Sulu is injured by the damaged console so that his scream, his fall, his subsequent grunts are not unnecessarily alarming to the viewer.

Please find some other way for Dr. McCoy to put Christine out of function, as slamming her hard enough across the face to render her unconscious is not acceptable.

Please delete the underline: ". . . but to govern a population of idiots . . ." Suggested substitution: simpletons. †

Tonia's seductive manner necessitates deleting the following part of her speech: ". . . as the instrument of your pleasure?" ‡

It will not be acceptable for Finnegan to kick Kirk, as

---

* A constant request.

† Either way, *no* open-mouthed kisses.

‡ You keep your mouth shut, Tonia!

this would be considered brutality; let's find some other way for him to humiliate Kirk.*
Caution against showing extensive shots of the snake; such reptiles are upsetting to many viewers.

In the meantime, the revised script is going through further agonizing reappraisals and scrutiny on the part of the Executive producer, producer, associate producer, and script consultant. Even though the script has been revised, further changes are almost always necessary. The following comments, by the various staff members involved, offer a graphic indication as to why this is so:

I think all dialogue and usages of terms such as "Roger," "Wilco," and "Over and out," should be gone over and brought up-to-date with the terminology we have established in the series.
On page 30 we establish a pterodactyl on a rocky cliff and also flying and swooping down. Since there might be some slight difficulty in getting the correct color stock footage of pterodactyls, we might make a substitution here and instead use the airplane that we have also established in the show.
Scenes 16 through 20 are very nice to read. And they would be fine in a movie. They show a certain filmic style. Do we need scenes 16 through 20?
Please examine scene 49. Examine it carefully. Open-mouthed Broadcast Standards will examine it very carefully.
You get me a horned koala creature that has been trained and won't excrete on the actor's shoulder, and I will be pleased to use it in the show.
On page 55 we see Benton riding a digging machine toward his cabin. Let's eliminate this device right now. I think it is pretty lucky for us that Dr. McCoy doesn't get killed by the open-mouthed Creature, although everybody else the Creature contacts really gets it where it hurts.

---

* You wouldn't dare, Finnegan!

Since this story premise results in an immediate "Mexican standoff," we would not be able even to get out of the teaser. Therefore, we would need a commercial message of approximately 57 minutes' duration. This is against all FCC regulations.

It is also at this point that Joan Pearce, in Kellam De Forest's research company enters the picture. She very often recommends additional changes. The recommended changes may fall into one, two, or even all three of the following categories:

1. Necessary to maintain consistency with prior shows.
2. Necessary to maintain basic scientific validity.
3. Necessary to avoid potential legal problem.

Consistency from show to show is a big point of consideration in Joan's review of any given script. Once having established a capability or a concept in one episode, the capability or concept must forever more be adhered to in later episodes. Any deviation from this practice will inevitably result in a deluge of letters from viewers, calling attention to, for example, the fact that "Last week on your show it only took four blinks of the transporter to beam these people down to the planet surface. On all previous shows it's taken six. Have you improved the transporter?"

An example of verifying the scientific validity of a point made in a script is a situation that occurred in "Devil in the Dark." This episode dealt with a silicon life-form creature called the "Horta." Scientifically, there is nothing wrong with the premise. It is possible such a life-form exists, but it cannot exist in the *same* atmosphere as a human being, because of the chemical properties that would be contained within the silicon life-form. It would catch fire in an oxygen atmosphere; which would preclude its existing on an oxygen-atmosphere planet. (On this point, a compromise was reached, in which the entire story action took place underground, where the humans had an artificial oxygen atmosphere, and the Horta could tunnel to its heart's content.)

One of the more serious problems Joan must resolve deals with the use of fictitious words which the writer will dream up as part of his science-fiction dialogue. On one occasion Joan requested that the word "drek" be deleted from the dialogue. "Drek" is a German word, but it happens to be a four-letter word in any language, including English. This sort of thing is guaranteed to give Kellam De Forest's staff recurring nightmares. His staff covers a lot of linguistic territory, including French, Italian, German, Arabic, Spanish, Slavic, and Russian.

(Considering everything the script is subjected to once it reaches the studio, I am surprised the thing ever gets used at all.)

Contrary to popular belief, science-fiction writers do not necessarily make good STAR TREK script writers. The problem seems to be the fact that prose writers, science fiction or not, seem to find it difficut to make the switch to the visual medium.

As a result of the suggested changes submitted, the script is revised again. If the changes are not extensive, only the pages affected are revised. These new pages are then distributed to the same people who received the first script.

Sometimes the changes become so extensive that the script must be rewritten again, re-mimeographed, and re-distributed. The person normally responsible for these rewrites is the script consultant.

STAR TREK's recent script consultant was D. C. Fontana— a highly talented young woman. It would be difficult to estimate the number of scripts she has rewritten for STAR TREK, but the figure must be staggering, at the very least. Aside from Gene Roddenberry himself, no one individual contributed more to the development of the background for the series than did D. C. Fontana.

At the beginning of STAR TREK's third season, D. C. made the decision to leave the series. Among other things, she wanted more free time to pursue some rather intriguing writing projects of her own. Her departure made it necessary to find a new script consultant, and, as of this writing, that position is now occupied by Arthur Singer.

Although it hardly seems possible, the script does eventually reach the shooting stage, and filming finally begins. But by that time there are other scripts that need changes, revisions, and total rewrites.

Chapter 2

## Making the Scene

Most TV shows can use their sets over and over. We can't. Except for the *Enterprise,* we make our sets one week and throw them away the next! Each show has to be different. It's an insanely difficult proposition.

Matt Jefferies

The problem confronting STAR TREK'S Art Director, Walter M. (Matt) Jefferies, is a staggering one. Almost every week the show goes to a different planet, and every planet has to be different from every other. This means that every week Matt must design and create an entirely new environment. The landscape, the houses, virtually any object the viewer sees on the planet surface—everything must be entirely different from any other planet they have ever visited before.

When a writer submits a proposed story line, Matt Jefferies is one of the people who receives a copy. He reads it and then, if he can word it without profanity, he gives any comments he may have to the producer or associate producer. He may feel he can't afford to build the type or number of sets for that particular show, just on the basis of what is implied in the story. Or he may even go so far as to suggest the story is not a STAR TREK-type story (a comment he makes quite frequently).

When the mimeographed script is distributed, Matt attempts to formulate a rough cost estimate for building the sets. This is a "ball park" figure and is usually based on the number of sets that will be required, plus the available space in which to build them. If he feels it still can't be done, either through lack of space or lack of money—usually it's both— he will request that portions of the script be rewritten in order to eliminate certain sets. Once that is taken care of, as far as Matt is concerned, the set requirements are pretty well buttoned up. He knows the script will probably go through several other rewrites before it finally gets shot, but he also knows that any additional changes will usually be confined to dialogue or action within the sets already approved.

The next step is to try to figure out what the sets are going to look like. As a general rule, the script will provide some pretty good indications. With those in mind, Matt will confer with the producer, associate producer, and director for their specific ideas. By putting all the clues together, he can then begin to visualize what the sets will look like. As the picture becomes clearer in his mind, he will do several quick sketches and take these back to the same people for approval.

If he is lucky, his sketches will be approved with only minor changes, and he can then proceed with construction blueprints. These will include all the technical data and notes the construction department will need in order to build the sets. Blueprints are also sent to the set decorator and the paint department as well. If one or more of the sets happen to be particularly heavy on special effects, a set of blueprints will also go to Jim Rugg, the special effects man. In addition to the blueprints, Matt will also prepare "elevations." These are drawings, sometimes in color, that illustrate what the sets will look like if you are standing there looking at them when they are completed. Finally, the master floor plan for both Stages 9 and 10 is prepared, showing where each of the sets will be located on the stage involved. Copies of all these drawings and blueprints are then distributed to the departments involved in the construction or use of those sets.

In the meantime Matt and his assistants embark on a scavenger hunt. They make the rounds of all of the places at the studio where pieces of old sets are stored. They look for anything that can be fixed up, repainted, or in some way used in the sets. Depending on the type of show called for in the script, these pieces could include old fireplaces, store fronts, window units, wall panels, stairways, or different types of arches. Anything found usable is immediately set aside, so no one else (from another show) can come along and take it. Everything else needed for the sets must be built.

By this time, shooting is usually only two or three days away. If you were to pay a visit to Stage 10 (where all the

planet exteriors are constructed) the day before construction
started, you would see a huge empty room. If you went back
the next day, you would see the set beginning to take shape.
It always reminds me of a house construction project. Paint-
ers, plasterers, carpenters, all busily at work erecting floors,
walls, windows, false doorways, and a ton of overhead catwalks. These catwalks are not really nailed to anything in
particular, they are hung from the ceiling on long chains and
braced here and there with two-by-fours nailed to various
parts of the sets built on the floor below. Most of the overhead lights are hung from these catwalks, and the catwalks
themselves provide access to the lights for the men who will
operate them. All in all, the sets go up amazingly fast. One
day there is nothing there, the next day you're on Altair IV.

Even though the set has been built, it still is not ready for
shooting. It is only a shell and must be "dressed" with such
things as tables, chairs, rugs, lamps, or any of a hundred
other articles that may be needed. This is where the set decorator, John Dwyer, comes in.

John is literally a very commanding person. He is six feet
six inches tall, with a muscular build, a ready smile, and a
(fortunately) friendly disposition. If he weren't working for
one of the studios, he would probably make a rather exceptional (formidable?) interior decorator.

How do you find a chair that will look like a chair should
in the year 2300 on the planet Orion? Or a table? Or a
statue? Or a painting? These are some of the minor problems
John is faced with on every show. Anything not an integral
part of the basic set structure is in his bailiwick.

Under normal circumstances, John has only two or three
days in which to find all the items needed for a particular
show. Considering the exotic nature of most of STAR TREK's
props, it isn't easy. Occasionally an item can be rented from
one of the prop houses in Hollywood, but this is the exception rather than the rule. There aren't many prop houses that
stock items such as Vulcan wind chimes. Of necessity, the set
decorator's job on STAR TREK is one long continual search
for suitable items. John frequently spends many hours just
prowling the rental shops, property departments of other studios, furniture stores, and junk shops. In one show, "The

Trouble With Tribbles," he needed twenty-two chairs, all alike, and supermodern, to use in a bar scene. It took him three days to find all of the chairs. John works very closely with Matt Jefferies, and together they work out the overall visual approach to the sets.

Two primary factors that influence the decoration of a set are time and money (the same two factors that plague everyone else at the studio). If you have unlimited amounts of both, you can do almost anything. If you have limited time and unlimited money, you can do pretty close to anything. But in television you are working with both limited time and limited money. This calls for a high degree of ingenuity.

In addition, you can't put anything in a set that will detract from the action that will take place there. For instance, a plastic tube with a neon light in it would be so bright the audience's attention would be drawn to it and away from the actors. The same thing is true of mirror reflections or highly polished surfaces. Frequently John finds his work will involve Jimmy Rugg and special effects. For example, John may have to come up with a lamp that spurts blue flame. First he will locate the kind of lamp that will fit the theme of the set. Then he turns it over to Rugg, so he can rig the lamp to spurt blue flame. This is a typical example of how often one area of production must work very closely with another area of production and how each must therefore constantly be aware of the other's needs and requirements.

Like almost everyone else in the STAR TREK crew, John Dwyer will inject a bit of humor into a situation at the drop of a hat. During the filming of "The Trouble With Tribbles" there was a scene in which Captain Kirk was trying to find out how the Tribbles (little furry animals with voracious appetites) got into the storage bin of rather exotic wheat called "quadrotriticale." John was standing at the edge of the set, as Bill Shatner delivered Kirk's line, "I want to know who put the tribbles in the quadrotriticale?" John immediately spoke up in a loud voice: "Well, I don't know, but if you'll hum it, I'll try to pick it up on my guitar."

Aside from time and money, one of the major problems confronting both Matt Jefferies and John Dwyer has to do with color.

The problem lies in the fact that while STAR TREK is filmed in color, the majority of the TV sets in the United States receive only black and white. There are different shades of certain colors that will transmit beautifully over color TV sets, but at the same time will look exactly the same shade of gray on a black-and-white set. As a result, great care must be taken in the selection of colors used on the set. Matt even uses a special viewing glass through which he can check the colors in order to determine what they will look like on black-and-white TV sets.

Matt Jefferies is normally one of the nicest, most amiable men you would ever want to know, and certainly he is a past master in the art of diplomacy, insofar as getting a job done is concerned. There are times, however, when the tiger in Matt comes to the surface. Once I asked Matt if he ever experienced disagreements with the director over the way a particular set is used during the course of shooting. I had come to realize that the whole "feel" of a set can be changed by rearranging some of the set dressings or, as more frequently happens, by the use of what Matt feels are the wrong colored lights on the set. I was therefore curious as to how he felt about this type of situation. Matt replied, "Well, that is the time for artful questions, and if they don't work, then some artful suggestions. If that still doesn't work and I feel it is critical enough, then it's time for Uncle Matt to get his back up. I just stand in the middle of the set and yell for the director, or stand in front of the camera and ignore everybody until something is done. Nobody's picked me up bodily and thrown me out yet."

Since the basic *Enterprise* sets are not normally changed, Matt doesn't have to worry about them too often. It's probably just as well, in view of problems he's faced with in constructing alien sets. For the record, the following is a list of the *Enterprise* sets, and possible variations:

## STANDING SETS

Herewith a list of existing and projected U.S.S. *Enterprise* sets.

*INT. BRIDGE—*

A circular, platformed set where Captain Kirk presides over the whole ship's complex. Access is achieved to this set by means of a turbo-lift elevator which opens directly into the set. Kirk sits in his command chair in the inner, lower elevation facing the large bridge viewing screen. Directly in front of him, also facing the screen, sit the Navigator and the Helmsman at their combined console. In the outer circular elevation of the set are various positions for Communications Officer, technician crewmen and other ship's officers. Mr. Spock, our Science Officer, presides over a console which is known as the "library-computer station."

*INT. ELEVATOR—*

Throughout the ship are turbo-lifts which can be programmed for lateral and/or vertical movement. One can reach almost any section aboard by activating its controls vocally.

*INT. SHIP'S CORRIDORS—*

Curved corridors with various interconnecting sub-corridors. Various doors and hatches open upon a variety of areas within the *Enterprise* proper. We play these as existing on the different decks and levels of the ship, and, of course, all have connecting turbo-elevators.

*INT. TRANSPORTER ROOM—*

We assume there are various transporter rooms throughout the vessel. The one we use has access from a corridor. Within, there is a console, free-standing, which is controlled by the Transporter Officer and a technician. They, in concert or singly, can transport up to six people at a time and, of course, accomplish the return of said people. At certain times, objects out in space which are in close proximity can be brought aboard also, providing their mass and size are not too great. At one end of this set is the transporter chamber itself. It is a circular platform with several steps leading up to its six positions. Each person to be transported stands upon one of six light panels. There is a light panel above each position also. Within this chamber people are made to disappear and appear optically as they are "beamed" to and from vessels or planet surfaces.

## INT. SICKBAY AND DOCTOR'S OFFICE

A four-room complex. The Doctor's office has direct access to a ship's corridor. There is access from his office to an examining room, also to sickbay proper. Access to sickbay can also be made directly from the corridor. Within the sickbay, there are built-in bed positions with a complete diagnostic panel above each. This medical device scans the patient continually, takes readings, and registers same upon the diagnostic panel instrument face. Thus, blood pressure, pulse rate, heartbeat, respirations, and various other readings are continuously recorded and displayed for each patient without the necessity of physical contact between doctor and patient. Adjoining the Doctor's office is a medical lab.

## INT. ENGINEERING DECK—

A section of the ship's innards, wherein we find the basic components of the ship's motive force and energy. This is a large set, the main province of the Engineering Officer (Scott). Access to the main feed of the starship's circuitry is available here. A smaller set, "Emergency Manual Monitor," is an adjunct to Engineering.

## INT. BRIEFING ROOM—

A large set where Kirk and Spock can convene all department heads aboard for briefings, discussions, and staff meetings. A large table with sufficient chair positions. There is a viewing screen device on the table. This set can double as a wardroom. Access directly into a main ship's corridor.

## INT. RECREATION ROOM—

A redress of other sets to give us a variety of mess and recreation facilities. In these, crew members can relax and enjoy their leisure time. Various games, such as three-dimensional chess, can be played here. A larger, totally new recreation room has been added.

## INT. CAPTAIN'S QUARTERS—

Captain Kirk has a two-room complex. One room contains his working area when he is away from the bridge. There is access from this room to the next room where his sleeping quarters are. There is direct access to the ship's corridor from either room. There are viewing and communications devices here as in most major sets.

## INT. MR. SPOCK'S CABIN—

A redress of Captain Kirk's cabin. It will, of course, be distinctly "Spockian" in nature and suggest something of his homeland.

## INT. PASSENGER QUARTERS—

Again, a redress of Captain Kirk's quarters unless a larger area is required, at which time it will be constructed out of a redress of briefing room.

## INT. SHIP'S CHAPEL—

Redress of transporter room.

## INT. DINING ROOM—

Redress of other sets as required.

## INT. GYMNASIUM—

A redress of another set. It is sufficiently sized to allow various forms of physical exercise and limited-area sports, such as wrestling, fencing, etc.

*EXT. SHUTTLECRAFT—*
Full-sized mockup of a six- or seven-passenger ship which can be sent out on intrasolar system missions. This craft can be duplicated in miniature.

*INT. SHUTTLECRAFT—*
Full-sized interior mockup of above craft.

*INT. HANGAR DECK—*
A miniature set, optically created to be a "huge football field" size area where our shuttlecraft or crafts are stored. It is at the rear of the thick cigar-shaped "engineering section" of our vessel and on the scale model are visible the huge hangar doors which roll open when a shuttlecraft departs from or returns to our vessel. Caution—miniature and optical work like this is expensive and *must* be a vital element in the story when used.

*OTHERS—*
Obviously, various stories may require specialized "one time" sets. Past examples of this have been a botany section, a computer bank area, an observation deck (with stars visible through a window), and so on. Again, completely new and unusual sets are costly and should be vital in the story if used. If planet sets and interiors are required, then new ship sets should be minimized—the writer must use experience and common sense in keeping construction costs within a normal television budget.

Excerpt from STAR TREK Guide

Chapter 3

## Feinbergers, Tribbles, and Other Things

If STAR TREK's fan mail is any indicator, one of the most popular areas of interest (aside from the stars of the series) is the unique props and special effects used in each show. People are continually writing to the studio, wanting to know how the phaser works, how the communicator works, and, in general, all the ins and outs of STAR TREK's futuristic equipment. (One fourteen-year-old boy wrote in and requested a *working* phaser. Another high schooler had built a Laser and wanted a phaser casing to mount it in!)

Irving Feinberg is the property master on STAR TREK. Theoretically, he buys or rents whatever he needs for a particular show. If he can't, Jimmy Rugg's Special Effects Department builds it for him. Once having acquired the necessary props, Irving stores them until such time as they are needed by the actors on the set. Irving, therefore, has charge of all such props as the phasers, communicators, tricorders, McCoy's operating instruments, the universal translator, etc.

Aside from this futuristic equipment, Irving has also found himself from time to time in charge of such mundane things as fruits and vegetables. This happens whenever there is a scene involving food. Naturally, our space travelers of the future cannot be seen with ordinary fruits and vegetables, so Irving dyes the edibles a variety of space-age colors. Thus STAR TREK people eat blue celery, bright kelly-green melons, and so on.

Over the period of time since STAR TREK first went on the air, Irving Feinberg has done such a great job of coming up with nifty futuristic props that everyone has gotten into the habit of calling his props "Feinbergers." Whenever a director or someone else needs a new kind of prop, they simply say, "We need a Feinberger for this scene." Or during a production meeting in which various requirements are being discussed on an upcoming episode, Irving will be asked to "provide a selection of Feinbergers." This practice is not at all in keeping with the scientific nature of the series, and prompted the following exchange of memos between Gene Roddenberry and Bob Justman:

TO: Bob Justman                 DATE: March 20, 1967
FROM: Gene Roddenberry          SUBJECT: S.F. TERMI-
                                         NOLOGY

Suggest we invent straight scientific names for our gadgetry, rather than calling it "Feinberg this or that." The reason is obvious: although we know and understand the joke ourselves, it encourages others to take a less than serious view of these items and objects.

We can't afford to let down in any direction in this second year, and one of our most important goals will continue to be creating and maintaining high believability.

                                Gene Roddenberry
cc: G. Coon
    D. C. Fontana
    E. Milkis

TO: Gene Roddenberry            DATE: March 20, 1967
FROM: Bob Justman               SUBJECT: S.F. TERMI-
                                         NOLOGY

Dear Mr. Roddenberry:

I am in receipt of your memo of 3-20-67, in which you suggest that we use "straight scientific names for our gadgetry. . . ." I think you are correct in your feeling that we should encourage others to take a more serious view of our items and objects. Therefore, I feel that we should no longer use the term "Feinberg" as a substitute name for gadget. You are right in insisting upon our attempting to create and maintain high believability on STAR TREK.

Therefore, I, for one, intend to dispense with all the jokes and levity I have undertaken this past season. I feel that in this way I can set an example for the rest of our fellow workers.

Very truly yours,

Robert H. Feinberg
Associate Producer


Working very closely with Irving, although in a totally separate activity, is Jim Rugg, in special effects. Although the correct title for his activity is actually "mechanical effects," everybody seems to refer to it as "special effects." Special, or mechanical, the effects Jimmy comes up with are often astounding—to say the least. (His devices are called "Ruggisms".)

Having observed Jimmy at work on several rather fantastic devices, I have a healthy respect for his ability. He is an absolute genius at creating the multiplicity of mechanical, electronic, and electrical devices constantly required for STAR TREK episodes. One of the more complex devices he was required to bring to life last season was a four-foot-high deep space probe called "Nomad" (seen in the episode "The Changeling"). According to the story line, Nomad could "think" and "speak." Before he was through with the project, Jimmy had wired the device with a complex array of lights, relays, motors, and a complete voice-actuated circuit which allowed certain lights to blink on and off in synchronization with the voice coming from the device itself. As a result of his achievements in the first season, Jimmy was nominated for an Emmy in mechanical special effects.

Jimmy Rugg and Matt Jefferies work pretty close on devices like Nomad. Matt will design the basic device, and Jimmy will add whatever circuitry is necessary in order to create the special effect required. Although most of the hand props used on the show are nonfunctional dummies, some are functional to a certain extent. For example, some of Dr. McCoy's operating instruments have very small motors in them, so that when he presses a button, you actually see something moving on them. A typical example of Jimmy Rugg's ingenuity occurred during the filming of "The Trouble With Tribbles." The Tribbles were small furry creatures about five inches in diameter. The story line required that some of them actually move about, or at least appear to move about. Jimmy put small balloons inside some of them, with air hoses that ran offstage, out of sight. By alternating the air pressure, the Tribbles could be made to appear as though they were pulsating. In others, he inserted small wind-up spring motors, so that they would actually move a short distance. For the larger-size Tribbles, he used Japanese-made battery-operated toy dogs. He simply cut the dog away, leaving the mechanical action intact, and inserted that inside a Tribble. The result was self-propelled Tribbles complete with battery packs and all. Many of the component parts for his special devices are found by frequent rounds of the surplus stores. Very often these forays will produce component parts not available anywhere else.

One of the continuing problems Jimmy faces is what he terms the "battle between sight and sound." Generally speaking, a mechanical thing such as a waterfall, or almost anything that moves, will make noise. The more it moves, the better the cameraman likes it, because, for him, the more interest it adds to the scene. On the other hand, the more it moves, the more noise it makes, and the less the sound man likes it, because the noise interferes with his recording of the dialogue. So Jimmy Rugg is caught in the middle, with the sound man saying less noise, and the cameraman saying more movement.

A big part of Rugg's job involves special effects maintenance of the interior sets for the *Enterprise*. Although the bridge is by far the most complex, almost all of the other sets contain some type of view screen or equipment requiring electrical or mechanical devices. These devices have a tendency to wear out, or break down under constant use, and Rugg continually finds it necessary to rebuild or repair them.

He won't even begin to hazard a guess at the total number of switches, relays, or miles of wiring involved.

In the area of special effects, Jimmy Rugg considers STAR TREK the most difficult by far, on a continuing basis, of any television show now in production. The difficulty of it all does not leave him unaffected. He frankly admits that when he goes home Friday night, he dreams about doing special effects all night long, and says that it isn't until Sunday that he really gets it out of his system.

Chapter 4

## Hunting for Aliens

Yes, we do have a casting problem. Suppose we need a seven-foot-tall alien that looks like a reptile. Where do we get a seven-foot-tall lizard? Making the Hollywood actor look something other than human is a terrible problem for us.

Joe D'Agosta,
STAR TREK Casting Director

Casting for STAR TREK must certainly be a strange experience, one that does not happen with most television shows. Ordinarily, it is simply a matter of choosing the type of actor or actress required to fit the part. The majority of the casting for STAR TREK, on the other hand, involves aliens, and with aliens, you really don't know what type you're dealing with.

About seven days prior to shooting the episode, casting efforts (for speaking parts) really begin. Until that point it would be useless to go into casting, since the script is normally still being revised. If you cast a part any earlier than that, you might find yourself in a situation in which the part you cast no longer exists in the script by the time shooting commences. Also, the director must be included when casting, and he does not report in until a week before shooting.

When casting is ready to begin, the executive producer or the producer notifies the studio casting director. A joint conference is then held, attended also by the associate producer and the director. Everyone expresses an opinion as to what they think the characters in that particular show should look like. When a consensus has been reached, the Paramount Studio casting director (in this case, Joe D'Agosta) makes copies of the script available to the talent agents around town, who then read the scripts and submit the names of their clients whom they feel could fit the part. The casting director sorts through these names and selects those he feels will be best suited for the type of alien needed in the show. He then makes his recommendations to the front office staff. (The studio casting director has no power to cast a part. He can only recommend.) If his recommendations are accepted, the actors or actresses under consideration are called in for interviews. A final decision is then made on the basis of those interviews.

This whole process takes a number of days, and it is not at all unusual for the final decision on a part to be made the day before shooting is scheduled to commence. This situation inevitably creates horrendous problems for the costume and makeup departments, but there doesn't seem to be much anyone can do to speed up the process.

When STAR TREK began its first season of production, Gene Roddenberry drove studio executives up the walls with his casting decisions. While Gene contends the studio's problem was simply one of adjusting to thinking in alien terms, I have no doubt he took a certain amount of delight in seeing their reactions.

The very first show shot (in regular production) was a classic example. It was titled "The Corbomite Maneuver," and it called for a situation in which the *Enterprise* (947 feet long) was endangered by a vessel so large and so powerful that it made the *Enterprise* look like a fly in comparison. Near the end of the show, Captain Kirk goes aboard the alien vessel and comes face to face with the Captain of the ship. He is three and one-half feet tall, dressed in robes. During the casting meeting, there was a great deal of discussion as to what this Captain should really look like, and a number of strange ideas were tossed around in an attempt to resolve the problem. Gene, who had taken very little part in the discussion, was sitting back in his chair, puffing a cigarette and not saying a word. Finally he said, "I think if you cast anyone over seven years old, you're in trouble."

If studio heads are not prepared for this sort of thing, they have a tendency to come unglued!

The next day Joe D'Agosta brought in Clint Howard, a seven-year-old boy. He read for the part and was immediately cast. He was made up with a skull cap and very bushy eyebrows to make him look more mature, and after the sequence was filmed, a man's booming voice was substituted for his own. It was very effective.

Still another example of unusual casting in an attempt to create an alien feeling in the characters occurred in "The Menagerie." The aliens were superior beings, and Gene visualized them as very thin and extremely frail. Although the script called for men, Gene cast slim, fragile-looking women in the parts. Their heads were covered with huge, false heads to give the impression of superior mental development, and their breasts were wrapped tightly to disguise their female form. Again, the results were extremely effective, when male voices were added.

It is easy to get the impression that every casting decision is carefully thought out in advance. Nothing could be further from the truth. There have been occasions when a casting decision was the result of pure chance. This was certainly the case with the episode entitled "I, Mudd."

It was an unusual casting problem in that a number of identical twins were needed for extras, as well as for the leading ladies. Joe D'Agosta soon found out Hollywood is unbelievably short on girl twins who are beautiful, have great figures, and can act. He simply couldn't find twin girls who were right for the part. The situation began to get desperate. Then one evening, on his way home, he was driving down Sunset Boulevard and by chance saw two lovely young twin girls walking along the sidewalk. He immediately stopped the car, jumped out, and accosted them, saying "Can you act? Have you ever acted?" Apparently he was really in a dither, and he hadn't even introduced himself. The girls thought he was trying to put something over on them.

Joe finally convinced the girls he was indeed a casting director from Desilu Studios, and if they would please, please appear the following day, they would get an interview for a part in a television show. When the girls came in, Joe brought them into a meeting with Dorothy Fontana, Gene Coon, and Bob Justman. They were lovely girls, about seventeen or eighteen years old, with great figures. They were both wearing low-cut dresses, with the skirt ending at about the hip, and they had a bobcat with them.

A real wild bobcat.

It was their pet and was about six weeks old at the time. Bob Justman was apparently somewhat flustered at the sight of these lovely young ladies in micro-mini skirts and tinkling peace bells, and not knowing where to fasten his eyes, he began staring at the bobcat. Bob made small talk, and since the bobcat was the thing he had been staring at, he talked about bobcats. (He also nearly had a finger gnawed off by the affectionate animal.) He told the girls that when bobcats get bigger, if they're not spayed, they kill dogs. One of the girls said very innocently, "Well, how do you know when they are old enough?" Bob replied, "When they start killing dogs."

(Bob says he doesn't remember that . . . probably because he was dazed at the time.)

Chapter 5

## Metamorphosis: Humans and Humanoids

Fred Philips, STAR TREK's wizard of makeup, has been a makeup artist longer than he cares to remember. As a matter of fact, his father, Fred Philips, Sr., was one of the eleven founding members of the Motion Picture Makeup Artists Association. I guess you could say Fred was practically born into the business. And *his* son is now also a young makeup artist.

As is everyone else connected with STAR TREK production, Fred is continually fighting the battle of time and money. There never seems to be enough of either one to go around. During the time Fred has been with STAR TREK, he has had to create a phenomenally wide variety of alien-looking creatures—all of whom have been quite human underneath it all.

Although Fred concedes that making Mr. Spock's ears back during the days of Pilot Number 1 turned out to be quite a problem, he no longer considers the ears a difficulty. Due to a number of minor modifications over a period of time, the ears fit so perfectly that the only problem, as far as he is concerned, is the length of time it still takes him to apply them. (There are times, however, when Leonard Nimoy considers them a pain in the ear.)

One of the most difficult makeup jobs Fred has had to tackle on STAR TREK was in connection with the episode entitled "The Deadly Years." In this show Kirk, Spock, McCoy, and Scotty were supposed to age to ninety years old, through four separate stages. The first stage could be handled with makeup, but the remaining three stages had to be accomplished by hand-making specially constructed pieces of rubber for each stage. These pieces of rubber were used to build up certain facial areas in order to create wrinkles, sagging chins, sagging jowls, etc. This whole process required twelve separate plaster models, just to make the special pieces of

351

rubber. On top of them, makeup had to be applied to create the wrinkled, papery skin of the elderly—not only on faces but on throat, neck, and hands. The last stage of "aging" required makeup time of three hours each on Kirk, McCoy, and Scott.

When the decision was made to shoot that particular episode, the first day of shooting was scheduled for eleven days later. Fred practically had a heart attack. Such an involved number of makeup changes, using essentially one makeup artist, was virtually impossible. Fred called frantically all over town, trying to enlist additional aid in getting the plaster molds made. He was turned down at every call. No one wanted to touch that many age changes unless they had at least thirty days to work on it. All Fred had was eleven. And the job had to be done; that's all there was to it. So he gritted his teeth, hired a mold maker to help him, and worked day and night—eleven days straight. He got the materials made, but it was a frantic race to the wire.

Fortunately, he was able to beg, borrow, or steal an additional eleven makeup artists from around town who could work the six days the show would be shooting. As it was, everything worked out fairly satisfactorily, but Fred shudders every time he thinks about the experience.

Not all makeup situations are that hairy. In fact, some of them are downright funny. One episode in the first season called for a seven-foot-tall android, and a very likable and talented actor named Ted Cassidy was hired for the part. (Viewers remember him as Lurch of "The Addams Family.") Ted was outfitted in the proposed costume and makeup he would use in the show and was taken over to Gene Roddenberry's office to see whether or not Gene approved. Fred had done a marvelous facial makeup job, using deep shadows, deep-set eyes, and a totally bald head. Ted was built up even taller by means of elevator shoes. He was the perfect epitome of a ghastly, pale android of monstrous proportions.

Those gathered in Gene's office to review Ted Cassidy's "image" included John D. F. Black, Bob Justman, Bill Theiss, and of course Fred Philips. As luck would have it, at that same moment a young man arrived in Gene's outer office from a local tailor's shop. The young man had been trying to sell Gene a suit, and Gene had finally agreed to see him. Gene's secretary notified him on the intercom that the young man was waiting. What happened next was a stroke of pure genius.

Ted sat down in Gene's chair, behind his desk, and everybody else (including Gene) backed out of the office, saying, "Thank you, Mr. Roddenberry, sir. We'll take care of that right away, sir." They trouped through the outer office, past the young suit salesman, and back down the hall to another door to Gene's office, which they had strategically left open. It was a grandstand seat. The young man was sent into Gene's office. (At that time, Gene's desk was screened from the front office door by a bookshelf divider, so anyone entering the office couldn't see Gene's desk too clearly until they were right on top of it.)

The young man came around the divider with his hand stuck out ready to shake hands and said, "Mr. Roddenberry, sir . . ." and stopped dead in his tracks. There was an eight-foot-tall, monstrous-looking Ted with the phone at one ear, playing the part to the hilt, saying, "Yes, yes, I'll take care of that. . . . Young man, I will take care of you in a minute." To everyone's surprise, the suit salesman recovered beautifully. The minute Ted put down the phone, he started his sales spiel, pulling out various swatches of fabric as he talked. Ted stood there, towering over him, looking at the fabric and saying he liked it very much. Finally everyone came back into the office and told him it was all a big joke—that this creature really wasn't Gene Roddenberry. To this day, no one is sure he ever really believed them, but Gene ordered two pairs of pants anyway.

Fred's day begins very early in the morning. He will usually be at the studio by six or six-fifteen in order to be ready and waiting for Leonard Nimoy, who comes in at six-thirty. Literally, no shooting can begin until the actors have been made up. With perhaps ten or fifteen thousand dollars riding on a day's shooting, Fred's job becomes a very important one.

Working in Fred's makeup department is a cute, perky blonde named Pat Westmore. Pat is the hair stylist and frequently has to exercise quite a bit of ingenuity in creating

widely different hair styles representing different alien creatures. Yet the hair styles can't be so far out as to be unbelievable or impractical. Pat uses very few wigs, working mostly
with falls, wiglets, and braids. Although the majority of her
efforts are directed to hair styles for the actresses, Pat also is
called upon from time to time to work on an actor's hair. Occasionally a director will request that an actor's hair be
changed to a different color, or shadings of gray added to his
temples.

One point that bothers Fred a great deal is the tremendous
pressure of time. He often worries about not having enough
time to do a particular makeup job to his own complete satisfaction. In the end, the only consolation that Fred has is the
knowledge that he is in good company. Everybody else on
the production crew is in the same boat.

Chapter 6

## Aliens—Dressed and Undressed

NO MATTER HOW MANY TIMES NASA DE-
SCRIBED THE OUTFIT OF THE FUTURE, IT AL-
WAYS SOUNDED LIKE LONG UNDERWEAR.

Gene Roddenberry

STAR TREK at least had the good sense to recognize that a
community of 430 people, working closely together, would
not ignore esthetics. Thus, they took the basic idea of long
underwear and added color and style. It wasn't necessarily a
knowledge of fashion design that influenced the uniforms, but
rather an appreciation of what fashion designing means and
why the human animal finds it necessary.

The style of clothing seen on every episode is the work of
Bill Theiss, the costume designer. Bill is a very bright young
man, sports an unbelievably bushy moustache, and is without
doubt one of the most talented, imaginative costume design-
ers in television today. He is no stranger to science fiction
costuming, either. Bill designs all of the costumes used in Ray
Bradbury's plays.

In designing costumes for STAR TREK, Bill is often in the
position of having to interpret what a script means or what
the producer says he wants. As in the case of all other areas
of production, Bill is continually fighting the battle of time
and budget. While he may have as much as two weeks in
which to design and execute a costume, he frequently has five
days or less.

Since the design of the uniforms worn by the *Enterprise*
crew members has by now been firmly established and does
not as a rule change, Bill's primary concern lies with designing apparel for the aliens and visiting humans encountered in
each episode. Dressing them—or in some instances "undress-
ing" them.

His approach to costume design is yet another factor in creating the uniqueness that is STAR TREK. When Bill Theiss receives his copy of the script, he reads it through the first time as rapidly as he can. If possible, he tries to project his own emotions into the story line as he reads along. Bill says this helps him quickly establish a mental picture, or strong feeling, of what the aliens in that particular show should be wearing, which, in turn, makes the designing easier and helps him achieve a fresh, new look in the clothing.

An alien's clothing is supposed to be "out of this world," but there are limits to anything. Bill must therefore weigh his first impression against several factors. He must decide if the clothing could, in fact, actually be worn on the planet in question. He has a pretty fair idea from indications in the script, and further details developed during production conferences, what conditions exist on the planet. The clothing he develops must be suitable for these conditions. For example, if the planet surface is covered with ice, he can't have the local inhabitants running around in loincloths (no matter what their social customs may be).

Another factor also influences the approach to costumes. They must be acceptable to the public, purely from a design standpoint alone. This is not easily achieved. While we say we are designing for the future, we are in reality designing for the present. The clothing must appear different and ultrafresh, but not so far out as to risk looking ludicrous.

Having taken these things into consideration, and feeling his visual impression of the clothing is on safe ground, Bill then begins a series of "doodles," trying to work out the physical appearance of the design on paper. As it happens, the majority of those doodles seem to be done on restaurant paper napkins and place mats. The doodling phase is usually sandwiched in between work on costumes for other episodes that are further along in production. As the design develops and comes more clearly into focus, these doodles become full-color sketches. A few never get off the place mat.

While an alien's clothing may be made of almost anything existing in the universe, Bill can work only with materials available here on Earth. (Until the next intergalactic trading ship drops anchor on this planet, anyway.) Fabric selection, then, is the next step, and always poses a problem.

Clothing that looks futuristic should ideally be made out of fabric that looks futuristic. Unfortunately, such fabrics are not available in great abundance. Trial and error frequently play a great part in fabric selection. Sometimes a fabric selected turns out later to be nothing but a headache. This has certainly been the case with the velour used in the uniforms worn by the series regulars.

"That rotten velour," as it is often referred to, was originally chosen because it has an attractive sheen under the strong lights used on the set—certainly a desirable quality from a visual standpoint. Much to his dismay, after having all the uniforms made and fitted to each member of the cast, Bill discovered a problem with the velour.

It shrinks.

Not just once, but every time it's cleaned. Since the uniforms are cleaned every day and some shrinkage occurs with each cleaning, the garments must continually be altered and realtered. The whole process has become one terrific pain in the neck. Needless to say, the velour is slated for replacement.

Budgetary limitations sometimes create similar after-effects. A case in point involves the boots originally worn by the cast. In order to achieve a somewhat futuristic appearance, the boots were designed with a semi-high heel, a snug fit to the ankle, and a top high enough to fit up under the short legs of the men's trousers. At the time filming was started for STAR TREK's first season, this type of boot was difficult to find. The only solution was to make them. Since the design indicated a close-fitting boot and there had to be some way of opening the boot in order to get the foot in and out, a long zipper was used. The boot itself was made of soft leather, strong enough to hold the zipper.

Fourteen pairs of boots were ordered, made, and delivered to the set. When worn, they conformed reasonably well to the leg and ankle, and at a distance looked fairly attractive. But because of limited funds, they were cheaply constructed, using lesser-quality materials. The end result was a cheap boot. The cast immediately began to complain that their feet hurt. The problem has since been solved by having a shoe-maker custom-fit each boot, using better materials and construction. The boots cost more, but at least they are both attractive and comfortable.

Fabric selection can sometimes force a change in the original design concept. An alternate fabric may be found that works better or at least as well, or with less labor, or that is less expensive. When this happens, Bill goes back to the drawing pad and revises the concept accordingly.

With the design firmly fixed on paper, and the fabric selected, the costume designer must now seek approval of the costume. Those who pass judgment on his design include the executive producer, producer, associate producer, and the director. By the time all concerned have expressed an opinion, changes are usually necessary.

Eventually the design receives final approval, and construction begins. As the costume begins to take shape, one major question mark still remains. Who will wear it?

Even though the design is firm, and construction has been started, Bill usually does not know the "body" that must fit into the costume. At this stage of the game, still several days away from shooting, the person who will wear the costume probably has not been cast. The individual involved, when finally known, very often dictates additional changes in the costume design, because of particular body problems. (Everybody has body problems . . . you rarely find a perfect body for clothes.)

The length of time needed to physically construct a costume varies from garment to garment and is greatly dependent upon the requirements of the individual show. In the case of a simple costume, virtually no time at all is required. One show called for a type of sarong (similar to the Hawaiian "lava-lava") to be worn by the men of a particular planet. Making the costume was simply a matter of cutting a length of fabric, wrapping it around their waists, and tying it off. Conversely, the more complex the costume, the longer it takes to make (thirty or more man hours) and the more expensive it is. By way of contrast, some motion picture costumes will cost thousands of dollars apiece, while most STAR TREK costumes will cost tens of dollars apiece.

to seeing it uncovered. It also raises doubt in their minds about what else they might see, and doubt plays a very important part in creating an interesting costume.

The use of revealing costumes does, however, present Bill with certain structural engineering problems. Breasts are the main problem. In terms of STAR TREK costume design, there are three kinds of breasts: no breasts at all (great), good breasts that are firm and need no support (rare), and the vast majority (terrible). Large or small, the vast majority need support, and in costume design that can be a disaster.

In order to achieve a fresh look through the use of nudity in unexpected places, the bra must often be dispensed with. This of necessity dictates a girl whose breasts do not need support. Bill then does not have to worry about straps, where they are going to go, whether or not they will show, whether one breast is going to be pulled higher than the other.

Small breasts are, therefore, far and away the best and easiest to work with. If more "volume" is required, falsies can be sewn into the costume or, as is often done, simply glued right to the breast. (There are a number of adhesives and tapes available for this purpose.)

One of the best examples of design, engineering, and provocative sexiness in a costume was the futuristic Grecian gown Bill designed for Leslie Parrish in "Who Mourns for Adonais." The material was soft pink chiffon, banded in silver fabric. The design was breathtaking and daring. The long flowing skirt was a hip-hugger in that the waistband of it came only to the top of the actress's hip line. The upper section was a carefully fitted piece of chiffon covering Leslie's bosom and anchored solely at one point on the skirt and by the weight of the chiffon cape falling over her shoulder. That was it—a top with a front but no back. The only visible means of support was the girl herself. Astoundingly she did not have to be glued or taped into it—it simply stayed in place due to strategic engineering. Leslie herself said the gown was completely comfortable, and she had no qualms about wearing it and moving in it. (The crew and set visitors had all the qualms.)

Chapter 7

## Quiet on the Set, Please!

When you see all those men on the stage working so hard, week after week, twelve hours a day, you have to excuse a lot of the horseplay that goes on, because there's a lot of tension there, a lot of tiredness. The weekends just aren't long enough to gain back that strength you have to have for the other five days.

Gregg Peters,
Unit Production Manager

To every studio visitor, the most glamorous aspect of television series production is the activity that takes place on the set—the shooting of the episodes. The fact that the series' stars are most easily observable on the set undoubtedly has something to do with it.

I, too, have found the "on set" activities glamorous, no matter how often I go back for another visit. But I have also become acutely aware of the enormous expenditures of blood, sweat, and tears represented by those "glamorous activities." What takes place on the set may be viewed as glamorous, but it is undeniably difficult, frustrating, tiresome work for the entire crew, including the director.

A director is a different kind of human being. He is many things at many times, including manipulator, tyrant, supervisor, father-confessor, and supreme ruler of the set. From the moment the director steps onto the set, the entire resources of every member of the production crew are supposed to be bent on seeing that he gets what he wants, so he can get the picture out on time.

Basically, the director's job is to tell a story. He is the one who must, in concert with the actors, make the show happen. For instance, suppose a scene in the script says,

362

"Full shot—bridge (overall view) Mr. Spock, Captain Kirk, Dr. McCoy, Scotty, and Sulu." The script does not say where any of them are standing, sitting, lying, or whatever. The script does not say what any of them do, in terms of movement. What is blank on the page must be filled in by the director. He must sit them in chairs, stand them up, turn them around, etc. It is a matter of creating three-dimensional life out of the scene and then getting it on film.

Most of STAR TREK's episodes have been directed by one of two men, Marc Daniels and Joe Pevney. In the second season Marc and Joe alternated shows. Normally, they prepare for as many days as they shoot. These preparation periods are actually part of the preproduction phase and involve work with the script, casting, set construction, and so forth. The preparation period, when properly used, will result in everything being ready by the time the director walks on the set. He can concentrate his time on making the picture, rather than preparing to make the picture.

As each scene is readied for shooting, the director will usually gather the actors around the rehearsal table (a small table located in some out-of-the-way corner of the stage) and attempt to work out any potential problems in the scene. This saves a great deal of time once the actors are on the set, in front of the camera. During these little rehearsals the actors will frequently offer suggestions on dialogue changes, movement changes, etc. If the director believes these suggestions are valid, they are incorporated.

No amount of advance preparation, however, can prevent the minor, unavoidable problems that inevitably occur from time to time. The film breaks; somebody makes a noise, spoiling the take and making it necessary to shoot the scene again; the camera dolly accidentally runs into something, shaking the camera and spoiling the take; an actor will forget a line he has said perfectly three times before. Overall shooting progress is measured in "pages per day." In order to shoot an episode in the required six days, production must average ten or eleven pages of script per day. Anything less than that, and the show is in trouble.

All footage shot one day is processed overnight and viewed in the projection room the next day. These viewings of the previous day's work are known as the "dailies." They act as a safety margin against the possibility that something went wrong during one of the takes and at the same time went undetected. Knowing about the problem the following day allows the director to reshoot the scene, if necessary, while the sets and actors are still available.

JERRY FINNERMAN IS TURNING OUT TO BE ONE OF THE FINEST TELEVISION CINEMATOGRAPHERS IN THE COUNTRY. THE SHEER QUALITY AND EXCITEMENT OF WHAT HE HAS DONE WITH LIGHTS IS ALMOST UNBELIEVABLE. VERY OFTEN WE DON'T HAVE TO REPAINT A SET TO MAKE IT LOOK DIFFERENT. JERRY WILL REPAINT IT FOR US WITH LIGHTS. HE WILL CHANGE THE WALLS FROM GRAY TO GREEN TO BLUE, DEPENDING ON THE MOOD AND THE PLACE WE WANT TO SAY WE ARE IN. ON OUR PLANET SETS, ONE DAY HE WILL CREATE A PURPLE SKY; ANOTHER DAY IT WILL BE LIKE THE HOT DESERT IN MARCH; ANOTHER DAY DEEP BLUE. AND HE DOES IT ALL WITH FILTERS AND LIGHTS.

As the cinematographer, Jerry Finnerman is in charge of most of the men working on the set. He is responsible for the way in which the set is lighted, as well as the way in which it is photographed. He is also responsible for the speed and efficiency with which the lighting crews and electricians set up the equipment for each shot.

Jerry's lighting crew averages about forty different setups per day. If each setup required an additional five minutes to prepare, by the end of the day those same forty setups would have required two hundred additional minutes to perform. Multiplied by five days, an entire day of shooting would be required to make up the lost time. The lighting crew, run by the chief gaffer, George Merhoff, moves with all possible speed on each setup in order to avoid such a problem. Two other key personnel help Jerry Finnerman's crew maintain a fast pace. One of these is Don Merhoff, who makes sure that the proper electrical equipment is on the set and the right color filters are available for the lights on which Jerry will use them. The second key man on Jerry's crew is the head grip, George Radar, who has the responsibility for making sure all necessary lighting equipment, including colored filters not normally available, are specially made up and brought to the set for use as needed.

In spite of the hectic pace at which they are forced to work, the entire production crew functions smoothly and displays a rather high degree of esprit de corps. One of the men who best exemplified the close-knit feeling among the crew was George Hill.

George was one of the electricians on the show, but retired at the end of the second season. Before his retirement George would bring a "goodie box" with him every morning. He would put the goodie box right next to the particular set the crew was working that day. The box contained an assortment of chocolates, candy orange slices, and various paper-wrapped candies. When the crew moved to another set, the box moved with them. What impressed me so much about George and this box was the fact that he paid for its daily contents out of his own pocket. It was a contribution he made to the overall enjoyment of those with whom he worked. It also struck me as being a reflection of a quality that seems to run through the entire production crew . . . more than an ordinary measure of concern for the product which they are involved in making, and a desire to do all those little extra things which, while not required by their job, nevertheless add in some small measure to the probability of its success.

Each show has a first assistant director, who is second-in-command on the set, after the director. The first assistant director's duties include preparation of the set shooting schedule, show budget, and coordination with casting, wardrobe, and art departments. All these duties are performed during the preproduction phase. The first assistant also generally hires or recommends the hiring of stunt men and extras.

Once shooting starts on the show, the first assistant director's duties include maintaining quiet and order on the keeping the crew informed of what set will be shot next, making sure those sets are ready in advance, having the actors ready at hand when needed in the scene, and, in general, helping to keep the shooting moving along as fast as possible.

Each show also has the services of a second assistant director, who functions as the right-hand man to the first A.D. The Second takes care of a number of details, including preparation of the call sheets, production reports, and making sure that the actors are in on time each morning and in makeup on schedule. He is in many ways a leg man and is a great help.

Until his retirement at the end of the second season, Leonard "Tiger" Shapiro was STAR TREK's most notable second assistant director. Tiger was a real sweet guy and helped make life a little more pleasant for a lot of people.

STAR TREK's new second assistant director is an energetic young man named Charlie Washburn, who was an apprentice A.D. during the second season. Charlie is a real go-getter and seems to radiate nothing but cheerfulness.

There is at least one member of the production crew who must have one of the world's most fantastic memories. This fellow is George Rutter, the script supervisor. George is responsible for "matching" scenes—i.e., if a prop is used or worn one way in one scene, it must appear exactly the same way in the next scene in which it is used. The same thing is true of wardrobe, makeup, mussed hair, etc. George has to remember what all these things looked like, even if the next scene in which these things will appear is not shot until three or four days later. His memory problem does not stop there, however. He must also remember details of a particular set and how the articles in that set were arranged, and must also remember the kind of lighting that was used to light that set.

As might be expected, George takes voluminous notes. He makes a record of all dialogue changes made as a scene is being filmed and times each scene in order to calculate how many usable minutes of film have been shot to that point.

Roddenberry has nothing but the highest regard for all the men on the crew, likens their relationship to a family, and tells the following story to illustrate the point:

YES, I THINK WE HAVE AN EXCEPTIONAL CREW. IT'S LIKE A FAMILY. WE HAVE OUR FIGHTS, BUT THERE IS A GREAT AFFECTION FOR EACH OTHER. IT'S LIKE BEING MARRIED TO THIRTY OTHER PEOPLE. YOU BEGIN TO SENSE THEIR MOODS, AND WHEN THEY ARE TIRED, YOU CARE. I WENT ON THE STAGE ONE DAY, AND THEY WERE ALL READY AND WAITING FOR ME, BECAUSE THEY KNEW I WAS REALLY EXHAUSTED FROM SOME LONG RE-WRITE SESSIONS. AS SOON AS I WALKED UP TO THE SET, BILL AND LEONARD BLEW A SCENE, BUT THEY BLEW IT ON PURPOSE AND BEGAN ARGUING VERY VIOLENTLY. BILL WAS SHOUT-ING AT THE TOP OF HIS VOICE, "LEONARD! WHAT DO YOU MEAN SAYING THIS IS A D-7 KLINGON SHIP! IT'S A D-6!" LEONARD SHOUTED BACK, "NO, YOU IDIOT, THE D-6 HAS FOUR DOORS OVER HERE AND THE D-7 ONLY HAS TWO!" BILL IMMEDIATELY SHOUTED BACK, "NO, NO, NO—IT'S THE OTHER WAY AROUND. YOU'VE GOT IT ALL WRONG."

WHILE ALL OF THIS IS GOING ON, I'M STAND-ING THERE, BEGINNING TO GET FRUSTRATED, WATCHING THE MINUTES TICK BY AND MEN-TALLY COUNTING THE MONEY WE'RE LOSING IN EXPENSIVE CREW TIME, BECAUSE THE CAMERAS AREN'T ROLLING. AND AS THE AR-GUMENT CONTINUED, I'M THINKING TO MY-SELF, "WHAT ARE THEY TALKING ABOUT? THEY'VE GONE TOO FAR!" THEN I BEGAN THINKING THAT I SHOULD REMEMBER WHICH IS THE D-6 OR THE D-7. FINALLY I COULDN'T STAND IT ANY MORE, AND SO I WALKED IN BETWEEN THEM AND SAID, "COME ON, FELLOWS, IT REALLY DOESN'T MATTER. LET'S GET ON WITH THE SCENE." THEN THE WHOLE CREW BROKE UP LAUGH-

ING. THIS WAS THEIR WAY OF SAYING TO ME, "HEY, TIME IS NOT THAT SERIOUS. RELAX A LITTLE." THEY REALLY ARE THE FINEST GROUP OF PEOPLE IN THE WORLD.

Chapter 8

## Beyond Human Ken

". . . minimizes special effects and process. . . ."

Excerpt from Series Format

A television episode is by no means complete once shooting has finished. With STAR TREK, it's a *long* way from being completed. The film must be "cut" (edited), sound effects created, opticals prepared, and the musical score recorded. These separate post-production steps must then be combined into one film . . . a strip of celluloid 4,351 feet long. The subtleties employed in this phase are manifold and, I suspect, beyond the public's conscious awareness and understanding.

The single most expensive part of STAR TREK's post-production activity is its complex opticals . . . "Photographic Special Effects." While most TV series make infrequent use of one or two opticals, STAR TREK may use fifteen or twenty per show. Almost $40,000 was spent for opticals on one episode alone. STAR TREK's optical requirements are so enormous that three, sometimes four, optical companies are needed, simply to keep pace with each episode.

Roddenberry apparently did not foresee such a heavy involvement in opticals. Perhaps it's fortunate he didn't. He might also have foreseen the staggering problems which went hand-in-hand with the opticals. These problems became progressively worse as STAR TREK got deeper into its first season's production. The situation became so severe that STAR TREK came frighteningly close to missing its very first air date.

ONLY A HANDFUL OF PEOPLE KNEW IT AT THE TIME. WE HAD A NEARLY DISASTROUS LAST-MINUTE PROBLEM WITH THE OPTICALS NEEDED FOR THE TITLE. A STAR TREK TITLE

CAN TAKE AS LONG AS TWO MONTHS TO PRE-
PARE. WE PUT ONE TOGETHER IN AN AFTER-
NOON, OUT OF REJECTS, JUST TO GET THE
SHOW ON THE AIR!

Fortunately, the enormous difficulties that have plagued
STAR TREK'S opticals from the very beginning have finally
been smoothed out. Although problems still crop up, time
and experience have developed reasonable methods of solving
them.

Before an episode begins shooting, either Eddie Milkis or
Bob Justman contact the optical house assigned to that show.
They go through the script, discuss each proposed optical,
and attempt to uncover any problems that may come up.
This allows the optical house to begin work immediately. By
the time the episode begins shooting, the optical house has
usually tested a number of alternate ideas and found a solution.

If all goes well, the optical house will have the effect completed and ready to add to the film by the time the episode
has been edited (usually about four weeks* from the time of
assignment to delivery of completed optical).

It takes an awful lot of coordination. They have to
have people who can lock in with our thinking. When
we say we want a blue man with green hair, they must
understand that's what we want. We might settle for a
pink man with orange hair—if it's going to be a helluva
lot faster and a helluva lot cheaper.

Eddie Milkis
Post-Production Supervisor

A typical optical frequently used, and one that is relatively
easy, is the "viewing screen matte shot." This is the type of
shot you see when something is being shown on the main
bridge viewing screen or almost any "viewing" screen used in
the show.

First step is to shoot the viewing screen, on the set. Prints

---

* Six to ten weeks for highly complex opticals.

of this footage are turned over to the optical house. A "mask" is then drawn, frame by frame, on a separate piece of film. This "mask" is a black area exactly the size of the viewing screen, as it appears on the film. A second "mask" is then prepared on another piece of film and blocks out everything else on the frame *but* the viewing screen.

The film supplied by the studio is then rephotographed, only this time with the first "mask" superimposed. The result is an exposed length of film with a "hole" in it where the viewing screen was before. Next, whatever is to be shown on the viewing screen is then rephotographed on still another length of film, this time using the second "mask." Now we have two exposed pieces of film, one with a "hole" in the middle, the other with only the center of the film (corresponding to the view screen) exposed.

Now it becomes simply a matter of placing both pieces of film in a special photographic unit called an "optical printer" and rephotographed both simultaneously onto a third piece of film. The end result is the viewing screen matte shot.

One of the earliest opticals created for STAR TREK was the *Enterprise* flying toward the viewer.* But before the optical could be created, miniature photographic models had to be built. Working form Matt Jefferies's renderings, Howard A. Anderson Co. created a four-inch wooden model. When Roddenberry approved, a larger size three-foot model was constructed. With a much larger size, more surface detail was possible, and more was added.

Ultimately, a fourteen-foot model was built using sheet plastic on all components except the engine nacelles, which were made of hand-carved hardwood. The saucer was ten feet in diameter. The model was later equipped with interior and exterior lights, and twin motors, emitting flashing lights in multicolored effects, spinning on the noses of the engine nacelles.

To make an optical showing the *Enterprise* flying toward the viewer, the fourteen-foot model is first set up on a special mount. The mount holds the model about three feet in the air and at one end of a long narrow set of tracks. A special camera dolly is mounted on these tracks. When the camera be-

---

* This shot is used at the beginning of each episode.

gins shooting, it zooms in toward the model, turning and tilting the camera head in the process. This simulates movement and, combined with movement of the model as it rotates, tilts, and changes positions, results in the illusion on film that the ship is moving, rather than the camera. Further realism is added, through mattes, by putting stars, planets, etc., in the background. The same basic approach is used for orbiting shots.

The dematerialization and rematerialization of crewmen (the Transporter Effect) is accomplished as follows:

1. The crewman to be transported steps into the transporter and is filmed.
2. As the camera continues to run, the crewman steps out of camera range and the empty set is filmed. Later, the action of the man leaving the set will be clipped out of the film . . . and the footage spliced into one piece.
3. On a duplicate piece of film shot in 2, above, a mask, exactly outlining the person's figure as he appeared in the transporter, is superimposed, creating a piece of film with a "hole" in it.
4. These pieces of film are then rephotographed simultaneously in the optical printer:

   a. The original film.
   b. The masked film.
   c. A length of film containing only the glitter effect * of the transporter.

5. The "glitter effect" goes through the "hole" in the second piece of film and thus coincides with the outline of the crewman. When the film is run, the man is slowly "faded" out of the picture, momentarily leaving the glitter effect in place of his body. The glitter is then faded ("dissolved") out as well.

Phaser beams are created by animation. A series of draw-

---

* To obtain the "glitter effect," aluminum dust was photographed as it was dropped from overhead, falling through a beam of high-intensity light.

ings is prepared, each showing the beam slightly larger and longer than the previous one. These are shot, one frame at a time, and when the film is run at normal speed, it appears as though the beam were being fired.

The post-production phase also involves the "cutting room." It is here the film editors, or "cutters," work in putting together some of the film shot each day on the set. If when finished, they will end up with the visual part of the story.

The day after shooting begins, the developed film is screened (the dailies) in a projection room. On hand are the front office staff, the director, the editor, and other interested parties. The dailies are nothing more than the individual strips of film that represent the scenes shot the day before. These scenes include close-ups, master shots, plus all of the "takes" shot for each scene. Thus, one scene might be viewed three or four times, depending upon how many times the director shot it before feeling he had what he wanted.

At the end of the dailies the editor, director, and producer discuss what was seen and try to arrive at a mutual understanding of what each scene should look like and how it should "feel." The editor then goes back to the cutting room, and working with copies of what he has just seen, attempts to put the various strips of film together in such a manner as to capture the "feeling" that is wanted. Throughout the six days of filming the editor will confer often with the director, at dailies as well as during visits to the set.

Editing is a big responsibility and a highly creative endeavor. An editor can save, improve, or ruin a show. Here again is another reason for STAR TREK's success—creativity in all areas—film editors like Fabien Tordjmann, Bill Brame, and Don Rode (Don was awarded an Emmy at the end of STAR TREK's second season).

Within about five days after shooting has been completed, the editor has the "first rough cut" ready—the full story, as complete as he can get it.

The first rough cut is viewed in the projection room by the director and production staff. Usually changes will be suggested. If so, the editor attempts to make them, and the second cut is then viewed. Eventually the film is approved and is cut to its final length of 48 minutes (the film would be close to this by now).

Occasionally the dialogue sounds that are recorded during shooting will need special rework before the sound track can be added to the film. It may be that an actor did not put the right inflection into a particular line, or that he mumbled it, or that some sudden background noise obscured the words of his line.

. To solve this type of problem, the length of recording tape containing the discrepancy is physically cut out of the reel and spliced with a piece of blank tape, forming a loop. The actor then goes to a special sound room called the "looping stage" and rerecords the line. He listens to the loop, times the words, and speaks the new words right over the top of the old words, in order to synchronize the sounds properly.

On those rare occasions when STAR TREK goes on location, it's almost a sure bet that every bit of sound recorded will have to be looped. The reason becomes clear when you consider that background noises, on location, are unavoidable. An airplane flies overhead, a car horn is heard, or any one of a hundred other noises are invariably picked up by the sensitive recording apparatus. All must be eliminated on the looping stage.

The looping stage is also used when another person's voice is to replace that of the person actually seen in the film. Since STAR TREK uses a number of aliens, the voice of the actor who played the alien will frequently be either raised or lowered electronically. This is another subtle touch that helps impart the "you are *really* out there" feeling.

Another example of the subtle touch concerns the "sound effects recording stage" where the sound effects are prepared. As the show is projected on a special screen, the sound effects man, Douglas Grindstaff,* selects specific background sounds which he will add to that particular spot on the film. Footsteps; doors closing; hums and clicks of computers; even such exotic subtleties as adding the faint sound of a tinkling bell to scenes depicting the surface of an alien planet. Grindstaff and his crew add the master's touch.

---

* Grindstaff was nominated for an Emmy at the end of STAR TREK'S second season.

A little-known area to the public, scoring is an extremely important factor in the overall dramatic effect of the show. The music editor screens the final cut with the composer and producer, and together they determine *every second* throughout the show where music will be heard. The composer then writes the music in such a way that each note will coincide exactly with a predetermined point on the film. This music becomes the overall theme of that show.

After the music has been composed, an orchestra is hired, and the music is recorded—but not in the ordinary way. The musicians sit in a room equipped with a large screen on the back wall. The conductor faces the screen and watches the show unfold as he conducts the musicians. He can thus insure that every note played will be timed to the proper scene and movement in the show.

If that isn't wild enough, there's more. The *same* approach is taken with each of the characters in the show! Although few people are probably aware of it, each character is given his or her own individual theme music, which is always played when they are on screen. Eventually it becomes time to put all of these various sound tracks together. This is done on the "dubbing stage." What follows is basically a massive rerecording job. As many as eighteen or twenty separate sound tracks are run simultaneously with the running of the film. Three men work a complex master control panel, monitoring the sounds on a variety of instruments and equipment. As they watch the film on the huge screen in front of them, they control the quality and intensity of the various sounds, blending everything into one single sound track on magnetic tape.

While all this is going on, the negative cutter is busily at work. As the film is shot on the set, "work" prints are made and distributed to the editors, optical houses, etc. The original negatives are stored safely in a vault. When the editor has completed his final cut, it is delivered to the negative cutter. He then removes the original negatives from the vault and proceeds to cut them in the same way in which the editor cut the work print. It must be a perfect match, frame by frame.

The completed cut negative is then sent to the lab to await processing with the sound track, which, when completed on the dubbing stage, is transferred from magnetic tape to optical film and becomes the optical track. The optical track and the cut negative are then processed together, making the completed film. Prints are made, and NBC gets another STAR TREK episode.

Part V

# WHITHER STAR TREK?

Chapter 1

## Seasons Follow

THE PHYSICAL AND EMOTIONAL COST IS
QUITE HIGH. IT IS THE ARTIST'S CALCULATED
RISK . . . LIKE THE CANDLE THAT WILL ONLY
BURN FOR JUST SO LONG. . . . YOU CAN
FORCE IT TO BURN BRIGHTER, BUT IT WILL
ALSO BURN FASTER. . . . YOU PAY FOR IT. . . .
STILL . . . I'D RATHER DO THAT THAN FLICK-
ER DIMLY IN A CORNER.

Gene Roddenberry

Despite the many problems that constantly developed, STAR
TREK made it through the first season and was renewed for
the second. The renewal came, in part, from the thousands of
loyal viewers who had expressed that loyalty in letters to
NBC. They believed in the show, and as far as I know, still
do.*

Insistence on believability in all aspects of the show, then,
has paid off for Gene. It has helped keep the series alive at
times when the great god Nielsen said it should be dead.

Gene is acutely aware of this and repeatedly reminds everyone of the importance of this point. For instance, at the beginning of the second season, he wrote a memo to the production
staff and crew, in which he remarked, in part:

Late last season and in many first-draft scripts coming
up this year, we are not seeing the "trained group efficiency" that should characterize a 20th century ship's bridge,

---

\* Roddenberry was finally forced to form a company, Lincoln Enterprises
(Dept. B, P.O. Box 38429, Hollywood, Calif. 90038) in order to
handle the continuing flood of fan mail and requests for actor photos
and for other STAR TREK souvenirs.

much less the U.S.S. *Enterprise* in the 23rd century. For
example, far too often someone reports to the Captain
that something is approaching the ship. The Captain asks
how far away it is and gets an answer. Then the Captain
must ask if they can make out the size of it, and he gets
an answer. Then he asks Mr. Spock for an opinion, gets
an answer. Hardly the kind of smooth, trained, and experienced coordination one would expect in a group of future-day astronauts aboard something like the U.S.S. *Enterprise.*

Kirk should never have to ask these questions. Sulu
should know what information from his instruments
should be immediately transmitted to the Captain. Same
with everyone else aboard the bridge. Just as even a co-
pilot aboard a present-day airliner knows he should constantly be making verbal reports to his Captain on the
reading of this instrument or that radio marker, or etc.

*Why is this important to us?* Believability again! Our
audiences simply won't believe this is the bridge of a starship unless the characters on it seem at least as coordi-
nated and efficient as the blinking lights and instrumenta-
tion around them. And we're not going to believe our
characters either unless there is a constant reminder they
are indeed the trained kind of individuals who would
have these posts of responsibility.

It has been said that if you repeat something loud enough
and long enough, people will begin to believe it. Perhaps
Gene's insistence on the Believability Factor has been responsible for the attitude I have observed in the cast and crew of
STAR TREK. Or perhaps it is a number of other things. At any
rate, time and again I have observed indications that those
connected with STAR TREK really do believe it all.

For example, I was on the set one day recently, observing a
scene that was taking place on the bridge. George Takei was
standing beside his Helmsman's position. The director was
going over some of the action that would take place in the
scene they were about to shoot. After reading through a few
lines of dialogue with Bill Shatner and Leonard Nimoy, the di-

rector turned to George and said, "Okay, and at this point Sulu fires the phasers. So you hit this button and fire the phasers." And the director indicated a particular button on Sulu's instrument panel. George promptly replied, "No, that's not the right button. The phaser button is this one over here." And George indicated a button on a different part of the panel. The director gave him kind of a funny look and said, "What are you talking about? What difference does it make? This is a set on a sound stage, remember? Push the button and let's get on with the scene." George steadfastly refused to push that particular button, saying, "If I push that button, it will blow up the *Enterprise!*"

On another occasion, during a scene in the transporter room, Jimmy Doohan refused to move a lever in the direction requested by the director. He argued with the director, insisting that he was being asked to do it the wrong way. You move the lever one way to beam a person down, and the other way to beam a person up. He actually refused to do it the way the director wanted it, even though the camera was all set up for the shot.

This sort of thing happens all the time. A director might ask an actor to activate a certain set of controls and then immediately report the results to the Captain. The actor will object and say he can't do that because it takes a couple of seconds for that to happen. Therefore, he will have to wait a few seconds before he can make his report to the Captain. No amount of pleading from the director will make them change their minds. They really believe it.

This feeling is by no means limited to the cast. Morris Chapnick once remarked to me, "Once you get on stage nine and the set is lit, you really believe for a moment . . . you sort of forget where you are."

I often wonder what visitors to the set must think when they talk to Irving Feinberg, the property master. He is very proud of the different props that are used on the show, and will readily offer an explanation of the use and function of any one of them. He will hand you one of McCoy's operating instruments, tell you exactly what it is for, and explain exactly how it is supposed to be used. If you hold one the wrong way, he will tell you, "No, this one goes this way in order to make it work. . . . You hold it this way when you pick it up, and you push this button over here to make it work."

Whether or not the scientific community believes as strongly in STAR TREK as do its creators is probably a matter of conjecture. There have been, however, numerous indications of interest and support. The following letter is typical:

DEPARTMENT OF THE AIR FORCE
USAF Aerospace Research Pilot School
Edwards Air Force Base, Calif.

5 May 1967

Mr. Gene Roddenberry
Desilu Productions
780 Gower Street
Hollywood, California 90028

Dear Mr. Roddenberry:

The students and staff of the USAF Aerospace Research Pilot School would like to invite you and members of your organization to visit our facilities at your convenience. Our mission here is to train experimental test pilots for the military services, NASA and NATO countries and to train astronauts for this Nation's space program. You apparently have some very loyal supporters in my organization, and they feel that possibly we can learn from your experiences. On the other hand, because of our mission and unique facilities here at the Flight Test Center, I feel you may find some material of value to you in your productions.

Feel free to contact me at any time and we can arrange a visit at your convenience.

Sincerely,

ROBERT S. BUCHANAN, Colonel, USAF
Commandant

Interest and support can also be expressed in another way. In June, 1967, Gene Roddenberry received a letter from the National Air Museum, Branch of the Smithsonian Institution, which read in part:

We believe the STAR TREK pilot would be a valuable addition to the archives of the National Air and Space Museum. Science fiction forms a definite segment of astronautics chronology.

As a result of that letter, STAR TREK became the only series in television history to have an episode * placed in the archives of the Smithsonian Institution.

Another thing I find quite interesting is the way the cast and crew always refer to Mr. Spock. I am convinced Spock has had a definite influence on them, and I'm not at all sure they are consciously aware of the degree to which they have been influenced. For example, whenever any one of them uses the word "logical" or says some very exacting phrase, a reference is invariably made to Spock. It's almost as though Spock had said to each one of them, "These are my words, my phrases. They belong to me." And the STAR TREK people seem to be acknowledging it. Frankly, I don't quite understand it. It just (as Mr. Spock would say) isn't logical.

This doesn't mean they are above teasing Leonard Nimoy. In fact, they seem to take special delight in putting him on. For instance, the incident with his bicycle.

The studio is such a big place and it takes so long to walk from one place to another that the stars of a series are usually given bicycles in order to let them take advantage of the precious little time they have free during the course of a day. Each bicycle has the name of the star on a sign attached to the frame, and it is considered verboten to touch the bicycle. For a while it became standard procedure to hide Leonard's bicycle. Anyone who happened to see it standing unattended was duty-bound to hide it.

Leonard began to complain he was having trouble finding his bicycle whenever he wanted it. Apparently he decided the only way he could be sure of locating it when he needed it

---

* "Where No Man Has Gone Before."

was simply not to let it out of his sight. That is why one afternoon Leonard rode the bike into the sound stage and parked it right next to the set, where he could keep an eye on it. Naturally, a plan was quickly formed to hide it. As soon as Leonard's back was turned, one of the crew members on the catwalk overhead dropped a rope to waiting hands below, and in no time at all the bicycle was securely lashed to the catwalk overhead. There it hung, about eight feet above the floor, nestled in between a couple of arc lights. The word spread rapidly, and soon everyone but Leonard knew about it.

About fifteen minutes later Leonard decided to check on his bike. He walked over to the place where he had left it, saw immediately that it was gone, and yelled, "Hey! Where's my bicycle?" Immediately there was a loud chorus of, "What bike? You mean your bicycle? I haven't seen your bicycle. Your bicycle was on the set?"

Leonard began to frown noticeably and said, "Now wait a minute, I left it right here." Someone suggested he look outside, as it could have been removed from the stage in order to get it out of the way. His jaw set, Leonard stalked out the door. He was back in a moment, still yelling, "I can't find my bicycle." He then shouldered a broom, apparently determined he was going to clobber the guy who took his bicycle. He walked around the set, waving the broom in the air, saying, "All right, where's my bike? Who's got my bicycle?" As he passed beneath the bicycle securely fastened overhead (the broom barely missed hitting it) someone said, "You're getting warmer." As he moved a few steps away, someone else said, "You're getting colder." For a moment, Leonard looked slightly bewildered, then it began to dawn on him that he was being put on. He turned around, slowly looked from left to right, then tilted his head back and looked up. There was his bicycle neatly suspended from the catwalk. He immediately dropped the broom, started to grin, and then broke up in laughter.

The next day some of the crew got a tow truck and towed his car away so that he couldn't find that, either.

If STAR TREK put-ons became the talk of the studio, STAR TREK parties became legend. There are birthday parties, Friday night parties (on Stage 9, celebrating survival through another week), end-of-the-season parties (usually very tearful affairs), parties to celebrate every holiday imaginable, and last, but not least, the August party.

Either through coincidence or diabolical design, a great number of the staff and crew, including Gene Roddenberry, have birthdays in August. As a result, the month is virtually one big party. All year long, studio executives look at their calendars and heave a sigh of relief as one more month goes by. Then when August comes up, they look at their calendars and cry a lot. Actually the STAR TREK parties are not so different from any other kind of congenial gathering of friends; they are just nuttier. If you attend one, you do so at your own risk. Anything is likely to happen, and usually does. They are usually held in Gene Roddenberry's office, in a building bordering Gower Street. I remember attending a STAR TREK party not long ago and thinking to myself as I was leaving that it was not at all unusual to leave the party by climbing through the window and dropping down to Gower Street and the sidewalk below.

The end-of-the-season party (called the wrap party) is held at the end of the last day of shooting on the last episode for the season. There is always a huge turnout, by both STAR TREK and studio personnel. Everyone congratulates each other on making it through another season of production; many congratulatory speeches are made: humorous gifts and awards are usually bestowed upon certain members of the cast and crew; and, of course, there is food and drink in abundance. And sometimes a studio executive will ride a motorcycle wildly through the stage. These particular parties start out as cheerful gatherings, full of genuine feelings of camaraderie, but always end in many tearful exchanges between old friends. At the time the wrap party is held, no one knows whether or not the show will be picked up for the next season. It may therefore be the last time the group is together as a production unit. Since they have poured their hearts into the production effort, day after day, for months, a kind of closeness develops between the cast and crew, welding them into a type of close-knit family. It is understandable they should express feelings of regret at the prospect of not working with each other again in the future as they have in the past.

But if they play hard, it is because they also work hard. Television series production is, among other things, a long, hard grind. The pressure is always on. There is no stopping the clock, and the air dates must be met at all costs. It is not at all unusual for many of the staff to work late into the night, come back in very early in the morning, and on numerous occasions, work right around the clock with no sleep at all. This routine goes on, day after day, throughout the production season. At times there is no such thing as "a good night's sleep," or the welcome respite of a weekend off.

It is a highly creative effort, but its physical and emotional cost to the individual is enormous. At one time or another, members of the staff have been hit with cases of uncontrollable hemorrhaging of the throat; severe back pain, requiring complete bed rest; acute fatigue and nervous strain; and complete physical exhaustion. The casualties have mounted steadily, and many members of the crew who launched STAR TREK on its voyage through the stars are no longer working on the show today.

I DON'T THINK THERE IS A PERSON WHO HAS WORKED ON THIS SHOW WHO HAS NOT SAID TO HIMSELF, "I AM TAKING A CALCULATED RISK WITH MY HEALTH. I COULD DIE OF A HEART ATTACK BECAUSE OF THE STRAIN OF THIS WORK." IT'S A RISK, BUT A CALCULATED ONE. IT'S ONE OF THE RISKS YOU TAKE, JUST AS AN AIRPLANE PILOT OR DEEP SEA DIVER TAKES ANOTHER TYPE OF RISK. THERE IS A COMPULSION WHEN YOU ARE A CREATIVE PERSON. A COMPULSION THAT DRIVES YOU TO DO WHAT YOU ARE DOING, AND YOU JUSTIFY WHATEVER PRICE YOU HAVE TO PAY WITH THE KNOWLEDGE THAT THERE IS SOMETHING ABOUT WHAT YOU ARE DOING THAT YOU LOVE VERY MUCH. AND PARTICULARLY WITH MEN—IT'S A PART OF WHAT MAKES A

MAN A MAN, AND IF HE DIDN'T DO IT, HE WOULD BE CONSIDERABLY LESS THAN HE IS.

I have no doubt the whole situation is made more bearable, at times of particularly great stress, by the humor, which is deliberately encouraged, even at the risk of a temporary loss in production efficiency. For example, at a particularly hectic point last season people were working extremely long hours, and one morning Eddie Milkis came into the office about 6:00 A.M. Bob Justman had been there since about 5:30 and had left the following memo for Eddie Milkis and Gregg Peters:

TO: Ed Milkis & Gregg Peters   DATE: July 12, 1967
FROM: Bob Justman   SUBJECT: WEDNESDAY

Gentlemen:
   I intend to be very mean today.

Regards,

Bob

Again, the following exchange of memos indicates the light-hearted atmosphere that can prevail, even in the midst of turmoil and chaos:

TO: Morris Chapnick   DATE: May 15, 1967
FROM: Gene L. Coon   SUBJECT: OFFICE FURNITURE

It has come to my attention that because of the great volume of scripts and other paper work that passes through my secretary's office she is at present equipped with a desk which is not only too small and inefficient, but terribly outdated and far too Battle Creek-ish for the secretary of so important a man as myself.
I find myself averting my eyes as I pass through my

outer office. This hurts the feelings of my secretary, who is trying to seduce me. Obviously she cannot, as I refuse to look in her direction. I refuse to look in her direction until she gets a more suitable desk. This is a matter of utmost importance. I have calmly accepted the fact that I don't have my own toilet, but equipping my office with a desk which was first manufactured for Charles Dickens is ridiculous.

I am, after all, a Television Academy award nominee.

Aggrieved,

Gene Coon

TO: Herb Solow          DATE: May 15, 1967
FROM: Gene Roddenberry   SUBJECT: TELEVISION
                                  ACADEMY
                                  AWARD NOM-
                                  INEE COON

The attached from the distinguished Mr. Coon speaks for itself.

We are thinking of expanding his memo into a STAR TREK episode.

It seems to me that anything that would help his secretary seduce him would be well worth the money. I am entering into this matter late because until recently I had not believed any help was necessary.

Gene Roddenberry

cc: M. Chapnick

TO: Gene Roddenberry DATE: May 16, 1967
FROM: Herb Solow      SUBJECT: TELEVISION ACAD-
                                EMY AWARD NOM-

INEE COON—
RELATIONSHIP
WITH SECRETARY.

I have read the questionable memos. I think we are
approaching this matter unscientifically. We are fighting
the end result of the problem as opposed to getting to its
cause. The cause is apparently the relationship between
Mr. Coon and his secretary. I have, therefore, assigned
Mr. Chapnick the additional responsibility of watchdog
of nonbusiness intraemployee-employer behavioristic
patterns based on the fundamental analytical occurrences when metaphysical protestations veer heavily on
the Calvinistic doctrines of predestination. In other
words, Morris is to find out whether or not Gene Coon
is Jewish.

H.F.S.

cc: Gene Coon
    Morris Chapnick


TO: Gene Roddenberry, Gene Coon, Morris Chapnick,
    Bob Justman
FROM: Herb Solow
DATE: June 1, 1967

Will someone please tell me whether or not Andee
ever got a new desk. The suspense has been killing me.

H.F.S.


(To my knowledge, she never did get the new desk.)
The game of television is played by some rather strange
rules, and among these rules are some rather interesting tell-
tale signs of success. These are unmistakable indications to the
Producer that either his series is successful or, because of it,
he has come to the attention of the powers that be and probably has something else they want.

Perhaps one of the first signs that indicates things are going well is when, on a trip to New York, three or four bottles of liquor arrive at your hotel room, accompanied by nice little notes from the network. Another, even stronger indication is when a young man in a dark coat walks up to the airplane and says, "Hello, Mr. Roddenberry." When this first happened to Gene, he was surprised, as he had never seen the fellow before. But he stuck out his hand anyway, exchanged greetings, and was then taken to a black Cadillac limousine for a chauffeured drive into downtown New York City. He later learned the network has a file of pictures, and the young man had studied Gene's picture so he would recognize him as he got off the airplane.

Perhaps STAR TREK's first season was similar to a shakedown cruise—possibly like that which any vessel (even the *Enterprise*, more than likely) must undergo before all the problems are ironed out. In any event, the first season must have provided much additional knowledge and a wealth of experience in operating a Starship because, by comparison, the second season was a breeze.

Problems, yes. There will always be difficulties and times of crisis where television production is concerned (that much I *have* learned). But the second season had very little of the extremely harsh pressure, the daily cliff-hanger fight just to survive "till the end of this episode," that was so much a part of the first.

As time went by, there were changes in staff, for the same range of reasons that any organization experiences them. John D. F. Black left the series to do a feature. He was replaced by Steve Carabatsos as the script consultant. When Steve left in December, 1966, Dorothy Fontana was promoted to script consultant, having demonstrated an exceptional ability at rewrite as well as original scripts.

Dorothy's promotion left a vacancy in Roddenberry's outer office, which was later filled by Penny Unger. She is a personable young woman and a highly efficient secretary. She is also tough, which is exactly what a producer's secretary must be. A producer is constantly being harassed from all sides with dozens of details and problems. Like any other harried human being, he needs to escape once in a while. A tough secretary will run interference for him, head off the phone calls and visitors, and give him a chance to catch his breath. Were this not so, the "normal situation" during production would eventually drive him up the walls. That Roddenberry has avoided this fate is a credit to Penny.

About midway through the second season Gene Coon departed the fold. Coon was brought in as producer after Roddenberry was satisfied he had firmly established the series format during the first thirteen or fourteen episodes. Roddenberry had moved up to executive producer, thus allowing him additional free time to develop future properties and commitments and yet maintain strong guidance at the helm of his Starship.

As a tremendously creative writer, Coon had done his job well. Producer on STAR TREK is no easy task and demands more than most are willing to give. But after almost a year as producer, he wanted a change of pace. John Meredyth Lucas took up the task until the end of the season neared, at which time Roddenberry once more resumed the double role of producer/executive producer.

The end of shooting for the second season came in mid-January, 1968. Tension and uncertainty was running high. Nielsen ratings had not been the best, and many blamed the apparent poor showing on the shift from the first season's Thursday night time slot to the second season's Friday night time slot. Rumors were rampant that STAR TREK would be cancelled. Few were openly optimistic about the chances for a third season.

The wrap party was a strange affair—a mixture of party atmosphere and half-voiced despair. Everyone gathered on Stage 9, listened to the familiar funny speeches, and laughed at the humorous awards presented. The possibility that this might be the last such gathering hung heavy in the air. Some openly discussed the subject, others openly avoided it. As the evening wore on, the little knots of people, huddled close in conversation, began to fade away, and by midnight the stage was deserted.

I remember standing there, alone in the middle of the darkened stage, after everyone had gone. It was an incongruous sight—paper cups, plates, and napkins scattered about—the make-shift bar standing beside the engineering room—the remnants of a 20th century party mixed in with the interior of a 23rd century starship. A starship that might never again go avoyaging through the uncharted reaches of space. I experienced the sadness then—I knew how the others felt—and understood.

For perhaps the last time, I walked through the corridors of the Starship *Enterprise,* my solitary footsteps echoing in the stillness. There had been high adventure here. Alien beings from strange worlds. Narrow escapes from incredible dangers. Men and women experiencing the heady exhilaration that must surely accompany a voyage among the stars. Now there was nothing. Only deep shadows among the sets, and an enormous feeling of empty loneliness. I pushed open the heavy stage door, and the night air rushed in. It was cold. I turned up my collar, thrust my hands deep in my pockets, and walked slowly through the dark empty street, toward the gate.

Chapter 2

## Bits And Pieces

STAR TREK is a show highly popular among young
people. The imagination behind the scripts and the tremendous uniqueness in each adventure give the stories a
range of vitality rare in a series program. And its scientific basis is as authentic as expert advisers can make it.
A crew of men in the spaceship *Enterprise* encounters
new worlds, new kinds of beings, situations which would
be unthinkable outside science fiction—and even there
surprising in their originality. Yet a number of intriguing
questions arise, which have a lot to do with what is happening in American society today . . .

> William Kuhns, writing in the
> February 23, 1968, *Young Catholic Mes-*
> *senger* (Teacher's Edition)

STAR TREK was renewed for at least the first half of its
third season, but not without a fight. As the rumor of impending cancellation spread among fans of the show, a
ground swell of protest began to rise. During the months of
January and February that ground swell assumed the proportions of a tidal wave. A highly articulate and passionately
loyal viewing audience participated in what is probably the
most massive anti-network programming campaign in television history.

NBC-TV (both New York and Burbank offices) was de-
luged with letters of protest. Most of these letters were personally addressed to Mort Werner. A sizable number were
also addressed to Julian Goodman, President of NBC. All de-

manded, pleaded, or urged that STAR TREK be kept on the air.

The furor increased with each passing day. STAR TREK's chances for renewal became a topic of discussion in newspaper columns across the country. Student protest movements were organized. Cal Tech students marched, along with other STAR TREK supporters, against NBC's Burbank office, carrying a petition urging the renewal of the series. At first the marchers were ignored. When it became apparent that the passage of time would only swell the crowd to larger proportions, worried network officials appeared, accepted the petition, but said only that the matter was up to "New York."

On the East Coast, meanwhile, reaction was equally vocal. For the first time in network history, pickets were marching up and down Rockefeller Plaza, carrying placards, handing out leaflets and bumper stickers, publicly protesting the rumored cancellation. NBC executives were astounded and periodically would send someone outside to see if "they" were still there.

The mail count began to reach alarming proportions. NBC's policy is to answer every piece of mail received, but at the rate cards and letters were pouring in, no one could begin to keep pace. Extra people were hired to help handle the load. The flap got bigger and bigger. Every department began to buzz with talk about "the mail coming in."

On Friday, March 1, 1967, NBC shattered all television precedent by making an "on-air" announcement of renewal at the conclusion of STAR TREK's program. The following Monday NBC issued this press release:

MARCH 4, 1968

UNPRECEDENTED VIEWER REACTION IN SUPPORT OF "STAR TREK" LEADS TO ON-AIR ANNOUNCEMENT OF SERIES' SCHEDULING FOR 1968–69.

In response to unprecedented viewer reaction in support of the continuation of the NBC Television Network's STAR TREK series, plans for continuing the series in the Fall were announced on NBC-TV immediately following last Friday night's (March 1) episode of the space adventure series. The announcement will be repeated following next Friday's (March 8) program.

From early December to date, NBC has received 114,667 pieces of mail in support of STAR TREK, and 52,151 in the month of February alone.

Immediately after last Friday night's program, the following announcement was made:

"And now an announcement of interest to all viewers of STAR TREK. We are pleased to tell you that STAR TREK will continue to be seen on NBC Television. We know you will be looking forward to seeing the weekly adventure in space on STAR TREK."

The "Save STAR TREK" campaign, which culminated in NBC's announcement, must surely rank as the most phenomenal expression of viewer opinion ever recorded in the annals of television. It must also serve as a graphic reminder to the networks that people like to believe they have a voice in affairs that concern them, and will express that voice, sometimes in staggering proportions.

In retrospect, it probably is a matter of conjecture whether or not STAR TREK fans won a victory. Television is a hard dollars-and-cents business, and like any other, must make a profit. It cannot do that with shows that do not move the sponsor's products. Viewer reaction notwithstanding, it is doubtful any network would carry a program it did not believe would make a profit. But philosophical questions were completely beside the point. STAR TREK was given a reprieve, and that's all that mattered.

Shortly after NBC's announcement, Roddenberry received a letter and a package from two loyal fans at the University of Washington. The letter read, in part:

Dear Mr. Roddenberry,

We thought it fitting that you have something appropriate with which to celebrate last Friday's announcement. Therefore, enclosed are 785.7 cubic centimeters of genuine IBM Brand Computer Confetti. Please note that it is packaged in a box formed of the principle export of Aldebaran IV, Aldebaran Okapi hide.

By the way, computer confetti is a guaranteed effective antilubricant when inserted into bureaucratic machinery. If and when NBC again decides to go totally illogical and consider cancelling STAR TREK, we intend to send them one metric ton of computer confetti by special delivery mail.

Roddenberry is quite well aware of the impact made by STAR TREK fans and is quick to point out the invaluable support they have rendered. He knows full well the fans, both young and old, have been a prime force in keeping his Starship on course. One of the interesting aspects of the fans is the fact that they are indeed highly literate. Herb Solow commented:

When I was still at Paramount, I'd get letters from astronomers, chemists, doctors, medical schools, teachers ... an amazing number of professional people. I have read mail from viewers in which they comment on many different series, but I've never read more intelligent, thought-provoking mail as STAR TREK gets. It's by far the most literate mail of any show on the air. Most letters received by a studio, on any show, will start with, "I'd like you to send me a picture," and that's about it. Not STAR TREK. These people really follow the show. They comment on the story, the theories advanced in the stories . . . everything seems to be on more of an intellectual level. For instance, there would be an operation on the ship, and De Forest Kelley would use one of his medical instruments. This is a thing that used to grind pepper, but they painted it silver and changed it a little. I've read mail from doctors who have commented on the practicality of this, who believe that in the future such a device might very well be used by medical science.

There are, of course, many requests for pictures, particularly from the younger fans.* These are usually turned over to Howard MacClay for processing. Howard is Paramount's head of publicity and is well-acquainted with the interest expressed by these youthful STAR TREKers. According to MacClay and his assistant Frank Wright, 12,000 or more letters are received every month on STAR TREK alone! Howard and Frank both are warm, personable men. They, too, work under the pressure of time. Set "stills" must be shot, printed, and made available to newspapers and magazines all over the United States. Specific requests for photos or transparencies are received daily and must be filled. And, of course, there is an endless parade of reporters, writers, and columnists who want to visit the sets and interview the stars. (There is also an occasional nut who wants to write a book.) Things get so hectic around Howard's office at times that I suspect if it weren't for Jackie Nelson and Margaret Clark (very capable, attractive assistants) they'd never make it.

And then, if by chance things happen to get momentarily quiet, one can always read samples of Justman's "correspondence"!

Dear Harry:

I thought it would be fitting and proper to tell you how much Mrs. Justman and I appreciated your gift of the most beautiful orchids I have ever seen.

We found them delicious and not filling at all. Not only that, but a half hour later we were hungry again.

One of the members of the front office staff is Rick Carter, assistant to the executive producer. The position Rick holds is similar to that of an administrative assistant in function, but is more of a training ground for bigger and better things the industry may have to offer later on. The man holding this position is normally referred to as a "gopher"—"go fer this, and go fer that." Rick winds up doing a multitude of errands,

* "STAR TREK's policy from the first has been to answer every fan request.

small jobs, and tasks, and jokingly calls himself "head of Xerox" because he's forever being asked to Xerox papers and correspondence. He is a happy-go-lucky sort of guy, with a ready smile and an unbelievable talent for tracking down an item needed or a bit of information desired. Any young man who wants to learn the television business would do well to start as Rick has. The work is not too difficult, the hours are terrible, and the opportunities for learning are fantastic.

In early spring, 1968, during a conversation with Rodden- berry, the discussion turned to events surrounding the finaliz- ing of the series format back in 1964. Perhaps a little sheep- ishly, Gene related the following:

ONE OF THE EARLY PAGES OF THE FORMAT WAS SUPPOSED TO EXPLAIN HOW MANY STARS THERE ARE IN THE GALAXY, MATHE- MATICALLY HOW MANY "M CLASS" PLANETS THERE ARE, AND SO FORTH. I HAD READ A THEORETICAL STUDY ON THIS BUT COULDN'T REMEMBER THE FORMULA USED. I ASKED A FRIEND OF MINE AT CAL TECH TO LOOK IT UP FOR ME, BUT IN THE MEANTIME I WANTED TO SEE HOW IT MIGHT LOOK ON PAPER. SO I JUST MADE UP A COMPLEX-LOOKING FORMULA TO VISUALLY GIVE ME AN IDEA HOW IT WOULD LOOK. BEFORE I COULD GET BACK TO MY FRIEND AT CAL TECH, MGM BEGAN ASKING ME FOR THE FORMAT. MY SECRETARY TYPED IT UP THE WAY IT WAS, UNDER THE PRES- SURE OF TIME, AND WE SENT IT OUT THAT WAY. FROM THERE, THE FORMAT MADE ITS WAY TO RAND, CAL TECH, DUKE UNIVERSITY, AND A FEW OTHER PLACES. I GOT BUSY WITH OTHER DETAILS AND FORGOT ABOUT THE PHONY FORMULA. NOW, OVER FOUR YEARS LATER, NO ONE . . . SCIENTISTS, MATHEMATI- CIANS . . . NO ONE HAS EVER QUESTIONED

THAT FORMULA, AND YET IT'S BEEN PRETTY
WELL PUBLICIZED ACROSS THE COUNTRY.
PERHAPS SOMEONE HAS LECTURED ON IT,
FOR ALL I KNOW!

Chapter 3

## Whither Star Trek?

AN INTERESTING ASPECT OF THIS WHOLE
THING, THOUGH, IS . . . THIS CRAZY NEW
GROUP THAT CAME IN . . . AND DID NOTHING
BY THE RULES . . . WAS THE FIRST SUCCESS-
FUL SHOW THAT DESILU HAD HAD IN YEARS.
THERE WAS STAGNATION, BUT WE CAME IN
AND MADE IT WORK AGAIN. . . . WE
BROUGHT TURMOIL, EXCITEMENT . . . AND
BEST OF ALL . . . CHALLENGE.

Gene Roddenberry

The victory that had been so exultantly proclaimed by
NBC's March first announcement quickly paled before the
news of a change in time slot. Originally scheduled for Monday night viewing, STAR TREK would now open its third season on Friday nights at 10:00 P.M. Many were they who
gloomily predicted the end was at hand for the Voyages of
the Starship *Enterprise*. The late night spot was considered
certain death for the series. NBC's commitment was for sixteen episodes, and most studio personnel held little hope for a
mid-season pickup.

By then I was living in Hollywood (my company had
transferred my office from Phoenix at the end of January)
and was spending a fair amount of time at Paramount, trying
to complete the design of the new Klingon space ship. I
knew Roddenberry, most of the staff, and many of the crew
quite well by then, and I felt like a member of the family.
When your family suffers hurt, you suffer also. I had grown to
know and feel as they did, and the openly acknowledged "in-
evitable fate" saddened me at least as much as it did them.

I thought a great deal about the unique group of people

400

who were the driving force that had made STAR TREK what it was. Gene Roddenberry, pure creative genius, sometimes serious, often full of laughter, always with his mental motor in overdrive. Bob Justman, a sharp, creative technician with a critical eye for flaws in script or film, forever twisting and twirling his handlebar moustache. Gregg Peters, one great big, friendly, hulking smile. Eddie Milkis, always instigating a put-on—and always protesting innocently in the process. Dorothy Fontana, a real doll—and one hell of a fine writer. "Uncle" Matt Jefferies, smiling behind those silver-rimmed glasses even when the situation was grim. Bill Theiss, who was wearing mod clothes before the term was invented. Penny, Rick, Sylvia, Dale McRoberts, the friendly guard at Paramount's Gower Street entrance—Jerry, George, Fabian, Don—quite a group, quite a group.

As this is written, mid-season pickup is a long way off in the future. But just as STAR TREK projects an optimistic future, so, too, does the staff and crew as they enter production for the first half of. the third season. Despite the unknown ahead, they are determined to be tigers all the way.

The new producer, Fred Freiberger, is a "pro" with impressive credits from "Ben Casey," "Slattery's People," and other top shows. He's backed by Bob Justman as co-producer and both Milkis and Peters as associate producers.

Should Gene have pulled back, to confine his duties to administration and policy? He put in over a year on pilots, plus two more years in production. Perhaps as gruelling a three years as any man in the history of television. When you see a man work night after night, without sleep, until white with fatigue, it's hard to insist that he owes more of what few others give at all.

It is impossible to predict at this point what will ultimately be the outcome. If STAR TREK does, in fact, come to an end next January, millions of viewers will mourn its passing.

Even so, the starship launched by Roddenberry and manned by an extraordinary crew will not depart the scene without leaving some ripples in its wake.

STAR TREK has proved that it really does matter to the viewer what he sees on television. Contrary to what the networks may believe, people *do* care about television programming. And they do not at all mind learning while being entertained. Learning implies believing. Learning also implies intelligence—the ability to see relationships, in a Vulcan, a Gorn, or a Horta. The response to STAR TREK'S message is irrefutable proof of the totally inaccurate network concept of the viewer as a clod.

But STAR TREK has done far more than that. It has given us a legacy—a message—man *can* create a future worth living for. . . . a future that is full of optimism, hope, excitement, and challenge. A future that proudly proclaims man's ability to survive in peace and reach for the stars as his reward.

Whither STAR TREK?

It really doesn't matter. We have its legacy . . . all we have to do is use it.

# ABOUT STEPHEN E. WHITFIELD

Steve Whitfield is an ex-Marine Corps pilot and Intelligence Officer and holds a commercial pilot's license in both fixed-wing aircraft and helicopters. Since 1959 he has worked in the field of advertising and public relations. His current position is that of National Advertising and Promotion Director for AMT Corporation in Troy, Michigan.

He is thirty-two years old, single, and lives in Hollywood, California. Whitfield is an inveterate traveler, and he lists his other interests as writing, music, hunting, fishing, and sailing. *The Making of Star Trek* is his first book, although he has a broad range of writing experience in newspaper and magazine articles, technical publications, historical research reports, and trade journals.

# ABOUT GENE RODDENBERRY

Gene Roddenberry, executive producer of NBC's one-hour color science fiction series, "Star Trek," is a former combat bomber and commercial airline pilot, a one-time police sergeant, and an authority on narcotics, who has put an exciting background to work as a television writer and producer.

In 1948, Roddenberry moved to Los Angeles to become a writer. During this period, he earned his living as a member of the Los Angeles Police Department, eventually working his way up to head of research in the chief's office, where he prepared studies still being used on narcotics addiction. Simultaneously, he was steadily writing television scripts, using a pseudonym. In time, he sold scripts to the then highly rated police series "Dragnet" and to "Four Star Theatre." When he felt assured of a writing career, he left the force to concentrate on TV.

## STAR TREK SHOWS

*Regular Performers for the First Season:*

| | |
|---|---|
| MAJEL BARRETT | LEONARD NIMOY |
| JAMES DOOHAN | WILLIAM SHATNER |
| De FOREST KELLEY | GEORGE TAKEI |
| NICHELLE NICHOLS | GRACE LEE WHITNEY |

"Man Trap                                     September 8, 1966

*Guest Stars:*

| | |
|---|---|
| Jeane Bal | Alfred Ryder |
| Vince Howard | Bruce Watson |
| Francine Pyne | Michael Zaslow |

"Charlie X"                                   September 15, 1966

*Guest Stars:*

| | |
|---|---|
| John Bellah | Abraham Sofaer |
| Don Eitner | Charles J. Stewart |
| Patricia McNulty | Garland Thompson |
| Dallas Michell | Robert Walker |

"Where No Man Has Gone Before"   September 22, 1966

*Guest Stars:*

| | |
|---|---|
| Paul Carr | Lloyd Haynes |
| Andrea Dromm | Sally Kellerman |
| Paul Fix | Gary Lockwood |

"The Naked Time"                              September 29, 1966

*Guest Stars:*

| | |
|---|---|
| John Bellah | William Knight |
| Bruce Hyde | Stewart Moss |

**"The Enemy Within"**                    October 6, 1966
*Guest Stars:*
Jim Goodwin
Edward Madden
Garland Thompson

**"Mudd's Women"**                    October 13, 1966
*Guest Stars:*

Roger C. Carmel            Seamon Glass
Susan Denberg              Jim Goodwin
Gene Dynarski              Jon Kowal
Jerry Foxworth             Karen Steele
                           Maggie Thrett

**"What Are Little Girls Made Of?"**    October 20, 1966
*Guest Stars:*

Budd Albright              Vince Deadrick
Harry Basch                Sherry Jackson
Ted Cassidy                Michael Strong

**"Miri"**                    October 27, 1966
*Guest Stars:*

Kim Darby                  Michael J. Pollard
Kellie Flanagan            John Megna
Jim Goodwin                Steven McEveety
Ed McCready                David L. Ross
                           Keith Taylor

**"Dagger of the Mind"**                    November 3, 1966
*Guest Stars:*

Larry Anthony              Marianna Hill
John Arndt                 Ed McCready
Eli Bahar                  Susanne Wasson
James Gregory              Morgan Woodward

**"Corbomite Maneuver"**                    November 10, 1966
*Guest Stars:*
Anthony Call
Clint Howard

"Menagerie" (Part I)                    November 17, 1966
                    *Guest Stars:*

Hagan Beggs                     Sean Kenney
Peter Duryea                    Susan Oliver
John Hoyt                       Julie Parrish
M. Leigh Hudec                  Adam Roark
Jeffrey Hunter                  Malachi Throne


"Menagerie" (Part II)                   November 24, 1966
                    *Guest Stars:*

Hagan Beggs                     Jeffrey Hunter
Peter Duryea                    Sean Kenney
Laurel Goodwin                  Susan Oliver
John Hoyt                       Adam Roark
M. Leigh Hudec                  Malachi Throne
                                               Meg Wyllie


"Conscience of the King"                December 8, 1966
                    *Guest Stars:*

Marc Adams                      Arnold Moss
Barbara Anderson                Natalie Norwick
Karl Bruck                      William Sargent
Bruce Hyde                      David Troy


"Balance of Terror"                     December 15, 1966
                    *Guest Stars:*

Barbara Baldwin                 Stephen Mines
Paul Comi                       Lawrence Montaigne
Mark Lenard                     Garry Walberg
                                               John Warburton


"Shore Leave"                           December 29, 1966
                    *Guest Stars:*

Barbara Baldavin                Perry Lopez
Emily Banks                     Bruce Mars
Shirley Bonne                   Oliver McGowan
Marcia Brown                    Sebastian Tom

"Errand of Mercy"                    March 23, 1967
                    *Guest Stars:*

John Abbott                    Walt Davis
Peter Brocco                   David Hillary Hughes
John Colicos                   Victor Lundon
                               George Sawaya


"The Alternative Factor"              March 30, 1967
                    *Guest Stars:*

Robert Brown                   Eddie Paskey
Richard Durr                   Christian Patrick
Janet MacLachlan               Arch Whiting


"The City on the Edge of Forever"    April 6, 1967
                    *Guest Stars:*

Hal Baylor                     Bartell LaRue
Joan Collins                   David L. Ross
John Harmon                    John Winston


"Operation Annihilate"               April 13, 1967
                    *Guest Stars:*

Fred Carson                    Craig Hundley
Jerry Catron                   Maurishka
                               Joan Swift


*Regular Performers for the Second Season:*
MAJEL BARRETT                  NICHELLE NICHOLS
JAMES DOOHAN                   LEONARD NIMOY
De FOREST KELLEY               WILLIAM SHATNER
WALTER KOENIG                  GEORGE TAKEI


"Amok Time"                         September 15, 1967
                    *Guest Stars:*

Celia Lovsky                   Lawrence Montaigne
Arlene Martel                  Byron Morrow

"Who Mourns for Adonis?"          September 22, 1967
*Guest Stars:*

Michael Forest                    Leslie Parrish
                                  John Winston


"The Changeling"                  September 29, 1967
*Guest Stars:*

Barbara Gates                     Blais del Makee
Arnold Lessing                    Meade Martin
                                  Vic Perrin


"Mirror, Mirror"                  October 6, 1967
*Guest Stars:*

Pete Kellett                      Vic Perrin
Barbara Luna                      Garth Pillsbury
                                  John Winston


"The Apple"                       October 13, 1967
*Guest Stars:*

Keith Andes                       Shari Nims
Jerry Daniels                     David Soul
Mal Friedman                      John Winston
Jay Jones                         Celeste Yarnall


"The Doomsday Machine"            October 20, 1967
*Guest Stars:*

Tim Burns                         John Copage
Jerry Catron                      Elizabeth Rogers
Richard Compton                   William Windom
                                  John Winston


"Catspaw"                         Ooctober 27, 1967
*Guest Stars:*

Mike Barrier                      Maryesther Denver
Gail Bonney                       Jimmy Jones
Antoinette Bower                  Theo Marcuse
Rhodie Cogan                      John Winston

"I, Mudd"                          November 3, 1967
                    *Guest Stars:*
Alyce Andrece                 Kay Elliot
Rhae Andrece                  Mike Howden
Roger C. Carmel               Richard Tatro
                              Michael Zaslow


"Metamorphosis"                    November 10, 1967
                    *Guest Stars:*
Glenn Corbett                 Elinor Donahue


"Journey to Babel"                 November 17, 1967
                    *Guest Stars:*
Mark Lenard                   William O'Connell
James X. Mitchell             John Wheeler
Reggie Nalder                 Jane Wyatt


"The Deadly Years"                 December 8, 1967
                    *Guest Stars:*
Charles Drake                 Carolyn Nelson
Felix Locher                  Beverly Washburn
Sarah Marshall                Laura Wood


"Obsession"                        December 15, 1967
                    *Guest Stars:*
Jerry Ayres                   Stephen Brooks


"Wolf in the Fold"                 December 22, 1967
                    *Guest Stars:*
Virginia Aldridge             Charles Macaulay
Joseph Bernard                Judy McConnell
Charles Dierkop               Pilar Seurat
John Fiedler                  Judi Sherven
Tania Lemani                  John Winston

"The Trouble with Tribbles"        December 29, 1967
### Guest Stars:

| | |
|---|---|
| Stanley Adams | Michael Pataki |
| Paul Baxley | Guy Raymond |
| Charlie Brill | Ed Reimers |
| William Campbell | David L. Ross |
| | William Schallert |

"The Gamesters of Triskelion"        January 5, 1968
### Guest Stars:

| | |
|---|---|
| Dick Crockett | Angelique Pettyjohn |
| Victoria George | Jane Ross |
| Mickey Morton | Joseph Ruskin |
| | Steve Sandor |

"A Piece of the Action"        January 12, 1968
### Guest Stars:

| | |
|---|---|
| Anthony Caruso | John Harmon |
| Sheldon Collins | Sharyn Hillyer |
| Lee Delano | Steve Marlo |
| Buddy Garion | Victor Tayback |
| | Dyanne Thorne |

"The Immunity Syndrome"        January 19, 1968
### Guest Star:
John Winston

"A Private Little War"        February 2, 1968
### Guest Stars:

| | |
|---|---|
| Paul Baxley | Gary Pillar |
| Arthur Bernard | Janos Prohaska |
| Booker Bradshaw | Ned Romero |
| Nancy Kovack | Michael Witney |

"Return to Tomorrow"        February 9, 1968
### Guest Stars:

| | |
|---|---|
| Cindy Lou | Diana Muldaur |

"Patterns of Force" February 16, 1968

*Guest Stars:*

Paul Baxley
David Brian
Peter Canon
Chuck Courtney
Richard Evans
Gilbert Green

Skip Homeier
Patrick Horgan
Bart LaRue
Ralph Maurer
Ed McCready
Valora Noland
William Wintersole


"By Any Other Name" February 23, 1968

*Guest Stars:*

Barbara Bouchet
Carl Byrd
Julie Cobb

Lezlie Dalton
Robert Fortier
Stewart Moss
Warren Stevens


"Omega Glory" March 1, 1968

*Guest Stars:*

Frank Atienza
Morgan Farley
Roy Jenson
Irene Kelly

Lloyd Kino
Ed McCready
David L. Ross
Morgan Woodward


"The Ultimate Computer" March 8, 1968

*Guest Stars:*

William Marshall

Sean Morgan
Barry Russo


"Bread and Circuses" March 15, 1968

*Guest Stars:*

William Bramley
Lois Jewell
Max Kleven
Bart LaRue

Jack Perkins
Logan Ramsey
Rhodes Reason
William Smithers
Ian Wolfe

"Friday's Child"                    March 22, 1968
*Guest Stars:*

| | |
|---|---|
| Tige Andrews | Michael Dante |
| Robert Bralver | Ben Gage |
| Cal Bolder | Julie Newmar |
| | Kirk Raymone |

"Assignment Earth"             March 29, 1968
*Guest Stars:*

| | |
|---|---|
| Paul Baxley | Ted Gehring |
| Lincoln Denyan | Morgan Jones |
| Morgan Jones | Don Keefer |
| Terri Garr | Robert Lansing |
| | Bruce Mars |

(Additional information may be obtained by writing to STAR TREK Enterprises, Dept. B, P. O. Box 38429, Hollywood, California, 90038.)

# BY ARTHUR C. CLARKE
# IN BALLANTINE BOOKS EDITIONS

**EXPEDITION TO EARTH**                                    75¢

A first collection of Clarke's stories, which will grip you and haunt you for a long time to come. If you are a Clarke fan, you will not want to miss this collection.

**REACH FOR TOMORROW**                                    75¢

A second collection; "A dozen stories, all written with the sense of style one has come to expect from Clarke, all literate and all, in the best sense, entertaining."
*The New York Times*

**EARTHLIGHT**                                            75¢

A most timely novel about what life would be like on the moon. "I had the eerie feeling that I had just returned from an actual stay on the moon . . . a tale of supersonically high-keyed suspense." *J. Francis McComas*

**TALES FROM THE WHITE HART**                             75¢

Stories that might have been strung out to many thousands of words, but which are handled with economy and ingenuity in the space of a few pages. "Ingenious, hilarious, wholly delightful tales of science fiction told by a master." *Montgomery Advertiser*

**CHILDHOOD'S END**                                       75¢

A towering novel—the classic of science fiction. "A real staggerer by a man who is both a poetic dreamer and a competent scientist." *Gilbert Highet*

------------------------------------------------